Mahayoga

*The Mystical Path
of the Siddhas*

Mahayoga

The Mystical Path
of the Siddhas

A Personal Journey

Swami Prakashananda

Sarasvati Productions

Mahayoga
The Mystical Path of the Siddhas
A Personal Journey
© 2012 by Swami Prakashananda

All rights reserved. No part of this book may be reproduced in any form or by any means, electronic or mechanical, including photocopying, recording, or by any information storage and retrieval system, without permission in writing from the publisher.

Published by:
Sarasvati Productions
1625 Hollingsworth Dr.
Mountain View, CA 94040

www.SarasvatiProductions.com

First Printing 2012
Printed in the United States of America

Cover designed by Gargi of Di Maria Design
www.dimariad.com

ISBN 978-1-886140-11-0
Library of Congress Control Number: 2012906553

Table of Contents

Acknowledgments x
List of Photographs xii
Preface xv

Inner Awakening 1
My Early Life 6
The Adventure Begins 12
India 21
Roti Baba 32
Kashi — The City of Shiva 35
Vedanta 41
Yoga 50
Return To Roti Baba 54

On The Road Again 65
Kanpur 68
Cave Life 74
"Guru Will Be Met In December!" 94
The Guru Calls 100
The Auspicious Moment 103
The Ashram 107
Mahayoga 122
My Life In The Ashram 134

My Spiritual Experiences 145
Ganeshpuri 153
Baba Returns 160
Alandi 165
"Go On A Pilgrimage!" 172

Drive To Delhi *178*
Pilgrimage South *183*
A Trip To Venice *194*
Return To Ganeshpuri.. *211*

The Karmapa's Visit *217*
Baba's Second World Tour.. *225*
Meditation Revolution.. *230*
Travels Across The U.S. *233*
The Oakland Ashram *247*
Baba Is Hospitalized.. *253*
Return To India *262*
My Marriage *265*
Baba's Illness... *267*

My Return To America... *271*
Baba's Third World Tour.. *275*
Miami Beach *279*
Santa Monica *283*
Back To Ganeshpuri *288*
Winds of Change *292*
The Beginning of the End.. *296*
Baba's Mahasamadhi *301*
Period of Solitude *306*

India Pilgrimage *310*
Kashmir.. *312*
The Forest Ashram.. *315*
Goa.. *319*
Kanhangad... *320*
Chennai *329*
Back To Goa *331*

Problems in the Family 333
My Departure From The Ashram 337

My Sannyasa Initiation 340
The Kedarnath Temple 346
More Solitude 351
My Move To California 354
Kumbha-Mela 359
Period of Writing 372
Period of Intense Sadhana 394

Glossary 403

Other books by the author:

Baba Muktananda — A Biography

Don't Think of a Monkey — And Other Stories My Guru Told Me

Ask the Horse! And More Stories My Guru Told Me

*Dedicated in loving memory to my Guru, Baba Muktananda,
by whose grace my search came to an end.*

Acknowledgments

There are a number of people that I would like to thank. First I would like to thank everyone who has gone through the book at its various stages. The first to do so was John, a childhood friend, who was kind enough to go through an early draft. There have since been a number of others who have gone through it, and I have appreciated all of their comments and suggestions. I would also like to thank Diane (Sita) Dropik for her editing work and helpful comments.

I would also like to thank everyone who allowed me to use their photographs. I wish to particularly thank Ramkrishan V. Gadekar, and his son Dayaneshwar, who have over the years been very generous towards me with their photographs. I also wish to thank Amma (Swami Prajnananda) for sharing some of her photographs with me over the years, and allowing me to use them. I would like to thank Don Sharpe for the use of his photos, as well as the Swami Ramananda Seva Foundation (SRSF). Thanks also to Swami Gurupremananda, and all of the photographers whose photos I have used. The photographer's name is included next to the page number and photo description in the List of Photographs, located in the following pages. I am deeply grateful for their generosity in allowing me to share their photos with the reader.

I wish to thank Gargi (Margaret) Di Maria for her beautiful cover design. She is a talented artist and graphic designer, and has designed the covers of all my published books. I can't thank her enough.

I would also like to acknowledge my deep gratitude to Lakshmi and Ed (Umapati) Collins, along with Lakshmi's mom, Thelma, for their loving support and shelter over the years. They have cared for me with great love, and have allowed me to continue to do my Guru's work unhindered. I also want to thank Ed and Lakshmi for their comments and suggestion while

I was working on this book.

Lastly, I would like to thank Amma (Swami Prajnananda) for encouraging me to publish the book. Amma and I became friends from the first day I arrived at the ashram when she translated between Baba and myself. After Baba's death we remained in contact with each other, and I would always visit her whenever I travelled to India. We remained close friends until her death.

List of Photographs

Page
7   The author at age seven just before his departure of the U.S.A.
36 The ghats of Varanasi (Photo by Author)
46 Front gates of an Aghori ashram (Photo by Author)
79 Entrance to forest ashram (Photo by Author)
80 Forest ashram huts (Photo by Author)
82 The author sitting outside of cave (Photo by Author)
82 Entrance to cave (Photo by Author)
84 Swami Naradananda (courtesy: Naradananda Ashram)
92 Anandamayi Ma (courtesy: Anandamayi Ma Ashram, Varanasi)
108 Baba sitting under the Parijata tree (courtesy: SRSF)
109 Early morning chant (courtesy: Swami Prajnananda)
114 Group photograph—Baba with first foreigners (courtesy: Malou & Amma)
116 Baba and ashram dog Raja (courtesy: R. V. Gadekar)
117 The author building a wall (courtesy: Swami Prajnananda)
119 Nityananda Meditating (courtesy: M.D. Suvarna)
132 Ganeshpuri Shiva temple (Photo by Author)
132 Shiva temple's linga (Photo by Author)
155 Mandakini Mountain (Photo by Author)
156 Bhagavan Nityananda with checkered blanket (courtesy: M.D. Suvarna)
157 Bhadrakali (Photo by Author)
157 Nityananda's Mahasamadhi room (Photo by Author)
158 Nityananda's samadhi temple (Photo by Author)
162 Baba early morning darshan (courtesy: R. V. Gadekar)
164 Baba in Nepali hat circa 1971 (courtesy: D.C.)
164 Baba in Rome, August 1970 (courtesy: Luciano)
168 Jnaneshwar's samadhi shrine courtyard (Photo by Author)
168 Jnaneshwar's samadhi shrine Shiva temple (Photo by Author)
179 Great Stupa of Sarnath (Photo by Author)
179 The burning ghat, Varanasi (Photo by Author)
199 Baba Q&A session (1971) (courtesy: Swami Gurupremananda)
201 Baba distributing *prasad* after the Q&A session (courtesy: SRSF)
205 Swami Prakashanandaji, senior disciple of Muktananda (courtesy: R. V. Gadekar)
215 Baba and Viju, the ashram elephant (courtesy: SRSF)
218 Baba and Karmapa (courtesy: Don Sharpe)
219 Karmapa and the black hat ceremony (courtesy: Don Sharpe)
221 Baba working on Chitralekha's statue of himself (courtesy: Don Sharpe)
222 Chitralekha's finished statue of Baba (courtesy: SRSF)

251 The author with Baba, Oakland 1975 (courtesy: David DiMartini)
285 Baba's photo of Chitralekha's statue of Bhagavan (courtesy: Baba)
298 Baba holding up the cane he gave me (courtesy: R. V. Gadekar)
305 Baba's samadhi procession to Ganeshpuri (courtesy: R. V. Gadekar)
343 Mahamandaleshwar Swami Brahmanandaji (courtesy: Sannyas Ashram)
345 Sannyasa initiation (courtesy: Swami Vishudananda)
345 The author with Swami Brahmanandaji after sannyas initiation (courtesy: Swami Vishudananda)
349 Kedarnath temple (Photo by Author)
349 The author at Kedarnath (Photo by Author)
365 Overview of Kumbha-mela grounds (Photo by Author)
365 Kumbha-mela crowds (Photo by Author)
367 Naga sadhus huddled around the morning fire (Photo by Author)
368 Mahamandaleshwars at Kumbha-mela (Photo by Author)
368 The author with friends at the 1989 Kumbha-mela (Photo by Author)
371 The author with Swami Prajnananda (Amma) 1989 (Photo by Author)
373 The author with Sivaya Subramuniyaswamiji (courtesy: Diane)
386 Author with sadhus in forest ashram (Photo by Author)
388 Bithoor overview (Photo by Author)
389 Sita with sons Kush and Luv (Photo by Author)
390 Center of the World, Bithoor (Photo by Author)
390 The author with the Mishra family (Photo by Author)

(below) Map of India and surrounding countries. *(right)* A close up of the western portion of the state of Maharashtra. These maps show some of the cities and towns visited by the author during his travels.

Preface

This book came about after an experience I had one evening in the fall of 1987. As I sat for my evening meditation, the events of my life with my Guru, Baba Muktananda, suddenly began to appear before my inner eye, as if I were watching a movie. The vision started with the first mystical experience I had which led me to India in search of a Guru, and then proceeded to reveal, in great detail, my experiences with Muktananda over the years. As this was occurring, I heard my Guru's voice say, "Write these experiences down."

This was somewhat unusual because from the time of my arrival at the Ganeshpuri ashram in 1969, Baba or Babaji, as Muktananda was affectionately called, had always encouraged me to remain silent about my spiritual experiences. This was also the same instructions I had received from an inner voice before my journey to India even began.

But now I was being instructed by my Guru to write down some of my experiences. The book is therefore not about any worldly achievements, since in fact I have no great accomplishments to report. It is however about the inner life and experiences of a seeker. It records my first spiritual awakening, followed by my search for a Guru, and the experiences brought about by my association with a perfected master, known as a *Siddha* in *yogic* literature.

The particular path that I follow has been called by various names throughout its long history. It is known as *Siddha Yoga* (the yoga of Siddhas)*, Siddhamarga* ("the path of Siddhas"), *Mahayoga* (the "great yoga"), *Kundalini Mahayoga* (the "great yoga of *Kundalini*")*,* and *Gurukripa* ("Guru's grace"). Nevertheless, all these different names indicate the same path, the mystical path of the Siddhas.

In this path the Guru transmits his own spiritual energy into a sincere seeker at the time of initiation by a process called

Shaktipat. This initiation awakens the latent spiritual energy within the individual known as *Kundalini*. When awakened, it sets in motion a process of spontaneous spiritual transformation, which ultimately brings the seeker to the realization of his complete identify with the Supreme Being, who is none other than his own inner Self.

At first it was not my intention to publish the book, but events have their own mysterious ways of unfolding. My hope is that the book will inspire all seekers of Truth, whether already on the spiritual path, or who may have had even a brief glimpse into the larger meaning and purpose of life. And my wish and prayer is that the reader will have a direct experience of the great divinity which resides within their own hearts.

Here I would also like to acknowledge and thank two women. The first is my mother. Although I caused her much grief and sorrow by my departure from home at such a young age, all of her prayers helped guide my path. She passed away in February 2006, just a little over a month after her 92nd birthday.

The second person is Thelma DiMaria, who has sheltered and supported me in numerous ways over the years. She had met Baba a number of times, and has been like a second mother to me.

The reader should also note that all non-English words have been italicized the first time they are used. And although their meanings are usually given when they are first used, a glossary follows the text.

Inner Awakening

On January 3rd 1969, my twentieth birthday, I had an experience which changed my life completely. At the time I was living in an apartment in San Francisco's Haight Asbury district, just a block from Golden Gate park. It was a Friday morning, and I was preparing some breakfast. At about 9:40 a.m., while I was sitting at the kitchen table, I suddenly became aware of the presence of Jesus. I saw his form appear about ten feet away from me. His body was surrounded by a divine glow. I watched in amazement as his body, floating a few inches off the floor, moved slowly towards me, until he entered my body. As this occurred, a wave of ecstatic joy washed over me, pervading my whole being. Simultaneously, my awareness deepened and I felt a new faith in God had been kindled in my heart.

At the time, I also received some personal instructions as well. As days passed my attitude towards life began to change dramatically. Many of my unhealthy habits began to lose their grip on me, naturally, without any effort on my part. I felt myself being slowly drawn towards a spiritual path.

I had previously had some mystical experiences. In fact, practically every night during the previous year I had been having very powerful and vivid dreams, which contained many spiritual symbols. As I had been brought up a Catholic Christian, many of the initial visions and images I perceived were naturally associated with Jesus and his disciples. For instance, a number of times I dreamt I was accompanying Saint Peter and some of the other disciples. These were not ordinary dreams. I call them dream-visions.

Unlike ordinary dreams, which are often insignificant, dream-visions are true exalted experiences which have the power to inspire and transform the individual. They are like the visions one may experience during deep meditation, except that they are occurring in the dream state. These dreams are often full of light. In such dreams one may see divine beings and receive their blessings or instructions. In some dream-visions one may also experience an elevated state of consciousness.

Some of the dream-visions I had were prophetic. I would see events about to happen shortly, while some events would not occur until years later. But enough of them occurred within a short time to give me faith in these visions. In one dream-vision, I was moving about in space in my subtle body, until I came to the vicinity of the planet Uranus. As I got closer to the planet, it suddenly exploded, with fragments flying in all directions. Not long after the explosion some radiant celestial beings appeared and approached me. They were holding a piece of the exploded planet, which they offered me, saying it was the planet's heart. I gladly accepted their gift, and when I did so, I began feeling extremely joyful. The planet was a bright saffron-orange color, and the piece I was holding throbbed with energy, like holding a beating heart.

At the time I did not know this, but the color of the planet in my dream was the same color as the robes worn by most of Hindu monastic orders (sannyasis), as well as some Buddhist sects. In Hinduism, the color symbolizes the fire of renunciation.

In Western astrology, a subject I had studied, the planet Uranus indicates revolutionary changes, freedom, detachment, and intuition. A few weeks after the dream-vision I happened to visit the Philadelphia Planetarium. When I reached the exhibition on the planet Uranus, the planet was the exact color that I had seen in my dream-vision.

However, as powerful as some of these experiences were, none of them changed my life completely. They no doubt inspired me to contemplate life's deeper meaning, and better understand human nature, but they did not transform my perception of life. This inner transformation began only after that morning's vision of Jesus. I was filled with excitement and joy.

One of the instructions I received that Friday morning was

to return to Philadelphia, and wait for further instructions. Like many others in the 1960s, I experimented with drugs like marijuana, and psychedelics such as LSD, mescaline and psilocybin. However, I did not use these drugs merely for recreational, or social purposes. I was more interested in exploring the expanded consciousness and spiritual revelations they brought. After that Friday morning experience, I lost all interest in such drugs.

A transformation had already started in my life even before the vision of Jesus. Only a week earlier, I had stopped smoking what had become a two pack a day cigarette habit. In this period, I also became a vegetarian and started practicing meditation. I began studying in more depth various scriptures of the world's religions, as well as the lives of saints, both Western and Eastern.

But the transformation of that Friday was profound. I began to surrender my independence to God. I accepted only what came my way naturally, without my desire or demand. I felt an inner inspiration and faith that the Lord had taken full control of my life, and that He was now directing it. When I say Lord here, I am not speaking about any particular form of God, or any master, such as Jesus, Krishna, Buddha, or any other great being. I felt connected to the Universal Consciousness, who has taken all forms, and resides in the hearts of all beings.

I soon had a number of experiences which more clearly confirmed the belief that the divine was now manifesting in my life. One night, after I had returned to Philadelphia, I was in my room casually talking with some friends when all of sudden, everything became completely calm and quiet. I then felt a subtle, divine energy move across my body and through the room, like a gentle breeze. This breeze could not have come from outside, as both the window and the door were closed. The others in the room also felt this energy. They all looked at me in astonishment. I simply said, it is mother playing.

As this had happened, I suddenly had felt the presence of the feminine aspect of God. Because of my Catholic background, initially the image of Mary, the mother of Jesus, came into my mind. But then I became aware that it was the Divine Mother of all that I was experiencing. It was a sweet and gentle experience which filled me with great love and joy for the beauty of God.

Two months later, I had an even more powerful experience, which also brought further instructions. One night while I was sitting in meditation, my mind suddenly became completely one-pointed and I entered a super conscious state, called *samadhi* in the language of yoga. I later learned that this is the fourth state of consciousness, known as *turiya*. It lies beyond the waking, dream, and deep sleep states.

First, the awareness, "I am not the body" arose. This was followed by the awareness, "I am all of This." At that moment, the illusion of duality completely vanished from my consciousness. I saw matter in its primordial form, a shimmering energy composed of pure consciousness. And "I" was the source of that energy. Everything, the walls of the room, the kitchen table, the seat I was sitting on, all were one pulsating energy, One Being.

As I heard the local electric trolley cars pass by my residence, I could feel the surge of energy moving up and down my spine as the trolley car started and stopped. I then experienced the whole universe, with all of its innumerable galaxies, all existing within my own body.

I experienced pure joy as I realized my own true nature. I was now fully aware of my true identity. I felt like I had awakened from a dream.

I felt my unity with that Universal Consciousness that is the source of all of this creation. I understood the true meaning of the words "I Am That" in the scriptures that I had been studying spoken by the Vedic sages, along with lord Krishna, Buddha, Jesus, and other great beings. This "I Am" is not the individual ego or personality, it is that one same divine consciousness existing within all. All of creation arises from that pure consciousness as the Lord's play, the expression of His great joy. It is God's sacred dance of life.

This experience is impossible to fully convey through words, but on a certain level, this is everyone's experience. It is the ultimate truth, the very essence of life.

This cosmic awareness continued throughout the night, and then gradually my personality began to return. I once again became aware of my physical body. However, an inner inspiration remained, and my mind appeared to be permeated with inner light.

During that night, I also received instructions from an inner voice telling me to go to India and look for my Guru. Although I was not given the Guru's name or address, I felt I would know him when I met him. I knew that he would help me become established in that divine state.

Another interesting experience I had that night was seeing the whole world located within my own body, and India was its heart. I then heard a voice say that India was the spiritual heart of the world, and spiritual energy radiated to all humanity by the continuous presence there of sages and saints, both past and present.

However, although I had heard and read about India, and I had just finished Swami Yogananda's book, *Autobiography of a Yogi*, I did not even know where India was even located. So I mentally asked the question, "Where is India?" The answer came back quickly through inner space, "Look at a map!"

My Early Life

I was born in a small town in the mountainous region of Abruzzo (also called Abruzzi), Italy. The town is located between the two valleys of the rivers Tordino and Vomano, not far from the Adriatic Sea. It was a town of approximately one thousand families and a population of less than three thousand, most of whom lived in the surrounding countryside, including my family. With its fertile land the area's economy relied mainly on agricultural products, such as fruit, olives, cereals, and a variety of vegetables.

I was the youngest of four children. I have two older brothers and a sister, who is the eldest among us. My parents were hard working farmers who owned a small piece of property. On our farm we had a variety of animals, such as cattle, sheep, pigs, chickens and rabbits. As a child I enjoyed taking care of them and some even became my dear pets.

I lived in Italy for the first seven years of my life, when my family moved to America. I recall a number of events from my early childhood in Italy, but the clearest memory is my first out of body experience , which occurred when I was about four-and-a-half years old. It is quite common in Italy for country families to have their own wine sheds, since many make their own wine. Italian parents teach their children that a small quantity of wine during meals is healthy, and even young children often drink wine diluted with water.

One day a friend and I locked ourselves in my parent's wine shed. We drank a few quarts of home-made wine and made ourselves extremely intoxicated. I became so ill that I lost body consciousness. I found myself floating in the air above my body and I watched as my uncle carried my limp body home. They placed my body on a bed and tried desperately to revive me. My mother was in tears the whole time, certain that I was dead, or dying. From my space above, I could hear her shouting to my

(*above*) The author at age seven (1956), just before his departure for America.

body, "Wake up my child, come back to me, I have baked you a nice cake."

I felt sorry that she was so upset and I even watched her bake the cake, but I remained outside my body, which was lying on the bed. I was floating in the air in my subtle body, which resembled the physical one. I found that I was able to float out of the confines of our house to the surrounding area. I was also able to see other people and what they were doing. This all felt very natural to me. I felt peaceful and knew that everything was fine. After a couple of days, I was suddenly pulled back into my physical body and soon awoke. Although this made my parents happy, I felt a restriction being back in my physical body.

This was a significant experience for me. It made me realize that I was something other than my physical body and from that day onwards, I no longer feared death. The incident also created a revulsion for the taste of wine, which I never drank again.

On May 8, 1956, a few months after my seventh birthday, I set sail for America with my mother and two brothers from Naples, Italy. My father and sister had gone ahead of us, and were waiting for us in America. They were living in West Philadelphia, where I would spend my childhood. Although my mother had grown up in Italy, she was born in America.

We travelled on the famous ocean liner, the *Andrea Doria*, arriving in New York on May 16th. As we passed the Straits of Gibraltar, where the sea was extremely choppy, the ship began swaying violently. I recall walking on deck with my brothers when suddenly I found myself pulled uncontrollably towards the ship's railings. I almost fell overboard. My upper body was already beyond the rails when my brother Albert caught me, just in time.

Unfortunately, a few months later, on July 25th, while nearing the coast of Nantucket, Massachusetts on its way to New York, the ship collided with the eastbound *SS Stockholm* of the American Swedish Lines. Fortunately, with improvements in communication systems, and the quick response of other ships, over sixteen hundred people were rescued, while forty-six lost their lives. Originally we were booked to travel on that ill-fated July crossing, but there was a last minute cancelation in the May voyage, which was offered to my family. Luckily my mother took the offer.

A few months after my arrival in Philadelphia, I began attending a local Catholic school. This was natural since my family, like most Italians at that time, were Roman Catholics.

Adjusting to my new environment was not always easy. At first I spoke no English, but soon I could understand well enough to communicate with others.

From an early age I had an interest in art, and used to enjoy drawing religious subjects. I was not particularly interested in sports, but I did play some school football in my early teens. I was more attracted to weight lifting and the martial arts, because of the focus on mental concentration and physical discipline.

Although I was by nature non-violent, I could be very stubborn and there were times when I lost my temper. Unfortunately we lived in a neighborhood where racial tensions would often break out into violent fights. I personally tried to be friendly with everyone I met, black or white. Not everyone shared my belief in the brotherhood of man and I was sometimes forced to defend myself. My innate belief in the equality of all beings was affirmed in August of 1963, when I left my small violent neighborhood and traveled to Washington DC. With my close friend and his father, I participated in the famous march on Washington. At the Lincoln Memorial we listened, along with 250,000 others, to Martin Luther King, Jr. advocating racial harmony in his historic "I Have a Dream" speech. I felt happy to be with so many others of all colors, who also believed in the brotherhood of man.

When I was about fifteen years of age, I began leaving my neighborhood, to explore other parts of Philadelphia. I even went as far away as New York City. Sometimes this brought me face to face with danger, but mostly I had good experiences. I felt extremely independent, even for a teenager, and often left without saying anything to anyone, including my parents. They tried unsuccessfully to curtail this wandering habit of mine.

I knew there was more to life and so I dropped out of high school during my sophomore year and left my family's home in search of it. I continued living in Philadelphia, but would at times travel to New York city. I did not leave home because of any problems with my parents, but simply because I felt an inner call. However, the object of my search had not yet clearly formulated. My detachment from my family was very difficult for my parents to accept and it caused them much grief, especially my mother. They felt rejected and could not understand why I felt it was necessary to leave home at such a young age.

Although this was the era of Rock & Roll, I was more attracted to folk music, which usually had a social message. I frequented coffee shops in Philadelphia and New York City where musicians performed. Not long after my eighteenth birthday, two friends and I decided to join the wave of young people at the time, heading for San Francisco.

However, we decided to take a long route. Our journey first took us north to Canada, and then through the western United States. I felt it was the beginning of a new chapter in my life, one of expansion and learning. We arrived in San Francisco in June of 1967, just at the beginning of what would become known as the "Summer of Love".

Although I had already started experimenting with different drugs, it was during this period that I delved deeper into it. These brought very powerful experiences of consciousness which gave me a totally different perspective of life, quite different from the "normal" perception of reality. These experiences also awakened within me a deep desire to discover more about who I was, and the world around me. However in the long run, drugs was not a vehicle that could take me to my destination.

For the next couple of years I lived in San Francisco for about six months of the year, and the other six months in Philadelphia. And although I would visit my family whenever I was in Philadelphia, I usually lived alone, or with friends.

Some years earlier, a friend introduced me to astrology. The first time he mentioned the subject I told him that one day I would study the subject seriously, and see for myself what it was all about. I would eventually study and practice both the Western and Vedic methods of astrology. I found astrology to be a wonderful tool in understanding human nature and the rhythms of life. I soon began giving readings and teaching astrology.

I also started studying metaphysics, theosophy, and various religious traditions. I have had an interest in religion ever since my early childhood. I recall wanting to become a priest or monk when I was only about five years of age.

As a child, I had also performed the various rituals of the Catholic Church, and felt a deep love for God. But I craved a direct experience of Him, often contemplating my relationship with God. My mind never accepted anything merely on faith, and I thought very deeply about the teachings of the Church. I discussed this with the priests at my school, but none of them seemed to actually have had any personal experience of God. I would not settle for anything less.

Even with all my studies, I soon felt that the knowledge I was gaining was nothing more than dry book knowledge. I felt a deep dissatisfaction and restlessness, but that all changed on that auspicious morning of January 3rd.

The Adventure Begins

The day after I was instructed to go to India, I began studying a world map to find its exact location and to prepare for my journey. I decided to fly to Europe, and then travel overland through France, Italy, Yugoslavia. Bulgaria, Turkey, and the Middle Eastern countries. This would take longer, but it would be much cheaper and I would get to see more of the world and its people.

The night before I left Philadelphia my friends threw a farewell dinner for me. They were happy for me, but sad to see me leaving. The next morning I traveled to Manhattan and stayed with some friends for two days while waiting for my flight. I gave my astrology library to a friend who had an interest in the subject. Since my awakening, I had pretty much stopped teaching and giving astrological counseling, which I had been doing for the previous almost five years.

On the night of my departure, my friends took me to the airport and wished me well. I was in an ecstatic mood, excited that my adventure had finally started. I felt that I was in the hands of God, with a divine presence guiding me. In order to fully surrender to God's will, I vowed to accept gratefully whatever came unasked, but not to beg or ask for food or anything else. God's guidance and protection would be confirmed many times throughout my journey.

From New York I flew to Luxembourg, a tiny country in western Europe, bordered by Belgium, France and Germany. In the late 1960s, it was the first stop for many young Americans who wanted to travel cheaply.

On the flight I met an American from southern California who was on his way to Spain. Since we were both heading south, we decided to travel together through France. During the day we hitch-hiked, and at night we slept outdoors under the stars. Sometimes we were invited to spend the night in someone's home, which allowed us to get to know the locals better. We were enjoying each others' company but soon we reached the city of Lyon, where our paths would separate. I turned east, towards Italy, while he continued south. After we said our goodbyes, I traveled mostly alone. I felt that my companion had been sent by God, to keep me company until I became accustomed to life on the road.

Near the Italian border, I got a ride with an Italian family, who invited me to spend the night in their home. I had not spoken Italian for many years and my Italian was basically the local dialect of Abruzzi. It was spoken only in the area where I was born. I was not feeling confident of my language capabilities.

However, an interesting thing occurred just after I entered Italy. I set out hitch-hiking early on my first day in Italy, but I got only short distance rides. I did quite a bit of walking until finally got a ride with a truck driver, who would take me almost the whole distance across northern Italy. He had a brand new truck which had a spacious cab and very comfortable seats that folded all the way back to a horizontal position. I was extremely tired from so much walking. The truck driver noticed this, and told me that I could sleep if I wanted. He would wake me when we reached the destination.

I fell asleep and immediately began to dream. Interestingly, in the dream I was speaking and thinking in Italian but not the Abruzzi dialect of my childhood. I dreamed in Italian as spoken in northern Italy, which I had never spoken. When I awoke, the truck driver was surprised at how much my Italian had improved after a nap. I continued to dream in Italian for as long as I was in Italy, and could soon communicate fluently with those I met. But the moment I left Italy, crossing the border of Yugoslavia, the experience stopped, and my dreams returned to English.

So far my journey was going well and I was enjoying my travels. During the day I hitch-hiked, but I always continued moving, walking if I was not offered a ride. All but a few of people I met were friendly, but I looked at everyone with a friendly eye.

I met a few strange characters along the way. I recall a ride with a Frenchman who was constantly babbling to himself. Periodically he would stick his hand in a large plastic bag, pull out what appeared to be pieces of raw meat which he proceeded to eat with gusto. I politely declined his offer to share some with me.

Along the way, I also met other travelers who informed me of what lay ahead and warned me of any danger. I was told by some travelers that I may have some difficulties hitch-hiking through Turkey, and so I decided that I would travel by bus or train while in that country. There was general agreement that hitch-hiking was not recommended in the Islamic countries that I would be going through. I was grateful for the advice, which undoubtedly helped me to avoid difficulties.

Near the border of Yugoslavia and Bulgaria, I got a ride with an Italian man who was traveling to the capital city of Sofia. When we reached the Bulgarian border, he took my passport along with his to have it stamped by the border police. Because I was still an Italian citizen, traveling with an Italian passport, I did not require a visa for most European countries. We spent the night in Sofia and the next day I went to the train station and booked a seat to Istanbul that night.

That evening on the train I found that there were two other Westerners in my compartment. After talking for some time, we went to sleep. Around midnight, we were rudely awakened by two large border police. At first we thought that we had reached the border and they were Turkish border guards. They began collecting passports. We noticed that they were being arrogant and rude to all the passengers. While examining my passport, they asked me where I had come from and where was I going. I told them that I had boarded the train in Sofia and was going to Istanbul. They did not appear to be satisfied with my answers and returned the passports to the other passengers in my compartment but kept mine. They ordered me to follow them, against the protests of my new friends. As I stepped down from the train, I realized that I was at the Bulgarian border, and these were Bulgarian border police — not Turks. I also realized that I was not the only one being detained.

When I entered Bulgaria, my passport had been stamped with an image of a car, indicating that I had entered the country by car. The police wanted to know why I had left my car in Sofia. My explanation that I had only been given a ride by someone and the car did not belong to me fell on deaf ears. They insisted that I would have to return to Sofia to pick up my car and take it out of the country.

I began to sense that this was not the real reason I was being detained. I realized that this was some sort of scam. They questioned me in English, but when I tried to get information from them, they were suddenly unable to understand English. They would laugh and say, "No speak English, parlez-vous francais?" They seemed to be enjoying the game.

They had detained twenty or thirty other passengers with similarly vague reasons. The train was ordered to leave without us and we sat anxiously on the platform for most of the night, without understanding the reason we were there. We soon came to the conclusion that what they really wanted was money. We noticed that whenever they spoke to us, they would give little hints that money would help our situation.

Our suspicion was confirmed by a few of the detained passengers who had traveled through that border before. They told us that it was a well-known practice there. There was not much we could do, since they already let the train go, so we decided to play our own little game. Whenever they hinted at money, we pretended not to understand them. They became increasingly frustrated and huddled together, discussing what to do with us.

When the next train to Istanbul arrived early the next morning, the police gave up. Completely frustrated with us they returned our passports and put us all on the train without any explanation. We watched as they repeated the same little game on a new batch of passengers, detaining twenty to thirty on vague excuses. We also noticed that they did not detain passengers entering Bulgaria — only those leaving the country.

As our train pulled out of the station, those of us who had been detained all night stuck our heads out of the windows and laughed at the police, some making obscene gestures and shouting, "Excuse me, I don't speak English, parlez-vous francais?"

By the time we reached the Turkish border, I felt prepared for anything, but nothing extraordinary happened. Our passports were taken and returned to us within a short period all stamped and ready to go. I found the guards to be courteous and efficient. We soon reached Istanbul, and I immediately went to inquire about a bus to Ankara, a city near the Iranian border. I found that one would be leaving early the next morning so I booked a seat.

It was now only mid afternoon so I decided to look around that ancient city. Istanbul, known as Constantinople under Byzantine rule, now marks the crossroads between Europe and the Middle East. I wandered around its streets for a few hours and then sat on some steps near the waterfront. A cucumber salesman was standing nearby. He offered me some slices of cucumber, which I gladly accepted. As cucumbers are cooling, I found them very refreshing.

After enjoying the view for sometime, I thanked the man and began walking back to the bus station, where the manager had given me permission to sleep that night. As I walked back to the station, I noticed someone was following me. After making sure that I was indeed being followed, I decided to confront the man. I turned off the next street and waited for him to arrive. As he came around the corner, I stopped him, and asked what he wanted.

He was a young man in his mid-twenties. At first he denied that he was following me. But I threatened to turn him over to the police if he did not tell me what he wanted. He then told me the truth. He said that he was in fact a policeman, working in the drug division, and showed me his credentials. He said that I had been observed speaking to the cucumber man, whom he claimed was a known drug dealer. They thought I was interested in purchasing drugs. I explained to him why I had spoken to the man, and that I was not trying to purchase any drugs from him. He believed me, and apologized for the mistake, and he went his way. I continued to the bus station and was soon asleep in the manager's office.

The bus departed for Ankara at 4 a.m. the next morning. We took the northern route, which allowed me a glimpse of the Black Sea, where we arrived in the early morning mist. From Ankara, my journey continued on to Iranian city of Tabriz, which I reached early the next morning. It was actually around 3 a.m. I went into a local tea house and was surprised to see so many people sitting there. The tea house was full of men reading poetry, relating stories, and smoking *hookahs* — tobacco filled water pipes. They were all very friendly, and one of the groups asked me to sit with them. I had some interesting conversations with them about Persian poetry.

From Tabriz, I traveled by bus to the city of Tehran. By now I was becoming a little impatient to reach India. I started thinking that perhaps I should fly the rest of the way, but I found the fare to be too high, and so I continued on my way. In Tehran I was advised to travel by train to Mashhad, which is the last large city before the Afghanistan border. I took this advice.

At Mashhad I would take another bus which was supposed to take passengers to the Afghan border. In Mashhad a young boy around the age of twelve or thirteen began a conversation with me in broken English. He attached himself to me, and stayed with me until my bus departed. At the time I was wearing a pair of Western boots. They were practically brand new, but were not very comfortable for walking. I had noticed the young boy admiring the boots and so I decided to give them to the him as a gift. When I offered him the boots he thought I was joking. But when I took them off and handed them to him, he was ecstatic. It did not matter that they were a little too big for him. I began wearing a pair of sandals that I had with me.

When the bus was about to depart, I said goodbye to the young man, and took a seat. We were soon on our way. However, although the bus was supposed to take us all the way to the Afghan border, the bus driver made everyone get off the bus about two or three miles before the border. We would have to walk the rest of the way.

On the bus from Tehran I had met two boys from Sweden who were also traveling to Afghanistan. They were on the bus with me. We got down and started walking towards the border. It was a beautiful and clear night, with the stars shining brightly.

When we finally reached the Iranian border post with Afghanistan, the Iranian guards began to harass us. They asked for money, but we refused, saying that we had just enough for our journey. But they kept insisting, and one of the Swedish boys started to become angry with the guards. I tried to calm him down, but at the same time we continued to refuse to give them any money. So they started going through one of the boy's bags, and found two U.S. dollar bills, which they took. We were then able to convince them that we were not going to give them any more money. They finally allowed us to go.

It was around midnight. We continued walking until we reached a small border village in Afghanistan. That night we slept under the stars. The next morning we discovered that there was no bus to Heart, which is the first large town in Western Afghanistan. Unfortunately the bus ran only twice a week, and it had come the previous day. We were told that the next bus would come three days later, maybe. The only other way to reach Herat was by jeep so we decided to hire one. We felt a little uncomfortable with the driver, but decided to go with him anyway. After some negotiations, we finally left for Herat.

Along the way, the driver seemed to make it a point of stopping at every out of the way place, obviously visiting his friends and relatives, who happened to run little tea and snack shops along the way. We finally reached the town of Herat, where I decided to spend the night.

Although I had traveled through a number of countries, Afghanistan was unique. When I entered Afghanistan, I literally felt like I had traveled back in time about five hundred years. I liked the country and the Afghani people very much. They are a proud and generally friendly people, but there are also fierce warrior clans as well. A funny incident occurred while I was in Herat. The two boys from Sweden and I boarded a local bus. The two of them sat together in one of the double seats, and I sat in the seat in front of them. As others began boarding the bus, a large Afghani man, wearing a long sword at his side, and a dagger in hi waste, asked me to move so that he could sit near his friends. I said fine and got up and took one of the seats behind my friends. After sometime, that same man came to my seat, and again asked me to move. But by then, the bus was practically full, and so I politely refused. Through a young man who spoke English, I suggested that he just sit in one place instead of moving about from one seat to another. I reminded him that I had already moved once. How many times did he want me to move, I asked?

When the young man translated what I had said, the man's facial expression suddenly changed. He looked at me sternly, and pulled out the large curved dagger he had strapped to his waist. Then, looking into my eyes intently, he said something, which the boy translated as, "In my country, we cut the throats of people like you."

While he said this he made a gesture as if cutting his own throat with the dagger. By this time everyone on the bus was staring at us, and there was tension in the air. I then looked into the man's eyes, and making the fiercest expression that I could, I replied, "In my country, we not only cut the throat, but afterwards we feast on the body."

I don't know why I said such a strange thing, but I did. The young man then translated it. The man continued to glare at me as the boy translated what I had said. Then suddenly, he burst out laughing. In fact, everyone on the bus began laughing, and the tension was suddenly dissipated. The man patted me on my back, and went back to his original seat. The whole incident was very comical, and I was happy it ended peacefully.

The next day I said goodbye to my Swedish friends and started for Kabul. They were also going to Kabul but had planned to travel the northern route on horseback. I decided to go by bus along the southern route, via Kandahar, which would be faster.

When I reached Kabul, I decided to stay for a few days and rest. I liked Kabul very much. While there I spent some time wandering that ancient city. But after three or four days, I left for Pakistan, traveling across the beautiful Khyber pass. It was now just a matter of days before I would reach India.

I had planned to get a visa for India in the city of Lahore, but unfortunately the Indian office there would not issue me one. They told me that I had to return to Rawalpindi, a city I had already passed through. The visa would be issued there by the Indian Consulate.

Unfortunately it was late Friday when I reached Rawalpindi, and so I had to wait until Monday morning before the visa would be issued. But the moment I received it I left for the Indian border. I was starting to feel somewhat restless and anxious, but at the same time very excited. During my journey I began feeling a deep devotional longing arising within my heart. I felt as if I was separated from my beloved.

India

After many weeks of traveling I finally arrived in India. Mysteriously, the moment I entered the country I felt as if I had returned home after a long absence. I continued my travels and before long I reached New Delhi, India's capital. It so happened that on the day I arrived in New Delhi, India had elected V.V. Giri, as the country's fourth president since independence in 1947. So thousands of people were out celebrating the event.

I, on the other hand, wondered what to do next. I had been instructed to go to India by my inner guide, but no specific destination was given. After all, India is a large country. So I began making inquiries as to where I might find *yogis*, saints, or monks. I was told that Rishikesh and Haridwar, at the foothills of the Himalayas was a good place for me to start my search. So I left Delhi and started traveling north on foot, occasionally getting rides with *Sikh* truck drivers.

The word Sikh literally means "disciple." The Sikhs are therefore disciples or followers of Guru Nanak (1469-1539 C.E.) the first of ten gurus in this lineage. The tenth, and last Guru, Govind Singh (1666-1708 C.E.), gave the religion its present form. The Sikh men I met were mostly friendly and courteous individuals. Since there were few private automobiles on the Indian highway in those days, the Sikhs or *Sardarjis*, as they are respectively addressed, were the majority of truck drivers. They were therefore my main mode of transportation. I grew to enjoy their friendly and hospitable nature, and to this day, I remember them with great respect and fondness.

Before long I reached the outskirts of Meerut, a city about 40 miles north of Delhi, where I noticed the peaks of a beautiful white marble temple. It turned out to be the burial or *samadhi* shrine, as it is known in the Hindu tradition, of a saint who had lived there many years earlier. There was no living master or *Guru* there at the time, but it was a very peaceful place. I decided to stop and meditate there for a while. Although Hindus normally cremate their dead, a saint's body is usually buried. It is believed that a portion of the saint's life force *(prana)* remains in the body for the purpose of blessing devotees.

After my meditation one of the devotees who lived in a small hut within the temple compound invited me to have tea with him. Which I did. After our tea he showed me his small shrine room.

Even though Hindus have temples which they visit, there is also a shrine room or area of worship in nearly every home. If space permits, a separate room is used specifically for spiritual purposes, otherwise a corner of the living room may be used. The area is kept clean and the atmosphere pure. The shrine can be as simple as a few photographs, or as elaborate as building a miniature temple. Elaborate or simple, this is where the family members perform their daily rituals and prayers, worshipping God at various times of the day. It is where they meditate and do *japa* — the repetition of sacred words, known as *mantras*. Such *mantras* are usually given to the individual by his or her Guru at the time of initiation into the spiritual life.

Because of the many rituals performed by the Hindus some people, particularly westerners, have the misconception that Hindus worship many Gods. However this is simply not the case. Hindus place a great deal of emphasis on religion and philosophy, and they believe that God is one, but who can be worshiped in different forms. Although westerners call the Indian religion Hinduism, and its followers Hindus, the traditional name is *Sanatana Dharma*, meaning the "eternal or perennial religion."

The word Hindu is actually a corruption of the name of the river Sindhu. In ancient times, the area near that great river was a center of culture, and the people were called Sindhus by the Persians. However, they pronounced the word with an 'H', making it Hindu instead of Sindhu. Europeans later used the word to describe the religion of India.

The word *Sanatana* indicates that which always exists, and the word *dharma* is often translated as religion. But this translation does not really convey its full meaning. Dharma is actually a way of life. The word has also been translated as righteousness and divine law. The word dharma is derived from the root-verb *dhri-* meaning to hold, to establish. And according to the Indian conception, it indicates morality, ethics and justice, as well as the primary relationship between an individual, God, nature, and other beings. It is the basic fundamental law of creation. According to the *Bhagavata Purana*, dharma is said to have four legs: penance, purity, compassion and truth. These qualities are therefore the basis or foundation of dharma.

The practice of one's dharma is considered to be man's main duty. It is also the means of communicating with God. Therefore, unlike other religions, this way of life is not based on the personality or teaching of any one individual. It is derived from the direct experiences of many sages, who have conveyed their experiences in the sacred hymns of the *Vedas*, Hinduism's earliest scriptures. While respecting the scriptures of other religions, Hindus hold sacred the *Upanishads*, which are the mystical portions of the *Vedas*, the *Bhagavad Gita*, and the teachings of all saints. The Indian sages, known as *Rishis* (seers), have taught that although God is one, sages have called him by many names.

To the Rishis, it was not enough to know that God existed, he had to be directly experienced. But in their wisdom, they also understood that human beings could not conceive of God in the exact same way. Everyone has their own temperament and ability to understand things, and this fact must be taken into consideration. It is for this reason that one finds in Hindu scriptures the most simplest of ideas about God, as well as the most profound.

Stop for a moment and think about God, and see what happens. Imagine what God may look like, if anything at all. What image comes to your mind?

Christians may have some image of Jesus in their minds, because they believe that he is God manifest. But Christians also believe in God the father, an idea that will create its own images. Jesus addressed God as *A'ba*, meaning father, thereby indicating an intimacy with him. *A'ba* has its counterpart in the Hindi word *Baba*, which also means father.

Whatever image arises when one thinks of Jesus, it is that image that the devotee will meditate on, and pray to. Nevertheless, as there is no historical picture of Jesus, a variety of images will emerge. There will be differences not only from one Christian sect to another, but from one individual to another. Depending on their background and teachings. Of course this does not mean that simply because there are multiple images that arise in the mind that there is no value in meditating on them, because there is.

Muslims on the other hand think of God as formless. They do not use any images in their Mosques. In fact, many find it offensive to think of God as having any form. But during their prayers, all Muslims face towards the Ka'ba, the sacred shrine located in Mecca, Saudi Arabia. It is there that the sacred black stone is located. It is this symbol which unifies all Muslims throughout the world. But God is all-pervasive, and therefore no one place is holier than another.

Although Buddhists do not believe in a creator God, they nevertheless use various images for their spiritual practices. Even within Buddhism itself, there are several traditions. The Mahayana Buddhist will pray to the Buddha for his grace, and will also use various images of the Buddha for meditation purposes.

On the other hand, the Theravada (Hinayana) Buddhists do not see Buddha as a deity at all, and so they meditate on *sunyata*, the state of nothingness. And in India, the birthplace of Buddhism, there have been many teachers and traditions over its long history.

Buddha was himself a contemporary of the sage Vardhamana,

who is better known as Mahavira, a Jain sage. He was Buddha's senior by about thirty years. Mahavira, a name which means 'great hero,' is considered the twenty-fourth Jina in the line of Jain saints. He taught the path of complete renunciation of worldly desires, and emphasized *ahimsa* or non-violence towards all creatures.

Great beings like Rama and Krishna are also considered by their devotees to be God incarnate, known in the Indian tradition as *Avatars*. On the other hand some see God as the divine teacher, who manifests in the form of a *Guru*. To the followers of this path, it is the Lord Himself who manifests as the Guru or master. It is He who leads a seeker to liberation. Therefore in this path it is the spiritual master who becomes the focus of the disciple's meditation and prayers.

If we analyze the world's religions in a sincere and unbiased way, we will find that there are two basic approaches to God. One is that of love and devotion, and the other is that of spiritual knowledge. The majority of people follow the path of devotion (*bhakti*), which is in fact considered the easiest of the two. In this path a devotee may relate or perceive God in a form similar to their human relations. Some will consider God as a parent, and will address him as either father or mother. Others may see themselves as a servant and consider God their master and ruler. Still others see the relationship as friend-to-friend, or lover-to-beloved. The devotee's particular characteristics in regards to their relationship with God arises naturally out of the seeker's own nature, temperament, spiritual experiences, and understanding.

The path of spiritual knowledge (*jnana*), on the other hand, requires great self effort and concentration. This path is considered more difficult than that of devotion. Although the Buddha taught mainly the path of knowledge to his disciples, not all Buddhists follow this path exclusively. In fact, as we have seen, for many Buddhists, the Buddha himself becomes the object of their devotion.

One's path naturally arises according to the practices he or she has performed both in this life as well as in previous lives. Such feelings are therefore the result of accumulative impressions. The seeker does not actually think, "I will follow the path of knowledge," or "I will follow the path of devotion." Quite often, great beings will express both qualities, especially during the period of their spiritual practices (*sadhana*). To a true saint, there is no distinction between devotion and knowledge, both are expressions of the same goal. However the mind requires something to focus on, particularly at the beginning of the spiritual life. One can not know or understand anything unless one has an image of that object in their mind. In fact, the real purpose of all scriptures is considered to be for the sole purpose of purifying the negative qualities of one's mind.

From the above, we see that no two people will have an identical image of God. Even those who follow the same master. There will be differences whether they are devotees of Rama, Krishna, Buddha, Jesus, or Shankaracharya. They each have different ideas of what these individuals looked like, what they taught, and how they acted. These ideas are further colored by local customs and culture as the religion moves away from its original locality. Some Christians will visualize the baby Jesus, while others prefer him as teacher and master. The same is true for the followers of Krishna. Some like to meditate on Krishna as a child, while others see him as the divine teacher of the *Bhagavad Gita.*

Even those who do not believe in the incarnation of God, or *Avatar* in Hindu terminology, and the Messiah in the Jewish, Muslim and Christian traditions, will still view God in some form or other. Including those who say God has no form at all. Even agnostics, who say that we can never truly know whether or not God exists, must also have some image or idea about God.

Nevertheless if one is sincere all paths are valid. Because of God's greatness and compassion, he can be all things to his devotees, depending on their nature and needs. This idea is beautifully captured in the Hindu concept of the *'Ishta Devata'*, that is, one's personal ideal of God. Whatever form or name of God the devotee chooses, that will be their object of adoration. For it is one's feelings and longing for God which is the important factor. The idea of the *Ista Devata* further shows the open mindedness of the ancient *Rishis* of India. Because of this concept, the individual is taught to honor and respect all forms of God, while worshipping exclusively their own chosen ideal. *Ishvara* (God, Lord), the Supreme Monarch of the universe, loves this creation, and manifests himself to his devotees in the form that appeals to them.

Due to our own limited understanding, we project our limited view onto God. But God has no such limitations. God's revelation to a devotee may come in any form. Some people foolishly believe that God cares more for one group over another. Jews believe that they are the chosen people, while Christians often quote the Biblical verses where Jesus proclaims that he was "The Way" and "The Light." They interpret such words to mean that Jesus was claiming that he was the *only* way to salvation. Some followers of Krishna do the same thing when quoting the Bhagavad Gita.

Were these great beings referring to their physical bodies or limited personalities when they proclaimed, 'I Am That' or 'I Am The Way'? Not at all. They were in fact uttering the reality that divinity dwells within, and therefore resides in all beings as their very own Self. To truly understand such statements, we have to have a direct experience of it ourselves. Only then can one understand its true meaning. The 'I' that is speaking here is really one and the same being, who is the inner Self of all.

Lord Krishna told his disciple Arjuna that he had given this very same teaching which he was now imparting to him in ancient times to the sage *Vivasvat*. Perplexed at such a statement, Arjuna responded in a similar manner as the Pharisees did to Jesus' statement when he claimed that Abraham had rejoiced in having seen him. Arjuna says to Krishna:

> *Later on was Thy birth,*
> *And prior to it was the birth of Vivasvan;*
> *How am I to understand this,*
> *That thou didst declare it in the beginning?*

Krishna replied:
Although I am birthless and of imperishable nature,
And although I am the Lord of All Beings,
Yet, by controlling my own material nature,
I come into being by my own supernatural power.

Whenever a decrease of righteousness (dharma)
Exits, O Arjuna,
And there is a rising up of unrighteousness,
Then I manifest myself,

For the protection of the good
And the destruction of the wicked;
For the sake of establishing righteousness,
I come into being from age to age.
Bhagavad Gita: chap.4 v.4-8

Similarly, the Pharisees asked Jesus:

Thou art not yet fifty years old,
and hast thou seen Abraham?

Jesus replied:
Verily, Verily, I say unto you,
Before Abraham was, I Am.
John: chap.8 v.56-58

Again in Exodus, Moses asks God:

When I come unto the children of Israel, and shall say unto them, the God of your fathers hath sent me unto you; and they shall say to me, What is his name? What shall I say unto them?

The Lord replied:
I Am That I Am. Thus shalt thou say unto the children of Israel, "I Am" has sent me unto you. (Exodus: chap.3 v.13-14)

When that supreme divinity is realized within, the awareness "I Am That" arises naturally. We see this same view being expressed in the Vedas, the Bhagavad Gita, as well as the Bible, in both the old and new testaments. Jesus not only expressed a personal relationship with God, but proclaimed "I Am That" because of his own direct experience of that divinity within himself. That Jesus taught the path of knowledge, along with that of love or devotion is clear from his statements, "I and my father are one," and, "...the kingdom of heaven is within." These are certainly the echoes of the ancient Upanishadic teachings, such as, "Ham-Sa" (I Am That) and "Aham Brahmasmi," meaning "I Am Brahman", the Absolute.

When Jesus was accused of blasphemy by the priests for voicing such statements, he quoted the Psalm: "Is it not written in your law, I said ye are Gods?" This is the same as the Upanishadic statement, "Tattwam Asi," which means, "Thou Art That." Jesus also taught his disciples to become, "...perfect, as your father in heaven is perfect."

Interestingly, there is a verse in the Brihadaranyaka Upanishad which says:

*Om purnamadah purnamidam
purnat purnamudacyate,
Purnasya purnamadaya
purnamevasisyate.*

> Om. That is perfect. This is perfect.
> From the perfect springs the perfect.
> If the perfect is taken from the perfect,
>   the perfect remains.

The *sufi* saint Mansur Manstan suffered a similar fate to that of Jesus when he too proclaimed, *"Ana'l-Haqq,* "I am the Truth." Many claim to believe in one God, but if one hears someone call God by a foreign name they immediately become agitated, and try to convert the person to his own beliefs. How foolish man is. We see diversity where none exists. In fact, God is the author of all religions. Different religions are all paths to the same Lord. But when one reaches God, all paths are left behind. Therefore, instead of seeing differences in different religions, we should try and see their similarities. But now let us return to my story.

After a few hours at the temple, I said good-bye to my host and continued traveling north. By the time I reached the foothills of the Himalayas it was dark, so dark in fact that I could not even see where I was walking. I began bumping into cows that were standing in the middle of the road.

Looking ahead I could see a dim light in the far distance. But no matter how much I walked, it appeared that I was not getting any closer to that light. Then I noticed a car coming towards me, and stopped right in front of me. The two men inside asked me to get in, which I did. We proceeded to drive back down the hill where I had come from. They did not say a word the whole time, and since I was tired, I also kept quiet. At the bottom of the hill there were two roads. The one on the right was the road to Delhi, where I had come from. They pointed out the road to the left, which I had missed in the dark. They told me that road led to Rishikesh.

That's all they said. I thanked them for the ride and started walking again. I soon reached the well known ashram of Swami Shivananda, the founder of the Divine Life Society. I was invited to spend the night. At the time one of the *swamis* was giving a lecture, but I was so tired, and had such a bad cough that I did not hear much of the talk, so I decided to go and rest. But as I laid in bed, I began having the distinct feeling that I would not find my Guru at that place. I felt depressed and anxious, but I finally fell asleep. The next morning, a student showed me around the ashram, telling me its history, and something about its founder, Swami Shivananda.

Rishikesh, which means the place of *Rishis*, and nearby Haridwar, meaning the doorway to the Lord, are both located on the banks of the river Ganga. These two ancient towns are known for their many ashrams and temples. Haridwar is also one of the four holiest sites in India where millions of pilgrims gather every twelve years for the *Kumbha-Mela* festival. Many sadhus also pass through these towns on their way to the upper regions of the Himalayas. I wandered around the area for a few days, but feeling no attraction to any one spot, I decided to move on.

Roti Baba

I decided to travel south-east towards the ancient city of Varanasi (also known as Benares). I had heard that there were many *yogis* and saints living in and around the city. In order to avoid wasting any time, I decided to travel by train. Each day now I was becoming increasingly anxious and uneasy. The desire to find a Guru was becoming overwhelming. My mind gave me no peace and my heart was full of grief.

On the way to the train station, an unusual man attached himself to me, and was now traveling with me to Varanasi. He was acting crazy, and would not stop talking. I became so impatient with him that I got off the train at a small town called Rai Barelli. I had still planned to continue on to Varanasi, but I wanted to travel alone.

It was just before sunrise when I started walking from the train station, making my way out of town. I was happy to finally be alone. Looking at a map I calculated that I was approximately just over 150 miles from Varanasi. I had walked only a few miles when a car pulled up along side of me and stopped. The driver offered me a ride, which I accepted. He told me he was a local lawyer, and asked the usual questions that Indians are curious about. "Where did I come from?" "Where was I going?" "What was my purpose in life?" and so forth.

Although I was asked similar questions throughout my journey, the last question always fascinated me since no one outside of India had ever asked me such a personal and yet profound question: "What is your purpose in life?" Yet in India, I was asked this same question hundreds of times, mainly by Hindus. I was highly intrigued by this question and its implication. The wise say that the real purpose of life is to know the Self.

After telling the lawyer my reason for coming to India, I asked whether any great saints or yogis were living nearby. He mentioned that a great *Avadhuta* (or *Avadhut*) was living just outside town on the banks of the river Sai. And although he had not met him personally, he said that many people considered him to be a great saint. He asked if I would like to go and meet him, to which I said yes. Since the place was located in the opposite direction, he turned the car around, and we drove to the area. I felt excited, and thought that perhaps this was the place I would meet my Guru.

We soon reached a wooded area surrounded by tall grass growing on the banks of the river. We got out of the car and started walking towards the river. I soon noticed a small thatched roof resting on bamboo poles. This provided shade for the *"Baba"* and his devotees. As already mentioned. the word *Baba* means 'respected father,' and it is used by many devotees throughout India to address their spiritual master. The lawyer introduced me to Baba, and explained to him why I had come to India. Baba welcomed me warmly and invited me to stay for sometime. After sometime the lawyer left.

This *Baba* was simply called *Roti Baba*. Roti is actually the word for the flat north Indian bread. Later I was told the story of how he had received that name. Apparently, when Roti Baba first arrived in the area, he would stand outside one of the villages, and would begin calling out, "Roti!, Roti!, Roti!" If anyone brought him food, he ate it, otherwise he would go his way. As he continued to live in the area, and never revealed any other name, everyone began calling him Roti Baba. Roti Baba was considered an *Avadhuta*. Avadhutas are said to have reached the highest state of renunciation, and they often wander about practically naked. Having attained the highest state of consciousness, they are completely unconcerned about their environment, and are happy under all conditions.

Roti Baba was about six foot tall, and wore only a loincloth. He was clean-shaven, both head and face, and looked to be perhaps in his sixties, although his devotees claimed that he was nearly 110 years old. He also had a large stomach, but apparently it was not due to overeating, since he ate very little. I later learned it was due to the yogic practice of breath retention (*kumbhaka*).

No one knew anything about Roti Baba's past, or even where he had come from. He had suddenly appeared in the area about seven years earlier. Apparently he had left once, but returned after traveling in the Himalayas for a few months. He did not speak any English. Generally Avadhutas stay for only short periods of time at any one place, but sometimes they may stay in an area indefinitely.

When I arrived, Roti Baba was sitting on a typical Indian cot made of threaded rope, while his devotees sat on the ground in front of him. At night everyone had to leave Baba by 10 p.m., and were not allowed to return until 4 a.m. the next morning. I was told that I could sleep on the verandah of a nearby temple with his only monastic disciple, Swami Atmananda. Swamiji later told me that Roti Baba did not normally accept disciples, nor even allowed anyone to stay with him, and so I should consider myself fortunate. Swamiji told me that he himself had to plead with Baba for a number of days before he was given permission to stay. Although I felt Roti Baba was a great being, after three or four days I started to feel restless again, and decided to leave.

Kashi — The City of Shiva

After leaving Roti Baba I once again started walking southeast towards Varanasi. Having walked a few miles a truck driver stopped and gave me a ride. Sometimes walking, and at other times riding, I reached Varanasi the next day. I had heard of several saints living in the city and decided to visit them.

Varanasi is an ancient city located on the western bank of the river Ganga. For many Hindus the city is perhaps the most sacred place in India. It is considered sacred to Lord Shiva. Varanasi, also known as *Kashi*, meaning the "city of light," was considered ancient during the time of Buddha who lived in the 6th century B.C.E. In fact the first sermon he gave after his enlightenment was given at Sarnath, just north of the present city. Today the West knows Varanasi as Benares, which is really a corruption of the Pali name of the city, *Baranasi*. The word Baranasi, or Varanasi, is created by the combination of the names of the two rivers which flank the city. The *Varana* on the north, and the *Asi* on the south of the city.

I had heard about a great saint who lived in the city named Anandamayi Ma. She was considered an enlightened soul so I decided to visit her ashram first. But unfortunately she was traveling at the time.

I then decided to visit the grandson of the famous saint, Lahiri Mahasaya, who was the grandguru of Swami Yogananda, the author of the famous book, *Autobiography of a Yogi*. I had read the book the previous year. I decided to visit the grandson's residence. He graciously invited me to visit with him for about an hour. I found him to be a very pious man. We had a long discussion on the spiritual life, particularly his tradition, known as Kriya Yoga. As I was about to leave he blessed and encouraged me on my spiritual search.

After wandering around the city for a few days, I started becoming extremely agitated and anxious again. These feelings appeared to increase daily. I felt depressed and confused. The question would constantly arise in my mind, "Why haven't I found my Guru?" I began praying for guidance. "Where should I go to next?" I mentally asked God. I would often cry as well and would say mentally to God, "You are my guide and goal, have compassion on me."

Day and night this became my constant prayer. It is difficult to convey the agony I was feeling. I felt like a lost child crying out for his parents to rescue him. The feeling of separation was extremely painful.

I visited a number of other *sadhus* in the city, but I felt no satisfaction or relief. I would also go and sit for hours at the burning ghats, watching the cremation of dead bodies and meditating on the impermanence of life.

One day while wandering through the streets I noticed a sign on a door which said Astrologer. I decided to go inside and meet the man. When I first walked in and asked the astrologer for a reading, I did not feel very welcomed. He appeared somewhat

(*below*) A view of the Varanasi *ghats* during a boat ride.

aloof and unfriendly towards me, but said he would prepare my horoscope, and told me to return in about half an hour. I had asked him for a reading partly out of curiosity, and perhaps with the hope of getting some guidance.

The reason for his initial unfriendliness was because in the late sixties there were many hippies traveling around India, particularly in Haridwar and Varanasi. The local people apparently did not like them very much. And with my long hair and beard, many called me a hippie as well. Some were true seekers, but most appeared to be in India just for the cheap and abundant drugs.

While I waited, I decided to go for a walk. When I returned, the astrologer's attitude towards me had totally changed. He was now very warm and courteous towards me. He appeared to be very excited about my horoscope and gave me a life reading.

However, my only real question was, "When will I meet my Guru?"

He told me that in fact I had already met my Guru, and that he was now guiding me. I assumed that he was referring to the experiences I had had earlier that year. However, I asked him specifically when I would meet the *outer* Guru.

After studying my chart for a few moments, he said that it might be sometime in December, a period which he said would be very auspicious for me. But as December was still a number of months away, I felt no mental relief. The astrologer then gave me some specific information about the next four or five months.

While he encouraged me, saying that I would certainly reach my spiritual goal in this very life, I still felt restless. In fact I had already met a number of palmists and astrologers in the city who had studied not only my palms, but also my face and torso. They all told me that I had many signs of a *sadhu* — a spiritual aspirant. But none of this information gave me any relief.

I continued to wander around the city for a few more days meeting different *sadhus*. But one afternoon I decided to leave

Varanasi. I started walking through the city and soon reached the bridge which crosses the river Ganga, leading east, and out of the city. By that time I felt extremely depressed and was crying. Before crossing the bridge, I paused for awhile on the banks of the Ganges. Night was falling, and I continued to pray for guidance and light. How can I explain my mental anguish? I thought I was going mad. I did not want to live any longer. The following story may illustrate my mental and emotional state at that time.

There was once a seeker who approached a Guru and asked, "Sir, could you please tell me when I will be able to see God?"

The Guru did not say anything, but gently took the seeker's hand, and led him to a nearby river. They walked into the river, and when they were about waist deep, the Guru stopped. Then suddenly he grabbed the seeker's head and pushed it under the water. Caught by surprise, and unable to get any air, the seeker began struggling, gasping for a breath of air.

After a few moments, the Guru released the boy's head, and then asked, "My boy, how did you feel?"

"How did I feel?" the seeker asked in surprise. "I felt like I was going to die gasping for a breath of air!"

"My boy," the Guru said, "when you feel that way for God, then you can be sure that you are not far from having his vision."

The intensity of my longing was like the poor disciple in the above story, gasping for air while his head was being held underwater. I felt that if I could not experience union with God, there was no longer a purpose for my life, so I decided to end it. I looked around to make sure that there was no one in site. I started walking into the river, all along praying to God and mentally asking why he did not show me his mercy? I complained that although I had prayed for his guidance and light, he had not answered me.

Overwhelmed by such feelings, I began thinking that

God was uncaring. First he revealed himself to me, but now it appeared he had abandoned me. This was the degree of my mental anguish. But just as the water was about waist high, I noticed a young man walking towards me. As he got closer he called out and greeted me. He began speaking to me in broken English, asking where I was from, and where was I going. His sudden presence distracted my mind from what I was about to do, and we started talking.

I told him that I was searching for a real holy man (*sadhu*). He suggested I visit the ashram of Avadhuta Ram, which he said was located just over the bridge. He told me that this Baba was believed to have reached a very high spiritual state, and he would be happy to take me to his ashram. I agreed to go. I also felt a little hope again.

We were walking across the bridge before I realized that I had not even asked his name. I inquired what it was, and he said it was Prakash. I asked him what the name meant, and he said it meant, "Light", "God's light." When I heard this, my spirits immediately returned. I again felt uplifted, realizing that the Lord was still guiding me after all.

As we walked we conversed about spiritual matters. He also told me about a well known *yoga* school located in the city of Monghyr, in the modern state of Bihar. He suggested I visit that ashram as well. However, when he mentioned the place, for some reason I doubted that I would find my Guru there. But when a person is desperate, he will try anything to appease his suffering.

At the time I was not very familiar with the various Indian philosophies. I knew very little about *Yoga*, *Vedanta,* or any of the other philosophical systems. I had read the Bhagavad Gita and a few of the Upanishads, but that was the extent of my knowledge of Hindu scriptures. In fact, I knew very little about India or its spiritual culture, except for what I had read in books. However, I was learning more and more each day through my meetings with India's holy men.

As we reached the other side of the bridge, Avadhuta Ram's ashram came into view. It was just a short distance on the right side of the road, just past the bridge. It was now around dusk. Entering the ashram's main gate, we walked down a short path through a garden. This led to the main building, where Ram's room was located. On the left side of the path I could see a small temple dedicated to the Divine Mother. As we got closer to the main building, we noticed Avadhuta Ram sitting on the verandah outside his room, giving *darshan* to a number of people. The word *darshan* literally means "to see" or "to have a vision off." It is a Hindu's belief that great merit is gained simply by having a glimpse of a sacred shrine, or a great and noble soul.

Ram was sitting crosslegged on a typical Indian cot. He appeared to be in his late thirties or early forties. He had short curly hair and a beard. When we reached the verandah, Prakash introduced me, and explained my purpose for visiting India. A smile appeared on Avadhuta Ram's face, and he said that he was very happy to know that I had come to India in search of a Guru. He then invited me to stay in his ashram as long as I liked.

There was something about Avadhuta Ram that attracted me. Perhaps it was his smile, as there was something very enchanting about it. I thanked him, and decided to accept his hospitality for at least a few days. He then asked me to sit near him.

His devotees made room for me near his cot, and I sat down. One of the devotees spoke English, and he became my translator for the duration of my stay. After sometime, most of the people left, including Prakash. There were now only two or three devotees, and Ram began questioning me. His questions were all philosophical, and it appeared as if he were testing me. However, it was a friendly conversation, and it seemed as if we had known each other for a long time. And with that first conversation, Ram began teaching me *Vedanta*.

Vedanta

The word '*Vedanta*' literally means, "the end of the *Vedas*". It is that portion of the Vedas called the *Upanishads*. These writings deal with the mystical knowledge of the relationship between the Supreme Being, called *Brahman*, and the individual soul, called *Atman*. These are in fact two names for one reality. When the Upanishadic seer refers to the Lord in his absolute state, and without any form, he is called Brahman. When they refer to Him as the Lord within, he is called Atman.

The *Upanishads*, the *Brahma Sutras*, and the *Bhagavad Gita* are the basic scriptures for all Vedantic literature. A number of commentaries have been written on all three by different sages. And since people differ in temperament, and the level of their experiences vary, there has arisen about a dozen schools of Vedantic thought. From these there are three basic views among them. The two extreme perspectives in Vedantic philosophy are the non-dualistic (*advaita*) school, and the dualistic (*dvaita*) school. Central between these two is the *Vishishtadvaita* or "qualified non-dualism." These three varying viewpoints are represented by three of India's great scholars: Shankara, Madhava, and Ramanuja respectively.

Shankara or Adi Shankaracharya's birth is placed in the eighth century (788 – 820? C.E.) by most modern scholars, although some dispute this date. Shankaracharya established four main ashrams at the four geographical locations of India. Although Shankara's name is specifically associated with *Advaita* Vedanta, this non-dualistic philosophy is much older than Shankara. There is no doubt, however, that Shankara has been its most brilliant proponent.

Next comes Ramanuja, who lived in the eleventh century (1017 - 1137 C.E.). He taught the *Vishishtadvaita* or "qualified non-dualism" perspective. After Ramanuja comes Madhava, who lived in the thirteenth century. Of course there were many other Vedantic teachers as well, but these three schools are considered representatives of the three above points of view. Keep in mind that their philosophies are all based on their interpretations of the same three scriptures mentioned above.

Shankaracharya proclaimed that there was absolutely no difference between the Self (Atman) and Brahman, the Supreme Being. That in fact, this world was nothing but a manifestation of Brahman. He interpreted literally the Upanishadic statements, "All this is Brahman," "Thou Art That," and, "I Am Brahman." For Shankara, life's only goal is to know oneself, to realize Brahman. We must therefore constantly ask ourselves, "Who am I?" "Where have I come from?" and, "What is the purpose of my coming?" In other words, "What is the purpose of your life."

These questions do have answers, and according to Shankara, it is our duty to find them. Shankaracharya lived for only 32 years. He had written commentaries on the Brahma Sutras, Bhagavad Gita, and the major Upanishads before he was sixteen years old. He also wrote numerous other works in addition to organizing and forming the *dashanami*, or the "ten branches or order" of *sannyasis*.

After Shankara, Ramanuja is the most important Vedantin. He also wrote commentaries on all the important Sutras. His Vedanta is called, "The philosophy of Non-dualism of the Qualified Brahman (*Vishishtadvaita*)." This means that Brahman is considered non-dual, but yet is characterized by the world and the individual spirits, which forms his body. This tradition is devotional and theistic in nature, and is also known as the *Vaishnava* religion.

This school advocates the path of devotion and complete surrender to God's will. Ramanuja accepts God, nature (*prakriti*), time, and the plurality of souls as different entities, although together they make up the non-duality of Brahman. There is a beautiful story about Ramanuja's initiation which illustrates his compassion and detachment. It is said that when his Guru gave him the *mantra*, he told Ramanuja that it was very powerful, and that he should not divulge it to anyone. But after his initiation, Ramanuja went around giving the mantra to many people. When his Guru heard this, in order to test him, he began scolding Ramanuja, and told him he would go to hell because he had divulged the mantra.

"And what will happen to those who received the mantra?" Ramanuja asked his Guru. The master replied that they would of course attain Self-Realization. Ramanuja then said, "In that case, I will be happy to go to hell." His Guru embraced him, forgave him, and eventually made him his successor.

Madhava (1199? - 1278 C.E.) is the third most important Vedantin in the above division. He is also a Vaishnavite. Madhava, like Ramanuja, was a follower of the path of devotion. But not being completely satisfied with Ramanuja's philosophy, he proclaimed the complete separation between Brahman and the world. He taught that the non-duality referred to in the Upanishads must be interpreted as that found in the relationship between the king and his subjects, between one who is independent, and one who is dependent on the former. Because of this dualism or separation between God and his creation, Madhava's school of Vedanta is called *dvaita* — meaning, "duality, dualistic."

In reality there is no real difference between the various philosophical schools of Vedanta. When approached with an open mind, we discover that everyone is speaking about the same Divine Principle, differing only in the relationship between the individual and the divine. But such perspectives are based on one's personal experiences. A lover of God expresses his feelings through his devotional worship; a knower of truth through his wisdom; the practitioner of selfless service reveals the man of action; while the yogi reveals it through his silence and yogic vision. But these varying views are not exclusive of each other. A true man of knowledge is also filled with great devotion, while a true devotee is full of wisdom. After having studied these different schools of thought, and through my own personal experiences, I have concluded that they are all describing different aspects of the same reality. We all perceive the Lord according to our own understanding and experiences. Although Shankara's emphasized the path of knowledge (*jnana*), he was also a supreme devotee. One can see this by the many devotional hymns he wrote. Great beings teach in accordance to the needs of the individual. Ramanuja emphasized the need for both love and knowledge. He did not believe in blind faith, but a reasoned devotion which arises from pure actions and self discipline.

Avadhuta Ram was teaching me Shankara's Advaita Vedanta. Since I had personally gotten a glimpse of the reality of Brahman as discussed by Shankara, I was obviously not yet established in that divine state. Although I still retained the experiential reality of my true Self, at the time I was very much aware of myself as a limited individual soul. Like the whole world, I was still overwhelmed by God's mystic power of Self-concealment known as *Maya*. Although God has created the whole universe from his own Self, yet he remains hidden from everyone. I was still experiencing painful feelings of separation from God, but I continued my search for a Guru. A Guru whose very touch would awaken that inner divinity.

The reader may wonder why, if I had already experienced the unity with the inner Self, was I still suffering so much? All I can say is that this is a great mystery. It is the Self which appears to be in bondage, and it is the Self alone which is rediscovered. That is why the world is such a wonderful play or drama. It is the Self which is in search of the Self. By appearing in multiple forms, the Lord plays hide and seek with Himself. God has the power to conceal himself, as well as the power to reveal himself. This is called divine grace.

In my tormented state, I kept wondering when I would meet my Guru. I still did not know the answer to that question, and so I was feeling very impatient. I was experiencing such longing that it was impossible to concentrate my mind on the lofty idea of "I am That." Like a pendulum, my mind swung back and forth struggling with this problem. One moment I felt small and insignificant, while the next moment I was convinced of my unity with the Absolute (*Brahman*).

Nevertheless, it is said that when the disciple is ready the Lord comes in the form of the Guru. Patience is very important on the spiritual path, for without it not much can be accomplished. I felt God's grace for the first time on that day in January when my life changed completely. But I now had to learn to be patient, and wait for my spiritual life to naturally unfold.

Meanwhile I was enjoying Ram's company. I found him very interesting. I learned that He belonged to the *Aghori* sect of Shaivites, and was considered a *Shakta*. That is, one who worships the Supreme Being in its feminine form. He worshipped the Goddess in the form of *Sri Sarveshwari* — meaning the mother or ruler of all. His Guru was the head of the main ashram of this sect of Aghoris, which was located in Varanasi. The Aghoris do not always follow conventional practices, and in fact some of their practices can be quite strange to the uninitiated.

For real spiritual growth, the divine energy (*Shakti*) residing within an individual must be awakened. In India this divine energy is addressed by yogis as Mother, Goddess (*Devi*), or *Kundalini Shakti*. From the perspective of a limited individual, there are cycles of creation, preservation and destruction constantly occurring. This manifestation is the work of God's power (*Shakti*), which is symbolized as being feminine, and is called *Chiti Shakti*, or the power of consciousness. From the perspective of ultimate reality, there is no difference between the Supreme Being and his power. But from the perspective of creation, there appears to be differences. In reality the God is neither male nor female, but from our limited perspective, we

(*above*) The front gate of Avadhut Ram's Guru's *Aghori* ashram.

say "He" or "She."

That first night in the ashram I was asked to join Ram for dinner. It was obvious that this was a privilege, and an honor, since everyone else was standing around serving us. Shortly a plate of food was brought to Ram, and I noticed it contained some meat. Since I had become a vegetarian, I respectively passed on the meat dish. Some kind of alcohol was also served to him. It was also offered to me, but again I politely declined.

As we ate, Ram questioned me about why I had become a vegetarian. He did not ask this in a critical or sarcastic manner, but I felt that he was testing my understanding and reasoning behind my abstention. However, having seen the meat and alcohol, I have to admit that a slight doubt and criticism arose in my mind about Ram's habits. But at the same time I felt that there was something special about him that I liked.

After finishing our dinner, we again sat on the verandah. Soon one of Ram's attendants began to prepare a *chilum* or pipe containing *hashish*, sometimes mixed with either marijuana or tobacco. Sadhus who smoke hashish or ganja (marijuana) usually follow a special procedure when preparing a chilum. They assume an attitude of worship. The chilum was soon ready. It was of course first offered to Ram. He took two or three puffs, and then passed it back to the attendant, who took a few puffs himself, and then passed it on to the other devotees sitting there.

It was now considered *prasad* or consecrated food since it had been offered to God and the Guru. Because I had stopped using these drugs, I passed on the *chilum* as well. However, I observed Ram with great interest, and when I looked at his face, I felt that he saw all this as simply a play. With a twinkle in his eyes he appeared to say, "I am more than this." In fact, Ram appeared to be just playing a role. Actually he did not seem to be affected by the drug. It appeared to be merely a ritual that he was performing.

After awhile I excused myself and went to bed. The next morning, Ram and I continued our talk. He gave me a set of Ram Tirtha's books, *In Woods of God Realization*. It was a set of six volumes dealing with Advaitic Vedanta, as explained by Swami Rama Tirtha. Swami Rama (1873-1906) was a very interesting personality, and had lived an amazing life. Before becoming a *sannyasi*, he had been a mathematics professor. But after his initiation, he traveled all over the world, and even spent time in Japan and America. He had experienced the highest truth and was a free soul. His writings are sprinkled with many humorous stories which often convey deep philosophical meanings. He was also a poet and the author of some very moving poems.

Everyday I read some portion of the books, and during the evening, Ram would ask me questions about what I had learned that day. We would then have a discussion on the subject. During those sessions, we discussed all sorts of topics.

But after about a week or two, I still did not know what to think of Ram. Although I liked him, and felt he had achieved something, nothing had yet occurred to indicate that he was my

Guru. Once again I started feeling restless, and so I decided to leave the ashram.

However, an interesting incident occurred one night which gave me an insight into Ram's mental state. One afternoon I was told that Ram was going to the palace of the *Maharaja* of Varanasi for dinner. Since I was told that I would not see Ram that night, I decided to go to bed just after dinner, which was about 8:30 p.m.. I quickly fell asleep, but after about an hour, I was suddenly awakened by one of Ram's attendants. He was shouting, "...Come quick, Come quick, Ram wants you, come quick."

I got up, still a bit sleepy, and ran to see what Ram wanted. I thought something had happened to him. But he was sitting on his cot while someone was massaging his shoulders and neck. I also noticed that he was having trouble sitting up, and the person massaging him was actually supporting him so that he would not fall over.

"My God, he's drunk," I thought to myself. "He went to the Maharaja's palace and got loaded."

I asked if there was anything I could do for him. I was told by the attendant that Ram had called me because he wanted me to tell him some stories. "Stories," I thought to myself, "what stories?" I didn't know any stories, and I said so. But he insisted. So I frantically searched my mind for a story, any story, but I came up blank. I tried telling him a story I had recently read, but he did not like it. I next told him about the life of Edgar Cayce, an American psychic who would go into a sleep like trance and give advice to people on health matters and other subjects. Ram said he liked this story better than the first one.

While all this was going on, my mind was still pondering Ram's mental state. I wondered why drugs and alcohol were necessary for him? I began watching him very closely. Then he suddenly gave me one of those looks of his, and it was clear that he was not drunk, intoxicated yes, but not from alcohol.

As strange as it may sound, the smoking and drinking

were really used as part of his ritual and not for the purpose of becoming intoxicated. He always took the same amount each time. I had watched him very carefully on a number of occasions. Even before smoking anything he looked intoxicated, with his body swaying to some inner rhythm. Then after he took two or three puffs from the *chilum*, in a way, he appeared to be more normal or sober. It was as if he were smoking simply to keep from entering into a deep trance.

Yes, there was something interesting and mysterious about Avadhuta Ram. I enjoyed my stay with him, but I concluded that he was not my Guru. I decided to leave the ashram and asked his permission to do so. He gave me his blessings, and said to come back and visit him at anytime. That I would always be welcomed.

Yoga

From Varanasi I traveled north to the city of Monghyr, located in the state of Bihar. I was going to visit the *yoga* school which Prakash had mentioned. I started out walking and occasionally got a ride with a Sadarji. When I reached the outskirts of Monghyr, I was given a ride by a local Muslim lawyer, who also invited me to his home for lunch. Along the way we discussed religion in general, and he asked me a number of questions about my experiences. At the time I had not studied the *Koran*, and so was unfamiliar with the religion of Islam. The only contact that I had with Muslims was during my journey through the middle eastern countries.

By the time we reached his home, the conversation had turned to the topic of death. He asked me what I thought really happens when one dies. I told him that since we were spirits, we really did not die, but that it was only the body which died. He asked how did I know that this was true? I replied that having had a personal experience of this truth, I no longer feared death.

The moment I said that, the expression on his face suddenly changed, and he said sarcastically, "So, you're not afraid of death?"

At the time I was sitting in a chair, and he was standing near me. He continued, "Suppose I say that I'm going to kill you, what would you say then?"

"I would have to say the same thing," I replied.

At that point he turned and grabbed an old spear which was standing in the corner of the room, and placed its tip to my throat and said, "Now, I will kill you!"

I said nothing. In the past I would have responded quite differently. I would have been very angry at the man, and would have probably given him a good beating. But instead, at that moment, I felt a deep calm, and I was not bothered by his behavior at all. Nor did I feel any fear or anger towards him. I simply sat there smiling at him.

After a few moments, his expression changed once again, and he smiled at me. He then bent down to touch my feet and asked for my pardon for having tested me in that way. He soon started calling me "*Chota Baba,*" which means "little father."

I told him that there was no need for an apology, and to simply forget it. After this incident, he began asking me many questions, and we talked for a number of hours. Finally, he personally drove me to the yoga ashram, and told me to call him if I needed anything while I was in Monghyr.

Unfortunately when I arrived at the ashram I was told that Swami Satyananda, the head of the ashram, was traveling abroad. However, I was invited to stay if I wished. Since Swamiji was not going to return for a number of months, I decided I would stay for only three or four days. At the time a female sannyasi was managing the ashram, and I was given a bed in the men's dormitory. There were only a few people staying in the ashram at the time, which included both Indians and Europeans. I became friendly with a European sannyasi who told me a great deal about the ashram and their practices. Photographs of their Guru were hanging on the walls in the ashram's main hall.

The photographs showed a clean shaven sannyasi who appeared to be in his forties. The emphasis in that ashram was mainly on *Hatha-Yoga*, or physical postures. There was also meditation, but hatha-yoga was the main path. *Yoga* postures were practiced for the purpose of awakening the *Kundalini Shakti*. The word *yoga* means to "unite" or "join together," and therefore indicates the joining of the individual soul with the Supreme Being. The English word "yoke" is derived from the Sanskrit word yoga.

Besides indicating the final goal of unity, the word yoga also identifies the particular path or method to be followed for achieving that goal. But with all forms of *yogas*, in order for real progress to be made, the latent spiritual energy (*Kundalini*) must be awakened. The particular method used at that ashram was Hatha-Yoga or yogic postures (*asana*).

According to the famous treatise on the subject, *Hathayogapradipika,* the practice of *hathayoga*, with its numerous postures and breath control, purifies the body and leads to *Raja-yoga* or the royal path. According to teachings of yoga, there are countless *nadis* or channels in the human body through which the life force (*prana*) flows. Within this network of *nadis,* some are physical, while others belong to the subtle body. Out of all these nadis, the three most important are the *sushumna*, *pingala*, and *ida*. Of these, the sushumna is the most important. In the physical body, the sushumna-nadi is located within the spinal column. The pingala-nadi is to its right, and is indicated by the right nostril, while the ida-nadi is to its left, and is indicated by the left nostril.

The word *ha-tha* is made up of two Sanskrit letters. The literal meaning of the word *hatha* is "forceful." Therefore, this is also known as the "forceful yoga." However, the mystical meaning is that the letter '*ha*' represents the sun, while '*tha*' indicates the moon. The energy producing sun is associated with the right nostril and the pingala-nadi, while the calming and cooling influence of the lunar energy is associated with ida-nadi, and the left nostril. Ordinary breathing occurs alternately between these two nadis. However, when the Kundalini Shakti is awakened, the yogi's breathing starts to occur within the sushumna-nadi itself.

Therefore, according to hatha-yoga, in order to achieve the transcendental state of samadhi, one practices certain physical postures (*asana*) and breath control (*pranayama*) for the purpose of purifying the body, particularly the nadis. In order to achieve samadhi the yogi must bring about the even flow of his prana. The flow of his outgoing and incoming breath has to become even, and with practice, it will slow down, eventually appearing to stop completely. However, breathing is still going on internally, but it is very subtle, and is occurring in the sushumna-nadi.

With certain types of *pranayama* one concentrates the breath *(prana)* directing it to the base of the spine where the latent Kundalini resides. The word Kundalini is the feminine form of the word *kundala*, which denotes something coiled or circular. But to the yogi, Kundalini is the that supreme power (Shakti), which resides within all beings. With continued practice, intense heat is generated within, until finally the Kundalini begins to rise up the spine until it reaches the top most spiritual center in the head, called the *sahasrara*.

The word hatha therefore really indicates the balance or *even* flow of prana between the right (sun) and left (moon) nostrils so that one can experience the transcendental state. Another subtle meaning of breathing within the sushumna, is that the yogi experiences himself to be beyond the rhythm of ordinary time, indicated by the sun and moon.

Sadly, not everyone practices Hatha-yoga for this lofty purpose. Today many people practice it simply for physical health, and the reduction of stress. Nevertheless, the true purpose of Hatha-yoga is to experience the transcendental state.

Unfortunately I did not feel the ashram was my home. Somehow I intuitively felt that when I met my Guru, the awakening of Kundalini would occur spontaneously. During my three days in the ashram, I tried to plan a strategy as to where I would go next. I thought that instead of running here and there, perhaps I should just go somewhere and stay for awhile, practice meditation, and see what happened. Even though I felt impatient and anxious I also knew that everything would happen at the proper time.

I realized that my restlessness was making me too impatient. And while thinking about what to do next, I suddenly remembered Roti Baba, and decided to return to him. I felt that he was a great being and I would benefit from his company.

Return To Roti Baba
(Lessons in Detachment)

When I left the ashram I began traveling southwest towards Rai Barelli. I decided not to stop in Varanasi, and instead continue directly to Allahabad. Allahabad or Prayag — the city's ancient name — is considered to be a very sacred place. Many pilgrims visit the city for the Magha festival held each year in the month of Magha (January). At Allahabad three great rivers merge: the Ganga, Yamuna, and unseen Sarasvati, which is said to now flow underground. Every twelve years millions of people attend the *Kumbha-Mela*.

When I reached the outskirts of town I went to the place where the confluence takes place. I sat quietly for awhile. Then as I was about to move on, I met a Swami Krishnananda. Swamiji was staying in a cottage right on the banks of the river. He was a scholarly man, and at the time was working on an English translation, and commentary, on the Bhagavad Gita.

He was a kind and saintly man. He lived on only two glasses of milk a day, which a devotee would bring him. He invited me to stay with him, but said that he was so busy that he would not be able to spend much time with me. I thanked him for his kind offer, but I decided to move on.

I continued west, and was soon walking through the streets of the city of Allahabad. As I was walking, a man on a bicycle suddenly pulled up next to me, and dismounted. He began walking alongside of me, and after the usual introductions, we began a conversation about religion. He told me that he and his wife were Christians. He seemed to be a kind man, and invited me to his home for lunch, which I accepted.

When we arrived at his home our conversation continued. But after awhile the conversation started to become less philosophical and more critical. He began by pointing out the differences between Christianity and Hinduism, and that he believed that Christianity was the superior of the two. His attitude towards Hinduism was obviously one of disdain. He believed that Hindus worshipped stones and therefore were idol worshipers. Looking around the room I noticed a crucifix hanging on one of the walls and I pointed to it saying that it appeared that he too was committing the same offense. But instead of stone, he was worshipping wood.

He became indignant at my statement, and pointed out that he was not actually worshipping the wood, but Jesus, whose image it represented.

"Exactly!" I said. "It is the same with Hindus. They do not worship a stone, but what that stone represents. The devotee does not say, 'Oh stone please bless me,' but instead prays, 'Oh Lord, help me and bless me.'"

At first he did not like this answer, and began arguing with me, but soon he realized the truth of what I was saying. He then asked if I would read the Bible with him and give my comments on some verses he had questions about. So we went through the Bible together until lunch was served. After lunch he invited me to spend the night, but I politely declined, saying that I wanted to reach my destination quickly.

However, I rested for awhile before leaving, and then started traveling west again. I reached Rai Barelli early the next morning and went directly to meet Roti Baba. When I reached the spot, I went up to Baba and did a full prostration before him, and asked his permission to stay for awhile. He smiled at me, and welcomed me back, saying that I could stay as long as I wished. I decided to follow his instructions and see what happened.

As I have mentioned earlier, Baba was a large man who wore only a loincloth. A loincloth is usually made up of two pieces of cloth, one tied around the waist, with the other wrapped over one's private area. Roti Baba told me that as long as I stayed with him, that I too should only wear a loincloth. He then instructed one of his devotees to have a special one made for me, which he brought the next day. The loincloth made for me was sewn into one piece so it would be easier for me to put on.

Swami Atmananda, Roti Baba's other disciple was a sannyasi, and so he wore the traditional saffron robes. Usually this consists of one or two pieces of cotton cloth. One piece is wrapped around the waist and reaches either the knees or ankles according to personal preference. This is called a lungi. The other piece is wrapped around the shoulders and upper body as a shawl. Some sadhus use only one piece of cloth, which is longer, but is wrapped in such a way that it serves as both lungi and shawl. It is a very comfortable way of dressing in that part of the world, where it is usually very hot.

I lived a very simple life with Roti Baba. I would sit meditating quietly with him each day. There were always two or three devotees who visited Baba during the day, and more would come on Thursdays and weekends. Thursday is called the Guru's day (*Guruvar*), and so it is considered an auspicious day to visit one's Guru. Usually there was someone who spoke English, and would translate for me whenever necessary.

However, as soon as I became familiar with the daily routine, there wasn't much need for verbal communication. If Baba had something specifically to tell me, or he was answering some question, then it would be translated for my benefit. But I really did not have any pressing philosophical questions. I was searching for a Guru who would bring about an inner transformation, not necessarily with words, but through his spiritual power.

Roti Baba was a free soul who was indeed established in that supreme state. He was very loving to everyone and yet had no attachments at all. He owned absolutely nothing, and could come and go as he pleased. Yet, for some reason he had chosen to stay on the banks of that river. To him, all devotees were the same, whether they were Hindus, Christians, Muslims, or any other religion or sect. He would give spiritual advice to anyone who asked, and he taught me something important each day. He did not speak very much, nor did he give any formal lectures. He had a lot of love for me and always took the time to explain subtle truths.

But in those days it was as if my brain was on fire, and I felt impatient, and could at times become short-tempered. I felt discontented and was always watching and testing Baba. I looked at him for any flaws, as well as a sign that he was my Guru. There were no bolts of lighting, nor flashes of light, but I had committed myself to learning patience. I thought that even if he was not my Guru, he was a great being, and I would benefit from his company.

As I mentioned earlier, the only rule was that everyone had to leave Baba by 10 p.m., and not return until 4 a.m. the next morning. Baba would spend that time alone in quiet meditation. All devotees would leave at night by eight or nine, since they would have to walk back into town. Swami Atmananda and I would stay and meditate until ten, at which time we would go and sleep on the verandah of a nearby temple. It was located less than a quarter of a mile away. We were in fact the only two that Baba allowed to stay with him continuously. We would wake up just before 4 a.m. and go meet Baba. He would still be sitting quietly on his cot inside a tent. Before sitting for meditation, I would go to the river and take a bath. I would then go and sit near Baba. These were very deep and peaceful meditations.

Originally Baba used to stay outdoors all of the time. But some devotees had erected an old army tent for him. The reason they gave for doing this was so that Baba could stay dry during the four month *monsoon* season, which was then winding down. However, Baba used to jokingly say that the real reason for setting up the tent was so they (the devotees) could stay dry during the rainy season. When it rained, everyone would squeeze inside the tent, sitting closely around Baba's cot. Baba on the other hand did not seem to care whether it was raining, or the sun was burning bright. At times he sat on the cot outside the tent even when raining. Or he would lie on the ground under the fierce rays of the sun. He was completely oblivious to his outer condition. He was in his own divine state.

Baba started calling me Shukadev Muni. He said that I reminded him of that ancient sage. Shukadeva was the son of sage Vyasa, and the disciple of king Janaka. He is considered the ideal renunciate and is pictured as a young man wearing only a loincloth, a dark beard, and long black hair combed back, similar to how I looked at the time.

Since Baba used to clean his teeth using only sand, I began doing the same. But later he told me to use branches of the *Neem* tree instead. I would bathe in the river each morning. But an interesting incident occurred on the first day I arrived back, and took a bath in the river. I removed the few clothes I had on, and walked into the river naked. The river was a little distance from where Baba sat. All of a sudden, I noticed one of the devotees sitting with Baba got up and started calling out to me. He was yelling something and making wild gestures, but since I was about half way into the river, I could not hear or understand what he was saying. But then Baba called out to the man, said something to him, and the man sat back down.

When I finished my bath, I put on my new loincloth and went over and sat with the others near Baba. Someone asked me, "Do you know what that man was saying?"

I said that I did not know since I could not hear him. The man explained to me that it was the custom in India that whenever a man bathes in public, and particularly in a river, he should wear at least a loincloth. There is however an exception for certain sadhus, like Roti Baba. I was told that one should not go naked into the river. "That's what the man was trying to tell you," the translator told me, "but Baba stopped him. Baba told the man that you were a great renunciate, and that it was all right for you to bathe naked."

I did not say anything, but soon people began coming out just to see the foreign *sadhu* staying with Roti Baba. They would ask me questions, or just sit quietly in front of me. As

I have mentioned, the practice of *darshan* is very common in India. Devotees visit the Guru, and just sit quietly with him and meditate, or they may ask some questions. The Guru may or may not say anything. But even if he does not speak, that is not important. It is the company of the sadhu which is considered important and beneficial. This was all new to me, and I just directed those people to Baba, telling them to put their questions to him, as I too was only a seeker.

Devotees would normally bring food to Baba once or twice a day. However, he would distribute it among all the devotees who happened to be present. He might eat some of it himself, but mainly Roti Baba ate very little. He mainly drank a little milk, and/or some fruit. Baba had given me a bowl in which he would place some food for me from whatever was brought to him. Swami Atmananda, on the other hand, would have to go to one of the local villages and beg for his food, as is common among sadhus. But one day, while we were having our lunch, Baba asked me whether I would go with Swamiji the next day and beg for my food as well?

As you may recall, before leaving America I had vowed that I would not beg for anything. I wanted to depend completely on God, and eat only if it came to me without my asking for it. I felt that whatever came naturally would be what my body required at the time. If I was offered some fruit, I would think, "My body must need this fruit today since God has sent it to me." I had full faith in God's protection, and I felt that he was providing everything I needed. Even during the most trying moments, I still felt deeply that he was present with me.

I tried to explain this to Baba, but he simply remained silent, appearing uninterested in what I had to say. After awhile he asked me again, "Will you go with Swamiji?" I said that I would go if that was what he wanted me to do. "Good," Baba said, "you can go with Swamiji tomorrow."

I felt that this was obviously some kind of test. At first I thought that he was simply trying to see if I would obey him, but then I thought perhaps he wanted to see if I would become embarrassed by having to beg. At the time I did not feel any embarrassment or shyness about the idea, but then again, I was not yet standing at some strangers door begging for food. The next day, when I went to see Baba, he was smiling and appeared very happy. He said, "Aah!, today you are going to beg for your food, this is a very good thing, very auspicious."

We sat around Baba as usual until it was time to go. I went and got my bowl, and before leaving I bowed to Baba. Swami Atmananda was chuckling to himself and appeared to be amused by the whole affair. I thought to myself, "How hard can this be?"

When we reached a nearby village, Swamiji was going to show me how it was done by going to the first few houses himself. Often a sadhu chooses a certain number of houses, perhaps three, four, or five, and if he gets something from these, he eats that day, otherwise not.

Swamiji's method was to stand at some distance from the front door of the house and call out the mantra, "Hari Om!" If the residents wished to give something, someone would come out of the house and bring rice, *dal*, bread (*roti*) or vegetables.

After having gone to the second house, Swamiji told me that I should do the next one. But the moment he said that, I suddenly became paralyzed by a deep inner panic. I did not say anything to Swamiji. But when we reached the next house, I found I was unable to ask for food. I suddenly froze up, feeling completely paralyzed. Seeing my condition, Swamiji had to finish the round himself.

We were soon on our way back to Roti Baba's camp. When we got there, Baba asked Swamiji if I had begged for my food. Swamiji answered in the negative. Baba just remained silent.

I sat down near him, and after a few moments, a conversation started.

"Why weren't you able to do it?" Baba asked.

Instead of telling him the truth, that I simply became

embarrassed, I started to say, "Well, it's not necessary, I feel God will provide for me."

But before I could even finish the sentence, Baba interrupted me saying, "Who cares whether you eat or not, you're just a sadhu. Don't think this is just for your stomach. No one could care less whether you eat or not. When a sadhu begs at someone's home, it isn't important whether he gets food or not. Instead, he is creating an opportunity for the householder to give something in charity. These actions will uplift the giver. Some people may never get an opportunity to give in charity in their whole life."

Baba spoke in this manner for sometime, not with anger, but with love and compassion. And as he was speaking, it suddenly became clear to me that I had been thinking only from my own egotistical point of view. I saw it only as a means of getting nourishment for myself. Thoughts such as, "How can I get my food? Should I be begging this way? Won't God take care of me?" were actually arising from my ego. I had not even considered the person who was giving. I never considered how that person fit into the picture. Would they gain anything from their actions, or are they just parting with some food? Why was I thinking only of myself? If I had given everything up, then why did I feel so proud? Truly, the sadhu's path is to concentrate only on God. They should completely forget their personal interests. But at the same time, he should be of some benefit to the world.

Suddenly my attitude completely changed. I now saw the whole thing from a totally different perspective. I then started feeling a deep inner calm and understanding. It was as if a veil had been removed, giving me a new insight into everything. I knew that it was Roti Baba's influence which was giving me this experience. I felt deeply appreciative and very happy. The next day, I asked Baba if I could go with Swamiji again. He looked at me for a moment, and then said in English, "Yes."

Swamiji and I again went to a nearby village. Standing

outside of the first house I called out, "Hari Om!" This time I felt no embarrassment or shyness at all. Instead, I felt elated. A woman soon came out of the house with some rice and *dal* (a kind of lentil soup which is usually mixed with the rice) and placed some in each of our bowls. She was smiling, and appeared happy to be sharing her food with us.

We went to the next house, and I again called out, "Hari Om!" This time a young girl, who was about six or seven years old came out of the house carrying some vegetables. Her mother followed closely behind. The little girl became very excited when she placed some vegetables in my bowl.

Hearing the talk outside, another neighbor soon came out and brought us some mango juice she had just prepared. We soon had more than enough food, and decided to return to our camp. When we arrived, Swamiji told Baba everything that had happened. Baba laughed and said to me, "From now on you won't have to beg anymore."

During my stay with Roti Baba, I also met a few other sadhus. One day, someone who used to come and visit Baba asked if I wanted to meet a yogi who was living nearby. I said I was interested, but first I asked Baba's permission to go visit the yogi, which he gave.

This sadhu was living in a very unusual room at a local temple. It was actually the space between the ground and the foundation of the temple. It was like a cave, but was only about four feet high. All one could do was sit or lie down. I was told that he had been living there for the past two years. The entrance was a small opening about three feet off the ground. With my guide leading, I followed closely behind. At first it felt a little strange, however I soon got used to it, and thought it quite cozy.

The sadhu was sitting alone when we arrived, and invited us to take a seat. He had long matted hair and beard, and wore a simple piece of white cloth wrapped around his waist. He told me that he had heard that there was a foreign sadhu living nearby and had wanted to meet me. He too was addressed simply as *Baba*. Even though a sadhu has a personal name, with the exception of other sadhus, he is not usually addressed by it. They are often addressed as Baba, Maharaj, or Swamiji in the case of sannyasis. The suffix *ji* (pronounced jee) is added to these titles and indicates both respect, as well as a personal intimacy with the person.

I asked the sadhu some questions on yoga and the particular sadhana he was practicing. We spoke for sometime, and then he invited me to smoke some hashish with him, which I politely declined. I spent a few hours with him, and when I left, he invited me to come and stay with him. I thanked him, but said that I was staying with Roti Baba at the moment, and did not want to leave him yet. He told me that he knew Roti Baba, and said that he was a great being.

Another sadhu I met at the time was Baba Chandra Dayal. I met him just about the time I was thinking of leaving the area. This sadhu had an ashram in the Punjab but was now on a tour of India. I met him in the nearby town of Rai Bareli, where I had been invited to meet him by one of his devotees.

He was a short man, and at the time was perhaps in his seventies. He had white hair and a long beard. His face was very bright, and appeared to glow with an inner light. I spoke with him privately and told him of my search for a Guru. He then told me something about his tradition and its practices. One of his devotees also related to me what had occurred to him after he had been initiated by the saint. He told me that he had started having deeper meditations and also began hearing *nada* — a *yogic* term referring to various inner sounds which are sometimes heard by advanced seekers.

Some of these sounds are that of a conch, bell, cymbals, a stringed instrument called the *vina*, a flute, drum (*mridang*), as well as natural sounds such as thunder or the roar of the ocean. There are many more types of sounds, but these are some of the most important ones. When they are heard by the meditator, the sound helps to focus the mind, which then leads to deeper states of consciousness.

Baba Dayal was very kind to me, and invited me to his ashram in the Punjab, where he would be returning in a few months. He said that he would give me initiation and instructions there in the path of *nada*. I was impressed with him, and thought I would go and visit his ashram.

At around that time I had started feeling restless again, and something was urging me to move on. I had learned a great deal from Roti Baba, and to this day I still feel a genuine love for him. He was truly a great being and taught me with great love and compassion. However, I never felt the relationship to be that of a Guru and disciple, and so with sadness, I asked his permission to leave. It was difficult but I felt I had to move on. Roti Baba blessed me, and told me that I would find my Guru soon.

On The Road Again

While I was still feeling a deep desire to quickly find my Guru, I was now a little more peaceful. I felt I had to just continue my practices and keep on searching until the auspicious moment arrived. There was no doubt in my mind that it would arrive, but when that would be was still a mystery to me.

I also believed that this inner change was due to Roti Baba's blessing. I was feeling a deeper inner confidence, and I felt more strongly that whatever happened was for the best. In fact, all of life's circumstances are actually the results of our own past actions. The Indian sages call this the law of *karma*, the law of cause and effect. The word *karma* has become well known throughout the world and has even become part of the English language.

The Sanskrit word *karma* literally means "action." But it also indicates the cumulative effects of all our actions. Our present circumstances are said to be the results of our past actions. Actions performed in the present life will be experienced either in this life, or in some future birth. In this way, the process continues like the motion of a wheel. We play different roles in life, forever changing our costumes, like actors on a stage. Each time we leave this world empty handed having brought nothing with us.

Many people may disagree with this view. Some believe that they will no longer exist after death, while others hope to spend eternity in heaven rather than hell. Some believe that they have full control over their lives, but with honest reflection on life's circumstances, it becomes obvious that this is not the case. From birth onwards, we find ourselves placed in different circumstances, which are beyond our control. Indeed, it is the force of our past actions which creates our present environment. Can we say that we had anything to do with our own birth? Not really. Some are born male while others female, some in rich families, while others in poor ones. Some are talented and express this early in their lives, while others may never do so.

Normally, the first few years of our lives we spend at home totally dependent on our parents. When we finally leave our home we feel, "Yes, now I really will be able to do what I want." But is that really the case? It may appear that way, but on closer examination, we will find that our meetings with other people occur unexpectedly, whether they are wives, husbands, children, friends, employees, and others. Except in a superficial way, we have no control over these circumstances. Only when looking back on our lives do we see the perfect order of the events of our life. But during the process, events appear to be random and unrelated. In fact everything has a reason, which is determined by one's own past actions. For example, sometimes even after one tries his best to succeed at something, failure is his reward. However, during other periods, success comes even when the individual does not seem to be trying his or her best. We also find times when success is achieved in exact proportion to the amount of self-effort put forth. The reason for these differences are all due to our individual past karmas.

But does this mean that we have no free will at all, and that our efforts are useless? Should we not act at all? Of course not. It was in fact due to our past actions which has created the present parameters that we must work under. We must keep in mind that although we may try to improve ourselves, sometimes our present circumstances may not be in our control to change. The only control that we have is in our reactions to life's circumstances, and the ability to perform positive actions. In any case, it is impossible not to act at all. We will be driven to action by the force of nature, and our past karmas. Lord Krishna says in the Bhagavad Gita:

> *Even a wise man acts*
> *in accordance with his own nature;*

> *Beings will follow nature;*
> *what can restraint do?*
> chap. 3 verse 33

Because of the power of karma, we should add the practice of meditation to our daily life, so that we can learn how to act with detachment. We should try to remain as witnesses to the circumstances in which we find ourselves. Gradually our understanding will change. We will then have a true vision of the world.

Kanpur

Early one morning I began traveling in the general direction of the Punjab. Since Baba Chandra Dayal would not be returning to his ashram for a few months yet, I was in no rush. I also continued my search along the way since I really did not feel such a strong attraction towards the saint.

A few days later I reached the city of Kanpur. I was walking through town when once again a man riding on his bicycle stopped right beside me. He started walking along with me, which was not unusual since Indians are generally a friendly and curious people. After a number of such incidents, the experience was no longer unusual.

After introducing himself, the man asked me where I was going, and why I was not wearing shoes. I had abandoned my sandals in Varanasi, leaving them at the train station. I had been walking barefoot ever since. I thought of it as a kind of penance, or as the Hindus would say, *tapas* (austerities).

As we continued walking, he inquired as to my purpose for visiting India. When I told him the reason, he was quite fascinated by my interest in spirituality. We spoke as we walked, and as we approached a tea stall, he invited me to stop and have some tea with him. Tea is a staple in India, and tea stalls can be found just about anywhere. *Chai*, as tea is called from Turkey to India, is prepared in India by bringing milk to almost a boil, and then adding tea. You then let it simmer for a few minutes, strain, and add sugar. Some like a 50-50 mixer of water and milk, while others prefer less milk. However, the tea one finds on the streets often have a much higher percentage of water.

Finishing our tea, I thanked the gentlemen for the tea and his company, and once again started walking. But he continued walking along side with me, so we continued our conversation. After awhile he invited me to stay in Kanpur for a few days. He said that he too had an interest in spirituality, and often met with a group of friends in the city, who were interested in meditation and healing. Persistent in his request for me to stay, and as it was now dusk, it may be a good place to stay for a day or two. As he took me to the home of one of his friends, he told me that the man we were going to visit was well known in the city for his healing powers.

Arriving at the home, I was introduced to Mr. Pandey, the healer, and his family. The man was dressed in western clothes, as was the man who had brought me there. After talking with them for awhile, I came to know a little more about their small group. They were interested in meditation and spiritual topics along the line of Theosophy. Since I had studied the teachings of Theosophy, I was familiar with their ideas. The group also had an interest in using the power of meditation for healing.

After about twenty minutes Mr. Pandey went and made a phone call. I was told by the man who had brought me there that arrangements were being made for me to stay with another of their friends. When Mr. Pandey got off the telephone, he told me that someone would soon be coming to meet me. About two hours later the man finally arrived. And we were introduced.

He was a *brahmin*, and unlike these gentlemen, he was dressed in a traditional white *dhoti*. A *dhoti* is a single piece of cloth about nine yards long, which is wrapped around the waist and legs in such a way as to create a kind of pants. It is a common mode of dress among traditional Hindu men, especially brahmins.

The man's name was Shiva Dutta Mishra. I could immediately tell that he was a very quiet and peaceful man. Something about his face indicated to me that he was a wise man. Mr. Pandey and the man who brought me there began speaking to Mishra in Hindi. Mishra listened carefully and quietly, while they explained what I was doing in India, and my interest in the spiritual life. Every once in a while, Mishra would look over towards me, as if studying my face. After they finished speaking, Mr. Mishra asked me a few questions, and then asked if I would like to stay at his home. I said that would be fine, and thanked him for his hospitality.

After about half an hour Mishra and I left for his home, located about two miles away. We took a cycle *Rickshaw*. A Rickshaw is actually a human-powered stretched tricycle. The front portion is like any other bicycle with a seat for the driver, while in the back, over the two wheels, there is a seat where passengers sit. It seats two comfortably. It is a common mode of transportation in northern India, as well as many other Asian countries. They have since become popular in some American cities, where they are called Pedicabs.

Along the way Mishra and I spoke very little. When we reached his home, he introduced me to his wife, Swarup Nandini Devi; his teen-age son, Ram Rajesh, and daughter Abha. He then showed me a small room in which he said I could stay in. We sat down on the cots in the room and spoke for awhile about meditation, and then we began meditating together for awhile.

Mishra was a retired lawyer who was perhaps in his late fifties at the time. As it turned out, he was also an advanced seeker. He was a very wise and pious man, and I immediately felt a lot of respect and love for him. He also had a good sense of humor, which I liked very much. We quickly became good friends, and often sat together for many hours discussing spiritual topics.

But after a few days I decided it was time for me to leave. Mishra however would not allow me to go, and gave me one excuse after another of why I should stay. And although we had known each other for only a few days, they treated me as if I was part of their family. Interestingly, I felt the same way towards them. I had become good friends with Mishra's son, Ram Rajesh, who was about two years younger than me.

Mishra asked me to extend my stay, and said that he knew many sadhus, and promised to introduce me to them. This was true, he was really a seeker at heart, and had therefore met many great saints. I finally agreed to stay a few more days.

We were always having philosophical discussions, and he would tell me stories from the *Puranas*, *Mahabharata* and *Ramayana*. These ancient books contain many stories which sometimes convey deep philosophical and moral teachings, but in such a way that they are easy to understand.

I felt a lot of love for Mishra. It seemed like he really understood what I was going through at the time. My meditation had not yet stabilized, And at the same time, my knees would become very painful when sitting cross-legged. I could barely sit for fifteen or twenty minutes at a time. So Mishra began teaching me a method to heal or remove some of the soreness in my knees. It helped, and so I began practicing it daily.

One night, while we were meditating together, Mishra got up from his seat and came over to where I was sitting. He placed his hand close to my forehead, but did not touch it. My eyes remained closed, yet I could sense the presence of his hand there. After a few moments, I began feeling a warmth radiating from his hand. I just focused my attention on this warmth.

After awhile he returned to his seat. We used to sit together regularly for meditation. He taught me a great deal, but after about two weeks I again started feeling restless and began thinking of leaving.

During my stay, I had met several sadhus in the area, and even meditated with some of them. I had met a *tantric* yogi who was living on the outskirts of town. I had asked him for some teachings, and he gave me some meditation instructions, as well as information about the *tantric* tradition.

On another occasion, the man who had first invited me to stay in Kanpur took me to meet a *sufi* who was living in the city. I was told his name was *Mohan,* and he was considered by some to be a very advanced teacher. So one evening we went to his home to meet him.

When we arrived, Mohan was sitting outside in the courtyard of his home. He greeted me with great affection, and asked me to sit in the chair next to him. He appeared to be in his mid-fifties and had a beard, but no mustache, as is common among Muslims. We spoke for awhile, and he then asked me to meditate. I closed my eyes and soon I started to go into a deep meditation. I felt I was traveling a long distance down within myself. This went on for sometime, until I started to see an image appearing out of the darkness. The image turned out to be Jesus on the cross. As I saw this image, I started feeling a deep peace and contentment. I gazed at Jesus for a moment, and then started coming out of the meditation. Mohan asked me what I had experienced, and I told him. He said very good, and invited me to come again. I went and sat for meditation with him a few more times, and had other experiences, but I did not feel that he was my Guru.

One day, Mishra told me that a great saint had come to town and that we should go and meet her. Remarkably, it turned out to be Anandamayi Ma, the woman saint I had wanted to meet during my visit to Varanasi. However, by the time we reached where she was, we were able to have only a brief meeting with her since she was just leaving Kanpur. We saw her for only about fifteen minutes, but I felt that she was someone worth knowing.

Restlessness was once again gripping my mind, and I thought that I should leave Kanpur. Mishra still did not want me to leave, but I really felt it was time. However, he said that there was another saint coming to town in just two days, and that I should meet him before I left. He told me that if he considered anyone as his Guru, it was this man. So I agreed to stay, but told him that I would leave immediately after I met him. He told me that this yogi was a great being, and that he had practiced *tapasya* (austerities) for many years.

Two days later we went to visit the swami at his Kanpur ashram. His name was Swami Naradananda. He was a *sannyasi* who was going to celebrate his seventy-sixth birthday that November. Swamiji did a lot of traveling, constantly visiting one ashram after another. He apparently had over a hundred ashrams throughout northern India, but I was told that his main ashram was in the forest of Naimisharanya.

Mishra and I met Swamiji at his small ashram located on the outskirts of town. The ashram was really a school for *Brahmacharis* or students who were being educated according to the *Vedic* tradition. Mishra introduced me to the *Swami*, who asked me a number of questions. Mishra also told him that I was about to leave Kanpur, and Swamiji asked me where I was going? I told him that I had no definite destination but planned to travel towards the Punjab. He then invited me to stay at his forest ashram, telling me that in order for one's meditation to become deeper, the person has to stay somewhere and practice *sadhana* (spiritual practices) for some time. He said that his ashram would be a good place to do that, if I was interested.

At first I was not sure that I wanted to go, but I finally agreed. Since he had another engagement before leaving for his ashram, he asked me to stay in the Brahmachari ashram, and wait for his return which would be in a week. He said that we would then travel together to his forest ashram. However I did not feel very enthusiastic about staying in his Kanpur ashram, but I said that I would.

Cave Life

After our meeting with Swami Naradananda, Mishra and I returned to his home. I had decided to move to Swamiji's ashram the next day. This also gave me an opportunity to spend another night with Mishra's family. But I had grown tired of Kanpur and wanted to leave. I felt restless again, and began thinking that I was wasting my time there.

Overwhelmed by the desire to find a Guru, who I felt would bless me with inner peace and union with the divine, I moved about like a mad man. Those were extremely painful days for me. It was like mental torture, and I felt powerless to do anything about it. My mind continued to doubt even with all the experiences I had been having.

When doubt enters one's mind, the person forgets everything else; all positive memories are pushed aside and appear unreal. The only reality is the present agony. The great sixteenth century saint and poet, Ravidas, describes beautifully in one of his poems the sad condition of a seeker who experiences the intense feelings of separation from his beloved Lord. The poem clearly describes my mental state at the time. He writes:

> *If I am in agony, to whom should I tell?*
> *Without my Lord,*
> * how should I survive in this state?*
> *My heart knows no rest,*
> * it longs for Thee,*
> *O my Creator, pray, take care of me.*
> *The agony of separation burns me*
> * with its tremendous heat.*
> *No sleep do I have nor do I like to eat.*
> *This indeed, says Ravidas, is my fear,*
> *How will Thy lover survive without seeing Thee,*
> * O my Dear?*

I spent the next morning with Mishra's family and left for the ashram in the afternoon. When I arrived I was introduced to the manager who was already expecting me. His English was not very good, and at the time my Hindi was practically non-existent. So we started to communicate with words and gestures as best as we could.

He showed me the room where I would be staying, and I put my bag inside. Since I had only a few pieces of clothing, my bag was very small. However, ever since I was in Kanpur, at the insistence of Mishra, I began wearing Indian flip-flops. I walked around the ashram to familiarize myself with my new surroundings. As already mentioned, this ashram was mainly for young boys studying according to the *Vedic* tradition. Therefore, the ashram was filled with boys ranging from ages of about eight to twelve years old. They were all excited to see a western sadhu, and had many questions. Some knew only a few English words, and wanted to practice using them.

While walking around the ashram that day I reflected on my recent travels. Before sleep that night I prayed intensely for some kind of guidance. I mentally asked what I should do. Whether I should go with Swami Naradananda to his ashram, or should I go somewhere else? After sitting for meditation for sometime I went to sleep. At about 3 or 4 a.m., I suddenly awoke. I was not fully awake, but it was not sleep either. I would later learn that this state is called *tandra*. During meditation one sometimes slips into this state and may see different lights or hear various sounds. At times one may even have a vision of some saint or deity, and receive instructions from them. Whatever is seen in this state will come out to be true. The experiences are like the dream-visions which I have been referring to.

While in that state I heard a female's voice coming from within me. I would come to know her as goddess Kundalini, the supreme power, who resides in all beings. She always guided and protected me. That night she told me not to worry, that everything was going well. She said that I should stay in the ashram and wait for Swamiji's return, and then go to his other ashram with him.

The divine voice also told me that I would be traveling to another place soon. And although I was not given the name of that place, I saw myself fly over the area in my subtle body. It was somewhere near water, and I saw a number of boats and ships in a large harbor.

I was also told that when I awoke that morning, I would feel ill, and would have a high fever. But that I should not worry about it, since the illness would last for only five days. As I listened to all of this, I became very calm and soon fell asleep again.

That morning I awoke at about 6 a.m. feeling extremely weak and feverish. I had absolutely no strength in my body, and all I could do was lie on the cot. After sometime a young boy brought me tea. But seeing the condition I was in, he immediately ran off to call the manager. The manager quickly arrived and took my temperature. Becoming alarmed at my condition, he wanted to call a doctor. But I told him not to, and that I would be all right.

I did not feel that I should tell him about my experience, and so I did not mention it. I had previously received instructions not to discuss my experiences with anyone, so I gave him no further explanation. But I did ask him if there was another, more quieter room that I could use. Since there were mostly young boys in the ashram, it could get very loud near the room I was staying in at the time. I felt that I needed quiet. The manager told me that there was another more quiet room I could stay in, and sent someone to prepare it for me.

After awhile the manager helped me move to the new room, which was located on the second floor of another building. When we got there, he again said that he wanted to send for a doctor. I could see his concern but I told him not to worry, that this would last for just a few days, and that everything would be alright. I also told him that I wanted to fast during that period, and to also remain in solitude, so I asked him to please not allow anyone to visit me.

Interestingly, I felt a desire to study the Koran during that time, so I asked the manager if he knew where to get a copy in English. I realized that I was making an unusual request from a Hindu, but he was very understanding. He said that he would take care of it. Which he did. Later a local Muslim cleric even came to visit me after hearing about my request.

The manager was very helpful and started to take personal care of me. For the next few days, I slid in and out of consciousness, and then suddenly on the fifth day, I felt much better. On the sixth day, I was back to normal, as if nothing had happened.

Two days later, Swamiji returned to the ashram, arriving in the evening. I went to greet him along with everyone else. At the time I did not know very much about him, but I did like him. When I went up to greet him, he placed his right hand on my head, as he had done at our first meeting. He was obviously blessing me, but I was not conscious of any energy transfer. He told me that we would be leaving early the next morning. He tried to encourage me by saying that my stay at his ashram would be very good for me. He told me that the ashram had many caves and huts, and was quite conducive to meditation. He said the place had a long spiritual tradition, and that many sages had performed spiritual practices there for thousands of years.

Early the next morning, at about 3:30 a.m., I went over to Swamiji's cottage to meet him. Everyone had assembled there for a short talk he would give before he left. After the talk, everyone who was going with him piled into two cars, and we headed north towards the city of Lucknow. I was riding in Swamiji's car with about five others. The journey took the whole day with a stop for lunch at a devotee's home. By the time we reached the ashram it was already dark. But I could sense that it was a very beautiful place. I could also smell the many fragrant flowers growing naturally.

Swami Naradananda was a *sannyasin* who had spent a great deal of time practicing intense austerities. He was a Guru who taught people to live their lives according to traditional *Vedic* ideals. During those days he spent his time traveling between his many ashrams. But I was told that this ashram was his favorite, and I could see why. The ashram was situated near the banks of the river Gomati. As mentioned earlier, the place has a long spiritual history. It is mentioned in the Puranas, and according to tradition, it is the place where sage Vyasa wrote the Mahabharata and Puranas. In ancient times sages gathered there to hold religious and spiritual discussions. At such meetings a learned hermit named *Suta* would recite the various Puranic stories to the other sages. He would also answer their questions. In this way, ancient knowledge was being passed orally from generation to generation. Later, a line of minstrels developed called Sutas, who would recite the sacred lore

The ashram was divided into different sections. Near the main entrance, in the first section of the ashram, there was a small school for Brahmacharis. In the same area, there were a number of cottages belonging to householders who had retired from worldly life. They were now in the third stage of life according to vedic tradition. The ashram office was also located in that area. Following a dirt road further into the ashram, one reaches the boundaries of the forest. A large building is located there, with rooms on both the ground and second floor. These housed the permanent sadhus, and those disciples who traveled with Swamiji. In front of this building there was a huge and ancient Banyan tree. Sometimes lectures were held under its large canopy.

Going further into the forest, one comes across small cottages and caves scattered here and there. Most of the sadhus lived in the cottages, but one or two lived in the caves, which were actually small rooms about eight feet long and six feet wide, with a ceiling height of about six feet. There was also a smaller cubicle just large enough for a person to sit cross-legged in meditation. When Swamiji was in the ashram, he would stay in his own cave. I recall the first night we arrived. We all squeezed inside that cave while he gave darshan to his devotees and disciples.

At another section of the ashram lived those sannyasins who had taken their vows only after completing their family life. According to vedic tradition there are four aims or goals of life. These are: *dharma*, *artha*, *kama*, and *moksha*. *Dharma* includes meritorious actions, religious practices, and following the proper laws of conduct while performing one's duty to society.

(*below*) Entrance to Forest Ashram.

Artha indicates worldly prosperity and attainments. *Kama* is the fulfillment of one's desires, while *moksha* is the attainment of spiritual liberation. In order to fulfill and work out these aims, life is divided into four stages called *ashramas*. The first stage is that of the student (*brahmacharin*). The student lives with the Guru, serving him, and in return he is educated. He is taught the necessary sciences, arts, and other branches of knowledge which are required to fulfill his objective in life, and at the same time, to live harmoniously in society. During this first stage, the student is prepared for the proper working out of the four objectives of life. After his education, the student returns home, marries, has a family, and carries out his life according to the duty of his caste or station in life. This is the second stage called *grihastha* or the life of he householder. It is during this stage that the individual works on the first three life objectives, viz. *dharma*, *artha* and *kama*.

After fulfilling his duty to family and society, and thereby completing the second stage of life, the man and his wife

(*below*) Forest Ashram huts.

will retire to the forest, still as a couple, but now pursuing philosophical and spiritual aims. They prepare for the higher life by gradually detaching themselves from social bonds. This is the third stage called *vanaprastha*, or forest dweller. During this period, the couple will devote themselves to spiritual practices. An internalization of the mind starts to occur, and the deeper practices of yoga are initiated. The diet also changes and becomes more simple. The person detaches themselves more and more from external conditions.

After spending some years in this manner, the fourth stage of complete renunciation or *sannyasa* may be taken. This last *ashrama* is different from the formal vows of sannyas taken by renunciates. Although these ashrams are considered an ideal life, the scriptures declare that whenever the call for true renunciation arises, sannyasa should be taken no matter what age or stage of life they are in.

The first night I arrived at the ashram, Swamiji instructed one of his disciples to let me stay in a cave located just near his own. I was taken to the cave and was told about the river nearby, where I could bathe in the morning. The cave had a small wooden bed which was about two feet high. The disciple said good night, and left me some candles. Being tired from the day's long journey, I soon fell asleep.

But the next morning, at about 3 a.m., I was suddenly awakened by someone singing and playing a harmonium not far from the cave's entrance. I wondered what was going on, so I got up and went outside. After all, I was in the middle of the forest, and I thought it would be a quiet place to meditate.

I asked the sadhu what he was doing, and he told me that he was performing his morning worship. "Praying to God," he told me in English.

He was singing *bhajans* or devotional hymns. I enjoyed the singing, but at the time, I was more interested in silent meditation. Which was, after all, why I had come to the jungle. Anyway, he continued with his singing, and I went back inside

(*(left)*) The cave's narrow entrance, only about 3 feet high.
(below) The author sitting at the entrance of one of the caves he lived in.

the cave and sat for meditation.

After my meditation, I went for a walk around the ashram to familiarize myself with my new surroundings. It was a very beautiful place, and I felt that I would enjoy my stay there very much.

During my walk that morning, I also noticed another cave further into the forest, located in an isolated spot. I went over to inspect it, and found it was empty. I thought I would ask Swami Naradananda if I could move into that cave. On my way back, I also noticed a pit nearby the cave, which was about 15-20 feet deep. I was later told that Swamiji had practiced austerities in that pit for over twelve years.

Yogis often prefer living in caves, not only because they are far away from towns and villages, but because they are very quiet. One of the steps of yoga is to withdraw or shut off the senses. The imagery used to symbolize this process is that of a turtle which withdraws its limbs into its own shell. The cave atmosphere is therefore considered very conducive for this practice.

When I returned from my walk, I noticed Swamiji was outside. I went over and bowed to him, and said good morning. He again blessed me by placing his hand on my head. He also asked me how I liked the place, and I answered that I liked it very much. At the time he was overseeing the work that some disciples were doing. They were building another small cottage, and I asked Swamiji if I could help. He seemed happy with my request and said to go ahead.

After finishing that project, he instructed me to practice intense meditation while I was there. I then took the opportunity to ask him if I could move into the cave which I had seen that morning. At first he was reluctant, cautioning me that this was a forest, and there were wild animals around. I said that I would be all right, and if that was his only concern, to please reconsider. I told him that I wanted to spend time in solitude. He finally gave his permission, and I moved into that cave that

Swami Naradananda

very day.

Soon, word spread around the ashram that a foreign sadhu had arrived with Maharaj, as Swami Naradananda was referred to by he devotees. This was obviously an unusual sight for them, since I was told that I was the first foreigner to have ever lived there. As days went by, I also met a number of the sadhus who were living in the ashram at the time, and with whom I became friendly. They taught me a great deal about a sadhu's way of life. There were ascetics living throughout the ashram, and for the first few days I went around meeting them all. I also met Swamiji's main disciple, Swami Vivekananda. He was about twenty seven years old at the time, and would one day be Swami Naradananda's successor.

Naradanandaji remained in the ashram for only about five days, and then left for Lucknow, a city located about a hundred miles away. He was to give a number of lectures there, and after he would return to the ashram. But once again for only a few days. Whenever Swamiji was in the ashram, I would go and have his darshan and listen to his talks, even though I did not always understand them. I would then sit quietly meditating.

My days were spent mostly in silent meditation and study. There were a few friends that spoke English and who would visit me from time to time. Our conversations were always on spiritual practices and the monastic life. But usually I spent my time in solitude. And because the cave I had moved into was at an isolated spot, hardly anyone ever came there.

During my stay in the ashram, I also tried to perform some daily service for the aged resident sadhus. I would wash their clothes, sweep their simple huts, or go and get water for them. In particular, there was one old blind hermit who I used to serve regularly.

When I first arrived, I had become friends with a man named Tewari. He was a retired lawyer and was living in the householder's section of the ashram with his wife. He spoke English fairly well and so we were able to communicate very easily. Sometimes he served as my translator. He would also provide me with English translations of books on *yoga*, Hindu philosophy, the lives of Indian saints, and other spiritual topics. I was now also starting to understand the Hindi language a bit more, but I was still not able to speak it very well. Later, someone started giving me lessons, but unfortunately they were cut short.

Meals in the sadhu section of the ashram was extremely simple. Once a day, at noon, we would be served roti and dal. And on occasion, some white radishes. Personally I felt no attachment to any particular food or taste. Food was not very important to me. I ate only to live and did not care much about taste. Eating only once a day also did not bother me, and I would often fast for many days at a time. However, every once in a while, my friend Tewari, or one of the students, would bring me some special dish that his wife had prepared, or which came from the student's kitchen.

One day, Tewari came to visit me. He asked if I wanted to accompany him to the local town to visit a friend of his. I agreed, and we went to his friend's house. After a short conversation, the man started to prepare some kind of thick, green colored drink. I asked what it was and was told it was *bhang*, an intoxicant made with cannabis and curds.

Tewari asked me if I wanted to try some, but I declined. However, after awhile, for some reason I decided to try some. Tewari asked his friend to prepare a glass for me, and gave him some instructions in Hindi, which I did not understand. When it was ready, I drank the whole glass, and asked how long it would take to feel its effect. Tewari said it would take about half an hour.

We said good-bye to his friend and left for the ashram, which was about a twenty minute walk. But on the way back to the ashram, I started thinking that perhaps I had made a mistake in taken the drug. I soon began wishing I had not. But I did not say anything to Tewari. When I reached my cave, I sat for meditation, but I was still feeling uneasy for having taking the drug. I started praying, asking God that if I had made a mistake, and should not have taken the drug, then to not let me experience its effect. I continued sitting quietly, waiting for the drug's effect, but it never came.

The next day, Tewari came to visit me, and asked me what I had experienced. I asked him how much had he given me. "Why," he asked, "Was it too strong?"

"No," I answered, "not strong, but too weak, I never felt its effect."

He looked at me in surprise, and said he did not believe me. I said that I did not know what to say, but I never felt anything. He then told me that he could not believe this because he had specifically instructed his friend to double the dose. So it was very strange that I did not feel anything at all. But there was really nothing more to say, and so we did not speak any further about it.

Another person that I had met at the ashram was Swami Krishnananda. But everyone called him "Om Baba" since he used to respond only with "Om! Om!" whenever anyone saluted him. He spoke a little bit of English, and was an Advaitic Vedantin. He would always say to me, "Just remember, 'I am That,' 'I am not this body.'" Every morning you could hear him at 4 a.m. chanting, "Om! Om! Om!"

Although most of the monks in the ashram, including Swami Naradananda, were *Vaishnavites* or followers of Lord Vishnu, Om Baba was a Shaivite or follower of Lord Shiva. The two sects lived happily and peacefully in the ashram. In fact, since this was a place for spiritual practices, followers of all sects were welcomed. Besides, many of the people living in that part of India, followed Lord Rama as their chosen ideal. They always chanted his name and saluted each other with *"Jai Ram!"* or *"Jai Sita Ram!"* Throughout the night I could hear the chanting of *Sri Ram, Jai Ram, Jai Jai Ram!* In fact, there was a section of the ashram where this mantra had been continuously chanted without break for more years than anyone could remember. Some said over a hundred years.

Every day Om Baba visited a Shiva temple located in a nearby village. He used to go in the afternoon at 4 p.m., and soon I began to accompany him. Along the way he would pick a few flowers and some *bilva* leaves for his worship. In the temple courtyard, there was a very large and deep well, with steps that led down to the edge of the water. People would have their ritual bath there before entering the temple. The pool was so deep that a circular iron rail had to be placed at some distance from the center in order to keep people from going too deep.

Om Baba and I would wash our hands and feet before entering the temple. Once in the temple, Om Baba would place flowers and the bilva leaves he had picked on Shiva's image, called a *lingam.* He would then pour some water over the lingam.

Sometimes he would hand me his water bowl, and I would do the same.

In Sanskrit, the word *linga* (or *lingam*) means an emblem, mark, or sign indicating or pointing to something beyond form. This emblem is therefore a symbol or sign of the Lord, who in this tradition is called Shiva. The linga represents the impersonal, Absolute Supreme Being, or Brahman.

After finishing our worship at the Shiva temple, we would walk down the road to the other end of town, where there was a temple dedicated to the Divine Mother. During our walks, we would discuss different philosophical topics. Om Baba taught me many things about Indian philosophy, and its different traditions and sects. I personally did not feel any need to affiliate myself with any particular sect, but one day Swami Naradananda asked me if I wanted to take *sannyasa*. I told him that I did not know, but I would think about it.

I later mentioned this to Om Baba and he asked, "Well, do you want to be a Vaishnavite or a Shaivite sannyasi?" I told him that I did not know, and after thinking about it, I decided that I would wait until I had met my Guru before deciding such matters. I believed that everything happened according to one's destiny.

I no doubt had dedicated myself to the spiritual life, but the particular path that one follows will usually be the same as that of one's Guru. Although I went to the temple and followed this little ritual everyday with Om Baba, for me, Shiva, Vishnu, and Allah meant the same thing; they were all names of the One God. Shiva is not different from Vishnu. They are one and the same. The difference lies in name only. When travelers from different countries ask for water, they may call it by different names, yet they are all asking for the same thing, water.

The ashram was really a beautiful place, but there was one thing that really troubled me. This had to do with the caste system practiced there by the orthodox *brahmins*. This was mainly obvious during lunch time, when everyone gathered to get their food. Some of the sadhus would stay and eat near the kitchen, while others would pick up their lunch and return to their cottage or cave to eat alone.

The ashram management thought it best to use brahmin cooks because those who are orthodox Hindus would only eat food prepared by other brahmins. On the other hand, due to fear of pollution, some brahmins did not even like to hand food to someone belonging to a lower caste. Therefore, a third person was required as a kind of middle-man. That person would take the food from the brahmin, and hand it over to the lower-caste person, who in this case were mainly ashram laborers. Unfortunately they would always have to wait until everyone else was served. And if for some reason the person whose job it was to hand them their food did not show up on time, the poor laborers would just have to wait.

Most residents treated me like a high-caste person, and so I personally did not have this problem. But I always felt unhappy when I saw it. One day, it so happened that the person who was to hand over the food did not show up. The laborers just sat there, waiting patiently, but no one would serve them their food. I asked someone what the problem was? I did not know at the time that no one would give them food when the 'middle man' did not show up. When I heard this, I became so angry at the ridiculous situation that I got up and went over to the brahmin cook, and told him to give me the food, and I would distribute it to them myself. I told him that I was not afraid of being polluted. At first the brahmin cook started to protest, but he decided not to, and handed me the bread and dal. After that incident, I decided to eat alone in my cave.

Originally the caste system was a recognition of the natural laws of the universe. It is derived by one's personal nature and inclinations, as well as their social conditions. One's caste was based on the temperament and qualifications of the individual, and not on his or her birth alone. In the Bhagavad Gita, Lord Krishna explains this by saying:

The fourfold caste has been created by me according to the differentiation of guna karma;
Chap. 4-13

In other words, *guna* and *karma* determine the caste of an individual. The word *guna* means quality, or what can be called the nature or temperament of an individual. Karma indicates the kind of work determined by one's actions and interests. If the individual is a brahmin, then his duty is to teach and continue the cultural traditions. They also are to perform all social sacraments and rituals, such as birth and death ceremonies, marriages, name giving ceremony, and performing the blessings at the start of one's education. However, the real meaning of the word brahmin is, "one who knows Brahman," the Supreme Being. Therefore the real duty of a brahmin is to realize Brahman.

On the other hand, the warrior caste has the duty to protect society like the military and police of today. But this kind of life was not meant for everyone. It requires a certain temperament, and that is why the caste system is based on guna and karma.

The duty of the third caste, that of the merchant, was to provide goods and trade for the community. Today they are called businessmen. All castes were necessary for society to prosper, and did not indicate one person to be superior than another. But unfortunately, the caste system broke down and was used by some to discriminate against others. It has become so rigid that those of the lower caste were discriminated against and were not allowed the same education and benefits that society had to offer.

But the corruption of social classes or caste is not peculiar to Indian culture alone. We see the same thing occurring even today in various forms in just about every society around the world. People think that they don't have prejudices, but when put to the test, those prejudices will naturally arise. Unfortunately most people enjoy the security of belonging to a group, and feel superior by declaring another group beneath them.

As time went by, my meditation became a little deeper, and more regulated. I also had a few visions. In one vision I saw a yogi appear before me. He was very thin and had long matted hair. He wore only a loincloth. He blessed me with a raised right hand, but did not speak a word.

I also began practicing various *pranayama* or breath control techniques which I had learned. I began to practice *trataka* as well, which is a steady gazing on a small dot or point, or, one can focus on the flame of a candle. I would sometimes use a point or spot on the wall of the cave, and at night, I would use the flame of a candle. The yogi focuses his gaze without blinking until tears flow profusely from his eyes. This produces a deep state of mental quietude.

It was also during that period that I became familiar with the *Yoga Sutras* of sage Patanjali, as well as other books on the subject. In the Yoga Sutras, Patanjali describes various mental states and divides the path of yoga into eight stages or steps. These start with the physical posture (*asana*), and end with the last stage, that of *samadhi*, which is the transcendental state. These steps are called the eight limbs (*ashtanga*) of yoga.

The treatise also deals with the results one can derive from the practice of yoga. Although some may desire to achieve various powers, the true yogi practices yoga in order to experience supreme joy, knowledge, and the pure consciousness of the inner Self.

Although Patanjali organized the practice of yoga into a systematic scheme, he is not the founder of the yoga philosophy. The practice of yoga in fact is very ancient and can be traced back to at least 3,000 B.C.E., and even earlier. The knowledge of yoga is the great treasure of the ancient Rishis.

One day an unusual incident occurred. After sitting in meditation for a long time, I decided to go out for a walk. I was still feeling somewhat intoxicated from the effects of my meditation, but I got up and went out of the cave. Standing there for a moment, I suddenly noticed a large black snake come out of its hole, which was just above the cave's entrance. I stood there looking at the snake, and he at me. But I felt no fear. This lasted for only about twenty seconds, when all of a sudden, we both turned around at the exact same moment, and went back inside our respective holes. I went back inside my cave and sat for more meditation, and as it turned out, I had very good meditation that day.

I knew that there were other snakes around as well because I had seen their old skins lying about. To the Hindu, all life is sacred, but the snake, particularly the cobra, has a deep spiritual symbolism. It also has a symbolic meaning in the tradition of yoga. It is thought to be an auspicious sign to see a snake either physically, in a dream, or in a vision. Such experiences

Anandamayi Ma.

are associated with Lord Shiva, who is considered to be the Lord of yoga. Shiva's anthropomorphic form is often portrayed with cobras wrapped around his waist and neck like ornaments, symbolizing Kundalini awakening.

One day, during one of my walks, I learned that Anandamayi Ma had an ashram nearby, and was expected to visit it in just a few days. This made me very happy since I had wanted to spend some time with her. I therefore went to her ashram to meet her on the day she arrived.

She was a very beautiful individual, and I felt a deep peace in her presence. She was an enlightened soul who had lived in the transcendental state since her early childhood. Since we were in an isolated area, the ashram was not very crowded, and so she was quite accessible. She was scheduled to be there for about a week or two, and so I went to see her everyday.

But even though I felt that she was a great being, who certainly could lead me to the spiritual goal, I did not feel that she was my Guru. However, I was very happy that I had finally gotten the opportunity to meet her. It was definitely worth the wait. Then just before she left the area, I asked for her blessing, so that I would find my Guru soon. While blessing me, she said, "You will meet him very soon."

"Guru Will Be Met In December!"
(Indian Astrologer)

After staying for about six weeks in Naradananda's ashram, I again began feeling restless. At the time Swamiji was traveling. But I had heard about an old astrologer living in a small village about twenty miles from the ashram. I decided to go and visit him one day. I was told he had an excellent reputation for the accuracy of his predictions. Even though I had given up the practice of astrology myself, I still had an interest in the subject. The natal horoscope is indeed the map of one's destiny, and a good astrologer can easily decipher it. But finding competent astrologers is not always easy. During my travels I had met dozens of astrologers. A few of them were quite good, but most were far from the mark.

I arrived at the small village early that after noon. As usual, I was received with great warmth by the villagers. Having traveled through many different countries, I have never found such hospitality and friendliness as I have in India.

After making some inquiries, I was soon taken to the astrologer's home. He appeared to be in his late eighties and did not speak any English. But fortunately there was someone in the village who did, and so he translated for me. After a short conversation, I asked the astrologer if he would prepare my horoscope. He said he would. I did not tell him anything about myself, nor had I asked him any specific questions yet.

At first it appeared that there would be some difficulty in calculating my horoscope. In order to prepare an accurate horoscope, the astrologer must have the person's birth date, birth time, and the place of birth. But having been born in a small town in Italy, I had to help him with the coordinates for the place of birth. Finding the approximate planetary positions is not difficult, but to find the correct house positions of the planets, the Ascending sign has to first be calculated. This requires the exact time and place of birth.

At the time I was unfamiliar with Indian astrology, and so I was not of much help to him beyond that. Nevertheless, after questioning me for some time, he finally proclaimed, "It does not matter, let me see your thumb." He then proceeded to carefully study only my right thumb and its lines. After a few minutes, he began calculating the chart, based simply on the information he got from the lines of my palm and thumb. This was extraordinary. Although I had studied palmistry, I had never seen this technique before. It was very unusual but quite fascinating.

Indian astrology, or more accurately, Vedic astrology has a long history. In India, the apprentice astrologer has to study under a competent teacher for many years before earning the right to be called an astrologer. He must also live a pure life so that he can maintain his astrological abilities. And he must practice of meditation to develop his intuition.

The old astrologer soon finished preparing my horoscope. He appeared very excited, and the first thing he said was, "You will come face to face with God."

I told him that I was in search of a Guru who would help me see God.

"You have already met the Guru," he replied, "and he is now guiding you."

I said that I had not met him physically yet, and asked if he could tell when that would be.

"Very soon," he answered.

"How soon?" I persisted.

"In December," he said.

Interestingly this was the same month the astrologer in Varanasi had said. And it was now almost the end of November.

The astrologer also told me other things about my past and future, and said that I would attain spiritual illumination in this very life. He spoke for almost an hour about my horoscope, and after the reading, he spent sometime telling me about the Vedic system of astrology. I found him to be extremely knowledgeable about the science, and a very unique astrologer.

It was now late in the afternoon, and I thought I should start back to the ashram. But the person who had been translating for me invited me to have dinner with his family that night, and to also spend the night. He said I could leave early the next morning for the ashram. Since it was getting late, I decided to accept his invitation. Soon a large meal was prepared in my honor. After dinner, a conversation ensued with my host, and a number of villagers, which continued late into the night.

Early the next morning, I said good-bye to my host and thanked him for his hospitality. I then left for the ashram, feeling happy with the thought that I would soon meet my Guru. I reached the ashram by early afternoon. The walk back had been very tiring due to the extreme heat, and so I decided not to go to the temple with Om Baba that afternoon. The next few days went by as usual, and I continued to go to the Shiva temple with Om Baba. I spoke to him about my feeling of discontent with Swami Naradananda, and although I liked him, and considered him to be a great being, I did not really see him as my Guru.

Om Baba, who was himself a visitor to the ashram at the time, had arrived there about six months before I did. He was originally from Bengal. Many sadhus used to visit the ashram, each staying for a few days or a few months. There were of course permanent residents, those who were devotees of Naradanandaji, but there were also wandering sadhus who stayed in the ashram for only short periods of time. In fact, Om Baba had told me that he was planning to leave in a few months, and asked if I wanted to accompany him. He said that we could first go to the famous city of Puri, in the state of Orissa, where he would give me *sannyasa* initiation. Afterwards, we could go on a long pilgrimage to south India. I listened quietly to his suggestions but did not commit myself to any plan. Instead, I said that I would think about it.

Swami Naradananda was a very learned man, and knew all the scriptures thoroughly. It appeared to me that it was his mission to convey this knowledge to the general public. But Swamiji did not only have intellectual knowledge, he also had practiced intense yoga, and enjoyed its spiritual fruits. When he spoke, he was not speaking from mere book knowledge but from his own personal experience.

I also felt that he had the power to transmit this experience to others as well. However, this was not his usual method of initiation, and so that ability was kept a secret. All great beings who have achieved the highest state of awareness are intrinsically the same. But due to differences in their unique destinies, their individual work in the world also differs. Some teach while others do not keep any disciples with them. Some become prominent, while others pass through life known only by a few. Some live like kings, while others like beggars.

I had been told by a devotee that Swamiji, like the great nineteenth century saint, Ramakrishna, had the ability to transmit by touch or word the experience of the Self to the disciple. The devotee said that he had personally witnessed this once when Swamiji had touched one of his disciples, who then immediately entered the state of *samadhi*.

Whenever Swamiji placed his hand on my head, although I sensed that something was going on, I did not know what. And during most of my stay, he was away from the ashram, returning only for a few days at a time. But about the middle of December, while Swamiji was in the ashram, I happened to be sitting with him when he suddenly began giving me instructions on the nature of the *mantra*. He told me how it was to be practiced, and what the results would be as the seeker progressed. He covered the subject in great detail. A mantra is given by the Guru when he initiates a seeker. The mantra is then said to become a vehicle for the Guru's spiritual power.

After listening carefully to Swamiji's inspiring talk, I asked him if he would kindly initiate me with a *mantra*. He closed his eyes for a moment, and then said that he would initiate me the next morning.

However, the next morning, as I arrived at his cave at the appointed time, I noticed that he was just about to leave. I went up to him and bowed, and as usual he placed his hand on my head. He also apologized, saying that he would not be able to give me initiation that day, but asked me to come again the next morning.

The next day there was a similar occurrence, and he had another engagement that he had to attend. I did not know what was going on, but it was obvious that for some reason he was putting me off. But I believed that if it was meant to happen, it would, otherwise not. And so his actions did not disturb me, because I was sure that there was some reason for it.

Meanwhile, the day before this last meeting with Swamiji, Tewari had brought me some new books and a magazine to read. I went through the magazine first. It was titled, *Gurudev-Vani*, meaning the Guru's words or teachings. It was an annual publication of the Shree Gurudev Ashram, located in Ganeshpuri, a small town about fifty miles north of Mumbai. I opened the magazine's cover and noticed that it had been a gift to Swami Vivekananda, and it was signed by Swami Muktananda, the head of the Ganeshpuri ashram.

Apparently Muktananda had visited the ashram two years earlier while on a pilgrimage in north India. It was then that he had given the magazine to Swamiji. At the time it was Swami Vivekananda, Naradananda's disciple, who had received Muktananda, and showed him around the ashram. The magazine contained articles written by Muktananda himself, as well as by his devotees.

At first I just glanced at the articles, but then I started reading an article written by Muktananda himself titled, *Guru Kripa* — meaning "Guru's grace." While reading the article, waves of excitement started to suddenly arise within me. In the article, Muktananda was describing the different paths to God, but with a special emphasis on the path of Guru's grace, and what occurs once the disciple receives this grace.

I had imagined in my mind what my Guru would be like, and now I was reading practically an exact description of him in this article. I could barely contain myself. My mind started racing, and questions like, "Who is this Muktananda, and is he still alive?" started to arise in my mind.

When I finished the article I tried to control my excitement, and thought I should sit for meditation, hoping to get some inner guidance. I started speaking to my mind saying, "Be calm, don't rush here and there. Look at what all that running around has gotten you so far." But this did not help. I again picked up the magazine, and opened it randomly. Suddenly my eyes fell on the title of the article which read, "Ganeshpuri Beckons." That was all I needed, and at that very moment I decided to go.

The Guru Calls

I had planned to leave the ashram for Kanpur within a few days. I wanted to visit the Mishra family before leaving for Mumbai. I had also written a letter to Muktananda's ashram at Ganeshpuri, asking for permission to visit, and to make sure that he would be there. I asked them to reply to me at the Kanpur address.

Interestingly, all of this was occurring at the same time as the *mantra* incident with Swamiji. He was acting very strange. It was obvious that he was postponing the mantra initiation for some reason, but what made it funny was that he kept on rescheduling the appointment. But by then I had already decided to leave the ashram. And on the day that I was scheduled to see Swamiji again, he was once again on his way out of the ashram. Many of the ashramites had gathered around him to say goodbye. I went and stood underneath a tree at some distance behind the crowd of devotees. Swamiji was standing on a platform about two feet off the ground. When he saw me standing at the back of the crowd, he jumped down from the platform and walked quickly over to where I was standing. The crowd created a path as he walked towards me.

When he reached me, he began by saying how sorry he was that we had not been able to get together, but that when he returned, we would do so. However, I told him about my decision to leave the ashram, and my plan to visit Swami Muktananda at Ganeshpuri. I told him that I was planning to leave in a few days, and wanted to thank him for allowing me to stay in his beautiful ashram. I then formally asked his permission to leave.

When this was translated to him, a big smile appeared on his lips. He said that it was good that I was going to meet Muktanandji. He then placed his hand on my head again in blessing, as he had done many times in the past. But this time

I suddenly felt a great energy enter me, filling me with waves of joy, which weakened my knees, making it barely possible to remain standing. I felt extremely intoxicated. I thought to myself, "Now he does this! Why couldn't he have done it earlier?"

Nevertheless, as I recovered my composure, I said good-bye to Swamiji. He in turn invited me to visit the ashram whenever I wished. When the conversation was over, he turned and quickly left, while I wondered what had just happened?

Two days later I boarded a train for Kanpur and went to Mishra's home. They were happy to see me, but unhappy that I was going all the way to Mumbai. They tried to talk me out of it, given different reasons, but I finally convinced them that I had to go.

I was still feeling excited about the trip, and couldn't wait much longer. Then that night, I had a very vivid and wonderful dream-vision. I found myself in a celestial realm, surrounded by what appeared to be many devotees, all apparently waiting for someone important to arrive. There was an air of great excitement and devotion.

I was soon standing in a line, waiting for my turn to meet this mysterious being. Those waiting with me included both historical persons, as well as all the Hindu deities. The Buddha was also present, and so was Lord Vishnu, as well as many other deities. We were all waiting excitedly to greet this great Being.

Soon, the line I was standing in began moving closer, and I could see a bright radiance ahead. But I could still not see who it was. I then noticed that a few of the celestial beings were performing *arati* or the waving of lighted lamps before this Being. The atmosphere was charged with great excitement and devotion.

As my turn finally arrived, I found myself standing before a royal seat, face to face with Lord Shiva Himself. He sat on a throne which sparkled with precious jewels. An enchanting smile played on his lips, and His right hand was raised in the gesture meaning, "fear not". Everyone was bowing to him and singing hymns of praise. I felt ecstatic and bowed my head in reverence. Tears of joy streamed down my cheeks.

When I awoke the next morning, I was still ecstatic. The joy which I had felt during the dream-vision had stayed with me. I told my friends that I felt this trip was going to be my last. I also predicted that I would hear from the Ganeshpuri ashram that very day.

They obviously did not want me to go, and continued to try and persuade me from leaving. But I finally told them that Shiva was calling me, and I had to go. After I said this, they did not press me further.

As it turned out, a letter did arrive from the ashram that very day, inviting me to visit. The letter also mentioned that Muktananda was in Delhi at the time, but was expected to return any day now. It was a Thursday, and so I decided to leave that very night. I immediately went to the train station and purchased a ticket for Mumbai. Unfortunately, since I had been traveling mostly by road, I had not yet learned about the Indian train system, and the wisdom of reserving a berth on long journeys.

The train was scheduled to depart at 8 p.m. that evening. I left for the station about an hour earlier. The train was to arrive at Mumbai the next morning. I found the train ride long and tiring. I hardly slept at all that night. It was also extremely hot, and there was no drinking water on the train, so I felt thirsty throughout the trip. The next morning at around ten, we reached Kalyan station, a town still some distance from Mumbai. But I had decided to get off the train there, and take a bus to Ganeshpuri. However, since there was no direct bus, I would have to make a change along the way. I found that even though it was the middle of December, it was an extremely hot day. I found the weather in north India very pleasant, but this heat was overbearing, and I became disheartened.

The Auspicious Moment
(I Meet My Guru)

By the time I reached the ashram it was about 4 p.m.. The bus stopped right in front of the ashram gate, and I stepped down, exhausted and dirty from the intense heat and long train ride. A crowd of people were standing around as if waiting for something to happen. I was told by someone that Baba was actually on his way home from the airport, and was expected at any moment. Hearing this news, I once again became excited, and also appreciated the wonderful timing.

I immediately went to the ashram office and introduced myself. The devotees there welcomed me, and said they remembered my letter. I asked if it would be possible to bathe before Baba arrived. I was given permission, and shown the bathrooms, where I took a quick shower. The bath made me feel a lot better and much more alert.

Soon Baba's car pulled up in front of the ashram's gate. He got out and went straight inside the temple, where he prostrated himself before a life size oil painting of his Guru. He then got up and went to his bedroom. An ashramite told me that he would soon return and give darshan. I felt excited, and my heart was pounding quickly, even though I had gotten only a glimpse of this Baba.

About ten minutes later he came out of his room, and sat on a folding beach chair in the small courtyard, just outside of his room. Smiling, he greeted warmly everyone who approached him. His devotees addressed him as *Babaji*. He appeared to have a great deal of energy, and seemed full of joy. He was wearing the traditional orange lungi of a sannyasi, which was wrapped around his waist, reaching to his knees. He was not wearing any shirt or shawl since it was still extremely hot, and he was perspiring a great deal. He was wearing a gold threaded rosary or *mala* around his neck made from *rudraksha* beads. These are considered sacred to Lord Shiva.

Babaji appeared to be in his early fifties, but in fact he was almost sixty-two. His attitude towards everyone appeared childlike, and everyone seemed happy to have him home. Soon some devotees began performing *arati* to him by waving lights before him, which reminded me of my recent dream. "Was this Lord Shiva?" I wondered.

It was soon my turn to meet Babaji. When I reached his chair I did a full prostration. When I stood up, he welcomed me with the words: "Aah, so you have come."

I did not know if he had been told of my arrival, or if he was speaking from some other level of awareness. He then asked me a few questions through a female disciple who was known as Amma, a word which means "mother" in south India. Amma was a long time disciple, and had even spent time with Muktananda's guru, Baba Nityananda.

I told Baba that I had just arrived from Naimisharanya, where I had been living for a few months. He said that he knew the ashram, and mentioned Swami Naradananda and his disciple Swami Vivekananda. He then asked me what practices I had been performing there. I told him I was practicing meditation and some pranayama. He then asked, with what appeared to me to be a mischievous smile, "What about a mantra, do you repeat one?"

The memory of Swami Naradananda's little game immediately came to mind, and I thought to myself, "I'm not going to fall for that again," and so I answered by saying, "No, I'm waiting for my Guru to give me a mantra."

"Guru Om" he quickly shot back, and said to me, "Repeat this mantra always, and you yourself will become the Guru."

After receiving mantra initiation, I again bowed to Baba. I then got up and stepped back, continuing to observe him very closely. I began to feel like I was finally home. The feeling was a combination of relief, security, and inner peace.

As I stood there watching him, my mind flashed back to

Swami Naradananda. I intuitively felt that he had not initiated me on purpose. As Swamiji was a great being, I am certain that he knew I was going to Ganeshpuri, and would be initiated by Muktananda. And even though I considered him as one of my teachers, Swami Naradananda had always treated me like a friend, and never as his disciple.

I also recalled the dream-vision I had when I first went to his ashram in Kanpur. As well as the dream-vision I had the night before leaving Kanpur for Mumbai. It appeared that Swamiji's ashram was simply a stopover, a place to meditate quietly until the right moment arrived to meet my Guru, who according to my dream was somehow associated with Lord Shiva.

After sometime, Babaji got up from his seat and went inside his room. I was told by one of the ashramites that Babaji had invited me to lunch the next day. I told the person that I had come to stay in the ashram, but he insisted that I should sleep in the town of Ganeshpuri that night. and return the next day. Ganeshpuri was located about a quarter mile down the road. Not wishing to go very far, I decided to sleep that night in an empty flower stall across the road from the ashram.

I had also been told by some devotees that a hymn called *The Shiva Mahimnah* was going to be chanted in the hall that evening. So I decided to attend. It was a very beautiful hymn, and even though I did not understand it, I enjoyed listening to it very much.

Before going to sleep that night, I sat for meditation using my new mantra. This brought some new powerful experiences. The next morning I awoke at about 3 a.m., and again sat for meditation. I started repeating the mantra, and shortly a light started to appear at the spiritual center between the eyebrows. The light appeared to pulsate with divine energy and my mind became focused on it.

At 4 a.m. the ashram's loud speakers crackled to life with a tape of the *Vishnu Sahasranama*, or the "Thousand Names of God." This was followed by a hymn to Nityananda,

Muktananda's guru. Shortly after, the morning arati began, and I went into the hall and stood with the other devotees in front of the large painting of Baba Nityananda. I listened as everyone chanted the Sanskrit mantras, while a priest waved lights before the image.

There were pictures of Nityananda, along with other saints, on the walls of the hall. Nityananda was a large man, who wore only a loin-cloth and was referred to as an *Avadhuta*. He reminded me very much of Roti Baba, and there was even a physical resemblance. I was immediately attracted to him, and felt that he was a great being. His painted image, and the photographs on the walls, all appeared to vibrate with divine energy. My mind became very still as I gazed on them, listening quietly to the morning prayers.

The Ashram

Muktananda's ashram was located right off the main road leading into the town of Ganeshpuri. When you walked out of the ashram's front gate you were on the road. Surrounded by a wall, the ashram's front gate led into a small courtyard. To the left of the gate, on top of the wall, there was a sign which read: *Shree Gurudev Ashram*.

The sign was wrapped in red and white bougainvillea branches. Sacred Ashoka trees lined the inside of the front wall, and two *Parijata* trees provided shade in the courtyard. Each had a raised platform built around them. The Parijata tree or night flowering jasmine is also known as the wish-fulfilling tree. There are a number of myths about the tree's celestial origins in the *Mahabharata* and *Puranas*. The tree is believed to have emerged during the churning of the cosmic ocean (the Milky Way). It is said that although goddess Lakshmi accepts any flower a devotee may offer, the small white flower of the Parijata tree is especially dear to her.

Babaji would often sit under the tree closest to the front gate. The tree produced hundreds of small fragrant flowers with white spiraling petals around an orange center. The flowers would drop during the night, and in the morning we would arrange them in various geometric patterns, or spell out mantras like "Om", "Guru Om", or "Om Namah Shivaya". In Ayurveda, India's ancient system of medicine, the tree's seeds, flowers and leaves have all been used for medicinal purposes.

The front courtyard was actually a part of the original three rooms built by Muktananda's Guru, Baba Nityananda, who was affectingly called Bade Baba or "senior" Baba. Nityananda was often referred to simply as *Bhagavan* (Lord). Sometime in 1949-1950, Nityananda built three small rooms on that site. This was about six years before Muktananda would settle there. In the early 1960s, a two story building was attached to these

(*above*) Baba sitting under the Parijata tree.

three original rooms. The building's ground floor was used as the ashram's main hall. The veranda of the three original rooms had been incorporated into the larger hall. One walked into the verandah through a doorway from the front courtyard, and turned left to go into the hall. Baba's seat was located in the right hand corner of the room, facing east.

It was in this hall that all of the daily chants were held. It was also where Baba met visitors, and in the afternoons, Amma would read him his mail. As already mentioned. the hall contained a life size oil painting of Bhagavan Nityananda, which was placed against the south wall. During the chants the men sat in rows facing each other in front of Baba's chair. Generally men sat on Baba's left, and the women to his right. If there wasn't enough room in the main hall, the person would

(*above*) Morning Chant in the old hall.

have to sit in the verandah in front of the three rooms. But then one could not see Baba.

As is common in Indian temple architecture, the hall's front door faced east, giving a spectacular view of each sunrise. But one could see the sunrise only if they sat in the veranda, In the distance one could see a mountain range with one of its peaks resembling a Shiva lingam. I would often meditate on that beautiful peak whenever I sat there.

The path from the front courtyard to the back, led one through a smaller gate located to the right of the three rooms. This gate led into the ashram's main courtyard. If you continued to the right, it would take you to the lower garden. Going still further, and crossing a path which divided rice fields, you would reach the upper garden. There were a number of rice fields, and the grounds contained all types of fruit trees, such as coconut, banana, papaya, mango and cashews. There were also many fragrant flowers and shrubs. In the upper garden there were cottages scattered here and there. They generally housed long time devotees who visited the ashram regularly on weekends and holidays.

If one followed the path to the left in the main courtyard, they would arrive at the ashram's kitchen and dining area. But just before entering the dinning room, there was a smaller courtyard right in front of Baba's original bedroom. Opposite the bedroom, just across the small courtyard was Baba's bathroom. It was in that small courtyard where I had first met him the previous night. Around Baba's room there was an enclosed verandah, where devotees meditated. I recall feeling a great deal of energy in that area. Baba had spent many years meditating in his small room, and one could feel it pervasive energy.

A few months after I arrived, construction was started on a new building next to Baba's original room. The bottom floor of the new building was to be Baba's new apartment. But at the time I met him he was still living in his old bedroom.

Construction on a new meditation room was also about to start. Part of the room would be underground. It would actually be the bottom floor or basement of Baba's new apartment. It would eventually become known as the "Cave Room."

The morning after my arrival I too meditated in the veranda around Baba's room. I sat there for sometime, enjoying a peaceful meditation, until I heard a bell ringing in the front courtyard. This bell would announce that a program was about to start, usually within ten minutes. I therefore went to the front hall and took a seat with the others. Soon Babaji entered the hall, and everyone started chanting.

When I first arrived at the ashram, the *Vishnu Sahasranama* or the "Thousand Names of Vishnu (God)" was the morning chant. Later it would be replaced by the *Bhagavad Gita*, until finally the *Guru Gita* would become the morning chant permanently.

It was just before sunrise when the chanting started. The eastern sky was streaked with beautiful orange light, creating an enchanting sight. Since I had never chanted the *Vishnu Sahasranama* before, that first morning I just listened, and observed Baba very carefully.

During the chant, Baba was extremely alert. He kept an eye on everyone in the hall, making sure that they were all chanting. I also noticed that everyone was completely focused on him. If Baba noticed someone not chanting, or worse, sleeping, he would throw small wooden children's blocks at them, which he kept on his desk for this very purpose.

I was still feeling the excitement from my meeting with Baba the previous night. All kinds of thoughts were running through my mind. Watching him that morning, I knew, and felt deeply within me, that I had finally found my Guru.

The chant was almost two hours long. Afterward, Baba went back into his room, while everyone else went to have breakfast. Since it was a Saturday, and because Baba had been away from the ashram for sometime, there were many visitors that day and the next. I spent part of that morning talking to some of the Indian disciples, and the two Westerners who had been in the ashram for sometime. We spoke about the ashram and their experiences with Baba.

I also went for a walk through the lower garden, and then to the upper garden. Walking down the steps into the lower courtyard, I noticed a large cage to my left where the ashram peacocks lived. They would go about freely during the day, but at night they would return to their cage.

There was also a large well in one of the corners of the garden. There were two or three small rooms in the area as well. Walking further along the path, I arrived at a small shrine on the left with a statue of Lord Shiva in the form of *Nataraj*, the King or Lord of Dancers. Continuing further along the path, I arrived at the back gate, which led to the upper garden. On the other side of the gate there was a path which divided two rice fields. Having crossed it, I soon reached the upper garden. I decided to visit the ashram cowshed. At the time, the ashram had about thirty cows, and a few calves. There was one large Brahma bull named Nandi. I could tell by their appearance that they were all well cared for.

I continued my walk, following a narrow path along the perimeter of the ashram. At the time the ashram was situated on about eighteen acres of land. It was very beautiful, and the atmosphere was peaceful. After walking along the back perimeter of the ashram, I soon arrived at a large building named *Turiya Mandir*. The building consisted of a large hall dedicated to Bhagavan Nityananda. It also had a few guest rooms.

The word *turiya* actually refers to the fourth state of consciousness, and *mandir* is the Sanskrit word for temple. Therefore, symbolically, this temple represented the fourth state of consciousness.

On my walk that day around the ashram, there was something else that I discovered about Muktananda, and that was that he was not sectarian. I noticed photographs of great beings from various traditions hanging on the walls of the front hall, the kitchen dining room, the meditation veranda around Baba's room, in Turiya Mandir, and even in the cow shed. Photographs of Krishna, Rama, Zarathustra, Ramakrishna Paramahamsa, Ramana Maharshi, Sai Baba of Shirdi, Anandamayi Ma, and many others graced the walls of the ashram. Indeed, Muktananda showed respect for all true saints and yogis, no matter what their religion or tradition was. He had a universal outlook and philosophy.

After my walk, I returned to the main courtyard and noticed that Baba was sitting outside. There were only a few people there with him, and so I went over as well. He was talking to some devotees, and appeared quite animated. Then after a few moments, he looked at me, and asked if I had seen the ashram. I said that I had.

He began asking me questions about the ashram at Naimisharanya, as well as other places I had visited. When he had finished questioning me, I asked for his permission to stay in the ashram. He smiled at me and said, *"Bahut Achcha"* — meaning, "very good, or very well." He told me that I could stay, and said that for the time being I could sleep in the upper garden on the outside verandah of Turiya Mandir. I thanked him and bowed.

I also asked him if there was anything in particular that I should do for my spiritual practice.

"No, just continue doing what you have been doing," he told me, "but also repeat the mantra I gave you."

Baba then told me that I should go to Ganeshpuri and have darshan of Bhagavan Nityananda's samadhi shrine, which I immediately did.

Not long after my arrival, Baba showed me an old mud hut which was located in an isolated corner of the ashram, not far from the main courtyard. He told me that it was a good spot for meditation, and asked me if I would like to do my sadhana in that hut. I was very happy to hear this and immediately said yes.

The hut was made out of bamboo, mud, and cowdung. It needed some repairs so I put into practice what I had learnt while living in the forest ashram. Part of the roof was made out of tin, and so I knew that this was going to make the hut extremely hot. I therefore decided to add a few layers of dried grass on top of it.

One day, while I was climbing up onto the roof, I suddenly heard Baba's voice calling out to me from the distance. I looked around and noticed him walking to the upper garden. We were separated by rice fields, but I could see him waving his arms in the air, and doing a kind of dance while chanting, "Hari Rama, Hari Rama."

He waved to me and continued on his walk. Later, he arrived near the hut and came over to see how it was going. He told me that I was now living like Lord Rama when he had to live in the forest.

After living in that hut for about two or three months, one day Baba called me and told me to move out of the hut, and go and stay at Turiya Mandir again, which I did that same day. This time I would remain at Turiya Mandir for the next four years.

(*above*) Baba sitting with first foreigners (early 1970s). The author is standing in the back, second from left.

Interestingly, a few days after Baba had told me to move out of the hut, the monsoon started, and the rains became so intense that the hut was completely washed away.

In those days, only the women stayed in rooms or dormitories. Most of the men slept either in the temple, courtyard, or upper garden. In fact, there were only two other Western men staying in the ashram at the time of my arrival. And on the day I met Baba, two more Westerners had arrived as well. One was a French girl named Marie, and the other a Canadian named Dale. The two had been traveling together in India.

One of the two westerners living in the ashram was an American named Larry. He and I became close friends. He had been there for sometime, and spoke Hindi very well. At the time he took care of the front hall along with an Indian disciple named Markandeya. The other Westerner living in the ashram was an Italian/Canadian man, who happened to also be named Bruno. At the time he was working in the garden. As he was older than me, he was known as Bruno the elder, and I the younger.

After a few days, Baba instructed me to take care of the cows. At the time, Gopal Desai, who later became Swami Govindananda, was in charge of the cowshed. I started working with him. I would get up at about 3 a.m. each morning, meditate, and then go to the cowshed.

But after a few days, I began meditating in the cowshed itself. After my meditation, I would clean the stalls, and feed the cows, while Desai milked them. Then Dale and I would take them out to graze, and later, we would go to the river to wash them.

The cows were very gentle, and Baba had named them all. He would visit them in the morning and afternoons, at which time he would feed them bread rolls. They would see him coming from a distance, and they would suddenly run towards him in excitement. Baba would simply laugh, and ask them to be patient. After sometime, I began to notice that they appeared to understand Baba, and he them. I found this to be true with all the other ashram animals as well. They all seemed to understand and certainly love Baba.

There were also five dogs living in the ashram at the time. One was named Raja. He was temperamental and had a bad habit of biting people. Another dog named Gopal used to always follow Baba wherever he went. If Baba was out of his room, you could be sure that Gopal would find him. The other two dogs were called Shyam and Ramu. The fifth dog, Sanjay, always remained by himself in the upper garden. He was an independent spirit and did not hang out with the other dogs. The others stayed mainly around the main courtyard, while Sanjay remained mostly around Turiya Mandir.

Besides the cowshed, I also worked in the gardens, and eventually in other areas of the ashram, including the front hall. Baba loved discipline and he ran the ashram in a very strict manner. Everyone living in the ashram had to follow the daily routine.

After the morning chant, everyone worked at their respective

(*above*) Baba with ashram dog Raja

jobs for about two hours. The times would change slightly throughout the year according to the seasons. After my morning work or service (*seva*) I would meditate for about half an hour just before lunch. After lunch everyone rested until about 3 p.m., when we would again do some ashram work for another two hours. Some disciples would also chant the *Vishnu Sahasranama* in the main hall at around 2 p.m. when it was no longer the morning chant.

After my afternoon work, I would again sit for meditation until just before the evening arati, which started at sunset. After arati there was dinner, followed by the *Shiva Mahimnah Stotram*, or Hymn to the Glory of Shiva. This lasted until almost 9 p.m., at which time I would again meditate and finally go to sleep by about ten.

Even though I knew deep in my heart that Baba was my Guru

(*above*) The author building a wall in the ashram garden (circa 1971).

from the moment I had met him, it took about three months to fully realize this in my conscious mind. I was still feeling the pains of separation. During those three months, although I had numerous experiences, I also had many doubts which I would voice to Baba. He was always very affectionate towards me, and would answer all my questions. The problem was, that I would spend the whole day formulating my questions, but when I sat before Baba in the evening, my mind would become totally still. I could then not recall what I wanted to ask him. During those moments, there were no doubts in my mind at all. Meanwhile, the translator would ask, "Well, what is your question?"

I would look at him as if I did not know what he was talking about. Baba would just sit there and laugh. I began feeling a deep intoxication whenever I was around him.

My meditations were also becoming deeper, and the light I was seeing at the center between the eyebrows was becoming more steady. It would arise and subside in waves. But even more important, I began to have a powerful relationship with Bhagavan Nityananda.

The first experience occurred in a dream-vision I had just a few days after my arrival at the ashram. In the dream-vision I was standing in a room with Bhagavan. I then did a full prostration before him. I was then about twenty feet away from him, still lying prostrate on the floor, when suddenly I was overwhelmed by an extraordinary power. I then started to slowly crawl towards him, until I finally reached his feet. He then placed his hand on my head, and I noticed a blue light streaming from it. As the light entered me, my subtle body started to shake violently, and even the physical body shook as well. Even so, Bhagavan would not let go of me.

Soon his whole body changed into that effulgent blue light, and he then entered me fully in the form of that light. At that moment my body started to roll uncontrollably around the room. I felt so much power and joy moving through me, that I went into an ecstatic state. Tears of joy and happiness began rolling down my cheeks.

When I awoke, I still had the same feelings, and I was still crying tears of joy. I sat up for meditation, but after awhile I fell asleep again. I had a number of these experiences during that time, and I also started to experience the inner power of the mantra. The mantra is indeed a vehicle for the Guru's *Shakti* or spiritual power. By entering the disciple through the mantra, the Guru awakens the seekers latent spiritual energy.

Within a few days, I had another powerful dream-vision with Bhagavan Nityananda. This time he was sitting quietly with his eyes closed. I then noticed a divine light emanating from his forehead at the spiritual center between the eyebrows. The light began to shine on me, and I started feeling great joy. I then ran up to him excitedly. I took hold of his right hand and started pulling him, apparently trying to lead him somewhere. After I had taken his hand I saw myself as a small, impatient child of

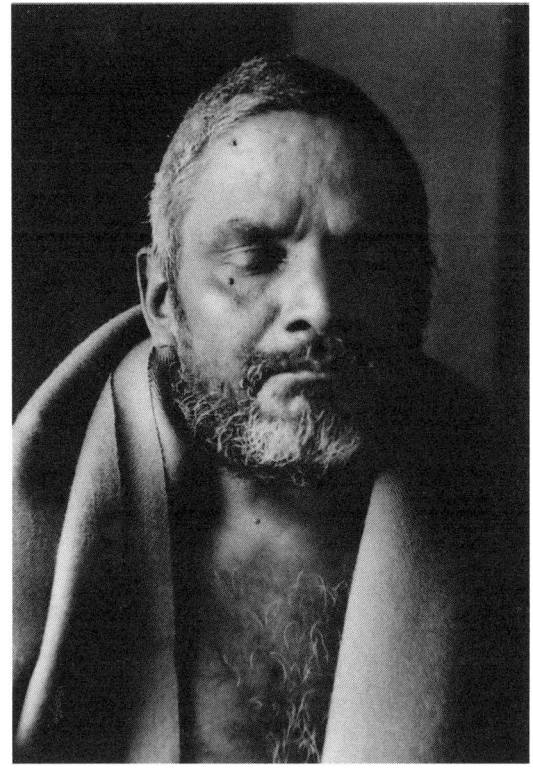

Bhagavan Nityananda

about five or six years of age. I was pulling him forward with the desire of introducing him to all my friends. Smiling like a kind grandfather, he followed me reluctantly. I then received a telepathic message from him, telling me not to be in a hurry.

Baba also appeared to be aware of my experiences with Nityananda, and encouraged them. After some months, Baba told me that I should take new visitors to the ashram, to visit Ganeshpuri on the first Thursday after their arrival. I was to show them the samadhi shrine and other sites, and tell them about Bhagavan.

But even with all the experiences I was having, the period was at times still quite difficult for me. I felt a lot of mental and emotional agitation during those early days. I felt like I still did not have that inner connection with Baba, and doubts continued to flood my mind. During the day my mind would constantly be agitated, and I would often cry for hours feeling a deep longing for the divine.

This longing for God is a very mysterious emotion. It is not like ordinary feelings. When a devotee is overwhelmed by the desire to merge with the divine, he or she can not think about anything else but God. And the mind is always thinking about what can be done in order to be closer to God.

In truth, this intense desire to know God is itself the manifestation of God's love and grace. During such periods, formal meditation may become difficult, or even impossible. But in reality, real meditation has spread into the devotees daily life, and this mental and emotional preoccupation with finding God, has itself become his meditation. The devotee has now entered into a personal relationship with God, and forgets everything else around him. He keeps to himself. His sleep may become irregular during this period, and at times he may feel like he is going mad.

It was only later that I discovered the mysteries of the mind, and how it adopts an attitude of self-surrender, love, and devotion for the purpose of spiritual progress. The more the disciple surrenders to the Guru, and the divine inner *Shakti*, the more powerful the experiences become. Eventually the mind gives up these moods or feelings (*bhava*), and the disciple becomes established in the knowledge of his own inner Self.

At night I would go and see Baba with all the questions that I had formulated that day. But as I have said, the moment I sat near him, my mind would enter a state of deep calm, and a feeling of intoxication would come over me. At that moment there were no questions, no doubts. It was then clear that Baba was indeed my Guru. And he always comforted and encouraged me saying that everything was going well, and that there was nothing to worry about.

This process continued for a while. Then one night, Baba told me that he understood my mental condition, and that I should not worry. He told me not to become overtly anxious and impatient. That I would receive everything there, which I interpreted to mean that I would receive everything from him. He explained to me that sadhana takes time, and that I should keep to myself and continue my practices with great intensity. He told me not to worry, that I would attain the Self in this life time.

He also told me that he would start to communicate with me from within, and if I had any questions, I would receive the answers there. I asked him if these answers would be clear to me, and not just vague mental notions?

Smiling, he said, "Yes, they will be very clear."

"And how long will it take to receive these answers after the question arises?" I asked.

He again smiled and said that I would receive the answer within two or three days.

After that night, I started experiencing the truth of what Baba told me. Now, all that I had to do was to continue my meditation, and follow his instructions, but most of all have patience.

Mahayoga

Baba belonged to the ancient lineage of perfected masters called *Siddhas*. The word *Siddha* indicates one who has achieved *siddhi* or spiritual perfection, as well as spiritual powers. This meaning will of course include anyone who has achieved enlightenment. But the word Siddha is also applied specifically to a lineage of masters, who initiate their disciples through the method known as *Shaktipat*. In this lineage, a Siddha transmits his or her own spiritual power into the seeker in order to bring about a spiritual awakening.

Muktananda was born in the modern south Indian state of Karnataka. He became a sannyasi or renunciate sometime in his teens, not long after a chance meeting with his future Guru, Nityananda, who was then a wandering Avadhuta. Shortly after that first encounter, Muktananda left home in search of God. He was about fifteen and a half years old at the time. He first stayed in the ashram of the famous Swami Siddharudha, where he was initiated into the monastic order, and given the name Swami Muktananda. While there he also studied Indian philosophies. After Siddharudha's death, Muktananda began wandering throughout India on foot, visiting many places of pilgrimage, and meeting different holy men. He was also in search of a Guru.

After many years of wandering, he again met Nityananda, who now had settled in the village of Ganeshpuri. Baba visited him for many years before Nityananda blessed him with *Shaktipat* initiation. When Muktananda received Nityananda's blessing in 1947, his wanderings finally came to an end. Then after a period of intense spiritual practices, lasting for about nine years, he became fully established in his own inner Self.

In 1956, Nityananda told Muktananda to settle permanently in Ganeshpuri, and had him installed in a small room just behind the original three rooms he had built years earlier. The room was originally built as a small temple to house the statue of Nityananda. This interesting event came about when a rumor began spreading that Nityananda was about to leave his physical body. When Nityananda was asked about whether the rumor was true, he responded with his characteristic "hum" sound. But as he rarely elaborated on anything, such remarks could be interpreted in a number of ways. The devotees who had asked him about the rumor interpreted the sound to mean that the rumor was true. That he was indeed about to take mahasamadhi. So they asked Nityananda if they could have a statue (*murti*) made of him, and install it in a temple. Apparently he gave his consent, and even told them where to build the temple in which the statue would be installed. Baba's room was that temple.

Later, when the rumor proved untrue, the devotees asked Nityananda what they should do with the statue. He told them to give it, "*jal samadhi*" — which is the immersion of the body in water at the time of death. The statue was dutifully submerged in the nearby river. Afterwards, the devotees asked Nityananda what deity they should install in the temple? Nityananda is said to have replied, "Muktananda." Baba was still living in that small room when I first met him.

Muktananda had achieved both the theoretical and practical aspects of knowledge. Besides being well versed in various scriptures, he also had a direct experience of his inner Self through the practice of *yoga*. And although Baba taught Advaita Vedanta, there is no doubt that the philosophy of Kashmir Shaivism was very dear to his heart. It is known as Kashmir Shaivism because this non-dual philosophy was developed in the valley of Kashmir by different sages, who called God by the name of Shiva, the auspicious and compassionate one.

In this philosophy, the universe is seen as the divine sport of Lord Shiva, and everything, from the highest principle down to a blade of grass is pervaded by that Supreme Being. This was in fact exactly how Muktananda had experienced the world in his own spiritual unfoldment.

Although Muktananda started out as a simple monk, in his later years he would become known as a renowned yogi around the world. But not long after he had received Shaktipat from Nityananda, he began having some strange experiences. Powerful experiences are not unusual after one receives Shaktipat, but little was known about them. Muktananda therefore at first became confused, and thought that perhaps something had gone wrong in his spiritual practice.

Just as Baba was having these doubts and feelings, Hari Giri Baba, a great Siddha and friend of Muktananda's suddenly showed up at his hut. Hari Giri Baba, who is said to have had the power of omniscience, began to comfort Muktananda before he was even told anything was wrong. He told Muktananda not to worry. That he knew what he was going through, and its meaning. As Hari Giri Baba was a strange character, he told Muktananda that he would explain it to him if he gave him two rupees (about a dime at the time). Muktananda handed over the two rupees, and Hari Giri Baba began telling Muktananda that the experiences he was having were all for his own benefit, and that he was no longer an ordinary sannyasi, but had become a *Maharaja* — a great king.

Years later, this prophecy proved to be quite accurate. Baba's external circumstances became more like that of a royal sannyasin instead of a simple monk, and his ashram looked like a palace. Astrologers had also been predicting from his early age that he had a great future, indicated by powerful *Raja-yogas* in his horoscope. According to Vedic astrology, such royal conditions may exist even in the life of an ascetic, when there are both *Sannyasa-yogas* and *Raja-yogas* in the person's horoscope. These yogas are special planetary combinations which produce royal conditions (raja-yoga) in the person's life, even if they pursues spiritual liberation because of the sannyasa yogas. Such beings may live simple lives, but it may be in the lap of luxury. In an attempt to describe such beings, the great poet-saint Bhartrihari wrote:

> *"It is impossible to say a word about the ways of perfected beings (Siddhas), or know anything at all about their Karma. Some live completely naked, lying on the earth without even a torn piece of blanket, and some live in splendor which outshines even that of kings. Some are serene and calm; others are mute all the time; still others never stop swearing and lie around like snakes."*

Muktananda's outer condition towards the end of his life was like that of the second type mentioned in Bhartrihari's poem. But even though these were the external conditions, Baba always remained very simple.

Like his Guru, Muktananda also had the ability to awaken the divine power lying dormant within an individual through *Shaktipat* initiation. The word *Shaktipat* literally means the descent of Shakti. The *Yoga Vasishtha* describes the characteristics of a true Guru (*Sadguru*) in the following words:

> *He who, by his gracious look, touch, or word, gives to the disciple an experience of his identity with the Absolute is indeed the true Guru.*

And in the *Kularnava Tantra* we read:

> *A discriminating person should choose as his Guru none else but one by whose touch he experiences the highest bliss.*

Within each individual there dwells a divine energy or power known as *Shakti*. This is the same energy which has created the entire universe. The energy residing in an individual is called goddess *Kundalini* by yogis. She resides in the human body in a contracted form. The Shakti is addressed as the Goddess (*Devi*), or simply as Mother. The Kundalini Shakti is said to reside at the root spiritual center called *muladhara*, located at the base of the spine in the subtle body.

As we have seen, Kundalini is symbolized as a coiled serpent, indicating its potential spiritual power when awakened. Even though it is said to be in a contracted form, and asleep in the majority of people, it is nevertheless the source of all functions within the human body. Sri Kundalini controls and silently guides all activities of ordinary life. The sleep referred to in the yogic language indicates spiritual sleep — that is, one's ignorance of their true nature. But when awakened, the person no longer experiences himself as a small and ordinary person, but recognizes his own inner divinity. This spiritual energy is that same power which is called the Holy Spirit in the Christian religion. The descriptions in the New Testament of the experiences people had with the descent of the Holy Spirit are strikingly similar to those found in the yogic literature.

Because of its importance in the attainment of spiritual liberation, it is therefore obviously very important to awaken this Kundalini. However, it is not an easy task. Yogic literature prescribes a number of methods to bring this awakening about, but without a doubt, the awakening brought on by the blessing of a Sadguru is considered the best, and easiest. Throughout its long history, this path has been known as *Siddha Yoga* (the yoga of Siddhas), *Siddhamarga* ("path of Siddhas"), *Mahayoga* (the "great yoga"), *Kundalini Maha Yoga,* and *Gurukripa* ("Guru's grace"). However all these different names indicate the same path, the mystical path of the Siddhas.

It is called Siddha Yoga because it is received by the grace of a Siddha. It is called *Mahayoga* or the "great yoga," because when activated, it naturally encompasses all other forms of yoga, such as *Hatha Yoga, Mantra Yoga, Bhakti Yoga, Jnana Yoga, Laya Yoga* and *Raja Yoga*. This means that in some individuals the Shakti may manifest as *jnana* or intuitive spiritual knowledge. And they may also receive knowledge of various sciences. In others it may manifest as deep love and devotion, which overwhelms the seeker with feelings of pure love for God, or in this case, one's Guru. In others, a yogic process may be set in motion which will influence both the physical body as well as the psychology of the individual. These various experiences all occur spontaneously, i.e., hatha yoga postures (*asana*) and/or different types of breath control (*pranayama*) may occur, even if the person has never even heard of them before. Some seekers may even experience these different paths one after the other.

The Guru not only awakens the inner Shakti, but can also control its movement in the disciple. Because of its sudden awakening, and the unusual experiences which often follow, the seeker may at first become confused and afraid. The Guru however will guide the seeker through it all. If the Shakti becomes too strong for the disciple to bear, the Guru will simply decrease its intensity. By associating with their Guru, and following their instructions, the seeker easily moves through the difficult path. The goal of this path is total spiritual perfection (*Siddhahood*). Baba would often say that one who has been blessed by a Siddha will also become a Siddha. In truth, the Guru is not an individual at all, but God's divine power of grace. Therefore, it is God himself who takes the form of the spiritual master in order to guide seekers.

I would watch Baba touch a person, utter a mantra in someone's ear, or simply glance intently at someone. All of these would have the same effect. They all brought about the arousal of the inner Kundalini. *Shaktipat* may be given in one of four ways: by look, touch, word, or thought. One day, I had a personal experience of Shaktipat by look. Baba was sitting in the small courtyard in front of his bedroom. There were just a few people standing near him, and I was standing at the entrance of the courtyard. The front hall was behind me. Baba was sitting quietly, and although his eyes were open, his gaze was within. All of a sudden, he turned his head in my direction, and looked straight at me with his eyes wide open, and a smile of pure compassion on his lips.

This was no ordinary look, but the expression of the transmission of Shakti by look. It was so powerful and tangible that it literally pushed me back off my feet. It immediately produced great joy within me, and suddenly a pure love began to arise in my heart for Baba. I felt like dancing, but controlled myself.

Later, someone who happened to be sitting in the front hall, looking at Baba through the window, told me that he had seen the look Baba had given me, and even he described it as a "tangible energy."

Not everyone received Shaktipat the first time they met Baba. Some people came just for a day or two, and expected to receive full *Shaktipat* before the day was over. Baba was amused at such "seekers". This is not the attitude of a real seeker. One must be willing to make any sacrifice in order to receive such a blessing. And after receiving it, some effort must be made to continue its unfoldment. In fact, the awakening is only the beginning of the journey.

One day someone asked Baba why in ancient times Shaktipat was given to only a few people, while he gave it freely to everyone. Baba said that it really did not matter how many people received Shaktipat, but what was important was how many could maintain it. He said that this was a divine state, which one receives only when a person is full of virtues. And that the purer one becomes, the more the Shakti reveals itself.

Sometimes the ashram appeared to be like a mad house. One person would be laughing, while another was crying. One would dance, while another would be completely still, in a state of deep absorption. Another person may be repeating Sanskrit mantras, which they had previously never even heard of.

One day a man came to the ashram to meet Baba. He had been brought by one of Baba's devotees. The man was shown around the ashram and later came to the courtyard where Baba was sitting. I happened to be standing near Baba with two or three other devotees. The man approached Baba and did a full prostration. With sincerity in his voice, the man asked Baba to please bless him. Apparently he was a seeker and had practiced meditation for sometime, but without success. Baba did not say anything. The man then stepped back, and remained standing there. After sometime Baba told the man to go into the meditation room and sit quietly, and asked me to take him inside. I did so, and then returned to the courtyard. Baba was speaking with one of the devotees when he suddenly stopped, turned towards the meditation room, and began shouting, *"Kula, Kula, Kula."*

Suddenly, a loud scream was heard coming from the meditation room, followed by hysterical laughter. It was obviously coming from the man Baba had just sent there. Later he reported his experiences to Baba with tears of joy rolling down his cheeks.

But then again, this does not happen to everyone. Another interesting incident occurred with a man who was visiting the ashram from South Africa. He was an elderly gentleman who had heard about Baba and his ability to give Shaktipat. He had a deep interest in the occult and decided to come and see what was going on, and hopefully receive Shaktipat himself. When he arrived he told Baba that he could only stay for three days. Baba just smiled and said nothing.

The first day went by and nothing happened. The man was a bit disappointed but took it in stride. The next day nothing happened as well. Now he became a bit anxious, and started doubting Baba. Of course Baba was not very helpful either, and would tease the man by asking in English every time he met him, "No Shaktipat?"

The man was told to continue to sit for meditation whenever he had the time. The third day came and went and still nothing had happened. He was scheduled to leave the next morning, and was now certain that he had wasted his time coming to the ashram. The next morning I recall him coming to say good-bye to Baba, who was sitting in the small courtyard just outside his bedroom. With a smile on his face, Baba asked, "Still no Shaktipat?"

The man answered in the negative, and Baba was told by the translator that he was very upset. Baba chuckled, and asked the man when he was leaving. He said he would be leaving the ashram within the hour.

"Why don't you meditate before you leave?" Baba suggested.

Thinking that by this time it was useless, the man said he had to do some more packing. But Baba continued to encourage him to try again, until finally the man went into the verandah, and sat for meditation. Previously Baba had touched him on the head, back, forehead, and just about everywhere else. But this time, after a few minutes, Baba got up from his seat, and went inside to where the man was sitting. I followed him. He then placed his hand on the man's head.

The moment he touched him, the man's body started shaking violently, and it appeared that he was about to erupt. He started crying uncontrollably, and was trying to speak but could not. Strange sounds started to come out of his mouth, and his face was also going through various contortions.

I could tell that his tears were coming from a very deep place within him, and I recall thinking that layers of darkness were being removed from his consciousness. After about half an hour of crying, Baba had me take him out of the meditation room, and walk him around the courtyard to calm him down. The man finally became calm, and went over to Baba, and fell at his feet thanking him profusely for his blessing. He was now ready to stay or go, as Baba wished. Baba teasingly said, "So, you have received Shaktipat?" Baba then told the man to return to South Africa, and continue to practice meditation there.

There were many such incidents which I personally witnessed over the years. Baba would often sit in the temple hall for hours at a time in total silence. He would sit casually while devotees meditated near him. During those periods, the energy was so powerful that it was difficult not to meditate. At such times I could feel the energy pervading the hall, and it would automatically pull me within.

In February of 1970, Baba went to Delhi for the *Shivaratri* festival. Shivaratri literally means the night of *Shiva*. It occurs on the fourteenth lunar night (*tithi*), during the moon's dark phase. Since it is based on the solar-lunar calendar, it falls in either February or March of each year according to the Gregorian calendar. The devotee usually celebrates the festival by remaining awake throughout the night, meditating, repeating the mantra, or chanting. On the day of Shivaratri, Gopal Desai told me that he was planning to go to the Shiva temple in Ganeshpuri that night, and asked me if I wanted to accompany him. I said that I would. He also told me that he wanted to pick some *bilva* leaves, which are considered sacred to Lord Shiva. I asked if I could help him pick them, as I also wanted to participate in the worship.

Although originally he was thinking of picking only 108 leaves, we got carried away, and instead picked 1008. That night we left the ashram at about 9 p.m. and walked down to Ganeshpuri. When we reached the town Desai wanted to have some coffee and talk to one of his friends before we went to the temple. By the time we arrived at the temple, it was about 10:30 p.m.

The Shiva temple in Ganeshpuri, called *Bhimeshwar*, is a very ancient temple. It is located next to Bhagavan Nityananda's tomb (*Samadhi shrine*). In front of the temple there are three hot sulphur spring pools. When we entered the temple it was empty. Desai sat down in front of the *linga*, and started to perform his worship.

The room is not very large and I decided to sit in the northeastern corner, and began meditating quietly. Sitting with my eyes closed I could hear Desai repeating the mantra, "Om Namah Shivaya!, Om Namah Shivaya!, Om Namah Shivaya!"

(*above*) The Ganeshpuri Shiva temple seen from the back; (*right*) The Shiva Linga inside.

over and over again. With each repetition, he would place a leaf on the *linga*. Meanwhile a brahmin priest came into the temple, and began chanting various mantras.

With my eyes closed, I was mentally repeating my mantra, when all of a sudden I felt a hand press down on my head. I quickly opened my eyes, but there was no one there. I again closed my eyes, and again I felt a hand on my head. I quickly opened my eyes, but again I saw no one standing or sitting near me. I again closed my eyes, and suddenly I saw fire all around me. But I felt no fear, and this time I did not open my eyes, nor did I move. Instead I went into a deep meditation, which lasted for quite sometime. And even after the meditation ended, I was still feeling intoxicated from its effects. I felt that Lord Shiva himself had blessed me on that sacred night.

After sometime Desai said that we should start back to the ashram. On the way home I was still in an exalted state. I therefore remained quiet, and did not mention my experience to Desai.

My Life In The Ashram

It did not take me long to get used to the ashram schedule and discipline. Besides the cowshed, I also worked in the garden, and soon started working in the main hall as well. I would become completely focused on my work no matter what it was. I had decided to follow Baba's instructions and see what happened.

Then one day, something occurred which would be a turning point for me. In those days it was the custom in the ashram that some of the male disciples would shave their heads and beards each full moon day. When I arrived at the ashram, I still had my long hair and beard. But then one day, a few months after my arrival, I felt an overwhelming desire to shave everything off. I recall that moment vividly even today. As I shaved my head and beard, I felt a great joy pervading me. I mentally offered my body and mind to the Guru, and started repeating the mantra Baba had given me. The action itself became a ritual, and symbolized a formal dedication and life long commitment to Baba, and the pursuit of Self-Realization.

My meditations were also becoming deeper, and I was enjoying the ashram's peaceful atmosphere. However, my inner turmoil would continue a little longer. The ups and downs would come and go. One moment I was feeling very happy, but in the next I felt the opposite. This finally came to a head while Baba was away in Delhi. He was expected to return within a few days. My mind was giving me so much trouble that I even thought of leaving the ashram.

Then one day, while out in the fields grazing the cows, I suddenly recalled something Baba had told me to do just before he left for Delhi. I had gone to see him one night to ask what to do about the constant trouble my mind was giving me. He asked me if I had studied the Bhagavad Gita?

I said that I had read it a number of times.

"No," he said, "I mean have you studied the Gita with some commentary?"

I said I had not. So he instructed me to do so. While sitting in the field that day, it occurred to me that Baba was returning the next day, and I had still not studied the Bhagavad Gita as he had instructed me. So that very afternoon I went to the ashram library to see what was available. I came across a book by Shri Aurobindo called, *The Message of the Gita*, and thought I would start with that.

Although I had read the Gita a number of times before, when I read it that day, I immediately began to identify my own mental doubts with Arjuna's emotional reaction to the eminent war which awaited him. Lord Krishna, with his divine wisdom, began reproaching Arjuna, and instructed him on what his proper attitude and behavior should be under the circumstances. By following Krishna's advice, Arjuna became successful in the ensuing struggle. It became clear to me that like Arjuna, I too should follow the spiritual path indicated by my Guru. I should also develop patience and self-discipline.

This was not simply an intellectual understanding that arose, but it was a very powerful experience. I felt deeply inspired by it. And that night, I also had a beautiful dream-vision of Sri Aurobindo. He was sitting in a chair wearing a white dhoti, with the top draped over his left shoulder. His hair and beard were white, and he appeared as an old man, but his face shone with a divine glow. I approached him with folded hands, and asked for his blessing in achieving my spiritual goal. He raised his right hand in the gesture of blessing, smiled at me, and told me that he would protect me.

After that experience, I studied more of Aurobindo's writings. He was indeed a great yogi, and his philosophical writings and poetry are the accounts of the divine inner journey. He also had a deep grasp of the English language, as well as Sanskrit and Greek.

After the above experience, things started to settle down for me. I began to really feel contented, and my experiences started to increase. During that time I also started having a powerful experience in meditation, which helped me understand an experience I had been having since my early childhood. Each night, just as I was about to fall asleep, I would experience a feeling of vastness, and a sense of having no boundaries.

The feeling would often be centered around the *sahasrara* or spiritual center at the top of the head. I never understood what was happening, but now it started occurring during my meditation, and I was fully aware of what was happening to me.

When one starts to experience the inner Self, one looses the sense of identification with the physical body, and starts to experience themselves as boundless spirit. After having that experience in meditation, my faith in Baba became one-pointed.

I realized more and more how important a true Guru was. The *Guru Gita* proclaims that it is devotion to the Guru which brings about grace, and one's spiritual unfoldment. By devotion to the Guru, one receives the knowledge the Guru possesses. When a seeker lives with the Guru for a long time, and practices sadhana with sincerity, he or she will always be guided by the Guru, even after the master leaves his physical body.

The importance of a true Guru can never be overestimated. The idea of God as the Guru may be alien to many in the modern world, but this is a very ancient concept. Although God is beyond all forms, the human mind requires some form in order to grasp the deeper levels of spiritual reality. And as we have seen, a religious person may perceive God as father, mother, friend, or even lover. But the spiritual seeker sees God in the form of his own Guru. Although there are many religious sects in India, all agree on the importance of having a personal Guru. There is a verse in the Guru Gita which says:

Gurubrahma guruvisnur
gurudevo maheshvarah
Gurusakshat parabrahma
tasmai shrigurave namah.

This verse says that the Guru is the creator (Brahma), preserver (Vishnu), and destroyer (Maheshwara). In fact, the Guru is considered the Supreme Absolute. Salutations to that Guru.

According to Kashmir Shaivism, there are five great acts of God. The act of creation, preservation, destroyer, concealer, and the fifth, considered as the most important, is the bestowing of grace, which releases the individual soul from the bonds of ignorance. Through this fifth act, the Lord reveals himself in the form of a personal Guru. Even if an intense spiritual awakening occurs directly within the heart, without the aid of an external Guru, the seeker is often guided to an appropriate Guru after the initial experience.

Besides declaring the Guru to be none else but the Absolute Brahman, the Guru Gita also warns of the rarity of such *Sadgurus*. Although difficult to find, one can succeed with God's grace. In the *Shiva Sutra Vimarshini*, the Guru is described as: *gururva parameshvari anugrahika Shaktihi*. That is: "The Guru is the grace-bestowing power of the Supreme Lord."

My daily routine would start at about 3 a.m. After my morning bath, I would sit in meditation for some time. Then at about 4:45, I would go to the dinning room where we practiced *hatha yoga*. In those days, Baba would often come out and teach us different postures, and make sure that we were performing them correctly. At the time there were only a few Indian boys and two or three Westerners practicing hatha yoga. I would have very good experiences while performing the various postures. When we were finished, we would all go and chant the *Bhagavad Gita*.

Around that time, Baba's book, *Play of Consciousness*, was

being translated into English. I had the opportunity of reading it as it was being translated. We were all very excited to read about Baba's experiences, as well as learning more about the workings of Shaktipat.

Also about that time, a funny incident occurred. Baba gave me a saffron colored cloth to wear. Up to then I had been wearing only white clothing. But one day, I happened to be sitting next to Dale in the dinning hall. Baba was also there but was sitting at some distance from us. He suddenly looked over to us, and then handed two lungis to an attendant. One was white and the other saffron. He also appeared to give the attendant some instructions, but Dale and I could not hear what was being said.

The attendant started walking in our direction. I soon realized that he was coming towards us. When he reached us, he handed me the white cloth, and Dale the saffron. But the moment he did this, Baba yelled something out to him in Hindi. The attendant then turned back to us and said, "Excuse me, I made a mistake," and took my white lungi, and gave it to Dale. He then took the saffron cloth from Dale and gave it to me.

At first I did not put very much emphasis on this incident, but I must confess that after a few days my ego got the better of me. The significance was that the saffron cloth is what sannyasis wear. So I soon started feeling somewhat proud. I began wearing that lungi all the time.

Then one day Dale and I took the cows to the nearby river to wash them as usual. It was our habit to remove our *lungis* before going into the river. But that day, just as we were about done washing the cows, I looked over towards the river's bank and noticed a scrawny white calf. He was chewing up my lungi. I yelled out to it, but he just ignored me. I then started running towards him, but being in the middle of the river, by the time I reached the spot the lungi was chewed to bits. Seeing it, I began laughing, and asked myself, "What is there to be proud of now? After all, it is just a colored piece of cloth."

I felt Baba was teaching me a lesson. I therefore decided that from that day onwards, I would wear only white clothing, symbolizing my student-ship. Interestingly, after that incident, Baba also gave me only white clothes to wear, although I had never told him what had happened.

It was soon Baba's 62nd birthday, and a large celebration was scheduled. Thousands of devotees from all over India and the world came to celebrate it with him. There was going to be a sacred fire ritual known as a *yajna*, as well as a continuous chanting lasting seven days. A *yajna*, or fire ritual is an act of prayer, worship, and devotion. The word is derived from the root-verb *yaj,* meaning to sacrifice. The performance of a yajna affects not only the participants but also the environment as a whole. The ritual creates a powerful force which allows many to get a glimpse of higher states of consciousness.

Yoga itself is also considered a yajna. However, the practice of yoga mainly benefits the practitioner. The yajna is an ancient form of worship which was practiced not only by the vedic brahmins, but also the priests of ancient Persia, whose descendants are today known as *Parsis* in India. They are followers of the ancient Zoroastrian religion.

Another important event that happened that May, was Baba's announcement that he had received instructions from his Guru to go abroad. There had been many invitations over the years for Baba to visit western countries but in the past he had always declined. But now he consented, and would leave for a three month tour starting on August 21, 1970. He would first fly to Rome, and from there to Switzerland, then France and London. From London he would fly to the U.S.

After his American tour, he would stop in Australia on his way back to India. Although Baba had been teaching and giving Shaktipat initiation for many years, according to his horoscope, his real spiritual work was just starting. He had entered a new cycle approximately a year and a half earlier which would last until the end of his life.

It can become extremely hot throughout India, but it appeared to be even more so in the humid and dusty regions of Maharashtra, the state where Baba's ashram was located. Fortunately the many trees and plants in the ashram helped to keep it cooler than the surrounding area. The ashram was like an oasis in the middle of a desert. By June, we were all anxiously awaiting for the monsoon season to arrive, so that things would cool down. However, if the rainy season did not produce much rain, it would create extremely humid conditions. Finally, by the second week of June, the rains arrived, and they would continue until about the end of September.

The rainy season became a special time for me. Sometimes it would rain steadily for days, or even weeks on end. I had never seen so much rain. During those days everyone stayed mostly indoors. During the rainy season, the cows were allowed to graze only within the ashram grounds. By then I had also been working more in the front hall, which I really enjoyed.

During the rains, I spent longer hours in meditation, and the repetition of the mantra (*Japa*). Japa became my constant companion. I would silently repeat my mantra for many hours at a time, until it became a part of my breathing. When I used to work in the gardens, I would work very hard. And when I felt tired, I found that if I repeated the mantra silently for some time, my fatigue would leave me. Unlike a mantra read in a book, one which is given by a perfected master becomes a vehicle for the Guru's own spiritual energy. Such mantras are said to be 'conscious,' and have the power to activate the seeker's latent energy.

Baba was also a strict master, and everyone had to follow the ashram discipline. He could also appear extremely angry, depending on the needs of the moment. But I had observed him on many occasions when he appeared to be angry, and without fail, I always noticed a sense of detachment on his part. I realized that it was simply what was required at the moment. It was all just a drama.

Usually when one becomes angry, the emotion of anger completely overwhelms the person's mind. But this was not the case with Baba. He used anger when it was necessary to teach his disciples some lesson. But the emotion of anger would never overwhelm Baba's mind. Once, after loudly yelling at someone for about ten minutes, he suddenly turned to a disciple and asked with a mischievous smile, "How do you like the show?"

I myself witnessed this incident. It began when someone stepped on a large sign with the sacred mantra, *Om Namah Shivaya*, which was about to be placed above a set of double doors in the small courtyard outside of Baba's room. He was telling the person to act more consciously.

During my travels I had met a few great beings, and I had learned that one had to be extra alert around them. One cannot judge a Siddha's actions in the same way one judges an ordinary person's. However, besides being strict, Baba was also full of love and compassion. He knew his disciples' weaknesses, and like a caring parent, he would guide them with love. The poet Bhavabhuti speaking on the subject of great beings said:

> *Who can fathom the hearts of great beings,*
> *which are harder than the thunderbolt*
> *and softer than the flower.*

Baba was very meticulous about everything. In fact, he ran the ashram like a military school. There was a sign near his seat in the front hall proclaiming the Vedic axiom: "Only he who obeys can command." So when someone once asked Baba why he was so strict, he told the person that when someone goes to the ashram, they should act properly, and not like as if they were at a club. Baba explained to the person that the ashram was not meant to simply be filled with people, but with virtuous qualities. "That is why I'm so strict," he told the person. "I am like the commander-in-chief of an army."

Baba said that a person should act in such a way in the

ashram that they become spiritually elevated. He would say that while living in the ashram one should live like a renunciate (*sannyasi*), and when they left they could return to their normal life.

Some visitors to the ashram did not like this strictness. But I had realized that not much could be accomplished without self-discipline. The ashram rules or dharma has great importance. By following it, one can easily achieve the spiritual goal. The word dharma is here used to indicate the rules of the ashram and the proper actions which are to be followed there. All places in fact have their own dharma. Even if one joins a club, or in one's work place, there are certain rules and regulations that must be followed. However, one should not get the impression that because Baba was strict and loved discipline, that he was harsh or mean spirited. In fact the opposite was true. People lived in the ashram with great joy.

Baba would personally oversee all of the ashram activities. He would walk around the ashram in the morning and afternoon, and observe not only what everyone was doing, but also how they were doing it. Although Baba had said that he would kick people out if they did not follow the discipline, he was very compassionate and fair. If someone was not acting properly, he would simply correct them. In fact, once you had become his disciple, it was not very easy to leave him.

Thinking about Baba's meticulous nature reminds me of a funny incident which occurred one day. I was sweeping the kitchen verandah, which extended from Baba's small courtyard to the end of the dining hall. I had started sweeping just outside of Baba's door, and was now near the end of the verandah. Baba suddenly appeared, and started walking towards me. He was alone, and was walking casually with his hands behind his back. I continued to sweep, but I kept him in my site from the corner of my eyes. When he was about fifteen feet from me, he noticed some bird-dropping on the ledge of the veranda wall, an area I had already cleaned. He nonchalantly walked over to the wall, and touched the dropping with his finger to see if it was fresh, or, if I had missed it. Seeing that it was fresh, he looked at me with a smile, and said "*Bahut achcha*" (very good), and continued on his way.

The attitude that Baba had about discipline was really to teach us to be always aware of our actions, even if they were small and appeared to be insignificant. He also believed that one could practice austerities and at the same time be constructive and creative.

The beauty and productivity of the ashram reflected this belief. In those days, the ashram grew its own rice, vegetables, and a variety of fruits. Baba oversaw all of the ashram activities. He would often be seen in the kitchen not only directing, but also preparing meals. He was an excellent cook and later trained all his kitchen staff. But above everything else, Baba did not like waste. If he saw someone waste food, no matter who it was, that person would get a real earful.

There were plans to start building a new hall after the rains ended. It would be a three story building with the ground floor serving as the new main front hall. On the second and third floors, there would be dormitories and guest rooms. The ashram was in the process of expansion, and quite a bit of construction was being planned to start just after the rains. In fact, the new construction had already started the previous year.

The meditation room beneath Baba's new apartment, known as the 'cave room,' had just been completed. A stairway led down to it from the verandah around Baba's old bedroom. I recall an incident that took place just after the room had been completed. One day, I felt drawn to the room, and went downstairs. When I got there, I noticed that Baba was standing there alone. He began saying something to me in Hindi. Although I had learnt a few words, I could not fully understand him. I thought he wanted me to do something, but I was not sure what.

He then started to make different gestures, like placing his hands and extended fingers on either side of his head, which appeared to me to indicate horns. He then bent forward, and started using one of his hands to indicate a flowing motion of something coming out of the rear end. It was like a game of charades, and very funny when I look back on it now, but at the time I took it very seriously.

I was frantically trying to figure out what he wanted. Then suddenly, in a flash, an image of a cow came into my mind, and I understood what he was saying. He wanted me to go to the cowshed and get some cow urine. The moment I understood this, I ran out of the room and up to the cowshed at top speed. The cowshed was located in the upper garden, and so it was at some distance from the cave room. As I got closer to the cowshed, I started thinking about how I was going to get a cow to urinate for me. But just as I was about thirty feet from the door, I suddenly noticed one of the cows spreading her legs, and lifting her tail, getting ready to go. I dashed in, picked up a bucket along the way, and held it out to catch the urine. When she was done, I ran back down to the cave room where Baba was waiting. Seeing that I had accomplished my task, he smiled and said, *"Bahut achcha"* (very good) a number of times, while patting me on the back.

He then made another hand gesture, indicating that I should sprinkle the urine around the room, which I did. He told me that cow's urine was good for purifying the atmosphere. When I was finished, he walked to the upper garden, and asked me to accompany him.

Before long there would be many chants held in that cave. It would become a very powerful place for me, and I would spend many hours there absorbed in deep meditation.

My Spiritual Experiences

About the middle of July, I asked Baba if he wanted me to return to America, and help with his tour. He told me that because he was going for such a short time, it was not necessary for me to go. However, he did tell me that I would be traveling with him on his next World Tour, which he said would be much longer. "Stay in the ashram and do your sadhana," he told me. I asked him to bless me and to deepen my meditation. He nodded his head in approval.

In those early days, Baba would often say that one day there would be many people living in the ashram, and that room would be limited. But at the time it was difficult to imagine such a prophetic statement coming true, since there were only a dozen or so people living permanently in the ashram at that time.

Although Baba had many Indian devotees, they came mostly on weekends and holidays. Some would come and stay for extended periods when possible, but at the time there were only a few people living in the ashram full time. Baba did not teach renunciation of the world, but to renounce our attachment to the world. Most of his Indian devotees were householders and professionals, who continued in their business and family life, but also added the practice of meditation.

When devotees heard that Baba was going to the West, many came for his darshan during the Guru Purnima celebration that year. In honor of all Gurus, the full moon which falls in July is celebrated as the Guru's full moon day. The celebration is traced back to sage Vyasa and his disciples. On this holiday it has become a tradition for devotees to go and have their Guru's darshan, no matter where he may be. However, as this festival occurs around the start of the rainy season, it sometimes makes the pilgrimage difficult.

But that year thousands of devotees came for Baba's

darshan, even with the heavy monsoon rains. And although the main road to Ganeshpuri had been washed out, it did not seem to deter people's enthusiasm.

It was soon August, and Baba left with five people for what was to be his First World Tour. Whenever Baba left the ashram, a complete silence appeared to pervade the place. It was a kind of emptiness. Nevertheless, the atmosphere always remained permeated with the divine Shakti, and the spiritual work continued. But there was no doubt that we would miss Baba, even though he would be gone for just a few months.

During Baba's tour, only a few individuals continued to live in the ashram. And even during the weekends, very few devotees would come from Mumbai. By then I was very much at home in the ashram. I continued with my practices but extended my meditation time. I have always preferred to meditate alone. And now that it was completed, I would often meditate in the cave room, and rarely upstairs in the verandah, unless Baba happened to be there.

In a way I was somewhat shy, and did not like others to see the spontaneous physical movements, known as *kriyas*, which may occur. I also felt that at times some people tended to exaggerate their kriyas. Baba would often scold such people, and would remind everyone that kriyas were a purifying process. And that they should occur spontaneously, without any conscious effort.

I had also started having a deeper understanding of the workings of Kundalini. A whole new world was opening up to me. I began receiving knowledge of various subjects during meditation. Although I had studied and practiced astrology professionally for a number of years before leaving America, I had given up its practice. But I was now receiving astrological knowledge and insights through my meditation, even though I was not making any effort to do so.

Many of my experiences started shortly after I arrived at the ashram, and would continue for a number of years. Here I will mention only a few of them. I would meditate sitting crosslegged in the yogic posture, with my hands resting on my knees. With practice, my knees were becoming more flexible. I did not try to control my breathing, but it would soon become slow and even. I would repeat the mantra mentally with the incoming and outgoing breath. And according to Baba's instructions, I also practiced the technique of "installing" the Guru within one's own body. The body would soon become relaxed. My thumbs and forefingers would join together in what is called *chinmudra*, locking the energy within the body. A pressure, created by the movement of the *prana-Shakti* would at times be felt in my chest, sometimes at the center between the eyebrows, or the spiritual center at the top of the head (*sahasrara*).

As the meditation deepened, my body would become stiff. If I became aware of it, it felt heavy like a wooden log. However, I was usually not aware of my body at all. I did not experience myself to be limited by the size or shape of my physical body. Instead, I felt myself to be all pervasive, unlimited, and endless. And sometimes I perceived my body as actually residing within Me. At other times, I would experience myself as being extremely tiny, and would see myself as residing within the heart.

My awareness would become focused mainly at the center between the eye-brows, but sometimes on the top of the head. One night during meditation, my awareness became focused at the third eye, where I saw waves of blue light. This was not unusual as I had often seen it, but now I noticed a hole starting to appear. And it was gradually getting larger. Suddenly I noticed two hands pulling the hole wider and wider apart. I recognized the hands as belonging to Baba.

At times I would see different objects at this center. For example, I would see the moon, stars, fire, precious gems, mountains, or different animals. I had also started seeing the *nilabindu*, the blue dot, or what Baba would call the blue pearl. Even though it was just for a few moments at the beginning, it brought great joy each time I saw it. The vision of the blue pearl would also occur while my eyes were open.

I also experienced different types of pranayama that would occur spontaneously. A variety of sounds would also come out of my mouth naturally, such as the roar of a lion, birds chirping, or the humming sound of bees.

The three yogic *bandhas* or locks would also occur effortlessly. These bandhas or contractions occur within the body in order to control the movement of prana, forcing it to enter the sushumna or central nadi. During this process my breath would be expelled, and the stomach was drawn in, while the diaphragm was lifted up high. The abdominal organs were then pushed back towards the spine. This is called *uddiyana-bandha*.

At the same time, my head would be bent forward while my chin would press down on my chest, in the notch just between the collar bones and the top of the breast bone. This bandha is called *jalandhara*.

When the anus starts to throb and contract powerfully, it is called *mula-bandha*. This occurs after the inhalation and retention of breath known as *kumbhaka*. The whole lower abdominal area is contracted backwards towards the spine. With the help of these bandhas, the prana is forced to constantly strike at the base of the spine, at the *Muladhara chakra*, thereby fanning the flames of *Kundalini*.

Before experiencing these bandhas I had never even heard of them. As time went by, and I found out more about them, I saw how difficult all these practices were. The *Hatha Yoga Pradipika* warns the reader not to practice them unless they are under the guidance of a competent Guru. But when one receives the grace of a Siddha, these yogic activities occur spontaneously, without any effort on one's part. And because it is Kundalini Shakti which is performing these kriyas, they are all performed with great accuracy. I was simply a witness to their performance.

I also experienced various *mudras*. *Mudras* or gestures are different types of inner techniques which also help in the control and movement of prana. Mudras are also expressions of subtle states of consciousness, and may manifest as different hand gestures. For example, one hand may be raised in the familiar gesture of "fear not," while the other hand opens downward in the gesture of bestowing blessings. These and other mudras all occurred spontaneously. I felt extremely happy, and my heart was full of deep love for Baba.

For some reason, in those days most of the physical kriyas appeared to occur during my meditation just before lunch. Due to the practice of meditation, and the powerful movements of prana, a great deal of heat tends to build up in the body. My body would naturally start to perspire a great deal. But strangely, a number of times I would start to perspire heavily, but the perspiration would occur only on the right side of my body. You may think this strange, or even unbelievable, but everyday for a number of weeks, when I opened my eyes and came out of meditation, I would find that the whole right side of my body, the right arm, half of the torso and right leg were totally soaked with perspiration, while the left side remained completely dry. There was a kind of visible demarcation line right down the middle of my body. The right side of my chest would be perspiring heavily, while the left side was totally dry.

But even with all the different types of kriyas, pranayamas, and even visions, the highest experience is when the mind becomes completely still. At that time there is deep peace and calm, with the awareness, "I am That" arising naturally. But there were also what I call dry periods. Times when the mind would not become focused. Those could be difficult periods. In order to get through them, I would do more japa and chanting.

At times, various diseases may also arise with the awakening of Kundalini. This does not mean, however, that the Kundalini causes these diseases, but her awakening may bring to the surface certain latent diseases. For all practical purposes, the illness appears like any other diseases. However, they do not always respond to normal treatment.

All one's past impressions created by one's action are said to be stored in the sushumna, or central spinal canal. So when the Shakti is awakened, some past impressions tend to rise to the surface in order to be expelled. One of the more interesting experiences of this kind began around the end of October when I got what appeared to be scabies. I asked someone in the ashram who had some medical knowledge about it. I was told not to worry, but that I should go to the hospital in Mumbai, and get some medicine for it. I was told that it was very easy to get rid of.

So I went to the hospital and the doctor gave me some medicine. They also applied sulfuric oil on my whole body while I was there, and gave me some to take with me. I was told to apply the oil all over my body and the disease would be gone in just a few days. Since scabies makes one itch a great deal, it was not a pleasant experience.

I returned to the ashram and followed the doctor's instructions, but there was no relief. Not even after a few days, nor even after almost two weeks. No one could figure out the reason why it would not go away. Not knowing what I should do about it, I prayed to mother Kundalini to guide me.

I remembered Baba saying something about this once, how some diseases may arise, but I was not certain that this was the case here. But shortly after praying for guidance, while meditating I received a clear intuition that this was indeed associated with the awakened Kundalini, and that it would stop when Baba returned from his our.

After receiving this message, I decided to stop using the medicine. This was about ten days before Baba was to return to the ashram. The itching continued until finally, on the very day that Baba returned, and entered the ashram gates, it suddenly stopped. And from that moment onwards the disease appeared to be gone. Within a few days, the scabs created from all the scratching also disappeared.

Now of course this does not mean that every disease which arises is necessarily associated with Kundalini awakening. One has to use proper discrimination, otherwise a simple illness may become worse without proper treatment.

As mentioned earlier, at the time I was working in the front hall, which gave me the opportunity to do more mantra repetition. In those days we were chanting the Bhagavad Gita in the morning, and after lunch some disciples would chant the Guru Gita. I enjoyed listening to that chant so much that I started to transliterate the hymn into roman letters, so I could chant it along with the others. This turned into a big project when Gopal Desai heard abut it. He was now the acting manager of the ashram. He was so excited that he wanted to publish the transliteration for the ashram, and present it to Baba when he returned. I therefore wanted to do a good job, and also make sure that it would be ready by the time Baba returned.

There were also other benefits of working in the front hall in those early days. Baba had a charming and melodious singing voice. He loved to chant various hymns and poems, and I really enjoyed listening to him. Some of these hymns were recorded over the years in the front hall, and a few would eventually become available on audio tapes. Initially they were played only on the ashram sound system, but some years later some of them would become available to the public.

One of the first recordings Baba made was of him chanting the Marathi Guru Gita. This version of the Guru Gita is from the famous Marathi book, the *Guru Charitra*. Although it is called the Marathi Guru Gita, it is somewhat misleading. Actually, in this version most of the verses are in fact in Sanskrit. However, there are some Marathi verses both at the beginning and end of the hymn, and because it is part of a Marathi book, it was known as the Marathi Guru Gita. Later Baba would also record a full Sanskrit version.

In fact Baba recorded a number of hymns, such as the *Devi Stotra* — one of my favorites, the *Shiva Mahimnah Stotra*, *Siddha Gita*, *Vedant Chanda*, and *Sunderdas* Poems. He recorded most of these in the Ganeshpuri ashram's front hall, and a few in his room. Some were even recorded in Mumbai at the home's of devotees. You can usually tell the one's recorded in the ashram by listening for the call of peacocks, the chirping of birds in the hall, sometimes hammering in the background, and the occasional bus or horse drawn carriage driving past the ashram's front gate.

I was fortunate to have been present during many of these recordings. During these sessions Baba would come and sit in the hall, and Amma (Swami Prajnananda) would set up the tape recorder for him. Sometimes Babu Rao would play the tamboura or harmonium. He even chants with Baba in the *Siddha Gita*. At times a small hand pumped instrument was used, which played a preset note in the background. Later someone brought a battery operated version. But often, the only musical instrument was Baba playing the *Ektara*, a one string instrument. Everyone had to be very quiet during the recording.

Ganeshpuri

While Baba was on tour, I often spent time in Ganeshpuri meditating at Baba Nityananda's samadhi shrine, as well as the actual room where he left his body. I would also bathe in the hot sulphur springs. The water of the hot springs has great healing powers, and it helps rejuvenate the body. However one must be careful not to stay in the hot water for too long.

The Ganeshpuri area has been considered sacred since ancient times. It is bordered on the northeast by Mount Mandakini (or Mandagni), and the river Tansa flows nearby. The ancient temple of Goddess Vajreshwari is also not far away. Legend has it that the great sage Vasishtha, the Guru of Sri Rama, chose the foot of the mountain to perform a great sacrifice (*mahayajna*). Legend says that before starting the yajna, the sage installed an image of Ganesh in a temple. And because of that it has been called Ganeshpuri, or the city of Ganesh ever since. However, at present, there is no temple dedicated specifically to Ganesh.

We are told that Indra, the king of the gods, along with his agents, decided to disrupt the sacrificial rites by inflicting various diseases on those who attended. In order to ward off any physical ailments or mental distractions, Vasishtha decided to create 365 hot springs so that the many sages who would attend could bathe in a different spring for each day of the year. Because Vasishtha managed the yajna without disturbance, Indra decided to throw his special weapon, the thunderbolt (*vajra-astra*) in order to destroy the sacred ritual. Vasishtha prayed to the Divine Mother for protection, who suddenly appeared on the spot, and absorbed the weapon into herself, thereby saving the yajna. In memory of this event, her image was installed at the spot as Vajreshwari, or the Goddess of the thunderbolt. A shrine was also erected for her.

The present fort-like structure in the town of Vajreshwari

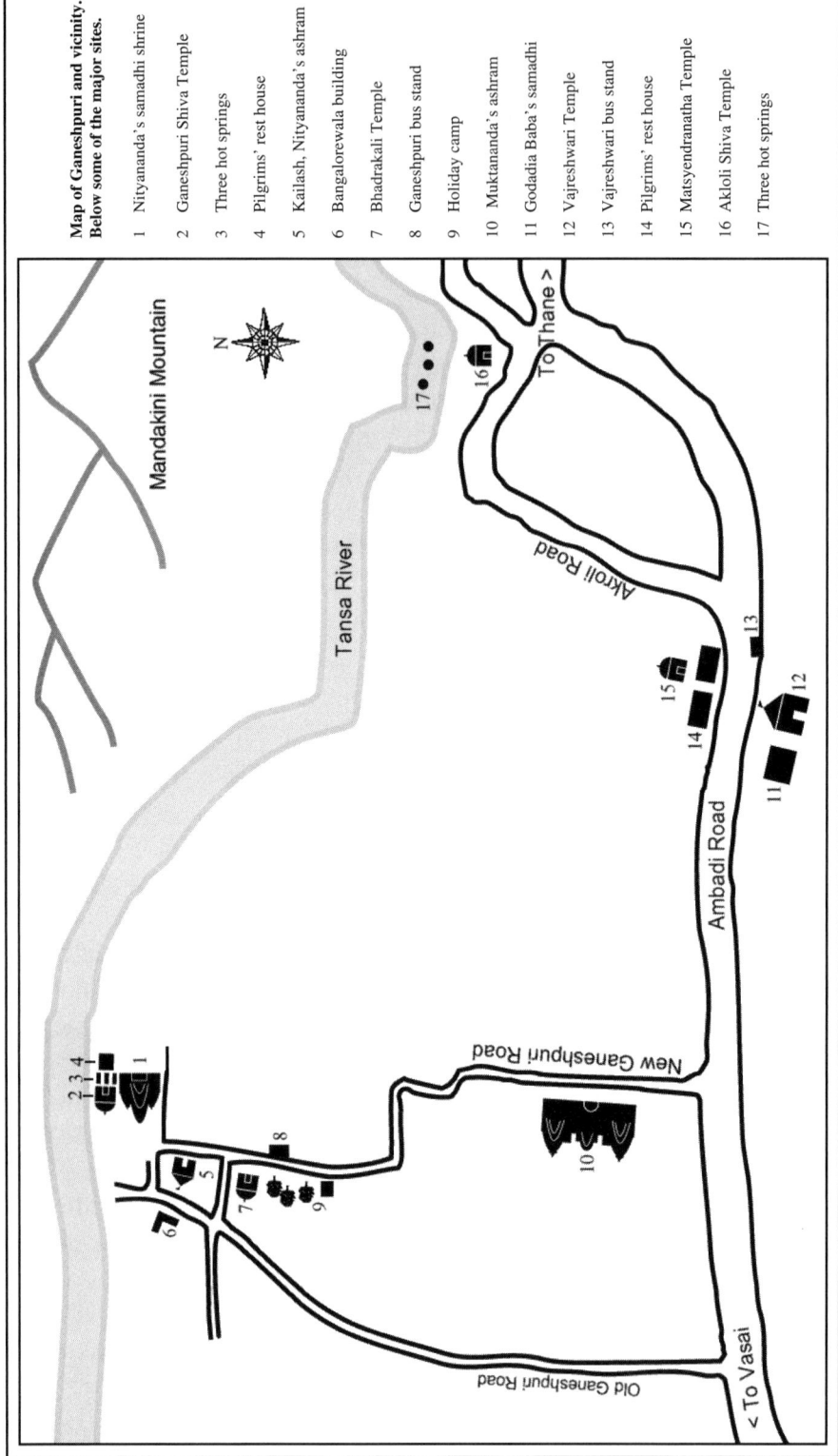

(*above*) Mandakini Mountain, Ganeshpuri

was actually constructed by the Peshwa ruler, Sri Chimanaji Appa in 1742 C.E.. Legend has it that he prayed to Goddess Vajreshwari that if he was successful in recapturing the Bassein Fort from the Portuguese, he would erect a new temple for her on the old site, patterned after the fort at Bassein. The original shrine was actually closer to the base of Mandakini mountain.

When Baba Nityananda settled in Ganeshpuri in the early 1930's, it was still a jungle filled with wild animals. There were no buildings except for the ancient Shiva temple, which was practically overrun by the jungle. But he soon renovated the temple, as well as the hot springs in front of it. Although he lived in a small hut next to the temple, within a few years a small township began to develop around him. By that time, Nityananda was usually addressed simply as Deva, or Bhagavan, which means God and Lord respectively.

Wherever Nityananda Baba had stayed, he would not only renovate an existing temple, but would also dig wells and build rest houses for pilgrims. When he first came to the area from

(*above*) Nityananda in Ganeshpuri (circa mid 1930s).

south India, Nityananda stayed in Akloli, a small village about three or four miles from Ganeshpuri. From there he moved to Vajreshwari, and then, sometime around 1934, he shifted to Ganeshpuri permanently. The small hut he lived in would eventually become the first ashram, and was called *Vaikuntha* (heaven).

As more and more people began visiting him, he had a road built so that they could reach the ashram more easily. He would remain in that ashram until 1956, when a new ashram was built just about twenty or thirty yards away from the old one. This ashram was called Kailash Nivas. Nityananda also built a few other temples in the area, one dedicated to Sri Krishna, and

(*above*) Bhadrakali temple in Ganeshpuri.
(*left*) The room where Bhagavan Nityananda took Mahasamadhi.

(*above*) Nityananda's samadhi shrine and Shiva temple on right.

another to Goddess Bhadrakali, which is located on the left side of the road just as one enters the town of Ganeshpuri. It is a beautiful image of the goddess.

In 1949, Nityananda had three rooms constructed about a quarter mile from Ganeshpuri. Initially they were not used, but as mentioned earlier, they would become the foundation of Muktananda's ashram. In 1956, after having completed his sadhana, and was staying at Chalisgaon in northern Maharashtra, he was called by Nityananda to move permanently to Ganeshpuri. At the command of his Guru, Muktananda moved into the small one room temple which had been constructed just behind the three original rooms. Later Nityananda made arrangements to purchase the land around the compound.

Even though Baba Nityananda lived in the new Kailash ashram until the end of his life, he did not die there. Just two weeks before his death he moved into a newly built pilgrimage house just behind the ashram. This was called the

Bangalorewala building since it was constructed by a devotee from Bangalore.

On the morning of August 8, 1961, Nityananda left his physical body and entered *mahasamadhi*. There are many stories related by devotees about how months earlier Nityananda had indicated to them in various ways about his eminent departure. I used to enjoy meditating in the room where he left his body, and felt closest to him there. Whenever I was troubled, I would go there and bare my heart to him. After awhile I would feel relief, and my heart lightened.

Baba Returns

Obviously everyone missed Baba very much while he was away. Every bit of news about him became precious to us, and we eagerly awaited the regular reports sent by Baba's translator. By October, some of those who had met Baba in Europe and England started arriving at the ashram.

Baba returned to the ashram on the 29th of November, at about 3 a.m. Everyone was very excited, and the whole ashram, including the new hall, had been decorated for his arrival. When Baba finally arrived, he was greeted with enthusiastic shouts of "*Sadgurunath Maharaj ki Jai!*" This phrase, meaning, "Victory to the true Guru, who is the Lord and great king," was enthusiastically shouted at all such events, as well as at the beginning or ending of any function. Bells were ringing, conches blowing, and drums beating.

Baba appeared happy to be home, and after having darshan of his Guru's portrait in the main hall, he went to his new apartment to rest. But to everyone's delight, he came out that morning for the Bhagavad Gita chant, which was now being held in the new larger front hall. The chant that morning appeared to be very powerful, and everyone seemed to be overwhelmed by the divine Shakti. Devotees from India and other parts of the world had come to welcome Baba home. Westerners who had met Baba on tour had already started arriving, and the ashram was completely full.

A few days after Baba returned, Gopal Desai, who had printed about seventy-five copies of my transliterated Guru Gita, offered them to Baba. Baba appeared pleased with them, and said that this would now allow Westerners wishing to chant the Guru Gita to do so. Some time later, he made the Guru Gita the ashram's morning chant, replacing the Bhagavad Gita.

After a week or so, the crowds became less, and things started to get back to normal. It was now December, my first anniversary with Baba. I reflected on the events of the previous year as I went up to greet Baba, and offer him an anniversary garland. By then I had full trust in Baba. I knew that whatever he asked me to do would be for my spiritual benefit. This understanding was now fully established in me. But the Guru is always testing his disciple, and one must therefore always remain alert around them. I found this to be especially true around Baba.

The relationship between Guru and disciple is a mutual one. That is, it has to be agreed on by both the disciple and the Guru. That is why Baba would often say when asked for his grace, that the disciple's blessing was also needed.

Even though Baba had achieved Self-Realization, he still expressed a deep love and gratitude for his own Guru. In fact, Baba maintained the attitude of a disciple until the end of his life. He considered those around him to be a part of his Guru's family, and he would welcome them all with great love and respect. This is the great secret of devotion.

Wearing only a cloth wrapped around his chest, which reached his thighs, each morning at around 3:30 a.m., Baba would come out of his apartment and walk out of the front gate. He would walk a short distance towards Ganeshpuri and bow to his Guru. He would then turn around and walk back to the ashram. Each morning I would open the gate for him, and many times found myself alone with him. He would be completely absorbed in his own inner state, and sometimes I would get a glimpse of that state by merely being in his presence. These were magical moments for me.

Once, while the evening program was going on in the front hall, Baba came out of his apartment and stood watching the chant inside from a window in the back wall. I was then on guard duty, and so he was standing only two or three feet from me. After a few minutes he turned and looked at me with a smile, then suddenly lifted up his dark glasses, and looked at me intently with wide opened eyes. As I stood there looking into his eyes, I saw two beams of white light. It seemed as if they were penetrating the deepest part of my being. At that moment, I felt completely intoxicated with love. This lasted for only about ten or fifteen seconds, but in those few moments, time appeared to stop. Baba then lowered his glasses, turned, and slowly walked back towards his apartment as if nothing had happened.

It was wonderful to have Baba back. On the day of his arrival, he walked around the ashram and inspected all the changes that had taken place during his absence. He also started visiting the cowshed again. It was obvious that they too were happy to see him.

During his absence, I had started to understand Hindi and

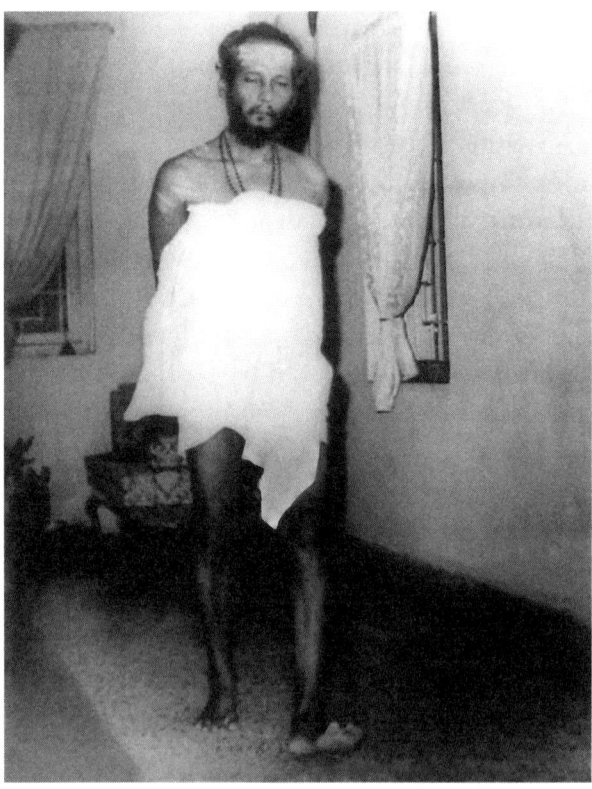

(*below*) Baba early morning darshan.

Marathi a little better, but I was still not able to speak it very well. But strangely, whenever Baba said something to me, I found that I could understand him clearly. At such times I had the distinct feeling that he was somehow helping me in a subtle way to understand him. The process was completely intuitive. When I was around Baba, I focused my whole attention on him alone. In fact, I can say that my mind would naturally become focused on him, without any effort on my part.

During darshan periods, which were mostly silent in those early days, my meditation would become very deep. Baba would often sit for hours in silence. But after his tour, because of the many foreigners that began visiting the ashram, things began to change.

(*above*) Baba circa 1971; (*below*) Baba in Rome, August 1970

Alandi
(Jnaneshwar's Samadhi-shrine)

Towards the end of December, I became seriously ill. The illness itself was mysterious. It was not due to a cold, flue, or any other obvious malady, But my temperature would quickly rise, and then suddenly drop. At times I felt like I was literally going to die, and even became unconscious a number of times.

I had not told anyone about this, thinking that it would get better on its own. At the time I had night duty at the front gate, and so I had to remain awake from 10 p.m. to 6 a.m. the next morning. By 10 p.m. the ashram was very quiet, as everyone was either asleep or meditating.

December, January and February are the winter months in Ganeshpuri, and it can get pretty cold at nights, particularly in the early morning hours. One night during my illness, I bundled myself up, and sat doing japa most of the night. But I felt extremely weak. My concentration was weak, and I often felt that I was about to loose consciousness.

The night had been a very long one, and so I was happy to see some of the ashramites arriving at around 4 a.m.. Markandeya was a young Indian man only a few years older than myself. He was in charge of the hall, and I would report to him. He was a sincere seeker and we had become very good friends. When he saw me that morning, and realized that I was very ill, he told me to immediately go and rest.

I was still living at Turiya Mandir at the time, and although it was not that far from the front hall, the walk there was extremely difficult for me. When I finally reached Turiya Mandir, I laid down and tried to sleep, but I could not. I started having very unusual experiences. When I closed my eyes I saw dark images, and I had the feeling that I was about to die. But, after about an hour of extreme restlessness, I finally fell asleep. I slept for about five hours, and when I awoke, I was feeling somewhat better.

Later that day someone brought me a message which was supposed to have come from Baba. The person appeared to have some difficulty explaining the message to me, but the gist of it was that Baba wanted me to leave the ashram immediately, and go to Mumbai for rest. When I asked the messenger if he knew the reason, he said that it was because I was ill, and I would get better there. He told me that Baba also said that I should leave the ashram right away, and that I should go and spend the night in Ganeshpuri.

At first I did not understand this and was wondering if Baba was upset with me for some reason. I tried to think of what I could have done wrong, but I could not think of anything. I was later told that someone had gone to Baba and tried to make some trouble regarding the fact that I had left an hour or so early that morning from my post. However, I did not put much value on that information.

In any case, I felt in my heart that if Baba wanted me to leave the ashram, then it must be for my own good. I knew that there was a purpose for it, even if that was not yet clear to me. I did feel however, that it was related more to my health, and the powerful experiences I was having. Baba would sometimes send a disciple away from his physical presence for awhile if the Shakti had become particularly intense. And it was not unusual that Baba would send a person to Ganeshpuri if they were going through a difficult period. So that night I walked down to Ganeshpuri and went directly to the Bangalorewala building, and the room where Bhagavan had taken mahasamadhi. That room had become a special place for me.

I did not know where I was going to stay that night, but I felt that Nityananda Baba would look after me. I had felt his presence very strongly in that room many times. I sat down and began praying for his blessing and guidance. After awhile I started to feel Bhagavan's presence, which made me feel calm and relaxed. It became clear that he was with me and guiding me. At the time, the only other person in the room was a sadhu caretaker. We had become friendly since I used to visit the place so often.

It was soon time to close the room for the night, and I was about to leave. But as I got up, I suddenly had the intuition that I was going to stay in that room that night. I asked the sadhu if that would be possible.

"Absolutely not!" he said emphatically. He told me that no one was allowed to stay in that room overnight. I said that it would be for only that one night, and that I would leave very early the next morning. He told me that there was a place where pilgrims could stay, and that I should go and stay there. I explained to him that I did not just want a place to sleep, but that I wanted Bhagavan's darshan.

He again said no, then turned and left the room. I thought that perhaps I was mistaken, and started to doubt about whether I was really going to be staying there or not. But when I looked at one of the photographs of Bhagavan hanging on the wall, a radiant glow appeared to emanate from it. When I saw that light and energy, I was certain that I would be staying. And just then, the sadhu came back into the room and asked, "You will leave early in the morning?"

I assured him that I would, and he finally gave me permission to stay. I was very happy and continued to meditate for awhile longer. I was very tired and tried to sleep, but found that I could not. So I continued to meditate. I felt very blessed that night, and also felt physically stronger.

Early the next morning I left for Mumbai on the first bus. I went to stay with a friend living in Juhu, which is a suburb of Mumbai. She was an American lady married to an Indian, and had been living in India for many years. She was also a devotee of Baba's, and her home had become a place where some of the Western ashramites would go to when they were ill or had to visit Mumbai for one reason or another. She had been inviting me to visit her home ever since I had arrived at the ashram, but

(*above*) Jnaneshwar's samadhi shrine courtyard; (*below*) Samadhi shrine and Shiva temple

I never did. I now decided to go and stay with her. I was already feeling much better, but I still did not know what had happened, or what my illness was.

The next day I decided to go to Alandi, a small town about twenty miles north of Pune. Pune is about 120 miles from Mumbai. The samadhi shrine of the great saint and yogi, Jnaneshwar, is located in Alandi. I had visited the shrine with Baba just before he left on his tour, and found it to be very powerful. I had also noticed the effect the place had on Baba himself. He often spoke about the greatness of the shrine, and so I decided to take this opportunity to visit it again.

When I arrived at Alandi, I immediately went to the samadhi shrine and sat for meditation. The tomb is enclosed within a small room, which is itself a part of a larger construction. It is there that the daily worship takes place. The public is normally not allowed inside this small room, but must remain in the adjoining room. Devotees have darshan of the shrine as they walk past the room's doorway. Although I had the opportunity to go inside that room with Baba, I now sat in the adjoining room.

After sometime I came out of meditation and sat quietly with my eyes open. The temple priest came over and began speaking to me. He was speaking in Marathi, which I was able to understand only a little. He asked where I was from, and I told him that I had come from Ganeshpuri. He said that he knew Baba, and invited me to stay at his home while I was in Alandi. He also invited me to accompany him each morning at 4.a.m. when he went to the temple to perform the morning worship. I thanked him for his hospitality, and the opportunity to visit the shrine with him.

We soon left the shrine and went to his home, where he introduced me to his brother, who lived with him. Interestingly, his brother was a mathematician and astrologer. He spoke some English, and so we had long conversations on these subjects until late into the night.

The brahmins of Alandi take turns each month in performing the daily rituals at the shrine. That month it was my new friend's turn. I felt that this was a special blessing since it was just a day or two before my birthday. I decided to stay in Alandi for three days, and each morning I would go to the samadhi-shrine with my friend. While he was busy with his worship, I would meditate quietly in a corner. This was inside the samadhi room, and it was more than I could have ever wished for. My meditations were very powerful there, and I felt blessed by Baba, Bhagavan Nityananda, and Shri Jnaneshwar.

There are two views regarding the dates of Jnaneshwar's birth and death. One, and perhaps the most accepted one, places his birth in the year 1275 C.E., with his death occurring in 1296 C.E.. The second view, based on the tradition of Janabai, places the year of birth in 1271. But if this date is used and the date of his mahasamadhi is 1296, this would have made Jnaneshwar twenty-five years old at the time of his death, which goes against the traditional view that he lived for only twenty-one years. The only date which is known for certain is the year 1290, the year he wrote the *Jnaneshwari*, which is a commentary on the Bhagavad Gita. The date is mentioned by Jnaneshwar himself in the last chapter of that work.

In any case, Jnaneshwar, also known as Jnanadeva, is recognized as a great yogi, poet and saint. His father was a renunciate (sannyasin), who had to return to his wife at the command of his Guru. In time four children were born to him, and the eldest son was named Nivritti, or Nivrittinatha, due to his association with the Natha yogis..

After receiving *Shaktipat* initiation during a chance meeting with the great Siddha Gahininath, Nivritti initiated his younger brothers and sister. Jnaneshwar was the next eldest son, and his younger brother was named Sopana, and the youngest child was their sister Muktabai.

Although all four had achieved great fame, it is Jnaneshwar who is best known. He has left behind a great masterpiece of mystical genius in the form of his commentary on the Bhagavad Gita. His commentary on the Gita is not like others. It is rather more like a continuation and elaboration of the dialogue between Lord Krishna and Arjuna. The details of the story are filled in by Jnaneshwar through his mystic vision.

After he finished the *Jnaneshwari*, his Guru, Nivrittinatha, commanded Jnaneshwar to write an independent work. The result was the *Amritanubhava*. In that philosophical work, Jnaneshwar expresses the Supreme Reality based on his own personal experiences.

Indeed, the real greatness of Alandi is his samadhi shrine. The unique quality of that samadhi is that Jnaneshwar, at the age of twenty-one, took what is called *sanjivan samadhi*, or live-samadhi. All great yogis come to know the time of their death, and Jnaneshwar expressed his desire to leave this world at that young age. At that momentous occasion, his family and friends all gathered around him. Then climbing down into a small cave underneath the front of the Siddheshwara temple, Jnaneshwar sat down and entered into samadhi. His brother Nivritti then sealed the tomb.

Shortly after this occurred, Sopana passed away, and then Muktabai, and finally Nivritti. Nivritti's samadhi shrine is located at Tryambakeshwar, near the town of Nashik. It's a place that Baba had often visited.

When great beings leave their bodies, it is said that they enter the hearts of their disciples. However, their *prana* is maintained at the burial shrine for the benefit of blessing devotees. Almost three hundred years after his samadhi, Jnaneshwar appeared in a dream to the saint, Eknath, and told him to open the tomb, and cut away the roots of the nearby tree which were strangling him. Eknath is reported to have opened the tomb, cut the roots from around Jnaneshwar's neck, and found that when he touched the yogi's body, it was still warm. Such is the power of that place.

"Go On A Pilgrimage!"

I returned to Mumbai after three days and went to Juhu beach to my friend's home. There was a message waiting for me that an American friend of mine was stopping in India to visit me on his way home from the East. He was scheduled to arrive the next day.

My host had also just returned from the ashram and had brought a cryptic message from Baba's translator, supposedly from Baba, which simply said that I should not bother to return to the ashram. The message both surprised and confused me.

My host, who understood Hindi, had not heard the message directly from Baba, and so she could not shed any light on the matter. She also did not know what to make of it. Unfortunately, politics exist even in ashrams. I had experienced this early on with one of the translators. So whenever I wanted to speak to Baba about personal matters, I would always choose someone that I was close to, and trusted. I followed this practice throughout my life with him.

I thought about the message very deeply and tried to think of what could have brought it about. Had I done something wrong? I could not think of anything, but I decided to go to the ashram and have Baba's darshan, and ask him directly what he wanted me to do. I wanted to get instructions directly from him, whatever that might be. I had already accepted Baba as my Guru, and I knew that he had accepted me as a disciple. I certainly did not want to leave Baba, but if that was his wish, then it was my wish also.

My friend John arrived in Mumbai the following day and we went out to the ashram together. When we arrived, I noticed that Baba was sitting in the courtyard with only one other person, a friend who had translated for me in the past.

I asked John to wait, and went up to Baba alone. I did a *danda namaskar*, which literally means to "prostrate like a stick", indicating my full surrender to him. As I did so, he made the sound of "Aah". As I stood up he greeted me with a smile, and asked how my health was. I answered that it was much better.

I then told him about the message that I had received, and said that I did not understand it. I told him that I was prepared to do whatever he instructed, but I also asked him if I had done something wrong?

As this was translated to him, Baba put on a serious appearance and asked, "Don't you know that discipline is my god?"

I said that I did know that, and asked if I had broken some rule. At first he did not answer, but then asked me, "Did you steal my coconuts? Someone told me that you have taken my coconuts, is that true?"

When I heard this, I almost started to laugh out loud, but kept my composure and said, "Baba, you know that I did not take your coconuts."

He said that he would check, and just then the ashram manager happened to come into the courtyard. Baba called out to him and asked him if I was the one who had taken his coconuts? The manager told him that it was not me.

The whole time this was going on, I could see a smile on Baba's lips, as if he was enjoying his little game. He then turned to me and said, "Very good." And that was the end of it. I never heard anything more about it.

After my talk with Baba, I told him about my friend who was visiting me. I said that I did not know how long he was planning to be in India, but I asked Baba if I could spend a few days with him. However, Baba said that since he had come such a long distance to see me, that I should take him on a pilgrimage. Baba told me that he was going to Delhi in about ten days, and that I should meet him there after my pilgrimage. After introducing my friend to Baba we returned to Juhu.

John and I immediately started planning a short trip through

India. And as luck would have it, that night we heard that a devotee of Baba's was planning to drive to Delhi, and was looking for someone to travel with her. She had already heard that we wanted to go to Delhi as well, and so we all met and decided to leave in two days.

My friend John had also heard of a teacher named Acharya Rajneesh, who was living in Mumbai, and wanted to meet him before we left. At the time, Rajneesh was living in an apartment not far from where we were staying, and so we decided to go and meet him. So that night John asked me to accompany him. When we arrived at the apartment, we were asked to wait a short time. We were then taken into Rajneesh's bedroom, where we sat on the floor along with three or four of his disciples. Someone asked him a few questions, and after answering them, he gave a short talk.

Rajneesh was perhaps in his early forties at the time, although he looked older. He had a long black beard, dark eyes, and would stare at a person very intently. He wore white robes. I had heard that he had previously been a professor, and while John and I were waiting in the living room to meet him, I noticed his large library. Most of the books were by Western authors, mainly on psychology. An attendant claimed that Rajneesh could read more than fifteen books a day.

When he finished his talk, I asked Rajneesh to say something about his practices. He said that he had been experimenting with a few techniques, and mentioned some of them. He also asked us to go and watch a film which was going to be shown that evening. We were told that the film was shot by devotees at one of his recent retreats. After the film, his instructors would demonstrate the techniques.

After some time, John and I decided to leave, and said goodbye to Rajneesh. John and I both felt a little skeptical about him, and I had perceived a dark energy around him, which disturbed me. But we decided to go ahead and watch the film since it was just a short distance from his apartment. There were about a half dozen people there including two of his instructors. They told us a little bit about the film, and said that afterwards we would do the practices.

The film started out by showing people sitting and practicing *bhastrika* pranayama, with intervals of retention (*kumbhaka*). This type of pranayama is performed by fast and forceful inhalation and exhalation. It is a very powerful breathing exercise, and like all pranayama, it must be done correctly, and under the supervision of a competent teacher. Otherwise it may have negative results.

After sometime, the people in the film started to dance and sway, as if under the influence of an awakened Kundalini. But soon, many of them started to remove their clothing, and began hugging each other, and rolling around on the ground, making various noises. This was quite unusual since the majority of the people in the film were Indians, who normally would never think of acting in such an undignified manner. At the time, Rajneesh had only a few Western devotees.

After the film, the instructors started to explain some of the techniques we had seen. The technique had a few stages, starting with bhastrika. As the breathing became more intense, we were told that we should repeatedly ask the question, "Who am I?", "Who am I?" Then we should let go, and do whatever came into our minds. They suggested that if you felt like taking off all your clothing, then go ahead. Whatever you wanted to do was fine.

All of this was really a bit too much for me. I saw that it was a little bit of yoga and vedanta, and a lot of hogwash. First of all, there were no instructions about how to perform the bhastrika correctly, or any other advice. The instructors appeared to know very little of pranayama, or that Patanjali, the author of the *Yoga Sutras*, gives the meaning of yoga in the second sutra as: *Yogas citta-vrtti-nirodhah*, which means, "Yoga is the control or inhibition of thought waves in the mind," and not, "Do whatever comes into your mind."

When we finally left, John and I had pretty much had the same impression about the whole thing. But the next day, another American came to the home where we were staying in Juhu, and since the talk at the house that day was about Rajneesh, he wanted to go and meet him as well. He asked if I would take him. I told him that I was not interested in seeing him again, and that he should go on his own, or with someone else. But after some persistence on his part, I finally agreed to take him. So that night, John, myself, the American, and a woman musician who was also a devotee of Baba's, all went to Rajneesh's apartment. Although I was not very interested in going, I thought that I would take this opportunity to see if I had the same impression as the previous night.

When we arrived, we were immediately taken into Rajneesh's bedroom, where he was sitting with about a half dozen devotees. He soon began talking about starting an army of sannyasins, and said that he would start giving sannyasa very soon. In fact, he said that he already had given initiation to a few people. He also said that he wanted to travel to the West, as well as change his name from Acharya Rajneesh to Bhagavan Rajneesh. The reason he gave for the name change was so that he could easily get past Indian customs.

Hearing about his desire to start an army of sannyasis I asked him who was going to perform the sannyasa initiation? He said that he would. I told him that since he was not himself a sannyasin, he had no authority to give sannyasa initiation to others. Therefore his followers would not be accepted by other sannyasins.

He told me that it did not matter, since this was going to be a new modern sannyasa. I told him that if it had nothing to do with traditional sannyasa ideals, then why let his followers wear the same monastic dress and call themselves sannyasins? "Would this not confuse people?" I asked him.

He simply brushed the question aside. But by the time we left, it became clear to me that Rajneesh would indeed change his name to Bhagavan, and have his army of 'sannyasins', and eventually go to the West, where, I predicted, he would become very popular.

Drive To Delhi

The lady who we were driving to Delhi with was a *parsi*, one of the few remaining followers of that ancient faith of Zarathustra, the prophet of Persia. Her name was Gorshed Gandhy. Her husband, Kekoo, was Baba's devotee, and I knew him very well. But I had not met Mts. Gandhy previously. They owned an art gallery in Mumbai, as well as in Delhi. She and her husband were both very nice people, and over the years I became very close to their family.

The three of us left Mumbai the next morning. Along the way I noticed how well organized Mrs. Gandhy was. She had planned out the whole trip very well, and as she belonged to AA, the Indian equivalent of AAA, each night we would stay in a beautiful cottage available to members.

Most of these cottages had been constructed by the British, and were used only by officials. Now they were being run by the Indian government. These buildings were kept very clean and in excellent condition, and they were very inexpensive to stay in, if you were a member. The problem is finding them vacant. But Mrs. Gandhy had already planned everything ahead of time.

We took about five days to reach Delhi. That gave us plenty of time to look at the many sites along the way. We stopped at Sanchi in the state of Madhya Pradesh, and visited the huge Buddhist Stupa, which was built over 2,000 years ago. The place was an important Buddhist center at the time of King Ashoka, who reigned at the end of the fourth century B.C.E. The present Stupa is dated from the second century B.C.E. It is believed to simply be an enlargement of a previous smaller Stupa. The Stupa was originally a burial mound, which housed the remains of the Buddha, or his disciples.

There are many forts, temples, and other ancient ruins

(right) The great Stupa at Sarnath; *(below)* the burning ghat, Varanasi.

along the way to Delhi from Mumbai. In the state of Rajasthan we stopped at the famous fort of Jodhpur, known today as Mehrangarh. The fort sits majestically on a hilltop dominating the surrounding plains. Its foundation was laid in 1459 C.E. by Rao Jodha, the fifteenth Rathore ruler. With its 68 feet wide, and 117 feet high walls, it soars 400 feet above the city of Jodhpur. We also stopped in Agra to see the Taj Mahal.

We had a very good time and enjoyed meeting the different people along the way. One day a funny thing occurred. Mrs. Gandhy, besides her name, had a striking resemblance to Mrs. Indira Gandhi, the then Prime Minister of India. At one point during our trip we were sitting underneath a tree relaxing when a number of villagers came over to meet us. A distinguished looking gentleman, who appeared to be the village leader, came closer, and saluted Mrs. Gandhy, thinking that she was the Prime Minister. When she told them that she was not Mrs. Indira Gandhi, they were all surprised, and somewhat embarrassed, but we all had a good laugh and shared some tea.

Finally we reached New Delhi. Mrs. Gandhy had invited John and myself to attend a wedding, which we did. Then the next day, John and I decided to go to Varanasi. We went by train and had planned to stay just for a few days. When we reached Varanasi we got a room near the Ganges. While John was resting, I decided to go over the bridge, and meet Avadhuta Ram.

I soon reached the ashram, and after speaking with a devotee, I discovered that Ram had been spending a lot of time in silence and seclusion. Someone went to his room to let him know that I was there. After a few minutes I was called inside. The room was dark and very still. Ram was sitting quietly on his bed, wrapped in a blanket, which was also partially covering his head. I could see that he had recently shaved his head and beard. He smiled and nodded gently on seeing me, and after saluting him, I sat down. As he was in silence, he did not say anything to me, and I just sat quietly meditating for about half an hour, and then left.

I returned to my room and met with John, who asked me to show him around the city. First I took him down to the river banks, and we walked to the burning *ghat*. As we got near the area where the bodies were being burnt, a deep calm suddenly overpowered me. I felt deeply intoxicated, and had to sit down and meditate. After about an hour, John and I went for a boat ride on the Ganges. The river had a very peaceful effect on both of us.

Like myself, John had an interest in astrology, so we decided to go and meet some of the local astrologers. We wandered about for sometime and met a few. I also took him to see the astrologer I had met the first time I was there, but unfortunately he was ill, and unable to do John's chart.

The next day we went to Sarnath, a place about eight or ten miles north of Varanasi. John considered himself a Buddhist and wanted to see the place. It is considered one of the four main Buddhist pilgrimage sites. It was at Sarnath that Lord Buddha gave his first sermon after achieving enlightenment.

The atmosphere there was very peaceful, and so we decided to spend the whole day. There are numerous temples in Sarnath, built by Buddhists from all over the world. We decided to return to Sarnath for a second time before leaving Varanasi.

After spending a few days in Varanasi, we decided to leave for New Delhi. We had planned to go by train but when we reached the station we found out that there was a strike. We found a similar situation at the bus stand. As John appeared to have contracted hepatitis, and was therefore not feeling well, he decided that we should fly to New Delhi. We therefore went to the airport and took a flight to Delhi, which stopped at Khajaraho and Agra.

We got off the plane at Khajaraho, and visited the famous temples there. We had also planned getting off at Agra to see the Taj Mahal again, but by the time we reached there, John's illness had worsened. We therefore decided to continue on directly to Delhi and find him a doctor.

When we reached Delhi, we got a room at a local hotel, and I went out looking for a doctor. Then just as I walked outside our hotel, I happened to run into a devotee of Baba's, who recognized me from Ganeshpuri. He took John and myself to a well known Ayurvedic doctor. Although I was personally very impressed with the doctor, John did not think much of Ayurvedic remedies. Eventually he would go to a hospital which practiced Western medicine.

Pilgrimage South

Baba was scheduled to arrive in Delhi in just two days. I was very excited. When the day arrived, John and I went to the home where Baba would be staying. Everyone was anxiously awaiting his arrival. There were brahmin priests chanting vedic mantras at the gate while waiting to receive him. When Baba finally arrived he was escorted into a large tent which had been set up on the lawn. After he was seated, a darshan line immediately formed, and I got in it.

When it was my turn, I went up and bowed to Baba. He said in English, "Hello," and asked how my pilgrimage had gone. I said that it went well, but that I was now happy to see him again. I asked him what he wanted me to do next.

He told me to say good-bye to my friend, and that I should move into the house he was staying at. He also told me that he was planning a pilgrimage to south India, "to his homeland," as he put it, and asked me to accompany him. He invited me with so much love that I actually felt it as a tangible force entering my heart. I was very happy. And since I had already brought my things with me, I went outside and said good-bye to John. He was planning to leave India for the U.S. in just a few days.

Programs were held each day during Baba's two week stay in Delhi. Baba Ram Dass had returned to India with Baba, and after having visited his own Guru, he returned to meet Baba in Delhi. Baba asked him to give some talks during the evening programs.

I had met Ram Dass briefly in Ganeshpuri just after Baba's return from his World Tour. I noticed that Baba treated him with a lot of love. I had also recently met his friend Bhagavan Dass during my stay in Mumbai. Bhagavan Dass eventually came out to Ganeshpuri to meet Ram Dass and Baba. Apparently he and Ram Dass had not seen each for a number of years.

During Baba's stay in Delhi, an interesting meeting

occurred. One night, a *Brighu* astrologer came to meet Baba. Baba's hostess in Delhi, Mrs. Rao, had come to Ganeshpuri in December to invite Baba to New Delhi for the Shivaratri celebration. But before she had come, she had visited a *Bhrigu-nadi* astrologer.

The *nadi* system is a special branch of astrology, and is not at all like regular astrology. In this system, the person's chart is not actually calculated by the astrologer, but is supposedly found in a collection of hundreds or thousands of horoscopes in the astrologer's possession. These charts, and their interpretations, are believed to have been written thousands of years ago by India's great sages. In this case, sage Bhrigu.

They have been handed down in certain families from generation to generation. The astrologer has to first locate the individual's chart, and then simply read what it says about the person's life. In north India, they are usually written in an old-style Sanskrit; and in the south, they are available in the Tamil language.

The reading often describes a number of aspects of the individual's life, and at times with incredible accuracy. It also gives details about the person's previous life or lives, and what specifically brought about the present life. Future predictions of the present life are also given, as well as any information about one's future birth.

Before going to Ganeshpuri, Baba's devotee had gone to one such astrologer, who found her chart, and gave her a reading. She had not previously met the astrologer, but he was soon telling her all about her life. But as he was doing so, the astrologer started to became very excited when he began reading the description the chart gave of her Guru. The chart also revealed her upcoming visit to the ashram, which the astrologer described by saying that it was a place that began with the letter 'G'. He went on to give her further details.

At the end of the reading, the astrologer asked her where her Guru lived, and said that he would like to meet him. She told him that in fact Baba would be coming to Delhi soon, and that he could visit him then. So when Baba arrived, a time was fixed for the meeting.

The astrologer had said that he had found Baba's horoscope in his collection, and wanted to read it for him. When he arrived, he greeted Baba and then sat down and started the reading. At the time there were about a half dozen of us present. The reading turned out to be very long, and so the astrologer had to return a second night.

The reading gave incredible details about Baba's present life, but more specifically about his spiritual work on earth. It also spoke about some of his previous lives. The chart further mentioned that Baba would visit the West a total of three times, and that he had recently returned from the first visit. The reading kept going on until Baba finally said it was enough.

I personally found the reading very interesting, and later I went to meet the astrologer at his home. I had known about this system of astrology, and on my recent visit to Varanasi with John, we tried to meet such astrologers. However, we were not able to find any reputable ones. We did meet one man who claimed that he had these charts, but he turned out to be a fraud. This is not unusual since these types of charts are very rare, and therefore one has to be careful.

As our stay in Delhi was coming to an end, the pilgrimage to the south was starting to take shape. I had spoken to a few friends and found out more about the places we would be visiting. It turned out that it was going to be a long pilgrimage, and I was very excited about it.

After New Delhi, some ashramites would have to return to Ganeshpuri, while others would continue on with Baba to the next stop, which would be the city of Hyderabad in the south. A group of us took a night train to Hyderabad, arriving in the city early the next morning. There were about a half dozen people who had arrived from America just after Baba returned from his tour. We all had a wonderful time on the train, and in the morning, we all chanted the Guru Gita.

In Hyderabad, I stayed in the house where Baba was staying. They had a very large house, and so they were able to accommodate everyone. I don't recall exactly how long we stayed there, but it must have been about four or five days. The actual pilgrimage was to start from there.

By the time we left Hyderabad, there were about four or five vehicles included in the caravan. Some ashramites would have to return to Ganeshpuri, while the others would continue on. The total number of people going on the pilgrimage would be around fifteen to twenty. But this number became smaller as the pilgrimage progressed.

The first to drop off the list was a young American. He had to return to Ganeshpuri after suffering a bad head injury the day before we were to leave Hyderabad. When we finally did get going, it turned out that we had quite a collection of characters. A few of them would keep everyone entertained throughout the pilgrimage. Baba was in a great mood.

One of the vehicles was an old American station wagon which was rented by a few western devotees. This group consisted of two Italians, a French lady, a large American man, and one or two Indians. There were also two Indian Ambassador cars, used by some of the Indian devotees. Ram Dass was also accompanying us, and Baba had instructed me to ride in the Volkswagon van he was driving. So it was Ram Dass, three of his friends, one of which was Krishna Dass, and myself in the van. Baba was riding in his own car, a Mercedes given to him the previous year by a German devotee.

On March 6th we left Hyderabad and were headed for Sri Shailam, a sacred mountain near the river Krishna, about 145 miles from Hyderabad. The Shiva temple at Shri Shailam is situated on a plateau of the Nallamalai Hills, located in the modern state of Andhra Pradesh. The plateau is about 1500 feet high.

The image in the temple there is a Shiva Lingam, considered

to be one of the twelve *Jyotirlingam* shrines in the country. The Linga in that temple is known as Lord Mallikarjuna. There is also a temple dedicated to the Goddess, who is known as Bhramaramba Devi. Her shrine is considered to be one of the 18 Maha Shakti Pithas or centers of power. Because of this combination it makes the site unique, and is the only one of its kind. Baba also told us that the place is considered one of three *Siddhapithas* or places where Siddhas dwell in a subtle form. Two of these sites are located in India. This one at Shri Shailam, the second is at Girnar, in the state of Gujarat, and the third is the sacred mountain Kailash, located in Western Tibet.

The origins and antiquity of the shrine is not fully known. But it has been mentioned in the *Ramayana*, *Mahabharata*, and a few of the *Puranas* (the Shiva, Matsya, Agni, and Vayu). There is also a hymn in the Skanda Purana called "Shrisaila Kandam," extolling the shrine's greatness.

The first historical reference to Shri Shailam is traced to the Pulumavi's Nashik inscription, dated to the first century C.E. Some believe that it began with the Sathavahanas, who were the first builders in Andhra Pradesh. However, they merely mention the shrine.

Over the centuries many kings of the south have maintained or constructed additional shrines at the site. Massive fort like walls some twenty feet high, and towers, enclose the temple compound. The compound is situated on the south side of the river Krishna, which flows down at the bottom of the hill. In the 14th century, Prolaya Vema Reddi, of the Reddy dynasty, constructed steps leading down the hill to the river. There are about three hundred and fifty steps. Ram Dass, his three friends, and myself decided to walk down the steps and bathe in the river.

The great Adi Shankaracharya is said to have visited the shrine, and it is believed that he wrote his immortal hymn, *Sivananda Lahiri*, there. Praise of the temple has also been sung by the Tamil poet saints of the past two millenniums.

We had planned to stay there for a few days, and arrangements had been made to rent some cottages. We would often have darshan with Baba sitting on the roof of one of the cottages. From the rooftop we had a panoramic view of the beautiful mountain peaks and the river Krishna flowing far below.

Each day Baba would speak on a variety of subjects: meditation, renunciation, knowledge, etc. He would also answer questions which were mostly asked by Ram Dass and his friends. This revealed a new side of Baba for me. Not that he did not answer questions before, but there were now actual question and answer sessions. I was very happy listening to Baba's answers, and I remember feeling grateful to Ram Dass for his many questions.

Baba told everyone to spend as much time as possible doing japa while we were at the temple. He also had a *Mahapuja* performed at both the Shiva and Devi's temple. I found the place to be extremely powerful, and my meditations were very deep. When I went to bow to the image of the Goddess, I felt a powerful energy coming from the image, which entered me through the top of my head.

On March 9th we left Sri Shailam and headed towards Chennai (Madras). But first we would stop for darshan at the famous Tirupati temple.

I enjoyed the company of my new traveling companions, and we had a good time together. However, they had a tendency to stop a lot, and so we were constantly falling behind the others. I urged them to keep up with Baba, but unfortunately, I was not the driver. I tried to explain to them that if we were late in arriving at the temple, Baba would not wait for us. I told Ram Dass that I knew that Baba was very fond of him, and would not scold him, but still Baba was a man of discipline, and so we should be on time.

Unfortunately we were late arriving at the Tirupati temple, and Baba had already left. I spoke to the temple priest, and he told me of Baba's visit. I also asked if we could go in for darshan, and he personally took us inside. He told me that if we were Baba's disciples, then we were more Hindu than some Hindus he had known. We were told that before this, non-Hindus had never been allowed inside the temple.

The deity of that temple is called Lord Venkatesa. Located on a high plateau the place is like a small city. It receives millions of pilgrims each year, and is considered to be the wealthiest temple in all of India.

After our darshan, we left Tirupati for Chennai, arriving there late that night. We found a hotel room and went to meet Baba the next morning. He was staying at a devotee's home and asked me to stay there as well. We apologized for arriving late at the Tirupati temple. He asked if we had been allowed inside for darshan. I said we had, and told him what the priest had said.

Baba stayed in Chennai for a few days, and from there we were scheduled to travel across the country, to the state of Kerala, located on the western coast of India. We were heading for a place called Dharmasthala, located near the city of Mangalore. Baba was born in that area, and there was a famous Shiva temple that he wanted to visit. Along the way, we would stop in the city of Bangalore, where we would spend the night. While in Chennai, two people in our party had become ill, and so they had to return to Ganeshpuri.

Ramana Maharshi's ashram is located just south of Chennai, and Ram Dass wanted to stop there. Baba gave his permission and said to meet him in Bangalore. We therefore left Chennai early enough so we could reach the ashram that night. We arrived very late, but went for darshan at Maharishi's samadhi shrine anyway. We sat in meditation for about half an hour.

Although it was late, the ashram authorities welcomed us with such great love, and offered us something to eat before going to bed. The next morning we again meditated at the shrine before leaving. I found this ashram to be very peaceful and felt the presence of Maharishi very powerfully. Especially in the meditation hall. The ashram is located at the foot of the sacred mountain, Arunachala.

From there we headed towards Bangalore, where Ram Dass wanted to meet Satya Sai Baba. So we went out to his ashram for darshan and spent the night. Ram Dass had also wanted Baba to meet Satya Sai Baba, and after repeated requests, Baba finally consented. Baba and the rest of the party drove out to the ashram the next morning, and met Satya Sai Baba for a brief time.

Unfortunately, when we met with the people on our tour, we found out that there had been a terrible auto accident the previous night. Before we had left Chennai for Ramana Maharshi's ashram, some people from Australia had come from Ganeshpuri to meet Baba. They were driving a van, and wanted to accompany Baba on the rest of the pilgrimage. Baba gave them his permission.

However, after we left, they decided that they too wanted to visit Ramana Maharshi's ashram, and asked Baba if they could follow us there. Baba gave his consent, but told them specifically not to leave until early the next morning. But as they were anxious to reach the ashram, the driver decided to leave that night, against Baba's advice. A few of the ashramites who had been traveling with us also decided to go with them. Along the way they had a terrible accident which killed the driver, and badly injured the rest of the passengers. They were now in a hospital in Chennai. This was indeed very sad news for us all.

Nevertheless, the pilgrimage continued on, and we drove through the beautiful state of Mysore. We would often stop on the roadside and have short *satsangs* with Baba. He was in a very happy mood, and we too enjoyed ourselves.

Since we had just met Satya Sai Baba, who claimed to be an *Avatar,* a question arose about *Avatars.* Baba spoke about the scriptural references to them, and then discussed the work of the *Avatar,* as well as the various signs that accompany him, both before and during his arrival. Baba gave some specific characteristics of a real Avatar.

This was a very intimate period with Baba, and he also appeared to be in a playful mood. I felt extremely fortunate to have been a part of that tour. I also realized, however, that with Baba's growing popularity, there would not be very many more intimate moments like these. We would often be driving around a curve and suddenly see Baba sitting alongside of the road. We would all stop and sit with him for sometime before starting off again.

These stops became more and more frequent as we got closer to Dharmasthala. The van I was riding in was always the last in the group, and at times we would make our own stops along the way. At one point, while we were far behind, we stopped and purchased some Indian watermelons. We began eating them as we continued to drive. But then, just as we were driving around a bend, we noticed further down the road one of the cars in our party. Suddenly there was panic in the van, and someone yelled, "Quick, get rid of the melons before we get there!" Someone slid open the van's side door, and out went the remains of the melons. I started laughing and said, "Lets see what happens. It's not easy to fool Baba."

As we got closer, we pulled our van off the road, and got out. As we walked towards Baba, who was sitting on the ground on the opposite side of the road, the first thing he said was, "Now don't drink any water for at least two hours, or those melons will make you sick."

We all just looked at each other and started laughing.

One of the most interesting characteristics of the temple at Dharmasthala is that it really is a non-sectarian temple. Although the temple is dedicated to Lord Shiva, the priests who perform the daily rituals belong to the Vaishnavite sect. And, the temple is administered by followers of the Jain religion. The temple feeds thousands of pilgrims each day, and on holidays many thousands more.

The temple is very special to the area's population, as it was to Baba's family. His mother had performed a special ritual (*puja*) for obtaining a son at that temple. She vowed to offer the child to God if her prayers were answered.

A devotee of Baba's had a special golden cradle and child made, which was offered at the temple to symbolize the completion of his mother's vow.

An interesting incident occurred while we were in Dharmasthala. Throughout the pilgrimage Ram Dass had been asking Baba about the power of a *chaitanya mantra* after Baba had mentioned it in one of his talks. Unlike a mantra read from a book, a *chaitanya mantra* has been enlivened with consciousness by a Siddha, thereby becoming a vehicle of his power to awaken the seeker. During the journey Baba would tease Ram Dass by saying that when we reached Dharmasthala, he would give him a direct experience of such a mantra.

So one morning after we reached Dharmasthala, Baba called me, and we went to where Ram Dass was sleeping. Baba awoke him, took him by the hand, and we walked to a nearby stairway which led up to temple. Baba told me to wait at the bottom of the stairs, while he took Ram Das to the top. When they reached a certain spot, Baba motioned to Ram Dass to sit down. After Ram Das sat down, Baba leaned forwards and whispered a mantra into his ear. He then sat down for awhile opposite Ram Das before leaving.

Upon hearing the mantra, Ram Dass suddenly went into a trance, becoming oblivious to his surroundings. He was not even aware of when Baba had left. Meanwhile, Baba reached the bottom of the stairs and told me to wait about half an hour, and if Ram Dass did not come down by then, that I should go and get him. After a half hour had passed, and still no sign of Ram Dass, I went up to get him.

When I reached Ram Das, I could see that he was in a semi-conscious state. He was kind of freaking out. And I could see fear in his eyes. Obviously he had never had such a powerful experience, and was unsure of what to do. I tried to calm him, and helped him back to our room. I then went and reported to Baba his state of mind. Laughing, Baba handed me some bananas and simply said, "He'll be alright. Feed him some of these."

I then returned to the room and hand fed the bananas to Ram Dass. After sometime he began to return to normal consciousness, but I could still see some fear in his eyes. I was sure he had an experience that he would never forget.

Even though there were more stops to make before reaching Ganeshpuri, for me, Dharmasthala was the climax of the pilgrimage. It was the pinnacle of the trip, and I felt very close to Baba. We stayed there a few days, and then headed north along the Western coast of India.

Along the way we made numerous stops, visiting different temples, and even an ashram. We also stopped at a few places along the seashore associated with Bhagavan Nityananda.

We finally reached Pune, where we were welcomed by Baba's devotees. We intended to be there for four or five days, and so daily programs were scheduled. A number of musicians also came to perform for Baba.

Some Westerners who were in Pune at the time also came to meet Baba. Among them was an Italian man named Radames, who was in Pune visiting his guru, the famous Hatha Yoga teacher, B.K.S. Iyengar. For some reason Baba made it a point to introduce me to Radames, and told him that I was also an Italian. Baba then invited the man to visit the Ganeshpuri ashram.

I spoke to Radames for sometime, and he happened to mention that he was returning to Italy soon. He also told me that he wanted to stop at Ganeshpuri when he reached Mumbai, and so I gave him directions to the ashram.

A Trip To Venice

We left Pune early one morning and arrived at Ganeshpuri that same evening. I had been traveling for a few months now, and so I was happy to be back home. I had hoped that everything would soon settle down again, and I could get back to my regular routine. But this was not to be, at least not yet.

A few days after my return, I received news from the government of India regarding my application for a visa extension. It had been denied. The previous year I had to briefly go to Nepal in order to get a new visa, now I was again being asked to leave the country. At first I thought that I would go to New Delhi and try to get the decision reversed. However, I knew it would be difficult. Once the Central Government had given its ruling, no one wanted to reverse the decision.

Baba suggested that I go and see a devotee of his in New Delhi, and see if he could help me. Baba told me only that the man worked for the government. I told Baba that I would go and see him, but if I was unable to get an extension, then I had planned to go to Pakistan or Afghanistan and get a new visa there.

I was given two weeks to leave the country. But there was one problem. Since I had no money, I did not know how I would get to Delhi. Then I remembered Radames, the Italian man that I had met in Pune. He had told me that he was coming to the ashram and would be driving to Delhi from there. I thought that perhaps I could get a ride with him.

A few days later Radames arrived at the ashram. I explained my situation to him, and he said that he would welcome the company. As I thanked him, I remembered how insistent Baba had been for me to meet him when we were in Pune. Radames turned out to be a kind and generous man, and we became good friends.

Before leaving the ashram, I went for Baba's darshan. He

told me, "Don't worry, you will not be gone very long."

Radames and I started out early the next morning. He was driving a British Land Rover which had all kinds of amenities. The roof popped up into a tent, and the windows had mosquito netting on them. It was a deluxe model Land Rover. However, we slept underneath the stars most nights. We had a very beautiful journey, and made some interesting stops along the way. When we reached the city of Jaipur, we went to the palace to meet a friend of mine who was staying there. She was also a Baba devotee. At the time she was working on a biography of the Rani (Queen) of Jaipur. So we spent the afternoon with her. As it was extremely hot, we also swam in the palace pool.

The journey was going well, but one day we had an interesting experience. While driving through the desert of Rajasthan, we noticed that we were getting dangerously low on gas. There were no gas stations in sight, nor would there be any for many miles yet. And soon the meter was at the empty mark.

Radames started to become anxious. But suddenly I became aware of Baba's presence, and had the feeling that he would take care of us. So I told Radames not to worry, that my Baba would help us. I told him to just keep on driving, and added the stipulation that he not look inside the gas tanks.

Since Radames was not Baba's devotee, it was hard for him to have faith in what I said. He wanted to see how much gas was actually in the tanks, and calculate exactly how far we could drive. But I saw no advantage in doing that since there were just no gas station nearby. Finally I was able to convince him to trust in Baba, and to keep driving without stopping. We continued to drive for about another hour and a half until finally we reached a gas station.

We were both very happy to have arrived safely. But Radames could not wait any longer to look inside the gas tanks. In that Land Rover there were two gas tanks. They were accessed from inside the cab. The caps for the tanks were so large that you could easily see inside the tanks. They were made that way so you could see exactly how much gas you had in case the meter was broken. When we looked inside each one of them, we saw that both tanks were completely dry. Not a single drop of gasoline. Indeed, not even moisture from vapors could be seen or smelled. Radames just looked at me in astonishment and said, "Your Baba is something!"

We finally reached New Delhi, and I immediately went to see Baba's devotee. He said that he did not know how he could be of help, but that he would try. Somehow he had access to the President's secretary, whom he called, and explained my difficulty. The secretary said that he was going on vacation the next day, but that he would call the person in charge of the visa department, whom I had met the previous year, and ask him to extend my visa. In any case, the secretary called back and said that he had spoken to the man, and that there would be no problem. He told me to go and see him on Monday morning, and he would take care of the matter. It was now late Friday afternoon.

Radames had decided to wait with me until I had the visa extension in my hand. It appeared that everything was going to work out fine, but you never know. As it turned out, on Monday morning when I went to see the man, he told me that there was nothing he could do. I had to leave the country immediately. It was of course his office that had issued the original order, and so, if he really wanted to do something he certainly could have. Since I had come to India on a tourist visa, the Indian government did not like to extend them for very long.

Radames was waiting for me just outside the office, and as soon as I told him what had happened, we immediately left for Kabul, Afghanistan. I had already obtained a visa for that country on Friday when Radames applied for his. We both had thought I should get one just in case something went wrong. It was fortunate we did.

I had been away from the ashram for only a few days now,

and I was hoping to get back in time for Baba's birthday in two weeks time. I was not sure if that was going to be possible, but I would do everything I could to get back in time. Once Baba told me that if I strongly wished for something, and prayed to Mother Kundalini, that she would fulfill my wish. So I prayed for her blessings.

My passport showed that I had been living in India for a long time. So it was possible that the Indian consulate in Kabul may not want to issue me a new visa. But I felt Baba's presence throughout the trip, and I had faith that Mother Kundalini would take care of everything.

From India we drove to Pakistan and then Afghanistan, crossing the Khyber Pass. We soon reached Kabul and checked into a local hotel. That same day we went and met with the Italian Ambassador, who Radames had met on his way to India. He had invited us to have dinner with him that night at his residence. It would be the first time in many years since I had genuine Italian food. The Ambassador had some special vegetarian dishes prepared for us since Radames was also a vegetarian.

The Ambassador was very kind to me, and with his help, I got a new visa for India right away. I knew that with this visa I could remain in India for at least another six months and perhaps longer. I was very happy, and decided to leave right away for India. I said good-bye to Radames, and thanked him for all his help. And before we parted, he invited me to come and stay at his home if I was ever in Italy. Little did we realize then, that this would be sooner than we both would have thought.

While Radames and I were in Delhi, I had again gone to meet the Bhrigu astrologer that I had met earlier when he read Baba's chart. The first time I met him he prepared a *Horary* chart for me, which is an astrological chart cast for the time a question is asked the astrologer, or, as in this case, to determine the precise time of our meeting. The chart was simply used to help him locate my horoscope from his collection. He had made some interesting predictions which turned out to be correct.

When I met him again that previous week, he prepared another Horary chart for me, and mentioned that in six months I would return to my place of birth. I explained to him that although I was born in Italy, the United States had actually been my place of residence, and that I had not lived in Italy for a long time. At the time, there was talk in the ashram that Baba might return to the west at around that time, and I thought that I might be going with him. So my question to the astrologer was whether he meant my place of birth, or my residence in the US?

"Your birth place," he said emphatically.

I had no such plans at the time to go to Italy, but I said, "Lets see what happens."

When I reached India from Afghanistan I headed straight for Ganeshpuri. From Delhi I took a train to Mumbai with money given to me by Radames. I had been gone from the ashram for only about ten days, and I would be back in plenty of time for Baba's birthday.

When I reached the ashram and saw Baba, I began to cry. He smiled at me and said, "It seems like you did not go anywhere." He then asked me what had happened, and I told him everything.

There was a lot of excitement that year about Baba's upcoming birthday celebration. A statue of Bhagavan Nityananda was going to be installed in the ashram's new temple. The statue had originally been made for the samadhi shrine in Ganeshpuri, but due to politics, some of the trustees of the Nityananda ashram decided that they wanted a different statue. This was after they had asked Baba to have one made. So Baba decided to install his statue in the main hall of the ashram, and had a temple built especially for it.

The Shankaracharya of Dwarka, and other sadhus, had been invited for the enlivenment ceremony. When a statue is installed, there is a certain ritual performed to instill the life force (*prana*) into the image. This ritual is called *Pranapratishtha*. If for some reason the statue later has to be worked on, or moved, then another ritual has to be performed which will remove the prana. Then after the work is completed, the *Pranapratishtha* ritual is again performed. This ritual is considered very important, and should be performed for any statue which is going to be used for worship.

There were also many new Westerners who had come to the ashram for Baba's birthday celebration. Ram Dass had returned,

(*above*) Baba during Q&A in his apartment veranda (1971)

and Albert Rudolph, known as Rudi, also attended. Rudi was an American disciple of Baba's, who was instrumental in bringing Baba to America during his first visit to the West. Rudi used to visit Baba each year around his birthday. That year thousands of people attended the celebration. I could see how Baba's public career continued to expand.

After the birthday celebration, things started to get back to normal for me. I was now working in the garden, as well as in the front hall. Desai, the manager of the ashram wanted me to also manage the Westerners, but I was not really interested in managing anything. I just wanted to do some simple work, and continue with my spiritual practices. But after some persuasion, I told him that I would do it temporarily, until he found someone else.

There were now also question and answer sessions each week, which were initially held outside in the courtyard. Baba would sit on what I call his perch. In the rainy season we would shift to the front hall. Every afternoon Baba's secretary, Amma (later Swami Prajnananda), would read any mail Baba had received from devotees. Sometimes he would give some response to the person's questions, and Amma would write the person back.

A question and answer session was held once a week just after the mail had been read. A formal Q&A arose because of the increase in foreign visitors, who had come after Baba's trip to the West. They naturally had many questions.

But one day, not long after the installation of Bhagavan Nityananda's statue, just after Baba had sat down in the front hall and was about to answer a question, he suddenly stopped and said, "Ever since we have installed my Baba here, I don't feel right speaking in his presence. I feel like I am gossiping."

Having said that, he got up and told everyone, "Come with me."

Everybody got up and followed him to the enclosed veranda of his new apartment. He sat down in one of the corners in a

(*above*) Baba distributing prasad after Q&A.

lounge chair. The women sat on his left and the men on his right. After getting settled, he said in English, "Ready!" And the question and answer period started. At the end of the Q&A Baba would distribute prasad.

Thane is a city located about forty miles southeast of the ashram. It is there that all foreigners living in that district had to go to register. I did not enjoy going there, especially during the rainy season. But one day, just after the rains started, I had to go there to apply for a visa extension.

After finishing my work with the police, I started walking back to the train station, where I was going to catch a train to Mumbai. During the rainy season the streets of Thane are often submerged under one to three feet of water. This was the case that day. I recall walking along the streets with my lungi folded up above my knees so it wouldn't get wet. I was also carrying an umbrella in one hand, and a bag over my right shoulder.

For some reason I started to feel agitated, and wishing I was back in Ganeshpuri. But just then, I felt something hit me on the back of my neck. Although I did not know what it was, I had a powerful urge to turn around and strike the first person I saw. But I decided to control myself. But by the time I reached the train station, my neck was itching like crazy. I still did not know what had happened. As I was scratching my neck, a man came up to me, and said that my neck was very red. He appeared to be concerned about me, and offered me a glass of water and told me to wash my neck. But before doing so, I took my shirt off, and placed my neck *mala* into the shirt's pocket. I then put the shirt into my bag, and began washing my neck with the water.

Meanwhile, the man who was supposedly helping me, took off with my shirt. However, I did not immediately know that the shirt was missing from my bag. The train soon arrived, and I got on and took a seat. When I finally opened the bag to get the shirt, I noticed it was missing. I suddenly realized the elaborate scheme the crook, or crooks, had played on me.

The crook had thrown some itching powder on my neck, which I was later told was an old trick. They then followed me to the train station, and watched to see where I kept my money bag. The bag was in my shirt pocket, where I had also put my mala. I did not have very much money, but it was now all gone. However, for me the most important loss was my mala. I didn't care very much about the money, but loosing the mala made me unhappy. But there was nothing I could do about it now. I took comfort in the fact that they did not take the bag as well, otherwise they would have gotten my passport.

When I reached Mumbai, I went to visit a friend of mine in order to borrow enough money to get back to the ashram. When I returned to Ganeshpuri, I mentioned what had happened to Desai, who was now the ashram manager.

The next day, Baba was sitting in the front courtyard just

outside the hall under the Parijata tree. We were standing near him when Desai told Baba what had happened to me the previous day. As he got to the part about the itching powder being thrown on me, Baba started saying, "No, no," in English, as if to warn me not to fall for the trick. Unfortunately it was too late.

Meanwhile, on hearing the story, a close friend had already purchased a new mala for me, and gave it to Baba for his blessing. As Baba placed the mala around my neck, he said, "Let this be a reminder to you that there are scoundrels and thieves in this world."

Interestingly, on that same day, I received a letter from Radames. It contained some money, which turned out to be the exact amount that had been stolen from me the previous day. I mentally thanked Baba for his blessings. The verse from the Bhagavad Gita also came to mind: "Mysteries are the ways of karma."

The monsoon season was a time for deep meditation. Baba would always encourage us to go deep within and practice more intensely during the rainy season. I was also doing more work in the garden, and had been supervising its maintenance.

I was still living at Turiya Mandir, except that I had moved to the top of a stairwell, which went out onto the roof. This was when Turiya Mandir was only one floor high. There was a door at the bottom of the stairs which was normally kept closed. In the summer months I would often sleep outside on the roof. I would always mentally thank Baba for the privacy, which I knew was becoming more and more scarce in the ashram. Most of the ashramites lived in dormitories near the front courtyard. And at the time there were two or three Indian men living in or around Turiya Mandir.

Turiya Mandir had originally been built as Baba's residence. Some of the ashram trustees had thought it would be a good idea for Baba to move to the upper garden. They thought that he could then retire to a quiet area of the ashram when there were large crowds down below in the front courtyard.

The large building was divided into three sections. The back section was to be Baba's apartment. This had its own entrance from outside, as well as an entrance to the main hall verandah. In between this door, and the one opposite, there were steps going up to the roof. That is where I was living. Just off of the verandah, there were a few bedrooms, which were used as guest rooms for sadhus. Normally these rooms were empty, except for one, which was used by a retired devotee.

These rooms were the second section of Turiya Mandir. Past the rooms is where the main hall was located. Originally this was to be the main hall where all the ashram programs would be held. It's a very beautiful hall and was kept very simple. The walls were covered with large photographs of Bhagavan Nityananda. There was also another life size oil painting of Bhagavan in a sitting posture, similar to the one in the front hall. A pair of silver sandals, and Baba's old water bowl from when he was a wandering monk, was also kept in front of the painting. When I first arrived at the ashram, I used to sleep outside of the hall's verandah. When I awoke each morning I would go inside the hall and meditate.

I was told that Baba had moved into the apartment briefly. But he thought it was too far from the main courtyard, where all of the activities were going on, and decided to move back down to his small room. He gave the use of the apartment at Turiya Mandir to one of his trustees and his family.

Part of my duty at Turiya Mandir was to also keep the sadhu rooms clean, as well as take care of any guest staying in them, including foreign sadhus. At times one of Baba's senior disciples, also named Swami Prakashananda, would come and stay at the ashram for extended periods of time. When Baba was away from the ashram, he would call Prakashanandaji to come and stay in the ashram during his absence. One of the rooms was especially reserved for his use alone.

Swamiji and I had become good friends ever since our

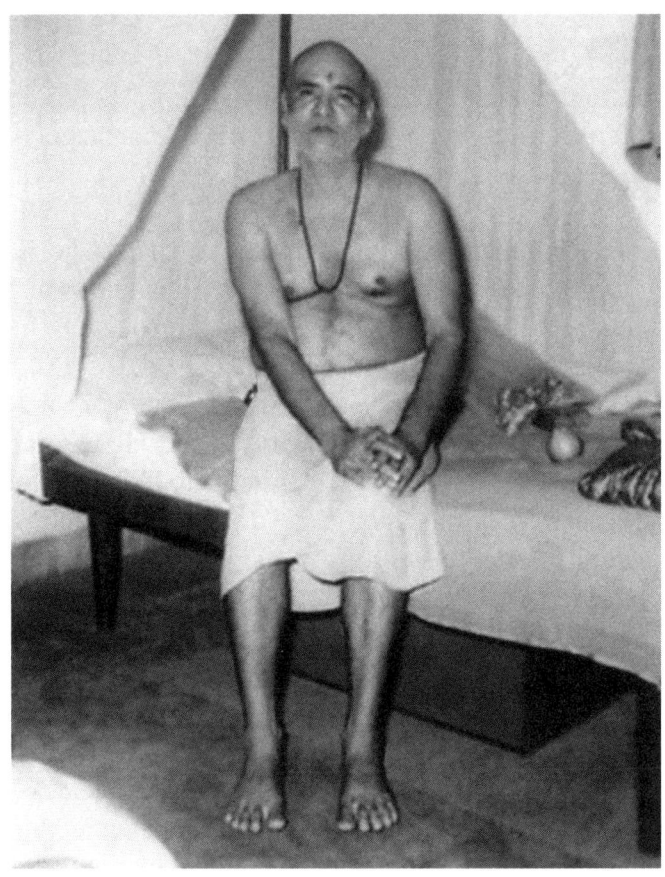
(*above*) Swami Prakashanandaji in his room in Turiya Mandir.

first meeting, just after I arrived at the ashram. I felt he was an enlightened soul, and treated him with great respect. He was also an excellent astrologer, and we often discussed the subject. Although he rarely looked at an individual's horoscope, he read my chart when I first met him.

In fact, Baba had a number of devotees who were good astrologers. They would often come to the ashram, and we would discuss different astrological techniques. They would teach me Vedic astrology, while I taught them the Western method.

In August, a large group of people traveled with Baba to Alandi for Jnaneshwar's darshan. I also accompanied him. As

I have already said, Baba had a very deep love and respect for Jnaneshwar. He once stated that he had learnt Marathi just so he could read the *Jnaneshwari* in its original language.

While at Alandi, an interesting incident occurred. One evening I was walking alone with Baba, when a Western devotee came up, and bowed at his feet. Suddenly the woman began having intense physical kriyas, accompanied with heavy breathing. Her body began moving very violently. Baba told me to grab her.

"Bend her head forward," he told me. He then gave me other instruction of what to do until her kriyas became less intense, and she began to calm down. It was an incredible experience.

My days were spent happily, and my meditations continued to deepen. But soon this routine would be disrupted. Although I had gotten a visa extension, it was now coming to an end, and it did not look like the government would extend it any further. By October, I had started getting notices to leave the country. But I was able to postpone my departure for sometime. The local immigration police suggested that I apply for a student visa, which would be good for at least one year, and which could be easily extended. They told me that they would grant permission when they were contacted by the central government with my application.

But unfortunately, this process would take about two months, and it had to be done from one's own country. I could not afford a round trip ticket to America, and in any case, I did not want to go. I did not know what to do, and so I discussed it with Baba. Meanwhile, I received a letter from Radames, who knew about the trouble I was having. He invited me to come to Italy and apply for a visa from there. I mentioned this to Baba, but he suggested that I first try New Delhi again, and if there was nothing to be done, then continue on to Italy.

Another problem that I had during that time was that the same disease that I had the previous year started up again. You will recall that although it had been diagnosed as having scabies, I had felt it was somehow related to the awakened Kundalini. It had not yet become too bad, but it was becoming very unpleasant, and so I spoke to Baba about it.

"What did you do for it last year?" Baba asked with a smile.

I had done a number of things, but as already mentioned earlier, nothing helped. It had stopped only when Baba arrived back in the ashram. I therefore had to tell him that I had done nothing for it.

"Then don't do anything about it this time either," he said. "It will be all right."

Finally the day arrived and I said good-bye to Baba. He blessed me by saying that he would be with me. The next morning I left for Mumbai, and from there took a train to Delhi. When I arrived, and made enquiries, I found that there was nothing I could do to reverse the decision. I had to leave the country. First I thought of going to Nepal again, but I decided against it. I really wanted a long term visa, and perhaps this was the way to do it. There had been a lot of rumors that Baba was returning to the west soon, but I was convinced that it would not happen for a couple of years yet.

I immediately started my journey overland to Italy, my place of birth, just as the astrologer had predicted just over six months earlier. I had very little money, and so I hitchhiked most of the way, taking buses or trains only when necessary. I was lucky and traveled most of the way with just a few rides.

I had also decided to avoid Bulgaria this time, remembering my previous experience. Since I had not been to Greece, I decided to go through that country, and then up into Yugoslavia, and from there into Italy.

Radames lived in Venice. He and his family had been expecting me, and graciously welcomed me to their home. Radames and his wife had two children. They all treated me like a family member, and showed me a great deal of love while I was there.

The first thing I did when I arrived was go to the Indian Embassy in Rome. At first they were reluctant to take my application, seeing that I had been living in India for such a long time. But I finally convinced them to take the application, and let the Delhi government decide. This time I applied for a student visa, and handed in all the required papers. I was told that it may take two months, but there was a possibility that we may hear something within six weeks. I also decided to write to the local police at Thane, and inform them of my application. I knew there was a trail of offices that these application would have to go through before it would reach their office.

After that, there was nothing to do but wait. While I was in Rome, I stayed with the Pozzis, an Italian family that had hosted Baba when he visited Rome on his first tour. I had met them when they visited Ganeshpuri. Their apartment became a meditation center after Baba's visit. Before I left the ashram, Baba told me to give some talks, and so while I was there, I conducted some *satsangs*. I would visit Rome a few more times to conduct programs before leaving Italy.

While in Rome, I also spent some time with Luciano. He was an unusual character but an excellent photographer. We had met when he visited Baba in Ganeshpuri about the beginning of 1971. He was very kind to me, and looked after me while I was in Rome.

During one of my visits to Rome, I was invited to someone's apartment, where Sri Jeddu Krishnamurti would be visiting. When I arrived, I noticed three or four people sitting around him on the floor, answering some questions. I had not met him previously but had read one or two of his books.

I found him to be a very gentle and warm man with a deep knowledge. I observed him very carefully, and I felt that he had attained an elevated state. However, I had heard that he did not speak well of gurus. He gave a short talk about witness consciousness, and afterwards, there were more questions.

I asked him why he had such a negative view towards gurus,

since obviously the very fact that he was teaching indicated that he was himself playing the role of a Guru. And obviously, many considered him as their Guru. He started giving an answer, but he did not really answer the question. So I jokingly said that even if he did not say so himself, I felt that he was a genuine Guru. He then started laughing and everyone joined in.

During my stay in Italy, I lived in a beautiful house outside of Venice. Radames had introduced me to a friend of his named Andrea. Andrea's family owned one of the largest glass factories in Venice. He and one of his brothers ran the shop. Andrea also had a great interest in yoga, especially hatha yoga. He lived with one of his brothers in a large apartment in Venice.

The rooms of that apartment were huge, and were filled with antique furniture, dating back a number of centuries. His brother Peppi was also an unusual and interesting man, whom I liked very much.

Andrea also owned some land outside of Venice, and had built a very large house on it, which he visited only occasionally. He said that if I didn't mind the solitude, I was welcomed to stay there. I told him that I would welcome the solitude, and thanked him for his hospitality.

I really wished that I was back in Ganeshpuri, but what could I do? This was my destiny, and I just continued with my daily practices. I spent most of my time in solitude, unless I went into Venice for lunch with Radames and his family, or Andrea. Once in a while they would come out to the house and spend the day with me.

I was still having my health problem, and at the beginning, Radames had some fears about it, thinking that perhaps his children might catch whatever I had. At first I did not tell him that I thought the disease was due to the activities of Kundalini. Since Radames was not a devotee of Baba's, and since he did not have the experience of an awakened Shakti, I was sure he would not understand. I therefore did whatever he asked me to do regarding the illness.

He took me to a local hospital which dealt specifically with skin diseases. They told us not to worry, as the treatment would take only three days, and I would be completely cured. They appeared very confident. I said wonderful, since the itching was driving me crazy. They admitted me into the hospital and started the treatment that very day. One day passed, then two days, and finally the third day, but I was still itching.

When the bandages were removed, the disease was still with me. The doctors were puzzled, but said that they would try another treatment, which would definitely get rid of it. This also took a couple of days, but at the end, the result was the same, no effect. Now they started to become upset with me, and a few of them wanted to study my condition. I said that I was not interested, and that I would continue the treatment at home.

They could not understand why they were not able to cure my disease since it was not considered difficult to treat. However, after my stay in the hospital, I told Radames that I felt the disease would go away on its on, and that he should not worry, that his family would not catch anything.

Return To Ganeshpuri

After six weeks I still had not heard anything about my visa. I wrote to my police friends in India, and they wrote back saying that they had not yet received my application from the central government. I asked the consulate in Rome to try and speed up the process, but all they could do was send a reminder to Delhi, which they did. But there was nothing else I could do. I had to just wait. However I was becoming restless, and I missed Baba a great deal.

Then there was the constant body itch from the disease. I still had it. If it wasn't for my friends in Venice, it would have been a more difficult time for me. I was also starting to doubt whether I would even get the student visa, and even if I did, it could easily take many months. I therefore decided to go back to Rome and try and persuade the Indian consulate to issue me a tourist visa instead. They told me that since I had already applied for a long term visa, they could not issue me a tourist visa. So I would have to wait for New Delhi to respond. But after some difficulty, I was finally able to convince someone at the embassy to issue me a visa, which I would be able to extend more easily once in India.

Meanwhile, Radames had purchased an air ticket to Mumbai for me. I was soon on my way back to the ashram. My disease was still with me, but I was in such a good mood that I hardly noticed it. I recall that I was still itching on the bus to Ganeshpuri, but mysteriously, the moment I entered the ashram, the itching stopped. And within a few days, there was hardly any sign that I ever had the disease.

The moment I entered the ashram I ran to the courtyard and saw Baba sitting on his perch. Only Amma was with him. I immediately went up to him and did a full prostration. He greeted me with a big smile and asked how I was. After answering his questions, he said something mysterious. He told me, "Now you have become an expert on visas. And because of your *tapasya* (austerities), others will not have to suffer."

At the time I did not understand the meaning of those words. It wasn't until a couple of years later, towards the end of the second World Tour, that I understood what he meant. One day Baba asked me to arrange for long term student visas for more than two hundred people that were planning to return to India with him.

Just before I had left Ganeshpuri for Italy, a devotee had offered Baba an elephant. When I returned from Italy, one of my duties was to take care of him. Baba gave him the name Swami Vijayananda. But he was affectionately called Vijay, or as Baba would often call him, "Viju." Viju was about 18 years old, just a teenager, when he came to the ashram. Elephants have a life span similar to humans.

Although the elephants' arrival was considered auspicious, taking care of him was hard work. At times Viju was like a spoiled teenager who happened to weigh more than a ton. My day with Viju started at about 3 a.m.. I would clean his shed, and afterwards wash and scrub him down. Washing an elephant is hard work. The skin is very tough, and one has to rub very hard. For this we used local volcanic pumice stones.

If Viju was in a bad mood, the job was even harder. After washing him, we would rub oil around his forehead, place a seat on his back, and decorate him. When we were finished we would take him down to the front courtyard where Baba would feed him.

After Baba fed Viju, the *mahout* — elephant keeper, myself, and sometimes a third person would take him out for a long walk. Usually two people would ride him, but sometimes Baba would have all three of us ride him at once. At times we would took him to the river and wash him there. He loved lying in the water, but he did not always cooperate. When he was in that mood, it was impossible to get him to do anything. It was particularly difficult in the spring when male elephants get into a rutting state which is called *maasty*, You could threaten him with a large stick, or even a spear, but he would not listen. At such times even the mahout could not control him. Nevertheless, Baba could control Viju by merely showing him a short whip, made out of braided cloth, less than two feet long.

One morning Viju had been extremely difficult, and had tried to grab me, and strike me with his tusks. The mahout told Baba what had happened. Baba picked up his whip and began scolding Viju for treating me the way he had.

"He gets up early in the morning just for you," Baba began saying. "He performs a great service to you by cleaning your stall, and washing your body, and you treat him this way? Shame on you!" Baba was saying to him. As Baba was scolding him, you could see that Viju was beginning to feel sorry for what he had done.

But one had to always be alert around him. I saw him grab more than one person with his trunk, and throw them as if they were nothing. I had both a feeling of trepidation, as well great love and respect for him.

Baba would come and visit Viju in the afternoons. He would sit in a chair just next to Viju. He would then feed him sugar cane stalks, which the mahout and I had cut into small bundles of about three pieces each. Sometimes Baba would tell me to climb on Viju's back, knowing that he did not like this very much. While laughing at my predicament, Baba would say, "Move more forward, come and sit just over his head."

Meanwhile Viju would be violently shaking his body trying to throw me off. Baba would be amused, and would start laughing out loud.

One day Baba came to the shed as usual. An old devotee had accompanied him. The mahout and I were the only other two people there. As usual I had prepared a stack of short sugarcane stalks that Baba could feed Viju. Baba sat down and began feeding him as usual. The devotee stood near the entrance, while the mahout and I stood near Baba and Viju. That day Viju had been overbearing, and difficult to handle. Baba also appeared to be more withdrawn that afternoon, and did not speak very much. When Baba was in that mood, the atmosphere around him would become very still and quiet. Although his eyes were opened, his gaze was inward.

Baba was sitting in the chair perpendicular to Viju. Viju was to his right. Baba's left leg and foot were resting on his right thigh. Viju was therefore facing the bottom of Baba's foot. Baba would hand Viju a bundle of sugar cane with his right hand, and then lapse into that inner state again. It took Viju just a few seconds to chew the sugarcane before he was ready for another. But since Baba was withdrawn, and was therefore taking some time to hand him the sugar cane, Viju became impatient, and started tapping the bottom of Baba's foot with his trunk. Baba, still withdrawn, handed him another bundle, but told him not to do that (tap his foot) again. But the same thing happened a second and third time. Baba then warned him to stop it, telling him to be patient.

We all began feeling the tension building, and I looked at Viju, and noticed that his eyes were widening. This was a bad sign, and always indicated trouble. Baba was still withdrawn when Viju tapped his foot again. Baba gently raised his right hand, indicating to him to wait. But Viju ignored him and tapped his foot again and again, until finally he tapped it so hard that it knocked Baba's leg off his thigh. Suddenly Baba jumped up from the chair, and holding a short bamboo stick in the air, as if ready to strike, he began shouting at Viju, "Don't you know me yet?"

Viju was huge next to Baba. But for some reason, at that moment, Baba's own stature appeared to have become larger. For about ten seconds Viju stared into Baba's eyes, which were now also wide open. I could tell by the expression on Viju's face that his mind was racing. Tension was in the air. We all stared at Baba in amazement. He appeared completely fearless.

Then, as if overcome by some unseen force, Viju's continence shrank down, and his knees bent low, as if bowing to Baba. Looking at his face and eyes, it appeared that he had suddenly realized who Baba was, and realized his mistake. He looked fearful and confused, and did not seem to know what to do. He bowed his head and kept making low squealing sounds.

The three of us stared at Baba in disbelief. The mahout and I both knew from experience that no amount of intimidation fazed Viju, whether you held a weapon or not. But here was Baba, holding only a short thin stick, which had struck such fear into Viju's heart. This was not simply our imagination. We could all feel the power coming from Baba as something quite

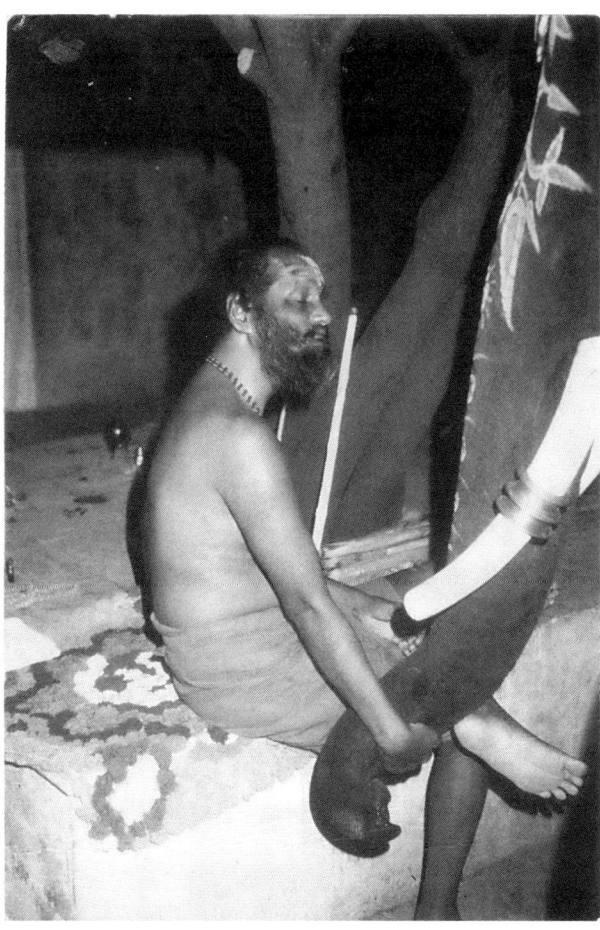

(*above*) Baba and the ashram elephant, Vijayananda.

tangible. And from Viju's reaction, it appeared he also felt it.

I had returned to the ashram just in time for Mahashivaratri. Baba was going to celebrate it in Ganeshpuri that year instead of Delhi, as he had normally been doing for a number of years. Part of the celebration was going to be a seven day chant.

There was also going to be the installation of a new gold dome cap over the Devi temple next to the ashram. This temple is dedicated to Goddess Durga, the Divine Mother, who is known locally as Gavdevi. The entrance to this temple is off the main road, just in front of the ashram. The temple was very dear to me, and I used to meditate there regularly, praying to the mother for spiritual liberation. I would also pray that she allow me to live my life as a sadhu.

After the Mahashivaratri celebration was over, things started to get back to normal. But it would soon be Baba's sixty-fourth birthday. Although the ashram was becoming more crowded, fortunately for me, Baba still allowed me to remain alone at Turiya Mandir.

With all the new Westerners living in the ashram, more of the upper garden was being developed. New paths were being created, and Baba named the main path, Nityananda-marg, in honor of his Guru. Baba was also traveling more those days, and he sometimes invited me to accompany him. Although I wished to be with Baba always, I knew that was not possible. In any case, I felt that the inner work was more important.

It was soon the monsoon season again, and things became very peaceful in the ashram. Baba was also very busy those days, and would often travel to Mumbai, or some village or town in order to inaugurate a new temple, or a devotee's new business. At the time there was still no mention of when Baba planned to return to the West. Personally I did not care. I liked Ganeshpuri, and preferred to stay there. But I knew that when the time came, I would do whatever Baba asked me. Looking at his horoscope at the time, I felt that the second World Tour would not occur until 1974.

The Karmapa's Visit

Sister Palma, an English lady who had been a long time disciple of the Tibetan Buddhist Guru, Gyalwa Karmapa, the sixteenth Karmapa in a succession of incarnations, had come to visit Baba a number of times. She wanted the Karmapa and Baba to meet, so when she came to visit the ashram towards the end of 1972, arrangements were made for his visit.

Baba had already invited the Karmapa to Ganeshpuri, and now it seemed that he was finally going to come. He arrived on the 1st of January 1973 with about 30 *Lamas*, monks and laymen. The Karmapa and his senior monks occupied all the bedrooms in Turiya Mandir, while the rest slept along the corridors, and in the large hall. For a few days the area looked like a Tibetan colony with their beautiful monastic maroon robes hanging everywhere. And although it was January, they kept all the fans and air-conditioners running, since they were not accustomed to the intense Indian heat. After his escape from Tibet, the Karmapa established his monastery in the cool mountains of Sikkim.

Although I had not previously met the Karmapa, I had heard of him from Sister Palma, who was a friend. And while they were there, I had to look after the group's needs.

One of the Karmapa's four main disciples, who are the designated successors of the Karmapa, also had accompanied His Holiness. I was asked by Sister Palma to show the eighteen year old Regent, Shamar Rinpoche, around the ashram. He was a pleasant young man, and spoke some English. During our walk, we noticed some clouds forming overhead, which were unusual for that time of the year in Ganeshpuri. The young Regent commented that Tibetans considered clouds as an auspicious omen. So I told him that the clouds must have come in their honor.

Baba and the Karmapa met a few times during the day, and

(*above*) Baba and the Karmapa (January 1973).

also exchanged gifts. They spoke about their common tradition, and appeared to enjoy each other's company.

It was sister Palma who introduced me to the Karmapa. I felt that he was a great being, so I went up and bowed down to him. As I was getting up, he said something in Tibetan, which sister Palma translated for me. She told me that the Karmapa had said I was a Lama.

The next day, which was the day before my birthday, the Karmapa was going to perform the sacred black hat ceremony. I had heard something about it from sister Palma, but I did not know what to expect. A raised platform had been erected in the front hall, facing the statue of Bhagavan Nityananda. A chair was also placed in the center of the hall for Baba to sit on. It faced the Karmapa's seat.

The front hall was packed. I was sitting against the back wall, with a clear view of both where Baba and the Karmapa would sit. Soon Baba entered the hall and sat in the chair. Then the

Karmapa took his seat on the platform. Before him was placed a kind of hat box, wrapped in silk cloth. He carefully unwrapped it, and unveiled the black hat, known as the Karmapa's *vajra* crown or thunderbolt crown. He also took out a crystal mala from a pouch, and with eyes opened, and unblinking, he began doing japa with it.

The lamas sitting to his right began chanting in a low guttural sound which reminded me of rolling thunder. At the same time, long Tibetan horns were also played. As the chanting and horns came to a crescendo, the Karmapa appeared to enter into a trance.

Suddenly, my own body started to contract. My eyes, now wide open, became fixed on the Karmapa. The Shakti started to rise up my spine with tremendous force. I could neither close my eyes nor move, but my body was been lifted off the floor. I first tried to control the movement, but it was not possible.

This experience continued for some time. I then began to feel a great inner joy. My eyes were now only half opened, and my vision was internal. While in this state I experienced pure knowledge and bliss.

After sometime, I started to return to body consciousness,

(*below*) The Karmapa performing the sacred *vajra* crown ceremony.

but by then the ceremony was already over, and the hall was practically empty. This was a very powerful experience, and from then onwards, I felt great love and respect for the Karmapa.

The Karmapa and his group were scheduled to leave for Mumbai just after lunch. As they were about to leave, a funny incident occurred. Everyone had gathered at the front gate to say goodbye. The Tibetans all got into their cars, and began to drive off. But just then, the Karmapa's car stopped abruptly, and began backing up until it reached the ashram's front gate. Then one of the Karmapa's attendants jumped out, and began running towards the upper garden, to Turiya Mandir. Before long he was seen running back down, carrying the sacred hat on his shoulder. They had forgotten it.

Baba was also scheduled to visit Mumbai, and he left later that day. He was scheduled to stay at a devotee's home for two weeks. Then in March, he went to Pune with a small group of devotees, and I also accompanied him. We again visited Alandi to have darshan of Jnaneshwar's samadhi shrine.

We stayed in Pune for only three days and then went to Shirdi for the darshan of Sai Baba's samadhi shrine. I had previously visited the place with Baba, and felt the shrine to be very powerful. Sai Baba's presence is very real there, and to this day he continues to bless his devotees.

In April, I went to New Delhi with Baba. There was going to be a ground-breaking ceremony for a new ashram. The Delhi devotees had been asking Baba to build an ashram there for a number of years, but he had always said no. He had finally given his permission.

Meanwhile, the Ganeshpuri ashram also continued to develop. Statues of different saints were being sculptured by different artists, both Indian and Western. They would eventually be placed along the new garden paths.

An Italian girl who had come to the ashram turned out to be an excellent sculptress. Baba gave her the name Chitralekha, a name indicating ones "artistic talent". During her stay she would make a number of statues for the ashram. When she first came to Ganeshpuri, she hardly spoke or understood any English, so I had to translate between her and Baba.

Baba liked her statues very much. But like many artists, she was very temperamental, and so Baba loved to tease her. She would eventually make statues of Bhagavan Nityananda, Hari Giri Baba, Zipruanna, and other saints. She also wanted to make a statue of Baba. Baba however tried to discourage her, saying that he did not want a statue of himself. And besides, he told her, she would not be able to capture his likeness. But she persisted, and Baba finally gave his consent.

However, just as Baba had told her, she just could not capture his likeness. No matter how much she tried, the statue,

(*below*) Baba working on Chitralekha's statue of him.

(*above*) Chitralekha's statue of Baba, the finished product.

particularly the face, did not resemble Baba at all. During his daily walk, Baba would stop at her work site to see the progress. Everyone would comment that it did not look like him. So Baba would make some minor changes here and there, or would add a little cement to the face, and voilà, it looked exactly like him. But the moment he left, and Chitralekha began working on it again, it would immediately loose his likeness. This went on for some time. I would tell her not to make any changes after Baba had worked on it, but she would not listen. Eventually, however, she took my advice, and finally finished it. Did it resemble Baba? Some said yes, while others did not think so.

A similar incident occurred while she was working on Bhagavan Nityananda's statue. She could not get the facial likeness quite right. But Baba would add a tiny amount of cement just in the right spot, and it would look exactly like Bhagavan. In the end, her statue of Bhagavan looked beautiful.

Being mystically inclined, Chitralekha would often take on some of the unusual characteristics of the particular saint whose statue she happened to be working on. She was such a great and inspired artist that her statues appeared to be alive.

I recall an interesting incident which occurred when she was working on the statue of Hari Giri Baba. Ever since she had started the statue, I had felt a strong attraction to it. The statue seemed very real and alive to me, and one night, Hari Giri Baba appeared to me in a dream-vision. He asked me to follow him. We went outside towards the back of Turiya Mandir, where the statue was being worked on. When we reached the spot, he turned and looked at me with a compassionate glance, and then started walking towards the statue, and entered it. The statue then appeared to become fully alive. After that dream, I have always felt his presence whenever I stood in front of it.

That summer's intense heat was finally replaced by the cool monsoon rains. In July we celebrated Guru Purnima with a seven day chant. And a week later it was the twelfth anniversary of Baba Nityananda's *mahasamadhi*. Then in August, about a thousand people accompanied Baba on a three day pilgrimage to Alandi and Pandharpur. This would be my first visit to Pandharpur. Baba however, had been visiting the place ever since his sadhana days.

In Pandharpur we visited the temple with Baba, and after I went off by myself to explore the town. After sometime, I sat near the temple and chanted the Guru Gita. While chanting, I suddenly started feeling pure joy arising in my heart, and at the same time, I found that I had a new and deeper understanding of the Guru Gita.

By then, we all knew that Baba would be leaving for his second World Tour at the beginning of 1974. Everyone was excited, and also relieved, since rumors of his departure had been going around ever since he returned from the first tour.

In October, Baba left for a tour of north India. He first went to Kashmir for a week, and while there he met with Shri

Lakshmanjee, a great saint and authority on Kashmir Shaivism. From there, Baba returned to Delhi, stopping at Amritsar and Ludhiana on the way. He stayed in New Delhi for about a week. While there, he opened the Delhi ashram. Although I had not gone to Kashmir, Baba had told me to meet him in Delhi. From Delhi he returned to Ganeshpuri, stopping at different places along the way meeting devotees.

Baba's Second World Tour

I had already spoken to Baba about what he wanted me to do for his upcoming tour. He told me to return to America and help prepare for his arrival there. He would be leaving Ganeshpuri at the end of February, and so he wanted me to leave by the beginning of the year. Money was going to be a problem for me, but fortunately I had left some money in a bank account, which turned out to be just enough for my return ticket.

I had also asked Baba what exactly he wanted me to do in America while waiting for his arrival. He told me to meet some devotees who were preparing for his visit, and visit others who had invited him to visit their area. He also told me to give some talks on Siddha Yoga. And interestingly, he told me to start doing astrology readings again so I could support myself during the tour.

Since I had been out of the country for so long, I had to re-apply for a resident green-card, a process which took a number of months. But by the beginning of the year, everything was ready, and I left for America. I had planned to visit my family before starting Baba's work. They were happy to see me after such a long time.

I then met with some of Baba's devotees in New York and spoke to those preparing for his visit in California. Baba had already sent word to them about my arrival, and that I would be helping them. I had already met most of these devotees when they had visited the ashram.

The first thing that had to be done was to plan a tour for Baba that would take him to as many parts of the country as possible. People from across America had written Baba inviting him to visit their homes, centers, and/or ashrams. These invitations came not only from devotees, but also from many different spiritual groups as well. We had to find out what was going on at each place, and then decide on whether Baba should visit or not. I was supposed to meet Baba in California when he arrived in April, and give him my report.

It was finally decided that a devotee of Baba's, named Michael, and I would drive across the country, visiting as many places as we could where people had invited Baba. We visited dozens of places. Along the way, Michael or I would give a talk on Baba or Siddha Yoga. Even though Baba had instructed me to give talks, I did not like to do so. Being reclusive by nature, I usually felt uneasy speaking about my personal experiences.

We drove across country in Michael's car. Initially we had no money at all, but along the way we would do odd jobs in order to pay for gas and other expenses. I also started doing astrological readings as Baba had instructed me to do. This helped a lot with expenses.

Baba left Ganeshpuri on the 26th of February. His first stop was Singapore, then on to Australia. He arrived at Piedmont, California on April 13, 1974. I was there to greet him, and was very happy to see him again.

Later, he asked me about the places I had visited, and I gave him a full report. I also told him that there were many people waiting eagerly to meet him. I suggested that some central cities could be chosen, and that way people could come from the surrounding areas. Eventually certain cities were chosen and dates set for Baba's visit.

Before Baba's arrival, I had been asked to be the general manager at the temporary Piedmont ashram. This was to be our ashram for the next month and a half. However, an incident occurred during that period which compelled me to speak to Baba about it. Someone had given me some instructions that were supposed to have come directly from Baba, but which turned out to be untrue. So I asked Baba what exactly it was that he wanted me to do. So he gave me some specific instructions, and then told me to always go directly to him in the future. He said to me, "Remember, you are working only for Baba."

On May 6th, a thousand devotees celebrated Baba's 66th

lunar birthday at the Fairmont Hotel in San Francisco. Baba gave many talks in the Bay Area, and also held a number of retreats in La Honda. Within a week of Baba's arrival, he gave the first of a number of talks to the followers of the Erhard Seminars Training, better known as *est*.

Werner Erhard, the founder of *est* had met Baba in Ganeshpuri the previous year while on a pilgrimage to India. Werner was so impressed by Baba that he had offered to sponsor his tour. An agreement was made that Baba would give a series of talks to *est* graduates in San Francisco, Los Angeles, Aspen, and New York City. Baba spoke at the Masonic Hall in San Francisco to a crowd of 4,000 people.

During his stay in Piedmont, a number of spiritual teachers also came to meet Baba. Many psychologists, authors, and healers came as well. They would come to love Baba as if he were an old friend. One day, Carlos Castenada, the well-known Mexican author came to visit Baba. They spoke together for about an hour and a half. He asked Baba a number of interesting questions about the spiritual life.

During that time, I used to sleep in a room just near the front door of the house. The room was also our main office. At five in the morning, I would open the front door and let people into the meditation room. Baba would often come down the stairs and walk around the room giving the touch to many of those who had come for meditation.

The meditation room was kept very dim, just enough light to see where you were walking. As Baba walked around the room, he would sometimes have me walk along with him. I would watch him very closely as he sometimes touched a person at the center between the eyes, or at the heart center. And at times he would touch the center located at the bottom of the spine (*muladhara*) with his toe.

After being touched by Baba, the individual would often start having kriyas. I had watched Baba give Shaktipat many times in India, but this was a new opportunity. If someone started to have violent kriyas, he would simply call out to them, say a few words, and the person would calm down.

Baba gave a number of programs and retreats during that period. But after having giving Shaktipat to so many people, his body would sometimes ache. I recall one morning sitting with Baba the day after a retreat, and his body was very sore. He explained to the few of us sitting there with him that the Guru has to often take on some of the disciple's karma when giving Shaktipat. As he said this, I began feeling sad that Baba had to suffer from these physical aches and pains, and so I asked him if others could help by taking some of this karma from him. He looked at me with great love and compassion in his eyes, but said that I would not yet be able to bear it. The moment he said that, he gave me a kind of demonstration. I suddenly felt like there was a great weight placed on me. This lasted only a few moments, but I got the message.

He then told me, "But don't worry, I just sit in front of my Baba's photo for a little while, and it's all gone. He takes it all away."

Each morning Baba would go for a walk, and he had asked me to accompany him. There were usually one or two others that would accompany us. These were very brisk walks, which he enjoyed a lot. He would walk in silence most of the time, and if someone tended to be a talker, they would not be invited again. I was feeling very close to Baba at the time, and wanted to only help his work. I knew that he had great work to do, and I felt happy to be a part of it.

In those days I had many responsibilities and sometimes I ran a little behind schedule. One day, about a half dozen people were going to accompany Baba to the home of the Indian Consul General in San Francisco. Although I was running a bit behind schedule, I thought that I still had enough time. I was then taking a shower, which was located in the basement of the house. While my head was under running water, I suddenly heard Baba's voice calling my name, and telling me to hurry. The voice was so clear, it was as if he were standing right next to me.

But of course he wasn't. In fact, no one else was in the basement at the time. Nevertheless, I jumped out of the shower, dried off as quickly as possible, put on my clothes, and ran upstairs. Just as I reached the bottom of the stairway, leading to the second floor, Baba started coming down the steps. When he reached the bottom of the stairs, he stopped next to me, and looked at me with a smile and said, "I see that you can also hear very well."

Meditation Revolution

In June. the tour moved south to Pasadena, California, where we stayed for a month. While in Pasadena many people from the entertainment industry came to meet Baba. Before leaving India, he had said that he was going to start a meditation revolution, *"For the happiness and progress of mankind."*

Looking at the tour so far, it seemed to me that this prophecy was already coming true. In the Bay Area, Baba had given Shaktipat to many people, and gradually his family began to expand, even though he would call it Nityananda's family. Daily programs were held during the month we were in Pasadena, as well as a few retreats at the Cottontail Ranch.

Los Angeles was actually the first stop of Baba's tour, which would take him to many cities across the country. In the next few months he would visit Aspen, Denver, Oklahoma City, Dallas, and many other cities. The sense of the 'ashram' was always with us, except now it was on the road. We continued with our daily programs wherever we were.

Many reporters and TV interviewers would ask Baba what his message was, and he would always tell them the same thing:

> *Meditate on your own inner Self*
> *Honor your Self*
> *Worship your Self*
> *Understand your Self*
> *God dwells within you as you.*

This was Baba's message to the world. A very simple but profound statement. Some understood this to mean that he was speaking about some type of ego trip, or personality worship. Those people obviously did not know Baba. There is an interesting story told in the Chandogya Upanishads which illustrates how one can misinterpret this teaching.

Once Indra, the king of the gods, and Vairochana, the lord of demons, independently had decided to go and meet Guru Prajapati. They were interested in knowing about the mysterious inner Self known as the *Atman*, and which they had heard was without disease and death. Prajapati told them that the person seen in the eye was the Atman. He then asked them to adorn themselves, and look at their reflection in the mirror, and told them that that which they saw was the Atman.

After receiving this instruction, the two started back home. Now Vairochana, following Prajapati's advice, saw the reflection of his own body in the mirror. So he began to worship the body as the Atman, and indulged in all types of sense pleasures.

Indra also followed the advice and saw his own body reflected in the mirror, but a doubt arose in his mind on how this perishable body could be the imperishable Atman. Having this doubt, he returned to Prajapati for further instructions. Prajapati then told him that the person in the dream state was the Atman, for even if the physical body was hurt, the dream body was not.

Indra thought about this, but was still not satisfied. He reasoned that it may be true that when the physical body was hurt, that the dream body did not have to be. But he still may suffer from some dream experience. For example, when a man is dreaming that he is being beaten by thieves or attacked by wild animals.

After voicing his doubt, Prajapati told Indra that the person in the deep sleep state was the Atman. But Indra again was not satisfied with the answer and said, "The person in deep sleep, being unconscious knows nothing, and so he is not a master of himself, Besides, even deep sleep comes to an end."

Prajapati then told Indra that the Atman, the witness of all, was beyond the deep sleep state. "It is bodiless, unattached, and beyond the reach of pain and pleasures," he told Indra. Indra finally understood.

Here, Indra represents the true seeker, and the quality of purity. He not only listens to the Guru's instructions, but also contemplates their meaning, until finally he arrives at the truth of the matter. Vairochana, on the other hand, symbolizing inertia and ignorance, does not bother to look past surface appearance. There is an ancient adage for seekers. And that is: First receive instructions from a true Guru, then contemplate those instructions, and finally realize its truth within yourself. Only if all three of these factors come together can one realize the true inner Self. Otherwise not.

Travels Across The U.S.

After Los Angeles, Michael and I were scheduled to travel to the south-eastern part of the country, specifically the states of Georgia and Florida. There were a number of invitations from these areas, and Baba wanted to visit them during the winter months. So we went to see what needed to be done. Meanwhile, Baba would be traveling towards New York City, stopping at different places along the way. He would reach New York in about two months.

Michael and I planned to first visit Atlanta, Georgia. But along the way we would also stop in Oklahoma City. We had already visited Oklahoma City, and had made arrangements for a retreat in the area. Baba was scheduled to arrive there in a few weeks, and he had told me that I should attend.

But we first had to go to Atlanta. In Atlanta Baba was going to be the guest of Mr. and Mrs. James Starnes. Their daughter, Bonnie Rama, had spent a few years in Ganeshpuri with Baba, and had asked them if they would be his host in Atlanta. Mr. Starnes was a mortgage banker, and somewhat conservative, but they were enthusiastic about Baba's visit. Michael and I stayed in their beautiful home while we were in Atlanta making arrangements for a retreat site. We also looked at a few large halls where Baba could give lectures in the city.

Our hosts were very kind to us and gave us all the help we needed. We went over the ideas we had for Baba's visit, and listened to their plans for renovating their basement so that it could be used as a large *satsang* and meditation room. We all agreed that that would be wonderful. We could see their enthusiasm at Baba's expected visit, especially Mrs. Starnes.

Unfortunately, one day when we were home alone, Michael managed to set off their alarm system not once, not twice, but three times. This exasperated the local police who had to come out each time.

But before long it was time for the retreat in Oklahoma City, scheduled for the first week of September. Michael and I left Atlanta and drove there, arriving the day before Baba. We went to the retreat site, which was located just south of the city, to make sure everything was ready. All the arrangements had been made by some devoted local seekers, who had invited Baba to visit them. We had first met them during our trip to California before Baba's arrival.

The next day Baba arrived, and inaugurated the start of the retreat. I was very happy to be with him again. Since I knew that I would not see him for almost two months after this retreat, I took full advantage of the opportunity to be with him.

Baba was also very affectionate towards me during the whole retreat. One day, he came out of his room alone, and told me to follow him. He told me to bring a chair. We walked into the woods some distance, until we reached a small clearing, where he stopped. I set the chair down for him to sit on, but first I placed my folded woolen meditation shawl on the seat. He sat down and told me to do the same. I sat on the ground just next to the chair. He did not say anything, but I soon started feeling a deep inner calm. In a few moments I began to feel a pure joy and love arising within my heart. And I felt completely intoxicated.

The feeling of intoxication continued for some time. But after awhile, Baba began speaking to me. At first it was nothing very important, but as I started returning to normal consciousness, he gave me some specific instructions about the tour. The whole experience lasted for about thirty-five minutes, at which time Baba got up and we returned to the hall. My mind was still very calm, and I remained in an intoxicated state of consciousness for a number of hours.

An interesting incident occurred during the Oklahoma City retreat. Since Baba had told me to do astrology readings, I had to get a small tape recorder so that the readings could be taped. I also had a small tape collection of Indian music.

Besides tapes of Baba's chants, I also had a tape by Hari Om Sharan — a singer-musician devotee of Baba's, who had become a successful singer of devotional songs. I had tapes of Panalal Ghosh playing the flute; some Tukaram Abhangas sung by Bhimsen Joshi; a Jalota tape; a tape with Pundit Surendra Rao singing *Jogi Mata Ja* — meaning "Yogi, don't go," — a favorite of Baba's; and a few other tapes.

One day, while Baba was sitting outside, he called me over. I happened to have the tapes with me in a bag I was carrying. I went over and bowed to Baba and sat down. He noticed the tapes in the bag, and asked which tapes I had. I showed him, and played some for him. Seeing all of them, he began saying Waa! Waa!

He told me that I had an excellent collection, and wanted to play some of the tapes during the *darshan* period — a time during the program when people would go up and meet Baba personally. I said that would be wonderful, and I made him copies of the tapes. From that day onwards, a number of those tapes became the background music during every *darshan* period. As time went by, and I became more familiar with the singers he liked, I would add to his audio collection. And whenever I was in New York City, I would go to music stores, and look for recordings of Indian music that he may enjoy.

After the retreat, Michael and I once again returned to Atlanta. We finished our work there in a few weeks and then left for Gainesville, Florida. This is a university town and some devotees were working very hard to get Baba to visit the town. We found that there was a lot of enthusiasm, and there were many people that wanted to meet Baba. So we made arrangements for a retreat to be held there. That retreat would in fact become the largest of the whole tour.

From Gainesville we traveled to Miami to see what was going on down there. Baba had told me on a number of occasions that he wanted to visit Miami. We found that there were many people who wanted to meet Baba and who wanted him to visit.

We therefore made arrangements so that when the visit was finalized, everything could be set in motion more easily. Since this was not going to occur for another few months yet, we would have to wait, and send someone down to Florida later that year to organize things.

While in Miami, we met many people who kindly offered their services in preparing for Baba's visit. I found that Baba was being welcomed by a variety of people, even those who followed other teachers. Michael and I experienced this everywhere we went. A number of spiritual teachers had visited Baba in Piedmont, and had become very friendly with him. Because of this, help was coming from many directions.

Throughout this advance work, I never felt like I was personally accomplishing or doing anything through my own efforts. I always felt that everything was being done by Baba through the divine Shakti. It was that Shakti which was arranging everything. This was not my imagination. I had many practical experiences of its truth. I would see that divine Shakti working through different people, who would suddenly appear and offer their service.

Sometimes I would enter the state known as *Guru-bhava*. This is a divine mood or feeling in which one's normal self-awareness is replaced by the personality and characteristics of one's own Guru, down to the smallest detail. This *bhava* is not mere mimicry of the Guru's mannerisms, but arises spontaneously due to the Guru's grace. It is not only a psychological change which occurs, but also a physical one as well. The disciple may walk or make gestures similar to those of his Guru. All this occurs through the unfoldment of the divine inner Shakti. At such times one experiences great joy, and has the full awareness of unity consciousness with his Guru.

Before long it was time to leave Miami for New York City, where we would join Baba. He was scheduled to arrive on October 6th from Ann Arbor, Michigan. While in Ann Arbor, he once again met with the Karmapa, who happened to also be touring the country.

By that time Michael and I really missed Baba, and so we were happy to be on our way. In New York, a four-story brownstone building had been rented. It was located on West 91st Street, between West End Avenue and Riverside Drive. This was to be our ashram for the next couple of months.

Since space was limited, I cleaned out a small room in the basement next to the boiler room, and lived there alone. It was an unfinished basement and there were dozens of pipes crisscrossing the walls and ceiling. But I did not mind it. It was very quiet. Hardly anyone ever came down there. I thought it was a perfect place for meditation and solitude.

However, there was a small financial problem. All the money that I had made from astrology readings had been used for our travel expenses. I now had absolutely no money left. I thought that since Baba had told me to do astrology readings to support myself, that perhaps I should rent a small room somewhere outside the ashram, where I could see clients privately. The basement would obviously not be inappropriate.

One day I had an opportunity to speak to Baba about this. I asked him what he wanted me to do next. He first gave me some instructions on what I should do in the ashram. I then asked him about the astrology, and what did he think about the idea of my getting a room outside the ashram?

When he heard this, he looked at me with shock and surprise and said, "What? Why do you need to go out of the ashram for a room? Use this room here for your readings."

At the time we were in the *Namastai* room. This was a room used only by Baba to privately meet visitors. His generous offer just hit me right in the heart, and tears started to slowly flow down my cheeks. When Baba saw this, he smiled and stroked my cheeks gently, and wiped my tears with his hand. He then jokingly said that now I would have to raise my prices since the *Namastai* room was a place that many people wanted to sit in. Any place that a Siddha stays at for sometime is considered to be charged with his spiritual energy.

I soon began doing more astrology readings. Baba also began sending people to see me. He would also ask me to fix auspicious dates and times for certain events. For me, our stay in New York was a very happy one.

Many people came to meet Baba, and as usual, other spiritual teachers would also visit him. This was not unusual because even in India Baba was recognized and respected as a great spiritual master, who had the ability to give Shaktipat. Once the great saint Zipruanna, while blessing Baba said, "Your fame will touch the skies." This prophetic statement was certainly coming true.

One day Ram Dass came to see Baba. Baba invited him to stay for awhile, but Ram Dass gave some feeble excuse on why he could not stay. Ever since his experience with Baba in south India, I had noticed that he kept his distance from him. He appeared particularly fearful of being alone with Baba.

After awhile Baba got on the elevator, which would take him up to his room. He was standing in the elevator alone, and before the door closed he again invited Ram Dass to accompany him upstairs. Ram Dass again declined. But just as the elevator doors were about to shut, Baba grabbed Ram Dass' arm, and pulled him onto the elevator with him. As the door closed behind him, everyone who was standing there began to laugh. About ten minutes later, the elevator came back down with Ram Dass, who was now wearing a new sweater and hat.

There was a new program that Baba had recently started, called the 'Intensive.' This was a two-day program, usually held on weekends. It included chanting, lectures, and lots of meditation. It was during the Intensive that Baba would formally give Shaktipat. It was not as if that was the only time that he gave Shaktipat, but those programs were specifically designed to be what its name implied, two very powerfully *intense* days. They became very popular and more and more people started to attend. There were also free daily programs as well.

People had strange ideas about Shaktipat. Some thought that they could simply make an appointment to see Baba, and he would give them Shaktipat as if it were a piece of fruit. One day I was riding down the elevator with Baba. As we got off, the phone rang in the corridor. Baba told me to answer it, which I did. It was a man on the other end, who told me that he wanted to make an appointment to come and receive Shaktipat the next morning at 10 a.m.. He said that it had to be at exactly 10 because he had an important business appointment at 10:30.

"Who is it?" Baba asked me.

I told him what the man had said.

"Tell him, why bother wasting his time coming here?" Baba said smiling. "I can give him Shaktipat over the phone!"

But then Baba became serious and told me, "Explain to him that Shaktipat is a divine initiation, and he should not treat it so lightly."

It was now December, and we would soon be moving south to Atlanta where we would spend a few weeks. Everything was ready there. The staff drove down while Baba went to Boston for a weekend program. I drove up to Boston with Baba, but I did not stay. I had to immediately turn around and drive his car directly to Atlanta so it would be there when he arrived. Along the way I stopped in Manhattan to pick up two other devotees. We arrived in Atlanta early the next morning. The hosts, and other devotees, had done a beautiful job in preparing for Baba's visit. I knew he was going to enjoy his stay there very much.

Baba arrived after the weekend, and the daily programs were once again started. He was also scheduled to give a number of public talks while in Atlanta.

One day, we took Baba on an outing to the famous Stone Mountain, located about sixteen miles east of Atlanta. It is one of the largest exposed granite domes in the world. At its base the mountain is more than five miles in circumference, and at its summit, the elevation is over 1600 feet. It therefore provided a spectacular view of the surrounding area, including the skyline of downtown Atlanta. On its northern face is the world's largest base-relief carvings of three of the Confederate leaders of the American Civil War: Stonewall Jackson, Robert E. Lee, and Jefferson Davis. The entire carved surface measures over three acres.

Baba really enjoyed the visit. At one point he took my hand and we walked slowly towards the edge of the northern face. He then carefully peered over the edge, hoping to see the carvings.

While in Atlanta, Baba was also scheduled to hold two retreats. Michael and I had found a beautiful retreat site in the mountains outside of Atlanta. I was looking forward to the Christmas retreat.

But that was not to be. As it turned out, the tour coordinator did not follow up on the plans for Baba's visit to Miami, and so nothing was ready there. All the work that Michael and I had done had been ignored. There was no house for Baba to stay in, no hall where programs could be held, and Baba was scheduled to arrive there in just a week's time. The tour coordinator did not really want to go to Miami, and was hoping that Baba would change his mind at the last minute. But in all my conversations with Baba, he had made it very clear that he definitely wanted to go to Miami.

There was now not much time left to make preparations. Then the night before the Christmas retreat was to start, Baba suddenly asked me to go to Miami to prepare for his visit. I said I would go. However, I did feel some anger towards the person responsible for this problem. But when Baba asked me to go, he placed his arm around me, and said with such love and affection, "*Sadhu*, do you mind going?"

What could I say? For a number of years Baba had been affectionately calling me Sadhu. There was so much love in his voice that all I could say was, "Of course I don't mind Baba."

I took a flight to Miami that very night. Baba said that he was going to send someone with me, and I met the person at the airport on my arrival.

The very next morning I started contacting the people that I had met during my previous visit, and by that night, I had found a house in Coral Gables. I first thought that we would use that house for Baba, but later changed my mind. In those days, since we were not yet a registered organization, everything: the house, telephone, etc. had to be put in my name.

I also visited all the neighbors and informed them that we would be in the neighborhood for about two weeks with a visiting meditation master. I invited them all to come and meet Baba. Everyone seemed very excited about his visit, and some even offered their assistance. I also called the tour coordinator and asked that he send some people to help with the preparation.

There were in fact many things yet to be done. Five people were finally sent down to help, and we immediately started working on the house. Since there would also be a few staff members that would be accompanying Baba, I began looking for a second house. I had decided that the house we now had would be used for daily programs since it had a fairly large living room. It would also be where the staff would stay.

Initially I could not find a house for Baba. But then the local Arica students offered their house for Baba's use. However, at first they offered only two rooms of the house, and also wanted to stay there with Baba. Since I felt this was not appropriate, I continued my search for another house. I wanted a house where only Baba and his immediate party could stay in. Keep in mind that we were not renting these houses. I was given absolutely no money by the tour coordinator. The house we already had was donated by a friend of someone I had met there on my previous visit.

Time was running out, and I still had not found another house. But the night before Baba's arrival, the Aricans decided to turn over the house completely to Baba. And through a generous donation from a devotee of Baba's, I was able to find other housing for them.

However, by the time all the negotiations were completed, it was almost 2 a.m., and the house had yet to be prepared for Baba's arrival the next morning. I woke the crew up, and we immediately got started. By 7 a.m. the next morning things were almost ready.

I was scheduled to pick Baba up at the Airport at 9 a.m. I had not slept the whole night, and thought I would rest for about a half an hour or so. I was exhausted, and fell asleep the moment I laid down. However, I began having a vivid dream-vision. In the dream I heard Baba telling me, "Get up, you have some other work to do."

I immediately awoke, and recalled something very important that had to be done. But even though I had only about a ten minute nap, I felt totally refreshed. I took a quick shower, finished the work I had to do, and left for the airport.

The two houses were about a half mile apart from each other. I had wanted to stay in Baba's house, but decided against it, thinking that I should be at the other house in case I was needed. I also did not want it to appear that I was taking advantage of my position.

Only a few staff members were coming to Miami with Baba. Most had already left for Los Angeles, which was our next stop. On the way to the airport, I began to mentally debate whether or not I should stay at Baba's house. But I decided to leave it up to Baba.

Baba arrived by plane from Disney World in Orlando, Florida, where the group had stopped for a few hours on their way to Miami from Gainesville. We had a reception at the airport for Baba. A number of devotees showed up, along with quite a few reporters.

After the reception, Baba came out of the airport and got into the back seat of his car. After I closed the door I sat in the drivers seat, and was waiting for someone else to get into the car. But Baba told me to go. Usually his translator, or someone else, would ride with him, but that day we were alone. Baba was in a good mood, and he was also playful. He asked about Miami devotees and the intensive hall.

After I gave him all the details of the arrangements, he laid back in his seat, and put his feet on top of the front seat's backrest. He placed each foot on either side of my head, and started rubbing it with his toes. While doing so, he told me, "You should stay with me at my house."

I first drove Baba to the staff house where everyone was waiting for his arrival. He went inside and gave a short talk, and afterwards we chanted. At the end of the program, Baba got into his car, and we left for his house. As we were pulling away from the curb, he said to me, "Don't come over to this house anymore."

Little did I know what was in store for me. The next day, the police went to the staff house and told them there was a complaint about the chanting being too loud. The manager of the house told them that they would keep it down. The police said fine, and left. But after the next program, the police once again showed up. Even though the chanting was not as loud, now they said that there were too many people staying in the house, and the programs would have to stop.

Apparently one of the neighbors, a judge's wife, was doing all the complaining. It was someone that I was not able to meet, although I had tried a number of times. Whenever I went to her house, which was right next door, I had the impression that she was inside, but would not come to the door. In fact, just about all the other neighbors had come to meet Baba, and they all seemed to like him very much.

Generally this was the case. Wherever Baba visited or lived for awhile, everyone in the area would come to love him. When it was time to leave, they would always ask him to stay longer, or come again. Baba truly cared for everyone he met, and always wanted to help uplift humanity. Even if he met someone walking on the street he would greet them.

However, there was someone who was obviously being disturbed by our presence, and so we stopped all programs at the house. I made arrangements with another spiritual group in the area to use their hall. The hall was not in the best condition, but it was very large, and would hold many more people than the house could have. So I was very thankful for it, and Baba also liked it.

The owners of the hall were followers of the silent yogi, Hari Dass. They were very helpful to Baba, and had offered their assistance to him with great love. Before the start of the program that first night, Baba and I went to their house which was located just across the street from the hall. Baba gave them a private darshan for about half an hour.

Now everything seemed to be ok. We had a better place for the programs, and we thought that we were no longer disturbing any of the neighbors. I had settled in over at Baba's house, and I was enjoying his company. I stayed at the house all day, and in the evening I would go to the program with Baba. We would also go for walks together near the house. These were very special moments for me. And as per Baba's instructions, I never went to the other house again.

Many people came to the house where Baba was staying, asking for personal instructions. I had also met an astrologer while I was there, and she wanted to do a reading for Baba. So I made arrangements for her to come and give her reading to Baba.

When Baba met her, he told the woman that besides being an excellent astrologer, I was also a good palmist. Baba then handed me his palm, and told me to read it. I pretended to study it carefully, and finally pronounced, "You will become a great Guru, and will travel around the world."

Hearing this, he quickly pulled his hand away, and we all started laughing.

One day, about a hundred devotees accompanied Baba on a boat ride, where we chanted the Guru Gita. It was a magical time, and everyone seemed to experience great joy that day. We had also made arrangements for Baba to be on television during his stay in Miami. He would be on the air for about half an hour with the show's host. Baba answered questions put to him by the host, and even gave him Shaktipat on the air after the man persistently asked him to do so. The man later came to meet Baba again, and told him about the experiences he had after Baba's touch. Many new devotees came to Baba during that time, and I could see that he was really enjoying his stay in Miami.

Meanwhile, the police had gone over to the staff house, looking to serve a warrant. Since I was the renter of the house, and everything was in my name, so was the warrant. When I first heard this, I did not feel any fear whatsoever. In fact, I was a little amused, and felt it was somehow Baba's play.

Baba's translator on the other hand, had become somewhat panicky, and decided to call a lawyer devotee in Chicago. The lawyer said he would look into the matter and call us back. After a few hours, he called back, and said that everything was taken care of, and that he had spoken to the District Attorney's office, whom he knew personally.

The next day, however, a second warrant was issued, and I was given until 5 p.m. that day to give myself up. The translator was once again on the phone with the lawyer; this time he was more frantic. But I was still not worried. Instead, I felt a deep calm. Baba was also being very playful the whole time. That day, about a half dozen of us were sitting with Baba after lunch, when he said to everyone, "Let us see if this astrologer is any good. Tell us," he asked me, "will you go to jail tonight, or will you still be here tomorrow?"

I told Baba that I would definitely be at home the next day, as well as the day after. I said that I would not be going to prison at all, because I had a very powerful Jupiter in my horoscope. However, I used the Sanskrit word for the planet, which is "Guru", thereby given a double meaning to my statement, which Baba understood. He laughed and said, "We'll see tomorrow!"

That day passed, and nothing happened. The next day, while we were sitting together again after lunch, Baba suddenly remembered what he had said the previous day and told everyone, "Oh! He must be a good astrologer since he did not go to jail yesterday, just as he predicted."

Everyone started laughing. Nothing ever did come from the incident, and it was eventually all straightened out.

The Oakland Ashram

After our stay in Miami, Michael and I drove directly to Los Angeles. Baba would fly there two days later. We arrived in Los Angeles just a few hours before I was to pick up Baba at the airport. It was now February, 1975, and we spent that month at a ranch just outside the city.

During our stay in Los Angeles, an old hotel had been found in Oakland, which we decided to lease, with the option to buy. It would require a great deal of work, and some major reconstruction had to be done. After Los Angeles, Baba would go to Hawaii for some rest. He then would fly to Oklahoma City, Houston, Dallas, Albuquerque, and a few other cities before reaching Oakland.

A funny incident occurred one day just before Baba was to leave for Hawaii. Baba had not yet told me where I would be going to after Los Angeles. I had a desire to go to Hawaii with him, but I did not say anything, thinking that I would probably be needed more in Oakland. Then one night, I had a dream in which I was on a walk with Baba, as well as his translator. In the dream, I decided to ask Baba if I could go to Hawaii with him. "No, you should go to Oakland where you'll be needed," he said.

The next morning, while on my daily walk with Baba, we reached a certain spot which reminded me of my dream. However, Baba's translator had been late that morning, and so we had left without him. Malti (later Swami Chidvilasananda) was with us. I thought that perhaps this would be a good opportunity to ask Baba about my going to Hawaii. I thought since the translator was not there, perhaps Baba's answer would be different than the one he gave me in my dream. So I started to ask the question, but before I could finish it, we heard someone shouting in the distance. It was Baba's translator calling out to us to wait for him. He soon came running up the hill, and when

I saw him I thought, "Oh boy, what bad timing."

After he reached us, Baba turned to me and asked, "Now, what was your question?"

Of course I now did not want to ask him, but I had no choice since he had already heard part of the question. So I asked him if I could go to Hawaii. He listened, just like in my dream, and then said, "No, you should go to Oakland where you'll be needed."

There was also another interesting incident which occurred during our stay at the ranch. When we first arrived in Los Angeles, we were staying in a large house. But due to lack of space, we decided to shift to the ranch, which was a few hours from the city. However, since all of our advertisement had given the house's address and phone number, someone had to be at the house at all times in order to let people know where Baba was. There were usually two or three people staying there in shifts.

It was during the last few days of our stay in Los Angeles, and it was my turn to be at the house. For some reason, the night before everyone was to leave, I was asked by the tour coordinator to drive one of the vans out to the ranch. As I arrived after midnight, I immediately went to bed. That night I had a vivid dream-vision in which I was walking to Baba's cabin for his darshan. He was standing outside on the porch. When he saw me approaching, he smiled at me, and then ran back into the cabin. Soon he returned holding a white woolen hat. He gave me the hat, and asked me to sit with him.

When I awoke the next morning, I walked over to Baba's cabin to have his darshan, just like in my dream. He was sitting alone on the porch, and when he saw me, he smiled and got up and went inside. When he came back out, he had a white woolen hat in his hand which he gave me, and then told me to sit down, just as it had occurred in my dream.

After sometime, I was about to leave, but he asked me to stay longer. Since this was the last day at the ranch, everyone was busy packing, and so there was no one else around. Baba's attendant was busy inside the cabin packing. I continued to sit with Baba for about another half an hour, until he went inside his trailer, which was being used as his kitchen.

While Baba went inside the trailer, I decided to clean up the area around his cabin. But shortly, I noticed a man walking towards the cottage. He had caused some trouble in the past, and had been acting extremely arrogant around Baba ever since he arrived at the ranch. He had also caused a scene during one of the evening programs, where he threw a large trunk in front of Baba. He would rudely ask Baba questions whenever he saw him.

Baba did not appear to be concerned, but a few of his disciples became so enraged at the man, that they wanted to give him a beating. Sometimes strange people would come to meet Baba, and a few were clearly mentally unstable. But Baba seemed to always overlook their apparent problems, and would take every opportunity to awaken the divinity within the person. However, the tension had been building, and everyone knew that if Baba gave him a beating first, the man would most likely receive Shaktipat.

That morning, the man walked towards me wearing no shirt, and carrying a dumbbell in each hand. He was about six feet tall, 220+ lbs., and very muscular. He appeared to be very proud of his physique. He asked me where Baba was, and I said that he was busy, and would not see anyone. He said that he would wait. I told him that instead of lifting those dumbbells, he should go and do some service by helping to clean up the place.

Since the area was very muddy, we had built a wooden walkway which led from the hall to Baba's cabin. I asked the man to help me move it. He stood at one end of the platform, and when he noticed my slender physique, he sarcastically said that I should get someone to help me lift my end up. I told him to just be concerned with his own end, and that I would take care of mine.

After sometime, Baba came out of the trailer. The man

started to walk quickly towards him, saying that he had some questions. Baba began yelling at the man, and told me to tell him to leave. I did, but the man refused, and said he wanted to ask some questions. Baba told him that this was not the time for questions, and that he should learn some self-discipline.

I conveyed all this to the man, but by that time he was standing very close to Baba. Baba started to walk towards his cabin, when suddenly, the man grabbed his wrist. At that point, I looked straight into the man's eyes, and told him to release Baba, or else. My full attention was on him alone, and I was ready to strike. The man looked at me with contempt, thinking perhaps that I could do nothing to him. As if reading his mind, Baba told him in Hindi, "Don't be fooled by his (mine) outer appearance. He has great Shakti (power) which you will experience shortly."

Obviously I did not translate this, but at that moment, Baba gave me a signal to be ready, and he suddenly yanked his arm free. At that moment I punched the man in the face. He fell back, and I hit him again. His cheek started bleeding.

Meanwhile, Baba's attendant had heard the commotion and ran out with a large umbrella, and struck the man on the head with it. Baba told me to grab the man and hold him, which I did. While I was holding him, Baba bent down, and took off one of his own shoes, and started gently tapping the man's forehead at the center between the eyebrows. He was obviously giving him Shaktipat.

After awhile, the man appeared to have had enough, and managed to run away. I started to chase him, but Baba stopped me, saying that the man was a coward, and had shown his true colors. From a distance the man called out to me, threatening to kill me.

Meanwhile, some of Baba's other disciples had returned. They felt sorry when they heard that they had missed the action. But actually the man was fortunate that they were not there, because they were all his own size, and could have easily hurt

(*above & below*) The author with Baba in Oakland, CA (1975).

him very badly.

Later that morning the man came and apologized to me. And during one of the programs, he shared his meditation experiences after Baba had hit him with his shoe. As I now look back, I see in my mind's eye a funny incident where punches were flying, while Baba gently tapped the man's forehead, blessing him. What a strange scene.

It was soon time to leave Los Angeles. Most of the staff members were sent to Oakland to work on the new ashram. It would be a huge project. The largest that we had encountered so far. We would end up working day and night getting it ready for Baba's arrival. But in the end, it was completely worth it. We had totally transformed it from a flop house, where people had been known to have been killed, into a beautiful temple where people would be meditating and chanting God's name.

Baba's birthday that year was celebrated on the 25th of May in the new Oakland ashram. Over a thousand people came to celebrate it with him. Also on that day, the Siddha Yoga Dham of America was officially formed. This would eventually become known as the SYDA Foundation.

Many people came to visit Baba at the Oakland ashram, including various spiritual teachers like Swami Chidananda of Rishikesh, and the well known Western Buddhist, Lama Govinda. The whole neighborhood also seemed to be responding to Baba's presence. Many of the neighbors were inspired to paint their houses, and even spruced up their gardens. Soon, the Mayor of Oakland, and other politicians, started to give Baba and the ashram awards for beautifying the area.

The city also provided plants, flowers and trees, and Baba had the ashramites plant them along the road divider in front of the ashram. Many of the neighbors also started to attend the daily programs. During the programs, Baba would give a talk, and afterwards, we would chant and meditate. When that was over, the darshan line would start, and people would go up to meet him personally.

Baba Is Hospitalized

We had been traveling for about a year now, so Baba decided that we should stay for sometime in the Oakland ashram. Eventually it was decided to purchase the building and make it into a permanent ashram.

Things were going well, but then I began to experience a lot of pain in my left arm, and I did not know what the problem was. For some reason the ulnar nerve had become swollen. Although I had gone to a number of doctors, no one was able to diagnose the problem. Of course I had told Baba about it.

Then one day, as I was walking with Baba, he told me that Dr. Thakkur, a devotee of his, would be visiting in a couple of days from India. Baba said that he was an excellent doctor and would know what the problem was. I had known Dr. Thakkur for years.

A few days later, Dr. Thakkur arrived, and Baba asked him to examine me. I remember us standing in the main hall when he examined my arm. It took him only about ten minutes to diagnose the problem. He told me I had leprosy, or Hansen's disease, as it is known in modern times. Doctor Thakkur then went and told Baba the diagnosis. Later Baba called me to his room, and told me not to worry. That as an astrologer I knew that what was destined to happen must happen. But he assured me that everything would be alright.

Within a few days, arrangements were made for me to see a specialist. As it turned out, the foremost specialist in the treatment of Hansen's disease, Dr. Faisal, was in residence at the Veterans' Hospital across the Bay in San Francisco. I went to see him one day and he confirmed Dr. Thakkur's diagnosis. Of the two varieties of the disease, I had the least serious, and fortunately it was not contagious. In my case the virus had inflamed the left ulnar nerve. Dr. Faisal said he wanted to admit me into the hospital right away and begin treatment. So

I remained in the hospital for about a month.

All of this was obviously unsettling, to say the least. But I felt Baba's protection and blessing. After all, I had the best doctor, and since Hansen's disease was on the CDC (Center for Disease Control) list of infectious diseases, all my treatment would be provided free. But most important was Baba's assurance that everything would be alright.

As it happened, during my hospital stay, Baba suffered a major stroke and had to be hospitalized himself. He was admitted to the UC Moffitt Hospital in San Francisco. One day I took leave from my hospital, and went to visit him. When I saw his weakened body, I started to cry, recalling how hard he had been working that previous year. He had given Shaktipat to literally thousands of people, which I knew had taken its toll. But Baba just smiled at me, and told me not to worry, that everything would be fine. He said that nothing was going to happen to him. This made me feel a little better.

He then asked me where my hospital was located. The Veterans' Hospital was visible from his bedroom window, and so I pointed to it. "Good," he said, "we can wave to each other each day." After visiting for awhile he told me to return to the hospital.

Before long we were both released from the hospital. Baba, however, still appeared physically tired, and older. He had always had a youthful appearance, even though he was in his late sixties. He appeared to throb with endless energy. But now he seemed tired, and when he went for his walks, he would often have to stop and rest. At such times he would have to lean on my shoulder for support.

I recall one morning walking around the block with him. After walking a short distance, Baba stopped to rest. He placed his hand on my shoulder, and I began gazing at his face, feeling sad that he had to suffer like this.

He saw the look on my face, and as if reading my mind, he said, "Don't worry, it is nothing. After this is over I will look even younger than before... all of this was meant to happen. Look at my horoscope and you will see it there."

He was of course right. And I knew it was indicated in his horoscope. Nevertheless, it pained me to see him like that.

That period was a difficult one for me as well. One of the drugs used to treat my illness was cortisone. This was mainly used to decrease the inflammation of the ulnar nerve. Unfortunately it had a number of negative side-effects. It made me feel restless, easily agitated, and short tempered. And unfortunately I was going to have to continue taking it for sometime yet.

Something else was going on in my life at that time as well. I was becoming close to someone. Until then, this person and I had only been friends. Her name was Lakshmi, and she was the head of the finance office. Lakshmi and I had been friends for sometime. But our personalities were very different, you could say opposites. Nevertheless, during our travels with Baba, we managed to become good friends. But that is all it was for me.

However, recently our relationship had become somewhat closer. It started while I was in the hospital in San Francisco. She began visiting me daily. I later discovered that Baba had told her to bring me lunch every day from the ashram kitchen on her way to meeting him in the afternoon at his hospital.

I was also aware that my horoscope indicated a destined marriage. And I knew that that time was quickly approaching. This created a deep conflict within me. Until then I had no interest in marriage, or any other type of personal relationships. I had only wished to live a monastic life. I was a seeker and a loner at heart, and had no interest in family life. But for some reason I felt a strong attraction for this person. I tried to resist the feelings, and so they would come and go.

The relationship gave me a great deal of trouble. At first I did not want to speak to Baba about it. I felt I was going against my true purpose in life, and I was therefore ashamed of it. I also had a feeling that Baba would tell me to get married, and then I would definitely have to do so. So I decided to wait and see what happened.

After almost a year's stay in Oakland, a hotel was found in the Catskill Mountains in upstate New York, where we would spend the spring and summer of 1976. This was to be the last stop on Baba's American tour. We rented a large hotel called the DeVille, just outside the small town of South Fallsburg. It was a huge place in comparison to the Oakland ashram, but it would soon become overcrowded.

I was still taking medication for the inflamed nerve, and I was still feeling restless and agitated. I had a lot of work to do during that time. Baba had told me to arrange for everyone's flight back to India, as well as getting visas for everyone on the staff. He told me that we would be in India for a few years, and wanted to get long term visas for those returning with him. So, after all of my own difficulties with visas, here I was trying to get long term visa's for about two or three hundred people. I was also doing full time astrological counseling in order to pay for my ticket to India. I had been doing readings all along, and Baba kept sending more and more people to see me. He also told me to bring my astrology books with me to Ganeshpuri because he wanted me to teach astrology there.

I was negotiating with Air India not only for the upcoming flight, but for future flights as well. But in the middle of the process, one of Baba's attendants decided to get involved, and accepted the airline's proposals without any further negotiations, nor did he speak to me first. Fortunately I had already made certain agreements with the airlines for the upcoming flight.

But then one day, Baba called me to his room to explain to him what was going on. Unfortunately, the very same person who had made the agreement behind my back was also going to be the translator at the meeting. When translating, he would only convey his own ideas to Baba, and would not translate my views. As my Hindi was never perfect, Baba kept asking him to translate what I had said. But I could tell that he would translate only a portion of what I said. As I heard this over and over again, it infuriated me. I became very angry, and shouted at the translator, forgetting for the moment that I was standing before Baba.

This had never happened to me before. I would have never thought of doing such a thing in front of Baba in the past. But still feeling angry, I left Baba's house, and went to my room. Baba had not said anything to me either way, leaving me feeling frustrated about the whole thing. But soon word came that Baba wanted to see me again. I went back to his house and was asked to wait by his attendant. It was torture. My mind was running at full speed, trying to figure out what Baba would say.

Finally, I was called into his room, and I went and prostrated before him. I then sat down in front of him. He first started scolding me, saying that I should not lose my temper, and that I should always remain calm. He then said that I should hand over the airline work to another person, and that I should just take care of the visas, plus a few other things that I was doing at the time. I was still angry when I left Baba, but I did what I was told. In fact, I took his command as a blessing, and felt it was one less headache.

The summer was passing quickly and thousands of people had come to the DeVille to meet Baba. The area was very beautiful and when time permitted, I would go for long walks in the woods, and along the nearby lake.

Not long after we had settled at the DeVille, an interesting incident occurred. Ron Friedland, a Chicago lawyer who had become Baba's devotee the previous year, was flying his private plane to New York to visit Baba. Lakshmi and I were sent by Baba to the local airport to pick him up. Ron had made many trips and loved to fly, but for some reason, Baba had told him on the phone that he should not fly the plane himself that day. We would soon discover the reason.

Although I had met Ron a number of times, I did not know

him very well. When his plane arrived, and he was getting off he said, "I'm having a heart attack. Take me to the nearest hospital."

We immediately rushed him to the hospital. After checking him in, we returned to the ashram, and Lakshmi and I went to Baba's house to report what had happened. It was late, and Baba's attendant said that Baba was already asleep, and should not be disturbed. We told him that Ron had a heart attack and felt that Baba would want to know. When we opened the door to his bedroom, to our surprise, we saw Baba sitting on his bed fully dressed, including socks and slippers. He was obviously waiting up for us.

After telling him everything that had happened, he asked me if I had looked at Ron's horoscope. I said I had not, and told him that he consulted another astrologer. Baba told me to get his birth data and prepare his chart, and let him know what I saw. Baba himself had some knowledge of astrology, but he would often ask me to look at a person's horoscope.

After getting Ron's birth data, I went to my room and prepared a chart for him. At the time, Ron was not even thirty-five years old. I immediately noticed that he was under some powerful afflictions, and death could not be completely ruled out. But after studying the chart more carefully, I felt that there was also a powerful protection in his life, and so I concluded that death would definitely not occur at that time, and that he would recover.

Meanwhile, the astrologer that Ron had been seeing came to visit me, and we discussed the chart. He told me that he was certain Ron was going to die and had already told his wife and Baba. After listening to the reasons for his conclusion, I told him what I thought, and why death would definitely not occur. Just as we were having this conversation, Amma came to see me, and wanted to know what I had found in Ron's chart. I told her that I felt Ron would be all right, and would recover soon. I said that he would be protected, and that he had some years left in his life. Amma said that Baba had just told her the exact same thing, and also said that he was going to be all right. Amma then went to tell Baba what I had said.

Meanwhile Ron's wife had returned from the hospital in a state of depression. The doctors had told her that Ron would not make it, and to get his affairs in order. They further told her that even if by some miracle he did recover, he would be an invalid.

But that night Baba sent her to see me. I spoke to her for some time, telling her not to worry. I reassured her that no matter how it appeared then, and even with the dire predictions made by the doctors, Ron's condition would soon change, and he would begin to recover. After our conversation she appeared to feel better. The next morning, as she was leaving for the hospital, I reminded her to have faith, that God had still some more work for Ron to do.

However, when she returned that evening, she was again depressed, having had to listen to the conclusions of the doctors. They were convinced that he was not going to make it. And she again came to see me. This went on for a few days, but finally Ron started to recover, and was eventually released from the hospital. In fact, he would go on to perform a lot of service for Baba.

In my conversations with Baba about Ron's chart, or anyone's chart for that matter, I felt that the discussions were always for my benefit. I never felt that I was actually revealing some information to Baba that he did not already know intuitively. In fact, I felt that whatever knowledge I had of astrology was due to his blessing.

As the summer progressed, and we were getting closer to our departure from America, I still had not spoken to Baba about my relationship with Lakshmi. But by then he had already heard about it. Finally, one day when I was in his house, I brought up the subject. I felt very nervous. In my heart of hearts I did not want to get married, however, I could not deny my feelings. My revelation did not seem to bother Baba at all. He told me not to worry about it, but to wait, and if I wanted to get married, I could do so in India. I told him that I was not sure that I wanted to get married, and he said, "Don't worry, what is supposed to happen will happen."

After our conversation, he got up and started for the *Namastai* room, where he was going to meet a well-known healer from Boston. He asked me to accompany him, and we walked across the field to the main building. When we reached the *Namastai* room, I sat down next to Baba's chair. The healer began a conversation with Baba. And after sometime, the man said that he had heard that Baba had diabetes, and said that he could heal him.

Baba told him that his disease could not be healed, but he added, "This person," pointing to me, "has some illness in his arm. Heal him!" The next thing I knew, I was lying on the floor with the man stretching and pulling on my arm. He then turned me over and started massaging and rubbing it. Meanwhile, I could see Baba quietly slipping out the door.

Our stay at the DeVille was a very productive time for Baba's work. Many people who were not going to India spent the whole summer with him. They knew that they would not see him for a number of years unless they visited him in Ganeshpuri. We held many Intensives, and by the end of the summer, the hall was absolutely packed every night. The last two Intensives accommodated 1,000 people each, and had been sold out since the beginning of summer.

In July, we celebrated Guru Purnima, and *Time* and *Newsweek* magazines both did articles on Baba, and the weddings that were performed at the ashram.

Ram Dass and other well known spiritual teachers came to visit Baba as well. There were also a few humorous moments as well. One day, a well known female teacher at the time told Baba that she had wanted to go into the lake to swim with the others, but that she was afraid that she would kill the fish.

"How?" Baba asked in surprise.

She explained to him that her body produced a great deal of heat, and that it would make the water boil, thereby killing all the fish. She told Baba that this had happened to her before in her bathtub.

With a smile on his face, Baba told her that under the circumstances, she should not go into the water. However, he advised her not to mention the reason to anyone else, because, he said, they would not understand.

By that time Baba had fully recovered from his illness, and he did look much younger, just as he had told me in Oakland. He had recovered his full strength, and was once again very active. He also enjoyed the area we were in, and told me that he wanted to return to that place again.

Return To India

It was soon time for me to leave for India. Baba was sending me six weeks in advance with a staff of about fifty people. Many others would be accompanying Baba when he returned to India. We left on the 28th of August. We would go directly to Mumbai, while Baba and about twenty-five others would get off in London, and then travel in Europe for the next six weeks. Baba would visit England, Germany, Switzerland and France.

Baba had been invited by Maharishi Mahesh Yogi to visit his International Headquarters in Switzerland. Mahesh Yogi received him with great respect, and in the traditional Indian manner. He introduced Baba to his students as a realized being who continuously lived in that supreme state of consciousness.

Meanwhile, the staff and I arrived at the Santa Cruz airport in Mumbai. We were picked up by Baba's Indian devotees, and were taken to the ashram. I was very happy to be back in India, and on the way to the ashram I was feeling a deep inner calm. We arrived at Ganeshpuri about two hours later at around sunrise.

We were under the impression that most of the work was done, and that we would only have to help with any last minute preparations. A new three-story building had been constructed to house the new arrivals, but it was far from finished.

The ashram had gone through quite a few changes since our departure. Lots of new construction had taken place, and the area across the road was now being developed as well. I was also shown the new building where the Westerners would stay. Although a lot of work had been done in the ashram, a lot more had to be done, with not much time left. It was going to be a very busy month for me so I got right to work.

I had to go to Mumbai a number of times during that period in order to help prepare for Baba's arrival at the airport. Unfortunately, at the time India was also under a state of emergency, imposed by the Central Government. The atmosphere was therefore extremely tense.

I had to also set up a system with the local government in order to register all the foreigners who would be coming to the ashram. Reports had to be submitted to three different government offices.

During that time, all the ashramites worked very long hours to prepare for Baba's arrival. Besides my own office work, I also had to supervise the progress being made in the new building. It was a project which was supposed to have already been finished. At least that was what Baba had been told.

Baba always taught me to be independent. If I did not know how to do something, he would tell me to apply myself and learn. Once, after our return to India, I needed some typing done. At the time I did not know how to type, so I got one of the ashramites to help me. Then one day Baba came to my office to see me, but I was not there. Since the office was closed, I locked the front door while my assistant was typing inside. Baba knocked on the door and called out my name. Hearing Baba's voice, the secretary opened the door. When Baba saw that I was not there, he left. Later that day I saw him, and he asked me why someone else was doing the typing. I told him that it was because I did not know how to type. He then told me that I should learn how, and again reminded me to always be independent. Because of this, I had to learn a number of crafts while living with Baba.

Turiya Mandir and my old stairwell had gone through major structural changes. A second floor had been added to the building. The second floor would be used for Intensives, and other programs. Even though I was staying in one of the rooms there at the time, I would soon have to move. Baba eventually gave me a small room off the main courtyard, which would serve as my office, as well as my bedroom.

Lakshmi was still in America and would arrive with Baba. I tried unsuccessfully to stop thinking about her. But I missed her, and was for the first time seriously thinking about marriage. However, I was confused about the whole matter. I had spoken to Baba briefly about it just before leaving New York. He again just brushed it off, saying not to worry about it.

But to confuse the matter, when I left his house, Baba gave me a saffron lungi, and said I would need it in India. You may recall that I had decided to wear only white clothing after the cow and lungi incident many years earlier. And Baba knew it. I began thinking that perhaps these feelings would pass soon, and that my path was indeed that of a sannyasi. I was feeling very confused about what to do. I was also still feeling restless and short-tempered due to the medication I was taking at that time.

On October 9th, Baba arrived at the ashram. Thousands of devotees had come to welcome him home. He first went into the temple and had darshan of Bhagavan Nityananda's *murti* or image. Afterwards, he sat for sometime with devotees in the courtyard. And then after awhile he went up to see the new *yajna-mandap*.

A permanent structure had been built in the upper garden at the spot where Baba had held all the previous yajnas. A *Vishnu-yajna* was now being conducted there in honor of his return.

Many Indian dignitaries also came to greet Baba and offered him their respect for all the work he had been done for the poor of India. Baba had built housing for many of the poor in the area, as well as schools, and medical facilities. More projects were also in the works.

During the program, Baba also introduced Werner Erhard, the founder of *est*. He too had come to the ashram to greet Baba on his arrival home. The next day Baba took everyone down to Ganeshpuri to his Guru's samadhi shrine, where we all chanted the Guru Gita.

My Marriage

A few weeks after his return, Baba introduced the Intensive to his Indian devotees. I was still very busy with ashram work, and as Baba was busy with his own work, I did not get a chance to speak with him about my situation. By that time I was seriously thinking of marriage, and thought that if it was destined to be, then I should surrender to it.

One day, I finally got a chance to see Baba, and I spoke to him about my confusion and doubts. I asked him what he wanted me to do. He said that I should get married, and that he would perform the ceremony.

That was not the answer I wanted to hear, but I did not say anything. He told me that I should ask Bhau Shastri, a brahmin priest and devotee of Baba's, to fix an auspicious day for the wedding. Someone who was there reminded Baba that I was myself an astrologer. Baba looked at the person sarcastically, and said that he was well aware that I was an astrologer. Nevertheless, he made it clear that he wanted Shastri to find a date.

After, I went to see Shastri, and he fixed the date for October 27th. In my opinion this was not an auspicious date for a long and happy marriage, but there was nothing I could do about it. The chart indicated that the marriage would be in trouble not only from the beginning, but it would have a life span of only four or five years.

I was in a troubled state, and things were moving as if I were in a dream. I knew deep within that I did not want to do this, but I thought that I should do whatever Baba said. The day finally arrived, and before long I was married. Baba blessed us and appeared to be enjoying the whole affair. He was very happy, while I was miserable. I felt agitated the whole day.

In those days married couples normally did not live together in the ashram, and so Lakshmi and I returned to our respective rooms after the wedding. I was not in a happy mood, and so I began meditating. But I soon began doubting Baba, feeling that he had abandoned me, knowing full well that I did not wish to marry. I therefore decided to leave the ashram, and everything behind. I knew that I would be hurting Lakshmi, and was sorry for that, but I felt driven. I left the ashram that very day for Mumbai without informing anyone. I stayed at a friend's cottage in Juhu beach. I wanted to think this out alone.

The next day, however, Baba sent Lakshmi to find me. Somehow he knew where I was staying. So Lakshmi came to the cottage and we talked for sometime. Finally, we decided that we would give it a try, and see what happened. We both felt that there must be some good reason for it, and that Baba always did things for our welfare.

You may think that having had astrological knowledge, that it would perhaps make things easier. And it did help. But it was still a very difficult time for me. We cannot escape our destiny. In any case, I returned to the ashram. When I went to speak with Baba, he told me that one had to bear one's destiny by going through it. He also told me to continue to live like a sadhu, even though I was married, and that everything would be all right. He then looked at me with a tenderness which only Baba was capable of, and said with great compassion, "Don't worry, you will get everything in this very life." I understood him to mean that I would get spiritual liberation in this life, since he had already told me that once before.

Baba's Illness

In February, just before the *Mahashivaratri* celebration, another plane load of devotees arrived from America. It was my job to get them through customs and back to the ashram. The ashram was now packed with people from all over the world. Baba had also told me to start teaching astrology. And I was still giving private readings as well. Baba wanted me to save money for the next tour, which he said would be in a couple of years. I had also surrendered myself to married life, and tried to continue my spiritual practices, and simply do exactly what Baba told me.

It was also during the *Mahashivaratri* celebration at the ashram that Hari Om Sharan, a long time devotee of Baba's, and a famous singer of bhajans visited Ganeshpuri. It was then that he sang his famous bhajan, *Mastana Yogi*, meaning, "Intoxicated Yogi", which he had specially written in praise of Baba and his yogic power.

I recall many wonderful bhajans led by Hari Om in the early years. Before Baba's second World Tour, Hari Om used to visit the ashram regularly. He would then sing bhajans or devotional songs and hymns for Baba. He would also lead the audience in the chants. He was a great singer, and I found his voice to be very melodious. I would often fall into deep devotional moods (*bhava*) during his performances. You may recall how at the Oklahoma City Retreat Baba had shown an interest in the tape I had of Hari Om Sharan singing bhajans.

At the end of February, once again Baba suffered from angina pains, and was taken to a hospital in Mumbai. After a few weeks, it was decided to move him to a private home at Juhu beach to recover. Baba stayed there for a month, and I visited him as much as possible. But I had responsibilities back at the ashram. Baba gave silent darshan sitting on the beach, while everyone sat quietly in meditation.

I was asked to look at Baba's horoscope regarding his health. Unfortunately there would be some difficult health problems for the next few months. Some feared it could be life threatening. I personally did not feel that that would be the case, however, I saw an extremely difficult period ahead.

All great *yogis* come to know about their *prarabdha karma* (destiny) beforehand. Baba had already warned us that something was about to happen. He had given Shaktipat to literally thousands of people, and it seemed to be a time to burn up any karmic residue the Guru had taken upon himself.

While recuperating in Juhu, an interesting incident occurred. One day a healer came to meet Baba. He was interested in trying to heal Baba's illness. Baba told him to go ahead. With great excitement the man got up, and started passing his hands over Baba's heart. But as he touched Baba, he suddenly started falling backwards, and was given a chair to sit on near Baba. Baba leaned over and started pinching the man on the bridge of his nose, and then moved his hand over his eyes. The man sat quietly, and soon became self-absorbed. Baba then jokingly said, "He is healed!"

Mahesh Yogi also visited Baba at that time, and read a beautiful poem he had written in praise of Baba.

Baba returned to the ashram just a few days before his birthday. There was a seven day *Om Namah Shivaya* chant started, and a five day *Maha-Rudra Yajna*. Baba went to the *mandap* for the fire lighting ceremony. The sacred fire is ignited by brahmin priests by vigorously rubbing two sticks together until it creates a spark. While all this is occurring. the brahmins are chanting vedic hymns.

The *yajna* or fire ritual is a very powerful and ancient form of worship. Yajnas had been performed at the ashram during Baba's birthday celebration for many years. He would tell us that the yajna not only benefited those who participated in them, but were performed for the good of all humanity. He said that yajna also influenced the environment. In his talk that day, Baba explained the purpose of the yajna, and then said that *Rudra* — the deity of that particular *yajna* — was He by whose power he gave Shaktipat. It was He by whose power we meditate. Rudra is the supreme being who destroys all of one's sins.

The final day of the celebration was on the full-moon day of May 3, 1977, Baba's 69th birthday. Maharishi Mahesh Yogi came for the celebration and gave a short talk. However, the day after his birthday, Baba suffered a major heart attack.

He had been telling the doctors for the past two weeks that if only a heart attack would occur, then the angina pain would subside. Later in the day Baba's heart slowed down to almost nothing, and at that point the doctors thought that he was gone. But after some time, Baba opened his eyes, and told the doctors that everything was now all right, and that they should go and have their lunch. After that, his heart and pulse became stabilized. Everyone in the ashram, as well as the ashrams and centers around the world started to chant the Guru Gita for Baba's quick recovery.

Unfortunately, during that time, another astrologer living in the ashram had started a rumor that Baba was going to take mahasamadhi in a few days. Many people, saddened and depressed by his prediction came to see me, and ask what I thought about it. I assured them that Baba's work was not yet completed, and that he would be around for a number of years yet.

Meanwhile, I was very busy registering all the foreign devotees that had come for the celebration. Another plane load of Americans had also arrived at the end of April, and I was now very busy registering them all. These plane loads of devotees had become a regular event.

My medication was still making me restless. Then one day, during a meeting with Baba, I told him that I was tired of taking the medicine, and that I wanted to stop. I felt it had made me extremely restless and short-tempered, and I had had enough of it. I told Baba that I felt that my arm was now healed.

Interestingly, he said that he too thought so. So I went ahead and stopped the medicine.

However, it was not a happy period for me. During Baba's birthday celebration, sannyasa initiation was given to about fifteen individuals. I recall wishing that I had been one of them, and felt sad and guilty that I was not.

After a few weeks, Baba's health started to improve, but he was still not very active. Then about the third week of May, Baba had an unexpected visit from his old Vedanta teacher, Swami Muppinarya. At the time, Baba had been bed-ridden, and so he received his old teacher, who was now about ninety years old, in his bedroom. It was a moving experience. Swamiji blessed Baba, and rubbed sacred ash on his forehead, arms, throat and chest. Meanwhile, with tears in his eyes, Baba wrapped a beautiful shawl around his old teacher.

My Return To America

Baba soon fully recovered from his illness, and once again started to oversee the ashram work. Even during his illness, Baba continued to remind us to look within, and not be concerned about the external body.

It was now almost a year since I had been back in India, and I had to speak to Baba about my American green card. A person with a U.S. green card could not stay out of the country for more than a year, unless they had applied for an extension before leaving the country. Which I did not do. If I stayed out of the country for more than a year, I would then have to give up my green card, and once again go through the long process of reapplying when I wanted to return to America. I had decided stay, but I thought that Baba would want to know.

The opportunity to speak to him arose one day when he called me into his room to tell me that Werner Erhard and Diana Ross were coming to the ashram. He asked me to go and pick them up at the airport. We also discussed some other ashram matters, and just before leaving his bedroom, I told him about my green card situation. I told him that I wanted to stay, and just reapply when we returned to the U.S..

He said that I should not loose my green card, and that I should return to America. I told him that I could go for just a few weeks, and then return, but he said that I should go and stay there until he instructed me otherwise. He also said that I should continue to do astrology readings, and save for the next tour, which he said would start very soon. However, since he did not give me a definite date on when that would be, I was apprehensive about leaving.

Nevertheless, about six weeks later, Lakshmi and I were on our way back to America. I was still feeling anxious about leaving Baba, even with all the encouragement he gave me before we left. I wanted to follow his instructions, and try to live happily. However, I must confess that at the time I found this extremely difficult.

Lakshmi and I moved to California and stayed with her mother. I continued with my astrological counseling. I also continued my spiritual practices while waiting for Baba's instructions. Things were all right for awhile, but I found it very difficult to live a married life. Lakshmi and I were good friends, but we had very different personalities and different priorities. I was becoming more anxious, and I started to feel isolated from Baba.

None of this had anything to do with Lakshmi. She was a good person who had served Baba with devotion for many years. And Baba had a lot of love for her. No, this was all due to my own temperament and the lack of desire for a married life. I was not suited for marriage, and so I became irritable and difficult to be with. At times I would argue with Lakshmi, but later that night, I would have a dream in which Baba would be scolding me. I would often wake up with tears of shame.

Finally, in February 1978, just a few months after leaving India, I decided to return alone for Baba's darshan. At the time he was in New Delhi for the Mahashivaratri celebration. When I arrived I immediately went up for his darshan.

"Why have you come?" he asked me in a somewhat sarcastic tone when he saw me.

"For your darshan," I replied.

He looked at me for a moment, and then smiled and said, "Aah! Very good."

After that initial test, he became very affectionate towards me, and told me to return to Ganeshpuri with him after Delhi. While in Delhi, Baba had me stay with an old devotee of his, who was also an old friend. In fact I had previously stayed at his home.

We stayed in Delhi for about six weeks, and as usual, there were daily programs. Baba was in good spirits, and many newspaper and television reporters came to meet him. He also met with the then Prime Minister of India, Morarji Desai.

While in Delhi, Baba inaugurated the new ashram which had been built while he was on his second world tour. He also had me do astrological readings for a number of his devotees.

By the time we returned to Ganeshpuri, it was almost time for Baba's birthday celebration. The ashram was therefore full of devotees. Baba's health was much better now, and looking around the ashram, I reflected on all that had happened over the years. I recalled the days when Baba used to say that one day there would be so many people in the ashram that there would hardly be any room. Well, those days had arrived.

In the previous year and a half, the ashram had gone through a great deal of expansion. The ashram's name was also changed from Shree Gurudev Ashram to Gurudev Siddha Peeth. Another twenty-five acres of land had also been acquired in the back of the ashram, which was named *Tapovan* — meaning "the place of austerities." Baba had wanted to one day build simple cottages on the hillside where people could meditate quietly. There were now many more plants and trees growing in the ashram, and the gardens looked beautiful.

Baba also involved the ashram in more charity work. He not only built houses for the local poor, a new mobile hospital was created, which would visit different villages providing free medical care. The hospital was staffed by volunteer doctors and nurses visiting Baba from India and abroad. In the previous year, India had suffered from massive floods, cyclones, and tornadoes. The ashram had made large donations for relief efforts.

Baba's birthday that year fell on the 22nd of May, and as usual, we celebrated it with the continuous chanting of God's name. Then, about a month later, he called me to his apartment and told me that I should return to America, and wait for him there. He said that he would be coming very soon. In fact his departure date had already been set for that summer. He told me to save my money so that Lakshmi and I could travel with him.

When I went to see Baba, he was relaxing on a lounge chair. I sat on the floor at the foot of the chair. As he was talking to me, he became playful, and started rubbing both sides of my head with his feet. As he did so, I began feeling a warmth in my head, and I started feeling intoxicated from an inner bliss.

When it was time for me to leave Ganeshpuri, I was reluctant to go. But Baba said that I would see him very soon, and so I packed up and left. Baba was scheduled to leave for his third world tour on the 18th of August. He would first fly to Australia, then to Japan for a week's stay, before reaching Honolulu.

Baba's Third World Tour

I returned to America and tried to live a happier life by trusting in God, and accepting the situation I was in. I felt that I had made a re-connection with Baba, and my spiritual practices continued to progress.

Although I had been feeling some distance from Baba, I never felt that his grace had left me. I knew that the suffering I was going through was due to my own mind. I had to go through it, and so I just had to accept it. Baba told me a number of times that I should see life's circumstances as a kind of spiritual austerity (*tapasya*).

In the middle of December, Baba finally reached the Oakland ashram. He told Lakshmi and me to leave everything and join the tour. We had in fact already completed our obligations, and were ready to go. We had been waiting anxiously for his return. When Baba arrived, we continued our regular work in the ashram. Baba also gave me many opportunities to spend time with him by inviting me to go on walks with him.

The Oakland ashram had been expanded to accommodate more people. When we celebrated Mahashivaratri that year, thousands of people came to meet Baba. Baba also gave a talk at the Palace of Fine Arts in San Francisco. And more than double the hall's three thousand person capacity showed up.

Baba had a gift for describing the highest truths in the most simple language. His talks would be sprinkled with stories that conveyed the fundamentals of the spiritual life, as well as the follies and antics of humanity. As Baba had a keen sense of humor, many of his stories were those of the comical but wise, Mullah Nasrudin. I used to love listening to his stories.

Baba stayed in the Oakland ashram for about five months before leaving for upstate New York. He sent me about a months earlier to help prepare for his arrival. We had just purchased a large hotel in the Catskills, not far from the old DeVille hotel.

The property had a hundred acres of land which included a lake. The hotel needed extensive repairs, but it was such a beautiful spot that it would be worth it. I was asked to pick the auspicious days for all of the important transactions.

Before I left Oakland I had asked Baba what he wanted me to do on the tour. He told me that I should continue doing astrological counseling, as well as some managerial work.

At the end of April 1979, Baba arrived at the new South Fallsburg ashram. When he saw the new property he was very happy. I would often go for walks around the property with him, and he would frequently say how beautiful the place was. He told me that it had all the natural beauty and qualities which makes a place suitable for meditation and worship.

Many of the local people once again came to meet Baba, and welcomed him back to South Fallsburg. One day the town's Sheriff came to visit. He welcomed Baba back to the area and then made him an honorary deputy sheriff. When Baba was given his badge, he immediately pinned it to his hat.

We celebrated Baba's 71st birthday that year. The new ashram was packed with the many people who had come to celebrate it with him. On father's day, Baba gave a talk at Carnegie Hall.

At the time there were about a thousand people living in the ashram. It seemed to just continue to expand. Throughout the summer we had to rent many local cottages and hotel rooms in order to accommodate everyone. We also completely occupied the nearby large TM center, which the Maharishi had so graciously offered to Baba for his use. There were also more Intensives as well. And Baba started to give more in-depth talks during the evening programs.

During the summer months, Baba also had many visitors, some of whom came from India. Ram Narayan, a well known Indian musician who had been to Ganeshpuri a number of times came to visit Baba. He gave a very beautiful concert during the evening program, playing the Indian string instrument, the

Sarangi. Baba introduced the old maestro by saying, "Even if you place the instrument (the Sarangi) in one room, and Ram Narayan in another, the Sarangi will begin to play."

Guru Purnima fell on July 9th that year, and as usual, we celebrated by chanting God's name. Werner Erhard also visited Baba, as did Rabbi Joseph Gelberman from New York, who had visited Baba on a number of occasions. He gave a short talk. That night there was also a fireworks display over the lake. It was a beautiful end to a wonderful day.

When we were in Oakland, a new type of program had been started. Many devotees began bringing groups of people from their respective professions to meet Baba. Special programs were therefore developed specific professions, such as doctors, lawyers, and scientists. These became very popular and a number of them were held in South Fallsburg as well.

Since Baba had visited a number of prisons during his travels throughout America, a program called the Prison Project had been started some years earlier. Devotees from across the country, who had participated in the program by visiting their local prisons to teach meditation, also came to Fallsburg that summer for a conference. At the time there were about 30 prisons across the country participating in the project.

On the 20th of July, we observed Bhagavan Nityananda's death anniversary. A rare film of him was shown. I had seen the film many times, and each time it had the same effect on me. It would produce a very powerful meditation.

On August 15th, Baba's initiation day anniversary, a play about his spiritual life was performed by some of his devotees from the acting community.

In the first week of September, Baba went to Philadelphia, and asked me to accompany him. He gave a talk at the Zellerbach theater at the University of Pennsylvania. This was an interesting experience for me since I had lived in Philadelphia during my youth. In fact, before my departure for India in 1969, I had lived for a short time only a few blocks from where we were.

The day of the talk, I happened to be with Baba in the waiting room along with two or three other disciples. Baba was sitting in a chair relaxing, and was asking me some astrological questions. It was just a casual conversation. But then I noticed him staring down at my bare feet. He then abruptly stopped speaking, and began removing his shoes and socks. When I saw this, I dropped to my knees, and removed them for him.

Ever since my first trip to India, I did not wear socks or shoes. but only flip-flops. This habit continued even in America. After I had removed his shoes, Baba told me that he had noticed my bare feet, and it reminded him of how much he used to enjoy going barefoot himself. Bust since his travels in the West, he mostly wore shoes and socks, saying that he was a "gentlemen Swami."

After his shoes and socks were off, he suddenly started to rub the sides of my head with his feet, as he had done on a number of occasions. As he did this, I became aware of an energy in the area he was rubbing. I began feeling joyful, and also intoxicated by the experience.

When Baba walked out onto the stage that evening, it was in his bare feet. He then spoke on, "How To Unfold Your Inner Power."

At the end of the month, Baba gave another talk at Carnegie Hall, where he was introduced by the well-known actor, Raul Julia.

Miami Beach

Ever since our arrival at the South Fallsburg ashram in New York, we had been looking for a place in the Los Angeles area where Baba could spend the winter months. Devotees had been trying very hard to find a place but nothing was available. Baba kept asking me and Chakrapani, another astrologer who was traveling with Baba, when would we find a place? But no matter how much I studied the charts, I saw nothing in the near future.

As time was running out, a search was also started for a place in Miami. Then one day, while we were walking through the South Fallsburg ashram lobby with Baba, he suddenly stopped and turned to Chakrapani and me. Then half jokingly, he gave us an ultimatum. He said that unless we gave him a date soon, something would happen to us. However he did not specify what that would be.

I continued to study the charts but saw nothing. However, after casting a chart for the time that Baba had asked me the question that day, I concluded that we would be going south that year, and not west. So I mentioned this to Baba. This soon proved to be true. Word arrived that a place had just been found in Miami Beach. Baba announced it to the public on October 21st during the *Diwali* celebration.

Before leaving for Miami, Baba went to the Boston ashram, where he held daily programs. While there, he was also a key speaker at the Fifth International Conference on Transpersonal Psychology. It was also at that time that tentative plans were made for the Seventh Conference to be held in Mumbai, India, in which Baba would also participate.

Baba arrived in Miami Beach on the 20th of November. I had arrived a bit earlier to help with the preparations. The hotel we had rented was about to be condemned. But one would never have known that seeing it on the day Baba arrived. The place had been completely transformed into a beautiful ashram, which was temporally called the Regency Siddha Yoga Dham.

The neighbors were all in shock, and could not believe the hotel's transformation. When Baba arrived, many of them came to meet the man who had inspired such selfless work in his disciples. When he arrived that morning, he was taken out to the roof of the hotel, and as he faced the ocean, he saw a small plane flying overhead towing a long banner welcoming him to Miami Beach.

There was a lot of activity during that time, and as usual, there were many visitors. M. P. Pandit, a well known *Tantric* scholar, and disciple of Shri Aurobindo, came to visit Baba. He had met Baba a number of times before, and had great respect and love for him. Baba asked him to give a talk during one of the evening programs.

At the time, Intensives were cut back to only one every three weeks, and the swamis were giving more talks. Towards the end of January 1980, I was asked to look at Baba's horoscope to see if there were any major health problems in the near future. Fortunately there were none.

That year, Mahashivaratri occurred on February 14th. And since it was also Valentine's Day, ten couples were married by Baba during the celebration.

At the time I was one of the managers. And I was also giving astrological readings as well. One day I was in the office when Baba came in during his morning rounds. He was alone and was questioning some people who were standing in one of the outer offices. When he saw me, he asked me to translate for him, which I did. Everything was going well, but at one point, he said something which I could not understand. My mind became completely blank.

Seeing my hesitation, he suddenly turned to me, and looking straight into my eyes said sarcastically, "You wanted to take *sannyasa*, but instead you got married. Now you can't even remember a little Hindi."

The moment he said that, I felt a sharp pain in my chest. It was as if a sharp instrument had pierced me. The intense pain of his words went straight to my heart. With a choked voice I said, "But you told me to get married!"

Suddenly a smile appeared on his lips, as he quickly turned and walked away. However the damage had been done. I felt awful, and went off to be by myself. He was of course right. I felt like I had abandoned my true path.

Such thoughts made my relationship with Lakshmi even harder than it had been, and I became very unhappy. Obviously this made Lakshmi unhappy as well.

About March of that year I received a notice informing me to be at an interview for my American citizenship. I had applied for it about a year earlier, so the process had taken some time. The interview was to be held in Oakland, California, and so I would have to fly out there for a few days.

Ever since Baba had spoken to me that day in the office, I began to reflect on all the events that had happened in the last few years of my life. I started to become more withdrawn, and I put more effort into my spiritual practices. I soon started to experience very powerful Kundalini activities within me.

Baba would soon return to New York, and in April I left for South Fallsburg. I drove from Miami alone, and stopped along the way to visit my family. I stayed for about a week before leaving for the ashram. Coincidentally, my brother's wife had a new baby that week, and I visited with them for a few days.

Meanwhile, the South Fallsburg ashram was going through a transformation as well. Work was going on in Baba's new apartment which was now located in the main building. The previous year he had lived in a house across the road. This meant that he had to go back and forth each time he wanted to walk around the ashram where all the programs were held.

The ashram grounds were also going through a lot of changes, and there were new statues being made by different sculptors. An artist was flown in from India, and the Italian sculptress, Chitralekha, who had earlier visited Ganeshpuri, also came from Italy to do a number of statues.

From Miami, Baba flew to Boston for three weeks. He returned to South Fallsburg towards the end of May. There were about two thousand people waiting to welcome him. His new apartment was completed, and the lobby of the ashram had been completely redone. The ashram looked absolutely beautiful. But more work was continuing in the gardens. In fact, throughout the summer this would become the main focus in the ashram *seva*.

When we first got the property, our initial focus was to take care of any immediate problems. We would later take care of the general design and appearance of the ashram. Also that summer, in honor of his Guru, Baba named the place, Shree Nityananda Ashram. It also became the official international headquarters of SYDA Foundation.

On July 6, 1980, the new International Fountain Plaza was inaugurated in the ashram by the Chief Justice of India, Sri Chandrachud. This plaza represented the international spirit of Siddha Yoga. Over fifty flags were flying, indicating the countries where there were Siddha Yoga centers.

During the summer, various statues were also inaugurated. Chitralekha had made a beautiful replica of the statue of liberty, which was inaugurated by the town's mayor. Followers of Martin Luther King came to the ashram to unveil his statue. Muni Sushill Kumar, a Jain monk, also unveiled a statue of Lord Buddha. And during that time, Pramukha Swami, the head of the Swami Narayan sect of Gujarat, India, also came with a large group of followers to meet Baba.

Santa Monica

By the end of summer 1980, a place had finally been found in southern California. The ashram would rent three hotels along the beach in Santa Monica, and try to somehow join them into one unit.

I had also just heard from the Immigration office that my application for U.S. citizenship had been granted, and that I would be sworn in on the third week of September in Oakland. This was perfect timing since I was scheduled to leave for Santa Monica within a week's time. I told Baba about the notice and he said, "Good, now you will not have to bother with that any longer."

I drove across country alone, heading for Oakland. I used to enjoy these few days of solitude and silence whenever we went from one place to another. I stayed in Oakland for about a week, and after becoming a U.S. citizen, I drove down to Santa Monica.

The temporary Santa Monica ashram was made up of three hotels in a row, with a large parking lot in between two of them. The center hotel would be used as the registration office, and some of the rooms would be for staff housing.

There was also a private apartment situated in the hotel which overlooked the ocean. It was closed off from the rest of the hotel with a high fence. This would be perfect for Baba's residence. And one of the nearby rooms would be used for the *namastai* room.

Even with all that space, there was still one problem. We had no hall. It was difficult to find a place in the Los Angeles area which was large enough to house all the people, and at the same time have a large enough hall to accommodate two thousand or more people at a time. This was not an easy task, and so the next best thing was to build our own hall.

The idea was to take the large parking lot and transform it

into a temporary temple. But the question was how to do that without constructing a permanent building. The answer was to use a tent. Not just any ordinary tent, mind you. On the outside it was a huge blue and white vinyl tent. But on the inside, a beautiful hall was built. It had a large lobby where people could leave their shoes before going into the hall. There was also a waiting room for Baba, and another room for the video department. Inside, the hall was spacious, with high walls, excellent lighting, and a good sound system. It even had air-conditioning. Baba really liked it.

Baba's stay in Santa Monica was very successful and many people came to meet him. On the night he arrived, the Mayor of the city gave a speech welcoming Baba on behalf of the city.

Within a few weeks, Baba sent for two of his devotees: Bhau Shastri, a brahmin priest, and Dada Yande. He wanted Bhau Shastri to perform the first portion of the sannyasa ceremony for twenty candidates. This would be only a preliminary ceremony, with the second portion to be performed later by Mahamandaleshwar Swami Brahmananda Giri.

At the end of November, John Denver came to visit Baba, and sang for him during the evening program. In December, he returned with Buckminister Fuller, whom he introduced to Baba. They spent some time together, and Mr. Fuller presented Baba with one of his mathematical formulas. Baba in turn presented him with a copy of his spiritual autobiography, *Play of Consciousness*, and told Mr. Fuller that it revealed *his* formula for the spiritual life. John was also an astrology client of mine, and consulted me a number of times during that time.

At the beginning of the year, Chitralekha started working on a life-size statue of Bhagavan Nityananda. Baba visited her daily, carefully watching the progress, and at times even helping. The statue looked great, but there was some problem due to the sea air, and the fact that someone had gotten her the wrong type of cement. And so it began to crack. Chitralekha became frustrated, but eventually it was completed, and it looked very much like Bhagavan Nityananda.

Interestingly, one day I was visiting Chitralekha and I had my Polaroid camera with me. Soon Baba arrived and saw my camera and asked if he could take a picture? I of course said yes, and prepared the camera for him. Baba then took a portrait shot of Chitralekha's statue of Bhagavan Nityananda.

During that period, Baba was also doing a lot of writing, and was working on several books. He had been giving in-depth talks on the *Pratyabhijnahridayam*, a very important work of Kashmir Shaivism. Kashmir Shaivism was no doubt Baba's favorite philosophy.

I also noticed at the time that Baba was placing more emphasis on the *Ham'Sa* mantra. This mantra is referred to as the natural mantra because every human being makes the sound of *Ham* with each incoming breath, and the sound *Sa* with each outgoing breath. It is a very powerful and mysterious mantra.

We were scheduled to leave for India in October, and so I

(*below*) Photo taken by Baba of Chitralekha's statue of Bhagavan Nityananda (April 1981 - Santa Monica, CA).

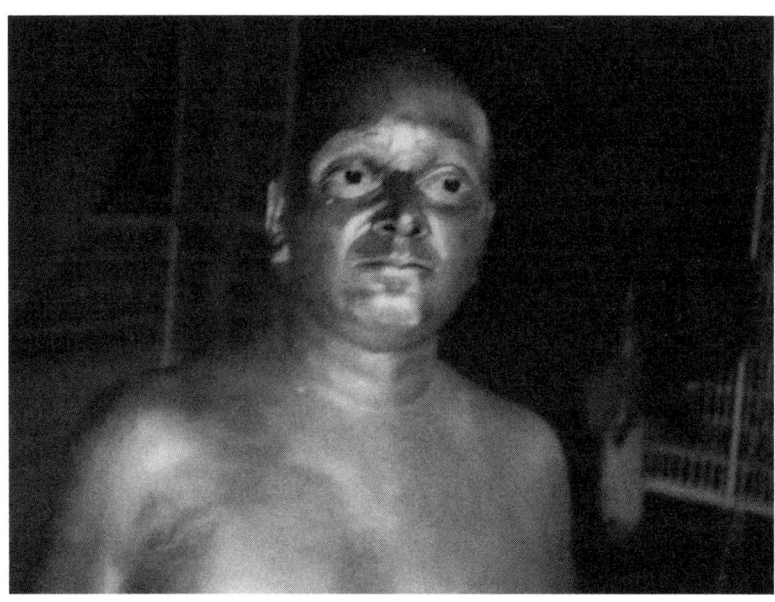

had to start the visa process once again. Baba told me that there would be many more people going with him this time. In the end, there would be about four or five hundred long term visas required. But the ashram had to be very careful with these types of visas since it was responsible for the individual during their stay in India. Because the Indian government had had problems with other ashrams in the past, they were very sensitive to its abuse, and could therefore refuse to issue them at any time.

Unfortunately my personal relationship with Lakshmi was at its lowest point during that time. We therefore decided to ask Baba if we could separate. Two days before Mahashivaratri, I went to speak to him about it. He told me that everything would be fine. But I wanted to know if it was really all right, and not just my inability to deal with it. I asked him if it was really over, or would we have to get back together again?

"She'll come to India if I ask her," Baba told me, meaning on the October flight. But I knew astrological that she was not going, so I said, "But Baba is not going to ask her, is he?"

He just smiled and said, "When one goes into a restaurant, he has to eat the food he has ordered. Now don't worry, it is all in the past."

A week later, Lakshmi left early for South Fallsburg. When I took her to the airport, we decided no matter what happened, that we would remain friends. It was a sad time for both of us.

I left for South Fallsburg at the end of April, stopping in Pennsylvania to visit relatives for a few days before driving up to the ashram. When I arrived in South Fallsburg, I immediately started my work. It was going to be a busy time for me.

I was also going to have to make many trips into Manhattan, visiting the Indian consulate, as well as doing other ashram work.

When Baba arrived at the South Fallsburg ashram on the 30th of April, everything looked beautiful. A great deal of work had been done by the ashramites, both on the outside as well as the inside of the main building. The summer months were very active, and the ashram was overflowing with people. A lot more housing was needed that year, and once again we rented local cottages and hotel rooms.

In June, we received news that Radbrook, a long-time German devotee of Baba's had passed away, as well as an Indian trustee, Mr. Vyasa, who was also a personal friend of mine.

Baba had also recently said a number of time that he would retire when he got back to Ganeshpuri. Although he had said this jokingly before, this time, for some reason I felt it was really true.

And, as if to confirm this, after his talk and darshan at that year's Guru Purnima celebration, Baba suddenly announced that there was one other thing that he had wanted to say. He then told Swami Nityananda, who was sitting next to him, to stand up. People had already started walking out of the hall, but they soon stopped and returned when they heard Baba speaking. Baba then said, "This person will be my successor," and then placed a garland around Swami Nityananda's neck.

Everyone was in shock for a moment, but then people started to applaud. Baba later explained that this did not mean that Nityananda had become a Siddha. But that he was just called to the University, and would have to work for that attainment, and be tested.

Although it was not a surprise to me, since Baba had told me of his intentions a month earlier when he asked me to look at the horoscopes of Swami Nityananda and his sister, Malti, it was still quite a revelation. And it began to confirm my growing suspicion that something important would happen when we returned to India.

Back To Ganeshpuri

I left for Ganeshpuri on October 13, 1981. Baba would arrive a week later. I was scheduled to be at the airport to meet all the devotees when they arrived. I also had some ashram work to do in Mumbai that week. Ron Friedland, the first president of SYDA Foundation, was also doing some ashram work in town, and so he and I would drive into the city together. Major construction work was also going on in the ashram.

On the day Baba returned, many devotees came to meet him. Darshan went on for many hours. I noticed him greeting each and every devotee in a special and personal way. At Diwali, which fell on November 15th that year, Baba held a *saptah* or continuous chant. It was the first to be held after a number of years.

As time went by I also noticed that Baba was becoming more self-absorbed, and it seemed to me that he was withdrawing more and more from ashram activities.

Then at the end of November, we received word from South Fallsburg that Ron Friedland had passed away. He was just forty years old. Baba asked all the ashrams to chant the mantra, *Om Namah Shivaya* for twenty four hours in his memory.

Ron's chart indicated an early death, but the event also had another meaning for me. I immediately began thinking about Baba's own health. I knew that I was about to go through a major change in my own life, as indicated in my own chart, and that things were about to change drastically in the ashram as well. I started to suspect that perhaps Baba would soon take mahasamadhi.

But those days I was kept busy with passport registrations and visa extensions. Planeloads of devotees were always arriving, and it was my job to get them safely to the ashram. I had to also travel to Mumbai quite often for other ashram work as well. In December, two more flights were scheduled to arrive with devotees coming for the Christmas holidays. My work at the airport, and taking care of the visas, became more difficult around that time.

Then about the third week of January of 1982, a unusual event occurred. One day I was standing with Baba in the courtyard discussing some ashram business. We were just finishing when suddenly a large European man walked into the courtyard, dressed completely in black, in total contrast to everyone else who was wearing white or saffron colored clothing.

Baba looked over at him with some interest. He then asked me who the man was, but I did not know, since apparently he had just arrived. The symbolism of the black clothing would take on a greater importance by the fact that the man would be dead before the day was over. We would later learn that he had visited the Devi temple in Vajreshwari shortly after his arrival. He also visited the tomb of Godadia Baba located on the hill just behind the temple. After that, he shaved his head and decided to climb the nearby Mandakini mountain with some friends.

We knew nothing about this at the time, and it was only later that day, when two of his friends returned to the ashram and told me that they thought their friend had had a heart attack on the mountain. I asked them to tell me exactly what had happened.

After getting the whole story, at about 7 p.m., I went to see Baba in his bedroom. After explaining to him what had happened, he asked, "Why did he climb that mountain, did he ask anybody? I have lived here for almost thirty years and never had the desire to climb that mountain," Baba said.

Baba then told me to organize a search party, and go and try to find the man. But by then it was already starting to get dark. Nevertheless, I gathered together a group of about fifteen people. We walked to the base of the mountain and started to climb. It took a few hours to reach the top. By then it was now very dark, but we started looking for the two missing men.

We had been told that a friend had stayed behind with the

man. So when we reached the approximate area, we started to call out, but there was no answer. After searching for a number of hours, and unable to see or hear anything in those woods, we decided to head back down to the ashram.

Two or three people who had previously been to the top of the mountain tried to guide us, but it was so dark that we got lost. And instead of walking straight down the southern face of the mountain, where we had come from, we went down the northern side. We therefore ended up circumambulating the south peak, in what is called *pradakshina*. It was as if we were performing a pilgrimage, or more accurately, a funeral procession for this unknown soul. And appropriately, the moon was waning in the sign of Scorpio that night, a sign specifically indicating death.

From the moment we had started that night, I felt that this was some kind of ritual that we were about to perform. One that was not planned but which occurred spontaneously. As we walked, I started to experience a deeper state of consciousness, and soon became very calm and quiet. I recall it all happening as if it were a dream.

We did not reach the ashram until about 4 a.m. the next morning. We had walked the whole night. A second search party was scheduled to start within the hour. They would eventually find the man dead. His friend had already returned to the ashram and would guide the group to the body.

An astrologer can gather information regarding coming events not only from the position of the planets, but also from the conditions of nature, or some unexpected event. These are known as omens or signs. One has to learn how to read the signs of the time, and lately, there had been quite a few unusual omens.

A week later I received a letter from Lakshmi, saying that she had come to the conclusion that it would be best if we got a divorce. This of course was not a surprise, but it was still very painful news. It is strange how the mind works. This was something which I had wanted for such a long time, but now

I was experiencing some sadness. Fortunately this lasted for a very short period of time. Baba had been very compassionate towards me during that time, which helped considerably. When he heard the news, he told me, "Now you are free to pursue your *sadhana*."

In the middle of February, two more flights arrived. Baba also went to Mumbai to speak at the Seventh International Transpersonal Psychology Conference. He spoke on the nature of the mind.

Many people who had attended the conference later came to the ashram to meet Baba. We celebrated Mahashivaratri on the 22nd of February that year, and on the 25th, Paul Horn, the famous flutist gave a very beautiful concert for Baba and the ashramites. On the 26th, we all went with Baba to chant the Guru Gita at Bhagavan Nityananda's samadhi shrine in Ganeshpuri. After walking around his Guru's statue, Baba sat down and meditated for awhile before we started the chant.

Many people had come to India on one-year visas. One day Baba told me that all those people who had this type of visa would have to stay for the whole year. But as time went by, a number of them wanted to leave early. When I told Baba this, he told me to give those people a hard time about leaving, and try to get them to stay. He even told me not to return the money they had to put down for their ticket home. I reminded Baba that we could not legally do that. So he told me to at least let them wait for it.

These were mostly people who had been with Baba for a number of years, and for some reason, he wanted them to stay. This made my job even harder. Because there were people who could stay, but did not want to, and there were those who wanted to stay, but could not do so because of the type of visa they had.

Winds of Change

One day around the beginning of March, Baba called me and asked about the planetary lineup which was to occur in about two weeks time. The event had been popularized in a book called "The Jupiter Effect." There was also an article about it in the March 8th issue of "Newsweek" magazine.

I explained to Baba that there was indeed going to be a lineup of planets occurring at that time, but that a more powerful combination would occur in the fall of that year, around September-October. I told him that at that time, the planets would be in a much closer configuration, and would therefore be more powerful.

As I was telling him this, I had the distinct impression that the information I was giving him had somehow confirmed something he already knew. And he agreed that the October lineup would be more important.

At the end of April, Lakshmi arrived for Baba's Birthday celebration, along with two more plane loads of devotees. In fact, people were coming from everywhere. Devotees that I had not seen at the ashram for many years unexpectedly arrived. These included devotees from India and abroad.

By then Baba had already announced that he was going to install as his successors Swami Nityananda, but now it would include his sister Malti, who would soon become Swami Chidvilasananda. She had become Baba's translator during the second half of Baba's second world tour. Both siblings had known Baba since their childhood. and their parents had been long time devotees of Baba's.

At the end of April sannyasa initiation was given to about twenty people, as well as the twenty-six from Santa Monica, who were now completing their final vows.

On the 4th of May, a yajna was started, and on the 5th, a *Rajya Abhishek* ritual was performed for Baba and the spiritual work he had accomplished. When a gold crown was placed on Baba's head by the brahmin priest, he immediately took it off, and walked over to Swami Brahmananda's seat, and placed the crown on his head. Mahamandaleshwar Swami Brahmananda Giri, affectingly known as "Maharaj" had performed all of the sannyasa initiations for Baba.

Although Baba could himself perform the initiation, as any sannyasi can, he was a traditionalist, and therefore always had a Mahamandaleshwar perform the ritual. With the exception of the first five sannyasis initiated in 1967, Brahmanandaji had initiated all the swamis around Baba, including Swamis Chidvilasananda and Nityananda. Baba had great personal affection for Swami Brahmanandaji.

On the 8th of May, Baba's birthday, the *Pattabhishek* or succession ceremony was performed. It was then that Baba officially named Swamis Nityananda and Chidvilasananda to be his joint successors. When Baba took his seat, there was a clap of thunder, and rain started pouring down in torrents, which lasted for about twenty-five minutes. This was considered an auspicious sign at a yajna, and everyone began applauding. Afterward, Baba lovingly placed both the swamis on his seat, while he himself squeezed next to Swami Brahmananda on his chair. This birthday celebration would certainly be one to remember.

The previous year in South Fallsburg, around the time Baba announced that Swami Nityananda would be his successor, he had called me and asked me to look at Swami Nityananda and his sister's charts. After I had studied their charts I went back to see Baba. He told me about his plans for them when he returned to Ganeshpuri. Now that he had decided to make them both his successors, he once again asked me to look at their charts and see what the future held for them. Which I did.

Baba had been saying for the past few years that he was going to retire. I had always understood that he did not mean it would happen right away, but at the same time, I could see that he was preparing us. During his talk on his birthday that year, he said that since he now had installed someone on his seat, he was free to retire. When I heard this, my heart sank. For some reason this time it sounded true. And with all the other events that had been occurring, this just seemed to confirm it. I began to reflect on all of this, and I also studied his horoscope and mine more closely. But I was still very busy at the time, and all the work kept my mind preoccupied.

At the end of May, Baba gave his first Intensive in Mumbai at the Taj Hotel. He was definitely more withdrawn at the time, and had the swamis give most of the programs at the ashram.

In the first week of June, I had to go to New Delhi for about a week on ashram business. While I was there, I visited a well known astrologer who had written me a number of times, asking me to visit him when I was next in Delhi. So I went to meet him. During our conversation he started to speak about my horoscope. I mentioned the planetary cycle change which was about to occur, and asked him what he thought the results would be. I voiced my fear that something was going to happen to Guru, and I thought he may pass away. But sometimes it can be very difficult to read one's own horoscope, or even of those one is emotionally close to.

The astrologer studied the charts for sometime, and then said that he did not agree with my interpretation. He said that nothing would happen to Baba for at least another five to seven more years, and gave me astrological reasons for his interpretation. I was very happy to hear what he was saying, but in my heart, I was not convinced. I had seen numerous signs, as well as having studied the charts of those close to Baba. The planet Jupiter has great importance in my chart, and its cycle, which lasts for sixteen years, was now in its final year. This indicated to me that there would be a major change in my relationship with Baba, which to me indicated his passing.

After finishing my work in Delhi, I returned to Ganeshpuri. Lakshmi left a week later for South Fallsburg, and we separated as friends.

For some time now I had been feeling restless, and thought that I was somehow wasting my time. I felt I should be focusing more on my spiritual practices. I had also lost all interest in my administrative work, and I was tired of the often petty politics. I was spending many sleepless nights at the airport, and would rather have been meditating or sitting with Baba. I somehow felt that time was running out. I wanted to return to the simple early days of the ashram, when I had time to fully devote myself to spiritual practices. I felt a powerful surge swelling up within me, urging me to break free. An inner voice appeared to be shouting at me, "Awake! Awake! Awake!"

The Beginning of the End

In the middle of August, I drove Swami Nityananda to the airport. He was on his way to Australia to conduct some programs, and Baba had asked me to drive him. Then towards the end of August something occurred which made me feel completely fed up with being an ashram manager, and all the politics that it involved. All I wanted was to meditate and realize the inner Self. I spoke to Baba about this, and even asked him if I could leave the ashram. I felt like I had reached the end of my patience with everything. I was just not interested in anything anymore. I was not interested in having any position or power in the ashram, and never had been. I wanted to live a simple life and completely focus my attention on spiritual practices. I told Baba that I did not want to leave him, but only the ashram politics. I will never forget what he said to me when I asked him if I could leave. He looked at me with great love and tenderness in his eyes, and told me, "But you have waited so long, and now there is such a short time left."

When I heard these words, I began to cry knowing full well their implication. He told me not to worry, and said that I should sit with him for darshan whenever he was out.

He then asked me to find an auspicious hour for opening a temple, a function to which he had been invited to bless sometime around the 9th or 10th of October. Whenever Baba asked me to do some astrological work, I would often do a quick mental calculation of the planetary positions for the time of the question. This is called Horary Astrology, and is used to predict the results or potential of the query at hand. Interpreting the planetary positions for that moment, I concluded that for some reason, Baba would not attend that function.

Also around that time, one of the office girls related to me a dream she had of Baba, and asked me to interpret it for her.

In the dream, she saw Baba removing a blue sapphire ring from his finger, a gem associated with Saturn, the planet of destiny. He had been wearing this ring recently for some time. He told her that soon his work would be finished.

As she was telling me the dream and her concerns about it, a number of other office girls had gathered around us. As I listened, I felt that this was a prophetic dream, and another sign of the impending tragedy. However, I did not tell the girl what I thought the real meaning was, but instead I tried to console her by simply saying that it did not necessarily mean Baba's passing, but could refer to his retirement.

At the end of August, I went to pick up Nityananda at the airport. He was returning from his trip to Australia. A few days, later Swami Chidvilasananda was going to Madras for a few days, and then to South Fallsburg. Baba asked me to drive her to her mother's house in Juhu, where she would stay until her departure.

Baba was going to give another Intensive at the Taj Mahal hotel on September 11th and 12th. He was scheduled to go to Mumbai on Friday afternoon. I had also been invited to go and attend the Intensive.

For some months, a small group of people had been chanting mantras in Baba's bedroom during the evening arati. That Thursday night, as usual, Baba had prepared some prasad in his kitchen, which he would distribute after the chant. When the chanting was over, everyone moved out of Baba's bedroom, and we were standing in the corridor waiting to go into his kitchen. I was standing just in front of Baba's door. The lighting was very dim, and as Baba came out of his room, he called out my name. I answered by saying, "Yes Baba."

But he again called my name, and I noticed that he had not seen me, even though I was standing only a few feet from him. So I went forward and took his right hand, which he then placed on my chest. He kept it there for a few moments. He then turned to Swami Nityananda, who was doing some cleaning nearby,

(above) Sadgurunath Maharaj ki Jai!
Babaji holding up the cane he gave the author.

and told him, "Give me that cane," and pointed to a corner where there were about a dozen canes.

Nityananda started to pick up one of the canes but Baba said, "No, not that one, the other."

After a few attempts Nityananda finally picked up the cane Baba wanted, and handed it to him. I immediately recognized it. It was the cane that Baba had been using ever since he had returned to Ganeshpuri the previous year. He handed me the cane, and told me to take it in my right hand. He then told me to raise it over everyone who was standing there in the veranda, and wave it over their heads. After I did this, he started to stroke my chest again, while saying, "*Bahut achcha, Bahut achcha*," — "Very good, very good."

He then touched me between the eyebrows. When he did this, I felt a subtle energy enter me, and I became very calm, and yet excited. It appeared as if he had performed some kind of ritual. When he touched me between the eyebrows, he bestowed a great blessing on me. I felt ecstatic.

When all of this was done, he told me to tell everyone to go into the kitchen and have prasad. After that evening, I noticed a subtle change starting to take place within me.

Baba had been very affectionate towards me ever since I had spoken to him. He gave me many opportunities to meet with him. He had also told me a number of times during that period that he was going to give me sannyasa initiation, saying that I now had no more worldly responsibilities. He had apparently told other devotees about it as well. Three or four people had already approached me, telling me that Baba had told them that he was going to give me sannyasa. Then one day, when I met with him, he again brought the subject up. But this time I asked him when exactly would this occur? "I will let you know," he replied with a smile.

I had wanted to take sannyasa from the very beginning, but Baba had told me to wait, that the time was not yet right. Shortly after I had first arrived at the ashram, Swami Prakashanandaji, Baba's elder disciple, had studied my horoscope and seeing the sannyasa-yoga it contained, decided on his own to ask Baba to give me sannyasa initiation. But in those early days, Baba did not give sannyasa so readily. In fact, at the time, he had given sannyasa initiation to only five people in the history of the ashram. So when Swamiji asked on my behalf, Baba told him that it was not yet time for me, because apparently I had other work yet to do. I recall Baba saying to me, "As an astrologer, you know that everything occurs at the right time, so be patient.

I will give you sannyasa."

Although he was not an astrologer himself, Baba intuitively had the ability to see a person's destiny. And having studied astrology, I knew the significance of his statement very well. Everything does occur at its destined time, and not before. I therefore never asked him again to give me sannyasa.

However, the subject was now being brought up by Baba himself. Over the years I had realized that it is not the outer dress which makes one a sannyasi, but inner detachment. I came to believe that if it was my destiny, then it would happen naturally. And if it was not meant to happen, it did not matter. I felt that true sannyasa was not attained by simply dying one's clothes a particular color. It is the heart which has to be dyed with the color of renunciation. And with that attitude, I tried to live my life as an inner sannyasi, by maintaining a sense of detachment under all circumstances.

The next day a number of ashramites, including myself, went to Mumbai and prepared for the Intensive at the Taj hotel. The Intensive was very powerful, and I was happy that I had the opportunity to attend.

On Monday, the 13th of September, Baba flew to Kashmir for a two week stay. While there, he again met with Swami Lakshmanjee, who is recognized as a genuine master of Kashmir Shaivism, and was also considered a great Saint. Baba also visited a number of places, including the famous rock on which the *Shiva Sutras* are believed to have been revealed to Vasugupta Acharya.

On the 26th, Baba returned to Ganeshpuri. After that, I noticed that Baba was giving special attention to everyone that went to meet him. There were people that had been with him for many years but with whom he had rarely spoken. But now they were getting special attention from him. He appeared like a father about to depart and was now giving something to each one of his children.

Baba's Mahasamadhi

On the 1st of October, a Friday, I had to go to the American Consulate in Mumbai and pick up Baba's green card extension papers. An extension had already been applied for in America, and I had to just pick up the certificate. I was also going to take someone to the airport the next morning at around 4 a.m., and so I booked a room at the hotel.

That morning I went to the American consulate and took care of Baba's passport and paper work. After, I had a lunch engagement with one of the American counselors. She was a very nice person and had come to the ashram to meet Baba with a number of other consulate staff. After lunch, we were talking casually when out of the blue she asked me if someone close to me had ever died. She then quickly apologized, and said she did not know why she had asked such a personal question. I told her not to worry about it, that it was all right. But no, I had not lost anyone close to me yet.

That night I did not get any sleep, and after taking the devotee to the airport, I went back to my hotel room, hoping to get some sleep before returning to the ashram that afternoon.

It was now early Saturday morning. I found I could not sleep, and for some reason, I felt extremely anxious, as if something ominous was about to happen. Although I was tired, I kept turning and tossing in bed. This was unusual for me since I normally slept lying flat on my back. After some time, I literally felt a bolt of energy push me off the bed, and I heard a clear inner voice say, "Return to the ashram immediately!"

I quickly got dressed, and went out and find some ashramites who were staying at the hotel and had planned to drive back with me. But since it was still early, no one wanted to go. So I left and drove back to Ganeshpuri. On my way home, the only thought in my mind was that I had to be in the ashram that day no matter what, and that I had to attend the evening chant in

Baba's room. When I reached the ashram, I went to my room as I now felt very tired. On the way, someone told me that they had tried to reach me at the hotel, but apparently I had already left. They had wanted me to pick someone up at the airport, who was arriving that night. But they had already sent someone else to pick them up. Only later would I see the significance of all of this.

I rested for a couple of hours and then did some office work. At about 5 p.m. I went to Baba's room for the evening mantras. The chant would start after Baba's return from his evening walk. However, that day Baba returned early, and for some reason thought that it was late. We were all puzzled and reminded him that it was still early.

In any case, we started chanting the mantras, but for some reason we went through them very quickly that evening. This surprised everyone since we normally chanted them very slowly. I watched Baba carefully since he seemed preoccupied with something. During the chant, I would often notice him looking around lovingly at the different people in the room. After the chant, Baba told me that he was very happy that I had returned from Mumbai. He asked me some other questions, and then we all had some prasad and left. I had some work to do, and so I returned to my room.

That night, at about 11:30, there was a frantic knock on my door. It was my friend Marie, the French girl who had met Baba on the same day I had. She told me to come quickly, that something had happened to Baba.

My heart was gripped with anxiety. I quickly got dressed and ran over to Baba's apartment, but when I got there, he was already gone. He had passed away at about 11:20 p.m..

The atmosphere in the room was filled with great power. I cried for sometime, but after awhile, I started to experience a deep inner calm. We began to wash and massage Baba's body. I soon entered a deep state of consciousness. The knowledge of what had to be done suddenly arose intuitively in my mind.

The first instructions that arose within me was that I should start fasting. I was to also remain with Baba's body until it was placed into the ground. Baba would be interred in a cubicle under his old bedroom. He had already instructed an Indian trustee the previous year to prepare the place for his samadhi. So the pit was ready, and now only the flooring had to be broken.

His body was put into the lotus position, and after performing the ritual bath (*abhishek*), we dressed and prepared him for the last physical darshan he was to give to his devotees.

It was now early Sunday morning. News of Baba's passing had quickly reached devotees all over the world, and thousands of people had already started to arrive. During darshan, I sat on the left side of Baba's seat, while devotees slowly passed by. I watched all of them, many of whom I had known personally, or had seen over the years. They walked slowly by, prostrating before their Guru for the last time. My heart went out to all of them.

After that morning's darshan, it was decided that the room should be kept closed until later that day, when darshan would again resume. For many of those hours, I was alone in the room with Baba's body, meditating quietly. As I sat there, gazing at his physical body, it appeared as if he would open his eyes at any moment. It looked like he was simply meditating and a deep peace shone on his face. Waves of sadness rushed into my heart as I recalled the many years I had spent in his company. I felt very grateful for that opportunity. I also recalled how once someone asked Baba what would happen to his disciples when he passed away. He replied that he would then enter their hearts, and inspire them from within.

In late afternoon, the darshan line was started again. People were coming from all over the world. This went on until about 2 a.m. the next morning, when the room was again closed. During those periods we would clean the room and prepare it for the next opening.

The next morning, the darshan line was again started, and

it went to about noon, at which time we again closed the room for some time. I sat for meditation until we opened the room again. This went on throughout the night until the next morning when we finally interred Baba's body.

The previous night brahmin priests had arrived from Mahesh Yogi's ashram. They began chanting vedic hymns in front of Baba. I was still sitting next to Baba's seat meditating. Darshan was still going on. My eyes were half open, and my breathing started to slow down, until it appeared to have stopped completely. A subtle breathing was going on inside the sushumna.

Although my eyes remained half opened, I was not seeing the outer world. My consciousness soon became completely focused, and then, all of a sudden, I saw a golden sphere come out of Baba's body, from the area of his heart, and it began floating slowly towards me. It soon reached me and entered my heart.

At that moment, who remained? It was difficult to tell. Was it me, or was it Muktananda? There was no difference between the two, they were now one and the same. The one that had become the outer Guru, had now returned to his seat within my heart, from where he had actually never left. A great joy arose within me, and I remained in an ecstatic state. The awareness of 'So'Ham' — "I Am That," arose spontaneously. The accuracy of Baba's words were coming true, he had now taken his seat within my heart.

After a few hours I started to become aware of my surroundings again. But the fact is, that even then I was hardly conscious of my body at all. The next morning there was another ritual bath, and afterward Baba's body was taken to Ganeshpuri for his final earthly darshan of his Guru's samadhi shrine. During the procession to Ganeshpuri, the road was packed with devotees. People could be seen shoulder-to-shoulder in a line stretching from the ashram all the way to the town of Ganeshpuri. Devotees from all parts of India and the world

came to have their final darshan of Babaji's physical remains.
When we returned to the ashram, his body was placed into the tomb facing east. The energy was very powerful, and Baba's presence was still felt throughout the ashram. Some disciples gave inspiring talks, but by late morning, it was all over.

Muktananda's Mahasamadhi procession to Ganeshpuri

Period of Solitude

The continuous chant of *Om Namo Bhagavate Nityanandaya*, which had begun after Baba's mahasamadhi, continued until the end of October. But by then, the chant had naturally changed to *Om Namo Bhagavate Muktanandaya*. The two had now become one.

About the middle of October, Swamis Nityananda and Chidvilasananda were formally enthroned by the Mahamandaleshwar, Swami Brahmanandaji. A yajna was also performed to help alleviate the sorrow that devotees were experiencing because of Baba's death. I found, however, that even though the devotees were going through an intense grief, many were also experiencing a deeper connection with Baba, and the inner Self. The emotions were a strange mixture of sadness and joy.

Within my own heart, a deep love soon began to arise, and I felt the need for solitude and quiet meditation. When all of the ceremonies were over, I began thinking about what I should do. I first thought of going on a pilgrimage, but the inner voice instructed me to go somewhere quiet and meditate. So I began contemplating my departure from the ashram.

At the same time, Swamis Nityananda and Chidvilasananda asked me not to leave the ashram. So in order to show my support for them, I agreed to stay in Ganeshpuri until the beginning of the year. Then, if permitted by them, I wanted to go and live in the South Fallsburg ashram. I also spoke to them about my desire for solitude and meditation, to which they gave their blessings.

Meanwhile, I continued with the ashram work the best I could, and helped those who were about to take over my responsibilities. But as time went by, I found myself spending more and more time alone, in quiet meditation.

In January 1983, on my birthday, I left India for South

Fallsburg, New York. When I arrived at the ashram I decided to first visit my family and friends before starting my solitary life. I felt that I was going to be spending a lot of time alone, and would not be able to see them for sometime.

However when I returned to the ashram a few weeks later, I felt somewhat awkward at first. Since I was not going to be working in the manager's office any longer, I did not know what I was going to do. So I began working in different departments, and doing various projects for the ashram. But none of them held any interest for me.

Then, an interesting incident occurred just after I returned from my trip. For sometime I had been attracted to the ashram prison project, but I never had the opportunity to see what was happening with it. I had read some of the letters written by inmates, and I was wondering how Baba's work was received in such a difficult environment. So I asked the person in charge of the project if I could accompany him to one of the programs. He told me that he was going to a prison not far from the ashram, and I was welcome to join him.

This was an interesting experience for me. At the prison, we were given a small room where we could chant and meditate. It was a maximum security prison. It was also a very noisy environment, and one could hear many of the other inmates calling or yelling at each other. But I found there quite a few dedicated seekers who participated in the program. When the program started, the head of the project introduced me to those present. He then asked me to give a short talk, and I spoke on the power of the *mantra*.

After my talk, we began meditating. I thought how wonderful it was that even there, Baba's work was still going on. A few minutes after we started meditating, I suddenly became aware of Baba's presence in the room. I then saw his form with my inner eye, walking around the room, giving the touch to the inmates. In his right hand he held the usual bundle of peacock feathers. I could hear its swishing sound each time he bopped someone on the head with them. I also began smelling *heena*, a fragrant oil that Baba often used. It suddenly became clear to me that a Siddha's power continues to work even after he leaves his physical body.

I soon began spending more time in meditation, japa, and chanting, and I remained mostly in solitude. The first year was difficult, and I felt a great deal of restlessness. I missed Baba very much, and often felt depressed about his death. But gradually my attention transferred from the outer form of the Guru, to the inner Guru, who dwells within the heart.

After that first year, things started to calm down, and a powerful longing for the inner Self started to develop within me. The mantra became very powerful, and the awareness, "I Am That" would arise naturally while in deep meditation. I decided to remain in solitude and observe silence for an indefinite period of time. Since I ate only once a day, I would leave my room only once to pick up my dinner, which I would then bring back to the room and eat alone.

I have always enjoyed the winter months in South Fallsburg. I loved the snow and clear skies, which I found very conducive for meditation. Sometimes I would go for a walk in the back of the ashram late at night when everyone was asleep.

At one point, Swami Nityananda came to the ashram to stay for awhile. I broke my silence just a day or two before his arrival so I would be able to meet with him.

Obviously, during that period I had not been doing any astrology. In fact I had not done any private reading in almost a year. I felt that the time would soon come when I could stop doing astrological counseling altogether. But many of my clients had been requesting appointments, so I decided to take a short trip to Texas and California at the beginning of the next year. The trip turned out to be a very positive one. Besides meeting with old friends, I made many new ones as well. Also during that trip, it became very natural for me to speak about Baba and meditation.

On my return trip to South Fallsburg, I felt inspired to stop in Michigan, and visit the Matrix Software company. They were pioneers in the development of Western astrological software. I had been using their software for a number of years, and had wanted to meet them. I had already spoken to Michael Erlewine, the company's founder, and he had invited me to visit. We soon all became good friends. I particularly became close to Michael and his family.

I arrived back at the South Fallsburg ashram about the middle of March. I was happy to be back. During that time, I was asked to help computerize the video department. This was an enjoyable project since I had to view many of Baba's videos.

India Pilgrimage

At the beginning of June 1984, Swami Chidvilasananda arrived at the South Fallsburg ashram for the summer. I had not seen her since I had left India and was enjoying her visit.

During her stay she asked me a number of times if I was going to Ganeshpuri that year for Baba's mahasamadhi anniversary. She told me that there was going to be a special yajna performed and encouraged me to attend.

She also asked me when I was going to take sannyasa. Knowing that the time for my sannyasa initiation had not yet arrived, I gave her the same answer that Baba had given me shortly after my arrival at the ashram, "Everything happens at the right time."

I decided to go to Ganeshpuri to attend Baba's mahasamadhi anniversary. Afterwards I would go on a pilgrimage throughout India.

At the end of September, I left for India on a flight full of devotees. When I arrived at the ashram, it brought back all the memories of Baba's mahasamadhi. At first this was very painful for me, but it soon became a powerful and positive experience. Whenever I sat for meditation at Baba's samadhi shrine, the mood of deep longing would arise naturally. This would often be accompanied by tears of joy. Then after sometime, the emotion became a focus of meditation for my mind. Afterwards, a deep calm would arise, and Baba's presence would be felt. The awareness that he and I were one and the same would arise naturally.

When I came out of the samadhi shrine, I often felt a deep intoxication, and even found it difficult to walk properly. Besides spending time meditating in the samadhi shrine, I also spent a great deal of time at the yajna. The sacred fire ritual had always had a powerful effect on me.

The ashram grounds had gone through major changes since I was last there. The upper garden had been changed dramatically. It looked very beautiful. There were thousands of people who had come for the anniversary, and tents had to be set up all over the ashram to accommodate them.

Kashmir

My solitary mood was still very strong, and so I had planned to go on a pilgrimage immediately after the celebration. Since I had decided to start my pilgrimage in Kashmir, I wanted to get there before winter arrived. So I left Ganeshpuri on October 10th, the day after the finale.

From Mumbai, I flew directly to Kashmir, changing planes in New Delhi. When I reached Srinagar, I found a hotel room with the help of a friend's relatives. The room was located just across the road from Dal lake.

As there were many places that I wanted to visit, I had planned to stay for about ten days to two weeks. I would plan out a day's trip to some particular area, and then choose a few sites to visit.

Kashmir has a long history, and there are many different traditions and cultures that have influenced the area. At the present time, Islam is the dominant religion. But Kashmir has also had very strong Hindu and Buddhist traditions from ancient times. Some even believe that there was a strong Jewish influence dating back to the time of Solomon. Then in the eighth century B.C.E., when the Israelites were conquered by the Assyrians, many were scattered throughout the Middle East, and some migrated to the Kashmir valley. However, at the time of my visit, there was a lot of tension in Kashmir due to terrorist acts. And government troops were visible throughout the whole valley.

Nevertheless, I visited many places that Baba had visited, like the Shiva Sutra rock, the Shankaracharya temple, and the *Ka Linga* temple in Bijabihara. I also visited the local mosques, and the tombs of a number of Sufi saints.

I visited Shri Lakshmanji a number of times. I felt he was a very great being, and also a great master of Kashmir Shaivism. At the time he was working on an English translation of some of the *Tantras*. I enjoyed my visits with him very much. He showered me with a great deal of love and affection during my visits. Although Lakshmanji was going to be celebrating his eighty-first birthday in a few months, he appeared young and radiant.

In Srinagar, there is a mysterious samadhi shrine, which according to local Muslim tradition, is believed to be the burial tomb of Jesus. This may sound strange to many people, particularly Western Christians, but the fact is, the burial site of Jesus is not known for certain. The sepulcher which is held sacred today in Palestine as Jesus' burial site is because he supposedly laid in it for two days after his crucifixion. Some Christians believe that Jesus ascended to heaven with his physical body, and therefore there is no burial site. But throughout the middle east, from Iran to India, and particularly in Kashmir and Pakistan, there is a long tradition which says that not only did Jesus visit India before his mission started in Palestine, but that he also returned to the valley after the crucifixion, and died there. References to this is found in both Muslim and Buddhist traditions.

In any case there is a tomb in Srinagar believed by some to be the final resting place of Lord Jesus. I had heard this account many times during my travels and had read the various books on the subject. I would now finally have the opportunity to visit the site myself. On the Friday after my arrival, I began making plans for the next two days. I would first visit some sites around Srinagar itself. The next day, Saturday, I had planned to visit an old fort on the outskirts of town which contained a Sufi's tomb, and there was a well known mosque nearby. I had not planned to visit that mysterious tomb until Sunday morning. But that Friday night, I was feeling tired, and decided to go to bed a little early. That night I had a dream-vision in which I found myself in the realm of the dead. I soon became aware of Jesus' presence, and I heard him call out in a deep and loud voice, "Awake, Arise!"

His call began to awaken the dead, and I saw their bodies suddenly move. The sound of his voice had set off a very powerful vibration, which I was able to feel inside the sushumna nadi. I started to feel the energy move up my spine, bringing with it a wave of joy. Shortly afterward, I awoke from the dream, but the rapturous feeling remained. There were tears of joy flowing down my cheeks, and the mantra So-Ham began to be repeated spontaneously. But it soon began to intermingle with "Guru Om". This went on for sometime, and I eventually went back to sleep, still permeated with inner joy.

The next morning, I started out according to the plans I had made the previous night. But as it turned out, on the way to the fort, I happen to pass by that mysterious shrine. Suddenly my rickshaw driver stopped right in front of it, and pointed it out to me. Since we were there, I decided to stop and have darshan. I went in and sat for some time in meditation. It was a very peaceful experience, and I also recalled that morning's dream. I can not say for certain who is buried in that shrine, but I felt it was someone great.

After Kashmir, I had planned to stop in New Delhi before my trip to south India. The main place that I wanted to visit in the south was Bhagavan Nityananda's cave ashram. I had also planned to visit an astrologer friend in the city of Chennai (Madras), who had invited me many times to visit.

I flew to New Delhi and stayed at the new ashram which had been built by Swamis Chidvilasananda and Nityananda. Nityananda had asked me to go and visit the ashram when I was in Delhi. But when I reached there, I found out that Nityananda was planning a visit in just a few days. Since I had planned to stay in Delhi for a few days anyway, I decided to wait and meet him

While in Delhi, I also visited some friends, as well as the samadhi shrines of the Muslim saint, Nizamudin, and his famous disciple, Amir Khusrau. Baba had visited these shrines a number of times.

The Forest Ashram

As it turned out, Swami Nityananda's visit to Delhi was delayed for about a week. I did not want to wait in Delhi that long, and so I decided to continue on my pilgrimage south. But after some persuasion by an ashramite, urging me to wait for Swami Nityananda, I decided to use that to visit the ashram of Swami Naradananda. You may recall that that was the forest ashram I had stayed in just before I met Baba.

I had not planned this trip, but for some reason, destiny was pulling me there. As it turned out, it was almost fifteen years to the day since I had last been at the ashram. A few years earlier, I had heard that Swami Naradanandaji had passed away. In fact, during my stay in Delhi, I had heard the same thing. So when I arrived at his ashram and found out that Swamiji was still alive, but was very ill and in a hospital at Lucknow, I was really surprised. Swamiji was now about 91 years old.

The first night I was there, I was given a small hut to stay in, not far from my old cave. The next morning at about 4 a.m., I heard someone chanting the mantra, "Om! Om! Om!"

This was not unusual since you could hear someone chanting just about any time of day or night. But this was a familiar sound. Later that morning I went to bathe in the nearby river. And as I was walking back to my room, I suddenly met Om Baba, my old friend. He had been living in the ashram ever since my first visit. We were both happy to see each other after so many years.

Swamiji asked me to accompany him to the Shiva temple in the afternoons while I was there, just as we used to do. I agreed to do so. I was very happy to see him again. I also noticed that Swamiji appeared more contented.

The ashram had not changed at all, with the exception that perhaps some of the huts had been shifted here and there. Om Baba asked me to stay in one of the rooms in the main building which was located on the second floor. It was close to his own room. For the first few days I walked around the ashram and met with the resident sadhus. They were all very kind to me, and there were even some who had been there when I had lived in the ashram, and they remembered me. I also met with Swami Vivekananda, Swami Naradananda's successor. He welcomed me with great affection, and told me to stay as long as I wished. I later met my old friend Tewari, the retired lawyer.

I had arrived at the ashram on a Saturday, and had planned to stay for about a week to ten days. At the beginning of the week, I accompanied Om Baba to a festival held about 20 miles away. Then on Wednesday, I made plans to return to Delhi that Sunday by going to the railway station to book a berth. A train was leaving on Sunday evening, and would arrive in New Delhi early the next morning.

However, on the morning of October 31st, we all heard the tragic news that Mrs. Indira Gandhi, the then Prime Minister of India, had been assassinated. She had been shot at around 9:30 a.m., and was pronounced dead at 2:30 p.m. that day.

Everyone was saddened by this news. But unfortunately it also brought a great deal of violence in some areas of the country. The Sikhs were mostly targeted since it had been one of her Sikh body guards who had assassinated her. People were being massacred, especially in the state of Punjab, and the New Delhi area. Her funeral was scheduled for that Saturday. Om Baba and I went to watch the funeral on television at a nearby villager's home. It was a sad time for the whole country.

Unfortunately, that same night we received news that Swami Naradananda had taken mahasamadhi. His body was brought back to the ashram just after 8 p.m. that night, and was placed in the traditional yogic posture, so that devotees make have their final darshan. Even though he had left his body, a peaceful radiance still appeared on his face.

Some disciples began chanting the Vishnu Sahasranama. Soon devotees from throughout the ashram started to come for darshan. For me, seeing the faces of his disciples brought back sad memories of my own Guru's passing.

Nevertheless, during that whole week my meditations had been very powerful, and the Shakti seemed to be more active. The awareness, "I Am That" would arise spontaneously. This experience had actually started in Ganeshpuri and continued during my stay in Kashmir, and now there. I was very happy.

Because of the violence and the possibility that my train might not be able to reach New Delhi, Om Baba. and some of the other sadhus, thought that perhaps I should cancel my departure date. There had been a great deal of violence reported, and they were obviously concerned for my safety. I thought about it, but felt that I would be all right, and that nothing would happen. I told Om Baba that my Guru would protect me.

He insisted that I reconsider, and so I said that I would ask my Baba on what I should do. So that night, before going to bed, I prayed to Baba to come into my dream and tell me if I should leave or not. When I fell asleep, I dreamt that I was having a conversation with Baba, and I asked him whether or not I should leave the next day. He told me, "Go! Everything will be fine."

The next morning I told Om Baba that I would be leaving, and that he should not worry, that everything would be fine. I told him I would write him a postcard as soon as I reached Delhi.

Before leaving that day, I decided to visit Anandamayi Ma's ashram. She had passed away in the summer of 1982, just a few months before Baba. While visiting her peaceful ashram, I recalled my lovely darshan with her in 1969.

That evening I boarded the train to New Delhi. But before the train departed, the station master told the passengers that the train may not reach all the way to Delhi. And if that were the case, we would have to make our own arrangements.

As it turned out, I shared my compartment with a soldier traveling to Delhi with his wife and child. As the train got on its way, we began discussing the possibility of not reaching Delhi. However, I told him that I felt that everything would be all right, and that we would reach Delhi safely.

After sometime, we all went to sleep. The next morning we still did not know if the train would continue all the way. As we got closer to Delhi, the train would slow down and come to a complete stop, wait for sometime, and then start up again. This happened a number of times. But finally we reached Delhi.

I took a rickshaw from the train station to the ashram. Along the way I could not help but notice the military presence on the streets. There was still a curfew, but by then, the violence had been mostly stopped. One could see that there was a lot of damage, and my rickshaw driver told me about some of the gruesome incidents that he had personally witnessed.

On the humorous side, during the last two days of my stay at the forest ashram, we had read in the paper that the Russians' were claiming that the CIA was somehow involved in Mrs. Gandhi's death. Although most Indians did not believe this, the damage had already been done. Many had believed it at first, particularly in the rural areas. So there I was, an American in the middle of the jungle, where some village people were starting to have second thoughts about me. The sadhus all tried to explain to them that I was a real sadhu, and not a CIA agent, but not all were convinced.

Swami Nityananda had already arrived in Delhi by the time I reached there. He was holding daily programs. I spent a few days with him before leaving Delhi. I had made reservations to fly to Mumbai that Friday morning.

Goa

My plan was to fly to Mumbai, and from there travel to Goa by ship. From Goa, I would take a bus to Mangalore, and from there a bus or train to Kanhangad. I was on my way to visit Bhagavan Nityananda's cave ashram, located near Kanhangad in the Indian state of Kerala.

When I arrived in Mumbai, I decided to visit some old friends before leaving for Goa. I booked a ticket on the Mogul line, a daily passenger service ship, offered by the local Government. Originally I had not planned to stay in Goa, but on the ship I shared a cabin with a man from Switzerland. He was on his way to Goa on vacation, and invited me to stay a few days.

I had heard about Goa being a Western hangout, and so I was not inclined to stay. However, my new friend said that he was not going to the main beaches, but to one that was more secluded, and peaceful. I had also developed a very bad cough during the end of my stay in Delhi, which unfortunately I had not taken care of. Now my throat was swollen so I decided to stay in Goa for a few days to recuperate.

Goa, actually the Union territory of Goa, Daman and Diu, which are three distinct geographic districts, was given independence in 1961, after 451 years of Portuguese colonial rule. Portuguese culture is still very prominent there. One can see it in its architecture, language, and religion.

The area is a very beautiful place, with its golden sandy beaches, and fields of rice, palms and coconut trees. I visited a famous Shiva temple, as well as a number of Christian churches. Also, an important Catholic festival was scheduled for the beginning of December, which was about three weeks away. I therefore decided to try and return in time for the festival on my way back to Mumbai. Since I had enjoyed the boat ride so much, I decided to return to Mumbai the same way. My stay in Goa was very enjoyable, and my cough was now gone.

Kanhangad
(The Cave Ashram)

One evening I left Goa for Mangalore by bus, arriving there very early the next morning. Although it was called Deluxe Tours, I swore that I would never again take another long bus ride in India.

I arrived at Mangalore at about 5 a.m.. After making some enquiries, I found out that there was no train to Kanhangad (pronounced as Kanchangad) until later that morning. So I decided to continue by bus, since one was leaving within the hour. But this meant that I would have to change buses at Kasarogod, for Kanhangad.

I arrived at Nityananda's ashram at about 9:30 a.m.. I met the manager and asked him for permission to stay for about five to seven days. After Kanhangad, I had planned to travel further south along the coast, and then on to Chennai on the eastern coast of India. The manager said that he remembered me from the Ganeshpuri ashram, which he visited along with Swami Janananda in 1982.

However, he told me that visitors were only allowed to stay for three days. This is a common practice in Indian ashrams, and sadhus generally stay only three days at any one place. But the moment I had walked into the ashram, I felt Bhagavan Nityananda's presence. For some reason I felt like I would be allowed to stay longer, but I did not say anything to the manager, except to thank him.

While I was speaking to him, my gaze suddenly went to a large photograph of Bhagavan Nityananda, which was hanging on the wall. It appeared to vibrate with energy. Just then, the manager suddenly turned to me and said, "You can stay the week if you like, after all, you're like family."

I was very touched, and very happy to hear that, and thanked him for his kindness. I also mentally thanked Bhagavan

Nityananda.

Before settling in Ganeshpuri, Bhagavan Nityananda lived in the Kanara area for a long time. We do not know for certain his place and date of birth, but there are many stories told by devotees about his early life in that area. It is believed by some that he was found abandoned in a forest when just a baby. Others believe that he was born in Udupi.

In any case, it seems that for about the first twelve years of his life, he was looked after by a Mr. Ishwar Iyer, who called him Raman. Mr. Iyer lived in Quilandi. It is also evident that Nityananda, or Raman, manifested advanced spiritual power from an early age, and was considered a born Siddha. His childhood was spent mostly in the area between Udupi and Calicut, along the western coast of south India. The town of Udupi is just north of Mangalore, and both are located in the southern tip of the modern state of Karnataka.

Just east of Mangalore is situated the famous Shiva temple at Dharmasthala. This was the temple that I had visited with Baba in our 1971 pilgrimage. Kanhangad is located just south of there, in the state of Kerala. The area appears to have been a favorite spot of Nityananda.

Sometime during his late teens, Nityananda returned to the area, and started wandering up and down the coast. This must have occurred just before 1920. He was very tall and thin, and wandered around mostly wearing only a loincloth. He kept no personal possessions with him, and was considered a supreme Avadhuta. He was called Nityananda, or just simply Swami or Sadhu.

He spoke very little, but when he did speak, it was in short cryptic sentences which were full of meaning. He ate very little and only when it was offered to him. Nityananda had attained the highest spiritual state, and had the ability to transmit that experience to others. His actions were often difficult to comprehend, but there was always a purpose to them. We are told that he also spoke about a half-dozen Indian languages, including English.

It was during that period, sometime around 1923, that Muktananda first met Nityananda. It was just around Muktananda's fifteenth birthday. When Nityananda saw the boy, he blessed him by lovingly stroking his cheek. This apparently had a dramatic effect on the young boy since he left his home within six months of that meeting to become a wandering sadhu.

As Baba Nityananda's divine powers became known to people, many of them started following him wherever he went. Some came for spiritual attainments, but many for worldly reasons as well. At times Bhagavan would disappear from the area in order to avoid the crowds. He would also climb trees to escape them, and would stay up on the tree for many hours. Devotees would gather at the foot of the tree, and beg for his blessings, at which time he would throw down leaves to them, which would be used for medicinal purposes. *Siddhis* or supernatural powers would manifest naturally in his presence. When questioned about these, he would simply reply that everything happened according to the will of God.

The train runs very close to the Kanhangad ashram. There are many stories told about Baba Nityananda and the trains. He used to ride them from Mangalore to Kanhangad, and became well known to the conductors. He was seen as an eccentric sadhu. After a number of unusual experiences with him, they allowed him to wander freely on the train. At times he was even allowed to ride with them in the engine compartment. They came to have great respect for this unusual sadhu.

Sometime in the mid 1920s, Nityananda settled in Kanhangad. At the time he may have been in his late twenties or early thirties. He soon started clearing an area on the outskirts of Kanhangad where the old Hosdrug fort was located. Over the years the place had been claimed by the jungle, but Nityananda soon cleared the area.

His attention was soon focused on a large rock which had

many small caverns. These were once used by soldiers during times of battle. Nityananda started to carve out small caves from that huge rock. He designed it in such a way as to allow the rising and setting sun to shine through the passageways, thereby bringing natural light into the caves. There are about forty-three completed caves, just large enough to accommodate about one, or possibly two people.

The outside is designed with terraced steps on either side, which looked to me like the human brain. I found the design of the place extremely interesting, and it gave me a new insight into Nityananda's artistic abilities. The "cave ashram" was completed about 1933.

Some interesting stories are told by eyewitnesses about how the project was being financed. After all, Nityananda owned absolutely nothing. And as already mentioned, he wore only a loincloth. But somehow he was able to pay hundreds of laborers. Where did all the money come from? The authorities also wanted to know.

The laborers were all questioned by the authorities, but all they could say was that when it was time to be paid, Nityananda would simply tell the foreman to go and look under a particular rock, which he would point out to him. Under that rock he would find the exact amount.

When a devotee finally started handling the ashram's accounts, he said that Nityananda would suddenly arrive each evening holding stacks of new currency notes, just the right amount for the next day's wages. Once, the devotee asked him where he kept all this money. Nityananda pointed to the ashram well, and told him to go look inside. When he did so, he was astonished to see bundles of currency notes floating on the surface of the water.

Now when the authorities heard that someone was doing construction work without permission, and that there were questions about the source of his funds, they decided to investigate. Initially some clerks from the local authorities went to meet Nityananda and inquire where he got his money, since everyone knew him as a simple sadhu. Nityananda is said to have taken them to a nearby submerged field, which was apparently infested with snakes and other creatures. Nityananda immediately jumped in, and when he came up from beneath the surface, he was holding brand new, and dry, currency notes. He then shouted, "This is my bank, do you want some, come in and get it."

The poor clerks apparently became frightened and ran off. Later a local British inspector named E.M. Gawne was notified. He was intrigued by the story and decided to personally go and investigate. Accompanied by other local authorities, he arrived on horseback, with his dog running along side of him. When he reached the cave where Nityananda was sitting, apparently sensing that he was no ordinary person, Mr. Gawne removed his shoes and went inside. When he asked Nityananda who he was doing all the work for, the Avadhuta is said to have replied in English, "Not for this one (pointing to himself). If you want, you may have it."

This answer, and Nityananda's presence apparently satisfied the inspector since he later gave an order to the local authorities, that they should not disturb Nityananda. And in fact should assist him in any way they could.

It appears that when he moved to Ganeshpuri, Nityananda followed a similar pattern. He had hired laborers to build a new road, and would pay them by directing them to look under nearby rocks. Or, he would simply stick his hand inside his loincloth, and when he pulled it out and opened his fist, the exact amount would drop into the worker's hand.

I realize how difficult this will be for many to believe, but I am only reporting them as I have heard them over the years from devotees, many of whom were eyewitness to these events. One should also remember that beings like Bhagavan Nityananda are unique individuals. They roam this earth in total freedom, manifesting divinity, and the full potential of man. In their vision, there is only unity, and their actions are for the sole benefit of humanity.

The caves of the ashram are not only beautiful, but also powerfully charged. Nityananda used to regularly meditate in them, and they developed a certain spiritual vibration.

After Nityananda left Kanhangad, his disciple Swami Janananda looked after the ashram, and also meditated in those caves. However, today there are only a few bats living inside. They are usually kept locked, and are opened only occasionally.

However, during my stay, the manager would open them for me whenever I asked. The first time I went in, I sat at different spots for short meditations. But the next day, I was attracted to one particular cave towards the back. I sat down and started to meditate. Suddenly, my body became gripped by the divine Shakti, which had started to move up my spine. I immediately started to experience Guru-bhava, but this time it was not *my* Baba's mannerisms that I experienced, but that of Bhagavan Nityananda's.

I felt ecstatic, and soon tears of joy flowed down my cheeks. My eyes were forced wide open, and I was riveted to my seat. I was not able to get up for almost two hours. One cannot possibly imagine what power lies within them unless they have hte experience of an awakened Shakti.

Later that day, when I met with the manager, I asked him if there was any special cave that Bhagavan Nityananda appeared to favor. He told me that there was one cave in which he had spent a lot of time meditating in. Swami Janananda also used it for many years of meditation. When I asked him to point it out to me, I was not surprised that he pointed to the very cave that I had sat in that morning.

The top of the Rock where the caves are is flat. A temple was erected there in 1963 in honor of Bhagavan. It contains a life-sized statue of Nityananda, with his right hand raised in a gesture (*mudra*) of blessing, and which means, "Don't fear".

When Nityananda left Kanhangad to settle at Vajreshwari, he told Swami Janananda to stay there and look after the ashram. Swamiji had been with Nityananda for a number of years, and had helped in the original construction of the caves. In September of 1982, Jananandaji, who was then about 92 years of age, visited Ganeshpuri for his last darshan of his beloved Guru's samadhi shrine. Swamiji passed away in December of that same year. He had stopped at Baba's ashram, who had welcomed him with great respect. Baba washed his feet, and later placed Jananandaji in his own car to be driven to Ganeshpuri, while he himself walked in front of the car.

The cave ashram is not far from the beaches of the Arabian sea. Devotees report that Bhagavan used to lay on the hot sands for hours at a time wearing only a loincloth. At times, he would be observed staring at the sun, which is an advanced yogic practice. It is said that he would often have a devotee bury him a few feet beneath the sand, where he would remain for two or three hours at a time. When he was dug out, he would sometimes relate some events occurring at distant places. But one day, it so happened that he stayed under longer then his usual time, and the devotee began to panic. But he knew that he could not disturb Nityananda, so he continued to wait patiently. After sometime, Bhagavan gave him the signal to dig him up. The devotee later voiced his fears to Nityananda, but Bhagavan simply said that some work had to be done at a great distance, and he could not return sooner.

Devotees from those early years relate how Nityananda would often indicate who would visit him that day. And sometimes he would instruct an attendant to prepare some special food, or to have a chair ready for some unknown guest.

Not far from the ashram there lived an old disciple of Nityananda named Swami Sadananda. I visited him one day, and stayed for a few hours. He related some of his experiences with Nityananda.

Another spot which is associated with Nityananda in that

area is Guruvana, a forest located about six miles from the ashram. It is believed that Bhagavan did some type of spiritual practices in a cave there. It is said that he had spent some years in the cave, absorbed in deep samadhi.

Apparently the area had no water, and devotees say that Nityananda created a stream of water using his extraordinary powers. Even though the cave has since been sealed up, a steady stream of clear water continues to flow out of it even today. The stream is locally called *Papanashini Ganga*, which indicates that a drink from it will remove one's sins. A small temple was erected nearby with a statue of a youthful Nityananda performing *kumbhaka* — breath retention.

That Baba Nityananda had extraordinary powers is a well known fact to his devotees, and to all those who have been blessed by him. Indian scriptures differentiate between the various powers one can obtain through the practice of yoga. The powers that manifested in Bhagavan's presence were not considered ordinary *siddhis*, the type which are achieved by practicing a specific type of sadhana. Nityananda did not practice any sadhana for the purpose of gaining powers. Such powers manifested naturally on their own.

In fact, Nityananda was so absorbed in the Supreme that he would often say that he had no desires at all, not even to help others. One of his favorite sayings was, *"Sub Mitti,"* meaning, "all is dust."

When commenting on his Guru's powers, Muktananda wrote:

"He visualized the same essence in himself as everywhere. He saw no distinction in a cat, a brahmin or a king. Having merged himself with the Supreme, he had no separate identity, he had become one with That. As a result, large and small miracles spontaneously manifested, without any deliberate effort on his part." Bhagawan Nityananda by Swami Muktananda *(1978)*

I was very happy visiting all the places associated with Bhagavan, and I felt his presence wherever I went. While in Kanhangad, I also went for the darshan of mother Krishnabai, the disciple and successor of Swami Ramdass of Ananda Ashram. She was a very beautiful person, and a great being. I enjoyed my visit with her very much, and felt very peaceful in her presence. She invited me to stay at her ashram. But when I told her that I was staying at Nityananda's ashram she said, "This ashram also belongs to Muktananda Baba."

This response touched me very deeply, and made me feel very much at home. I thanked her with deep appreciation, and decided to go and stay in her ashram for a few days.

Chennai

My original plan had been to travel further south and then up to Chennai along the eastern coast. However, after visiting Bhagavan Nityananda's cave ashram, I had lost all interest in visiting any other place. I had received an inner message from Bhagavan to quickly return to South Fallsburg and continue my spiritual practices there.

However, since I had already made arrangements to visit my friend in Chennai, I thought that I should go. From there, I would return directly to Goa, then to Mumbai, and finally to Ganeshpuri before leaving the country.

I took an afternoon train from Kanhangad to Chennai and arrived early the next morning. I went to meet my friend, and then got a room at a local hotel. My friend was an astrologer, and was also interested in using computers to calculate horoscopes. I spent some time with him, and at other times I visited different places around the city.

The last time I was in Chennai was with Baba in 1971. But at the time I did not get to see very much of the area. One afternoon, my friend, his wife, myself, and one of their friends went to visit Kanchipuram, one of the seats of the Shankaracharyas.

I had great respect for the current Shankaracharya, Swami Chandrasekharendra. He was in his nineties at the time, and had been maintaining silence for some years. There was a kind of radiance that shone on his face. He had long ago passed to his disciple the Kamakoti seat, while he spent his time traveling around India.

This is a common practice among all the Shankaracharyas. Traditionally, they have traveled around the country on foot, spreading the teachings of Vedanta. His disciple had also recently chosen his own successor, who was an eleven year old boy at the time. Therefore, on the day of our visit, we were able to meet three Shankarcharyas, which we all considered as very auspicious.

While in Chennai, I also visited the Theosophical colony and library at Adyar, as well as some of the local temples. I visited the Ramakrishna mission as well. This was something which I had done in Mumbai and New Delhi. I liked meditating in their shrine room where a beautiful marble statue of Ramakrishna is installed.

Chennai also has a long Christian tradition as well. Although many dispute this, tradition holds that it was saint Thomas himself who brought the teachings of Jesus to India in the year 52 C.E.. According to the Middle Eastern Christians, and particularly the Syrian Church, he was known as Didymos Judas Thomas, meaning Judas the twin.

He was considered one of the twelve apostles, as well as the twin brother of Jesus. In Mylapore, a Gothic style Cathedral was built in 1893 over the spot where St. Thomas is believed to have been buried. The tomb was supposedly rediscovered by the Portuguese in 1522. However, today only a tiny bone fragment the size of a finger nail remains. His relics are said to have been moved to the city of Edessa in the 4th century, but were again moved later. Some say to the town of Ortona, in the Abruzzi region of Italy, while others say they are located in the Syriac Orthodox Church in Mosul, Iraq.

I also visited Saint Thomas Mount, a hilltop overlooking the city. There, an old church is built over a cave said to be where the saint had meditated and eventually died.

I should add here that some believe that the visit of St. Thomas to India is a total fabrication and a myth promulgated by Christian missionaries. Indeed, there is no clear proof of his visit to that country at all, a fact which even the Catholic church has had to admit. However, I can only recount my own experience at the burial site, where I did feel a powerful presence.

Back To Goa

I stayed in Chennai for approximately ten days. The morning I left, a huge storm delayed my flight to Bangalore, making me miss the connecting flight to Goa. Since there was only one flight a day from Bangalore to Goa, I had to stay overnight in that city. I arrived about 10 a.m., and decided to take advantage of the opportunity to see something of the city. I also wanted to visit Mr. B. V. Raman, a well known Vedic astrologer. He had visited Baba a few times, and I had met him briefly during those visits.

I flew to Goa the next, which was a Sunday. I went directly to the hotel where I had previously stayed and got a room. I arrived just the day before St. Francis Xavier's death anniversary. The body of that saint, who is considered the patron saint of Catholic Goa, would be shown for the first time in ten years. And there was speculation that this may be the last showing.

Saint Francis Xavier had died in the sixteenth century, and for the first few hundred years his body supposedly remained uncorrupted. However, it eventually started to decompose, and there was now not much left. For one thing, body limbs and internal organs had been removed by over zealous devotees and church leaders, and had been distributed to churches throughout Europe.

Saint Francis Xavier's birth date is given as April 7, 1506, although this has been disputed by some. He was a young Spanish missionary who was influenced by St. Ignatuis of Loyola, whom he helped find the Society of Jesus, better known as the Jesuits. He arrived in Goa on May 6, 1542 and stayed for only a few months. While in India, he traveled to other parts of the country visiting Christian centers. He also made a pilgrimage to the tomb of Saint Thomas in Chennai.

He died on the 2nd of December 1552, on the island of San Cham, off the coast of China. His body was later unearthed and taken to Goa. He was canonized in 1622, the same year as Ignatuis of Loyola. His remains are kept in a silver casket in the Basilica of Bom Jesus, which was built in 1605. During the Exposition, the body was kept in the Se Cathedral, also built in the 17th Century. Frankly, I have never felt anything special about him. In fact, from everything I had learned about him, I found him to be a very narrow minded individual.

I remained in Goa for just three days before leaving for Mumbai on the same ship I took on the way down. I arrived the next morning, booked my flight back to the U.S., and then went directly to Ganeshpuri. I had planned to be in Ganeshpuri for only about a week. As it turned out, I arrived at the ashram only an hour before Swami Nityananda returned from his tour. Swami Chidvilasananda had already left for her trip west.

Problems in the Family

I left Mumbai for New York about the middle of December. It had been a wonderful pilgrimage, but I was now happy to be home again. I first had to catch up with some work, but otherwise I kept mostly to myself.

In February 1985, my spiritual practices (*sadhana*) once again became very intense. I began spending more time meditating, chanting, and mantra repetition. I also remained in solitude and observed silence. Silence (*mouna*) is a very potent spiritual practice, and its benefits can not be overestimated. It has great power. That period lasted until the end of March, at which time the intensity of my sadhana decreased a little.

Swamis Chidvilasananda and Nityananda were scheduled to arrive in June of that year. By that time I felt absolutely no interest in doing anything external. I wanted to just pursue meditation, japa, and chanting. Day and night I was attracted to nothing else.

At times I felt depressed and dejected. A deep yearning to fully know God would arise within me, increasing gradually until I felt I could no longer bear it. These periods would finally culminate with the full awareness of my unity with the Divine. The awareness, "I Am That", would arise spontaneously, and at times, I would hear the mantra *So'Ham* being repeated automatically within my heart.

During this process, I would experience a tremendous energy surging throughout my body, filling me with great joy. A variety of *kriyas* or spontaneous movements would also occur, including different yogic postures, various types of *pranayama*, and intense crying or laughing. Sometimes I would dance in ecstasy, or shout with joy. And while in deep meditation, I would often hear, or see, poetic verses within the inner sky of consciousness. These were all the play of the divine inner Shakti.

The last experience had started manifesting sometime in the previous year. Many of the poems were directly related to the deep feelings of anguish I was experiencing while in this divine state (*bhava*). However, from that suffering, a deep compassion for all humanity began to grow within me, and my love for Baba also continued to grow. I was extremely thankful for what he continued to reveal to me.

Swami Nityananda arrived in South Fallsburg about the middle of June. About ten days later Swami Chidvilasananda arrived. They were scheduled to spend the summer together in the South Fallsburg ashram. I had an urge to speak with them about my desire for complete solitude. However, I did not want any special treatment. I wanted to give them the opportunity to tell me whether or not they would mind, or if they thought that I should be participating more actively in ashram life.

A few days after Nityananda arrived, he came to see me for an astrological reading. Afterwards I discussed with him my desire to remain in solitude, and asked whether he and Chidvilasananda would be alright with that? He told me not to worry about it, and to just continue with my sadhana. Later when I saw Swami Chidvilasananda, she reaffirmed this message.

Since Swami Chidvilasananda had arrived on her birthday, there was a big celebration. So I briefly left my solitude to enjoy the evening programs with her.

That summer many people came to the ashram, and among them many were my astrology clients. After numerous requests for astrological updates, I decided to do some consulting work. During the previous year, I had given only a few readings. And I also had received an inner message that I would be giving up the practice completely within the year.

Nityananda left for India first and asked me to drive him to the airport. I had known for sometime that there were difficulties between he and Chidvilasananda. In fact, I had discussed all of this with him when he came for his reading. I was troubled by the planetary configuration I saw in his and her chart, and tried to warn him of its danger.

There had also been clear signs of animosity between his and her devotees. By that summer it had become quite obvious that their partnership had taken a tragic turn. A number of her devotees had behaved with open hostility, not only towards Nityananda, but also towards his close devotees. A number of devotees had personally complained to me about the mistreatment from her devotees. This saddened me very much.

I had felt obliged to help and support Swami Nityananda ever since an experience I had on the night of Baba's mahasamadhi. I did not reveal this to Nityananda, but on that night, while he and I walked into Baba's bathroom to get water and towels to wash his body after his death, I clearly heard Baba's voice tell me to help Nityananda. Ever since then, I had tried to help and guide him the best I could.

Now, during the drive to the airport, I again warned him of the upcoming danger, and predicted that within a few months there would be dramatic changes within the foundation.

Then, as if to test my loyalty, he asked, "Do you love me?"

I said that of course I loved him, but, I added, I also loved his sister. I told him that I saw them as two aspects of Baba's nature, and as long as they remained together, I had committed myself to supporting them. But I told him that if they were to split up, then I could not say what I would do.

From my perspective, Baba was the Guru, and we were all his children. Although I looked at them with respect and love, my heart belonged to Baba. He was my Guru. I felt neither the need nor inclination to follow either of them, or any one else. Shortly before his death, Baba had reminded me many times to always be independent, and to be independent of these two as well. I felt that I had always made this clear to them, and I did not want any confusion about it. However, I respected their position, and the work Baba gave them to do.

Since Baba's mahasamadhi, Nityananda had continued to come to see me for astrological consultation. But Swami Chidvilasananda began to keep a distance. She had previously come to see me personally for readings, but now she no longer did so. Instead, she began sending her close attendants with questions about her chart. I felt that this was not a good idea because there were often personal matters that I needed to discuss with her. And I did not feel comfortable discussing them with her messengers.

The tension thickened that summer, and many devotees felt pressured into choosing sides. I was not interested in choosing either side. I saw them as my Guru brother and sister, and tried to support each of them as best I could. They had been given special work to do by Baba, and I felt they should try to work together.

However, I also believed that everything happens according to one's destiny. And try as we may, what must happen will happen. I was not optimistic about their future together.

In the first week of October, Swami Chidvilasananda left for Ganeshpuri. Baba's lunar mahasamadhi anniversary would fall towards the end of October that year. The planets indicated that this would be a major turning point for SYDA Foundation and its heads.

My Departure From The Ashram

I had made plans to go on an astrological tour to Michigan, Texas, and California at the end of October. I left on schedule, and arrived in Michigan where I stayed for three days with my friends, Michael and Margaret Erlewine. I then left for Austin, Texas.

The previous few nights I had been having unusual and chaotic dreams. And for some reason, I felt a deep apprehension. I was aware that something was not right, but I did not know what.

The drive to Austin took two days. When I arrived at the house, my hosts were out, but the door was left open for me. So I went inside and started to unpack.

About fifteen minutes later, the phone rang. It was one of my hosts calling from his office. He told me that he had just received news that Swami Nityananda had stepped down from his position as guru. This had occurred in the Ganeshpuri ashram shortly after Baba's third mahasamadhi anniversary. This was of course not a total surprise to me. Nevertheless, it was a huge shock to many people, especially his devotees, which included my hosts. The report said that the change had occurred smoothly, however, there were no details about what had actually happened.

After about a week in Austin, I continued on my trip and stopped at the Santa Monica ashram for a few days. Afterwards I drove up to the Bay Area, and then across country, back to New York. I reached the South Fallsburg ashram about the middle of December.

My vivid and uneasy dreams had continued throughout my trip, and they were indicating that there was a strong possibility of my having to move soon. There was also a sense that there were more revelations yet to come, and that the changes going on in the ashram were not yet over.

When I reached the ashram, I felt a strong urge to go into solitude for an indefinite period of time. I wrote a note to Swami Chidvilasananda, who was then in Hawaii, requesting her permission and blessing to do so.

I soon received a note from her giving her blessing. She also sent me copies of some photographs of her, Nityananda, and myself, which had been taken in Ganeshpuri just after Baba's mahasamadhi. They were a reminder of better days, when we were all together as Baba's family.

Soon my meditation once again intensified, bringing with it many powerful experiences. And by the beginning of 1986, I came to know through my meditations, that I would be taking *sannyasa* initiation that year. But no exact date had yet been revealed to me.

Everything was relatively peaceful until the end of February, at which time, I received a phone call from Nityananda. He told me that he was going to be in New York, and wanted to see me, so he could tell me his side of the story. He had been accused of certain indiscretions. I decided to go and see him, and spent a few days with him, at which time he told me his version of what had occurred.

He also told me that he had just given an interview to a Mumbai magazine which was scheduled to come out in just a few days. In the interview he had made a number of accusations against Swami Chidvilasananda, and some other ashramites. I was saddened by this turn of events which was obviously going to create a lot of problems.

Over the course of three days I listened to everything Nityananda had to say. I also questioned him carefully about the accusations made against him. I was saddened by the whole mess. But there was now nothing to be done about that. Despite Baba's request of me, I could not help him with what was already done. Things would have to take their own course.

I did feel, however, that he still had some work to do. And I knew there was a reason why Baba had chosen him. I felt that although he may have stumbled, if there was a sincere effort made on his part, I saw no reason why he could not find his way again. The next day I decided to return to South Fallsburg.

A few days later, Swami Chidvilasananda arrived at the South Fallsburg ashram. I met with her shortly after her arrival. She proceeded to tell me her side of the story, and all that had happened, according to her.

Accusations of indiscretions were being made by both sides. Soon special meetings were called at the South Fallsburg ashram in order to counter the accusations being made by Nityananda. There was increasing tension and mistrust between devotees in the ashram. And no one appeared interested in finding a peaceful solution to the problem.

Although I felt a strong responsibility to help resolve the issue, I did not know what I could do. Feeling frustrated, I began thinking of leaving the ashram, but I heard Baba's voice telling me that it was not yet time. So I stayed on, but remained in solitude, not wishing to discuss the matter with anyone.

There were powerful emotions in the air, and many people suffered because of it. I tried to remain neutral and prayed to Baba for a peaceful resolution. But soon everyone knew that I had visited Nityananda, and a rumor was being spread that I was secretly his devotee. And observing Chidvilasananda's attitude towards me, it was clear that she believed this.

Nevertheless I stayed, waiting for Baba's guidance. But then one night, I heard Swami Chidvilasananda making some disparaging remarks about me during her evening program. I prayed to Baba asking how much longer I would have to wait, and the reply came immediately. The time had finally come for me to leave. So I immediately went down to the hall, where darshan was still going on. I got in line and waited my turn. When I reached her seat, I asked Chidvilasananda for her permission to leave the ashram, which she quickly granted.

My friend Michael in Michigan had been inviting me to move there for sometime. So I decided to first go there. After having lived in Baba's ashram for seventeen years, my departure was very difficult for me. Particularly under the circumstances.

My Sannyasa Initiation

Michael had recently purchased a second house next door to his own. He used this to house for visitors to his astrological software company, as well as visiting Buddhist monks. Michael and his wife were followers of a Tibetan Buddhist Master belonging to the Karmapa's lineage. They had also recently opened a small Buddhist center.

When I arrived, there were as yet no permanent residents in the new house. Michael and his wife Margaret, along with their whole family welcomed me with great love. They immediately made me feel at home. Although it was a painful period for me, I felt Baba's grace guiding me. I had complete faith that everything happened for the best.

Then about the middle of May, Baba appeared to me in a dream-vision, and told me that it was now time for me to take *sannyasa* initiation. He then gave me detailed instructions as to what I should do.

He told me to contact Mahamandaleshwar Swami Brahmananda Giri, and ask him to initiate me. However, because of the strained relationship between Nityananda and Chidvilasananda, I mentally wondered if Swamiji would even see me. Although I had met him on a number of occasions, I was not sure how he was dealing with the difficulties between them. The last I had heard, he would not even meet with Westerners. However, reading my mind, Baba assured me that he would not only see me, but would welcome me with great love, and would take care of everything.

Baba then showed me some events that were about to happen, both in the near the future, as well as some that would not occur for a number of years. When the vision of the future events ended, Baba gave me some further instructions and then said, "Now go!"

I immediately awoke. But although now wide awake, I was

still feeling the intoxication which I felt in Baba's presence during the dream-vision.

The next morning I told Michael and Margaret about the command I had received from Baba to go to India. I began to immediately make arrangements for my trip. Everything went so smoothly that it was obvious that Babaji was making all of the arrangements.

In the dream-vision, Baba had also instructed me to let Swami Chidvilasananda know that I was going to take sannyasa. I therefore called the South Fallsburg ashram to let her know. However at the time she was in New York city, and when I called there, I was informed that she was not available. So I just left a message about my sannyasa with her attendant.

By the 1st of June, I was on my way to India. I felt as though I was in a dream, and was watching everything as a witness. When I arrived in Mumbai, I went to Swami Brahmanandaji's Sannyasa Ashram, located in Vile Parle. The ashram was being taken care of by his disciple and successor, Swami Vishveshwarananda.

Swamiji greeted me with much love. He said that he remembered me from the Ganeshpuri ashram. Swamiji also questioned me on why I wanted to take sannyasa. After given him my reasons, he appeared satisfied with my answers, and seemed to recognize my sincerity.

I stayed in the ashram for a few days. He then wrote a letter for me to take to swami Brahmanandaji, who at the time was staying at his ashram in Haridwar.

The next day I left for New Delhi, and from there made my way to Haridwar. Actually, Swami Brahmananda's ashram is located near the small town of Kankhal, a few miles from Haridwar.

Out of affection, his disciples and devotees addressed him as Maharaj, and so I did the same. I gave Maharaj the letter from Vishveshwarananda, and explained to him personally the circumstances which had brought me there. I then asked him to please bless me with sannyasa initiation.

As Baba had assured me in the dream-vision, Maharaj welcomed me with great love and affection, and said that he would certainly give me initiation. He said that he would take care of everything, just as Baba had told me. That evening, an auspicious date was set for the ceremony, which would take place in about ten days.

While waiting, I spent my time in quiet meditation and visited the many interesting places around Rishikesh and Haridwar. It was now over fifteen years since I had first visited the area.

Maharaj's ashram was very beautiful and peaceful, with the river Ganga flowing next to it. The ashramites were all very friendly, and I was particularly helped during the ceremony by two swami friends, who were also disciples of Baba. They happened to be staying at the ashram at the time.

The first day of the ceremony finally arrived, and my head was completely shaved, except for a small tuft of hair at the crown of the head. This would be cut at the completion of the ceremony.

The first day's rituals are associated with one's social and family obligations. They are meant to put an end to such responsibilities. This is symbolically done by performing funeral rites for one's parents and ancestors. I was assisted with these rituals by a local brahmin priest.

Once the ceremony started, I was to remain within the *yajna mandap* or ritual pavilion for the rest of the day and night. At the conclusion of the first day's ceremony, my time was to be spent doing *japa* and silent meditation. At the same time, I had to make sure that the sacred fire was not extinguished.

During the night, one has to be careful not to fall asleep, but to continue doing japa and meditation. This continued until around 3 a.m. the next morning, when Maharaj arrived to perform the final initiation. This started with the final purification of the body, senses, mind, and *pranas*. In this portion of the ceremony,

(*above*) Mahamandaleshwar Swami Brahmananda

one is actually performing his own funeral rites. The body is symbolically offered to the sacrificial flames. From that moment onwards, one looks upon themselves as dead to the world, but alive in the inner Self.

After this ceremony, we walked over to the river's edge. At that stage only sannyasins are allowed to witness the remaining ceremony. Everyone else was asked to leave.

I walked into the flowing Ganges and offered the white garments I had been wearing, along with the sacred thread and staff I was holding. These symbolized not only the discarding of all worldly attachments and caste identification, but also the rigidity of religious dogma, symbolized by the staff.

The sannyasi worships the Lord in the form of their own

inner Self. Standing naked with arms outstretched overhead, while facing north, I repeated the ancient vow of renunciation. Maharaj then handed me my new saffron robes, and I was given the monastic name of Swami Prakashananda Sarasvati, the name indicated to me by Baba in my dream-vision. This was indeed a most joyous occasion for me and the fulfillment of my Guru's command.

(*above*) The first day of the author's (on left) sannyasa ceremony.
(*below*) Receiving Swami Brahmananda's blessings after initiation.

The Kedarnath Temple

After my sannyasa initiation that morning, I went inside the ashram's main hall and placed a flower garland around a large photo of Baba, which was hanging on the wall. I then went to Maharaj's room, and offered him a garland of flowers, as well as a basket of fruit. We spoke for sometime, and after giving me some instructions, he gave me his blessing by placing his hands on my head.

Maharaj had been extremely kind to me throughout my stay. As I was reflecting on this the night before my departure, I suddenly recalled the assurance Baba had given me in the dream-vision, that Maharaj would "receive me with great love."

Maharaj was scheduled to leave the ashram for New Delhi the next day for an extended tour. I had decided to go on a pilgrimage to Kedarnath, a temple located high in the Himalayas. I therefore also left early the next morning.

I had wanted to visit the Kedarnath Temple for a number of years, but for one reason or another, I never had the opportunity. I traveled all day by bus from Haridwar, and finally arrived at Gauri Kund. The distance from Haridwar to Gauri Kund is about 150 miles. Gauri Kund is the end of the line for cars and busses. It is a small village. From there one must trek the rest of the approximately eight and a half miles up to the temple either on foot, pony, or be carried in a palanquin by porters.

By the time I arrived at Gauri Kund it was dark, and so I looked for a room to stay that night. The moon was almost full, and the Summer Solstice would occur in just two days. I considered all of this to be very auspicious. As I stood gazing at the nearly full moon from my room's balcony, it appeared so close that I felt I could reach out and touch it.

Just before dawn the next morning, I started my trek up the path leading to the temple. I arrived at the temple at about 10 a.m.. After having darshan of the temple's ancient *Shiva-*

lingam, I went searching for accommodations. I had planned to stay for only a few days, or perhaps even a week. The area was very beautiful, with snow-capped mountains all around. It had been extremely hot down in the plains and so this was a great relief.

The Kedarnath Temple is located in the Garhwal district, surrounded by the Rudra Himalaya Mountain Range. Just behind the temple is the great dome known as Kedar peak. Because of its height, it is visible from great distances. The temple is at a height of approximately 12,000 feet above sea level.

The temple is only open for six months of the year. It opens sometime around the end of April, and closes towards the end of October, or beginning of November, depending on the weather. But the dates are mainly fixed astrologically. It is opened when the sun enters the constellation Aries (about mid April), and closes when it enters Scorpio (about mid November). The intense weather and snow-fall makes the temple inaccessible during the winter months.

The temple itself is built over the Kedar mountain peak. That is why it is called Kedarnath (Kedar+Natha) — meaning, "Lord of Kedar." The lingam is shaped like a pyramid or triangle, and appears to actually be the peak of Kedar mountain itself. It is known as a *Swayambhu* lingam, a word meaning self-created or self-revealed, indicating a naturally formed linga. It is also considered one of India's twelve *Jyotirlingams* or *"Lingas* of Light."

The present temple is believed to have been built or renovated by Adi Shankaracharya (788–820? C.E.), or at least under his guidance. This would make the temple approximately 1200 years old. The temple is built on a large rectangular platform with large grey stone slabs. The inside of the temple is decorated with carved figures of deities and scenes from various mythologies. The temple has been renovated many times over its long history.

The Kedarnath Temple has actually been considered a site

of worship since ancient times. It has been associated with the Pandavas, the heroes of the great epic, the *Mahabharata*. It describes a period somewhere between 4000 to 5000 years ago. Some believe that it was constructed by the Pandavas themselves, while others say that they simply renovated an older temple, one to which they often came to worship. The *Mahabharata* mentions a number of visits to the area by the Pandavas, especially Arjuna, and later his elder brother Yudhishthira during his journey to heaven. There are also legends in the Mahabharata associated with the temple's origins.

As we have seen, Adi Shankaracharya is closely associated with this temple as well. There is even a legend that he took *mahasamadhi* at Kedarnath, and there is a small shrine next to the temple purported to be his samadhi shrine. However opinions differ on this matter.

I went to the shrine to pay my respects to the great Master since I now belonged to one of the ten orders of sannyasis he organized. While sitting there, I had an intense feeling that I had previously visited the spot.

Shankaracharya is the founder of the particular order of sannyasins to which I now belonged. He organized sannyasis into ten branches or orders, each having a different name. They became known as the *Dashanami* sannyasins. The word *Dashanami* literally means "ten names." Names such as Giri, Bharati, Tirtha, Sarasvati, etc., These names are added to the end of a sannyasi's name. It becomes something like a last name.

Generally, the person taken sannyasa in the *Dashanami* monastic order will automatically belong to the same branch as their Guru. However, if one has no Guru, the person will be associated with the branch to which the person performing the sannyasa initiation belongs to. Since Baba belonged to the Sarasvati branch of sannyasins, all of his sannyasi disciples automatically belong to the Sarasvati branch. This is true even

(*right*) Kedarnath temple high in the Himalayas. (*below*) The author at Kedarnath (June 1986) after his sannyasa initiation.

though most of Baba's sannyasis were actually initiated by Swami Brahmananda Giri, who belongs to another branch, that of the 'Giris'.

While visiting Kedarnath I met a number of Naga sadhus. One sadhu was particularly knowledgeable of the monastic traditions, so we had many interesting conversations. I also unexpectedly met another Baba disciple, who happened to be on a pilgrimage. But I spent most of my time sitting quietly near the temple. I did however wander about in the surrounding area. I was feeling so much peace there, that I ended up staying for almost two weeks.

On the night of the full moon, which also happened to be the Summer Solstice that year, I was sitting for meditation. Suddenly, Lord Shiva graciously bestowed on me the vision (*darshan*) of the inner *lingam*. The temple *Shiva-linga* suddenly appeared before my inner eye. It then became illuminated by streaks of brilliantly colored lights, which appeared to be passing through a prism. The different colors were projected one after the other onto the sacred *linga*. Upon seeing this, I felt great inner joy and contentment. It also made me feel that Lord Shiva had blessed my *sannyasa* initiation.

I later heard a story that Shankaracharya consecrated one of five crystal *Shiva-lingas* at Kedarnath, called *Mukti Linga* or the "Linga of Liberation." The divine light I saw in my vision shining on the Kedarnath linga, through what looked like a prism, may have actually been that crystal linga. In any case, I saw my visit and experiences at Kedarnath as an auspicious beginning of my life as a sannyasi.

More Solitude

After almost two week's stay at Kedarnath, I returned to Brahmananda's ashram, where I spent the night. I left for Delhi early the next morning.

In Delhi I stayed with some friends. I also visited Amma (Swami Prajnananda) at her ashram, and spent a few days with her. Amma and I had been friends ever since I arrived at the ashram. It was she who translated at my first meeting with Baba. I always made it a point to visit her whenever I was in Delhi. A few days later, I left for Mumbai.

The day after I arrived in Mumbai, I went directly to Ganeshpuri for darshan of Baba's and Nityananda's samadhi shrines. Along the way I felt great excitement about having their darshan. However, I felt uncertain about my reception at the ashram, so I decided to first go to the town of Ganeshpuri and have Bhagavan Nityananda's darshan. And then go to the ashram for Baba's darshan.

I had not planned to stay in Ganeshpuri very long. Not wishing to have a confrontation with the ashram, I quietly made my way to the samadhi shrine, and sat for meditation for only about twenty minutes. I then immediately left for Mumbai.

The room where the shrine is located was still kept very simple, and I could feel Baba's presence. Still feeling joyful from my initiation, I mentally thanked Baba for all his blessings.

Since I would be leaving in just a few days, I took a hotel room not far from the airport. While there, I called some old friends who came to visit me. One of them was Anoop Vyas, the son of an old friend, and one of Baba's trustees. I had become close friends with his father after Baba had asked me to take care of him during a visit he made to New York to meet Baba during the second World Tour. When Anoop visited me at the hotel, he invited me to stay at his home whenever I came to Mumbai in the future.

Swami Vishveshwarananda, from Sannyas Ashram, and another swami also came to visit me, and congratulate me on my initiation. After a few days, I left for New York, and then back to Michigan.

By the middle of September, I was once again inspired to go into solitude and observe silence. Again my practices became very intense. Feelings of deep longing for the Self once again arose in powerful waves. I spent hours fluctuating between painful feelings of separation, and ecstatic joy.

As before, whenever this divine mood (*bhava*) arose, it was accompanied by various types of *pranayama,* as well as different postures (*asanas*), such as the *simhasana* or lion's posture. Sitting with the buttocks on my ankles, the anus would automatically start contracting in what is called *Mulabandha*. My mouth would automatically be forced to open wide, and my tongue would then be stretched downwards, towards my chin. At the same time, my eyes would roll upwards, gazing at the center between the eyebrows. The palms of my hands would rest face down on my knees, while the fingers would be outstretched. The anus would then start pulsating rapidly.

I could then feel the prana being forced into the *sushumna* canal. Sometimes a loud roar would arise, while at other times a hissing sound could be heard coming out of my mouth. Different mantras would also arise spontaneously.

When the feelings of longing became overbearing, I would feel totally exhausted. But when the Shakti became active, I felt a great deal of energy moving throughout my body. My hands would then automatically assume various hand gestures (*mudras*).

Towards the end of October, I ended my solitude. After a number of requests, I gave about a half-dozen talks on yoga and meditation to some of the local residents. Then at the end of November, I once again went into solitude.

However, a few weeks later I came out of my seclusion for the visit of Khenpo Karthar Rinpoche, a Tibetan Lama. He was Michael and Margaret's Guru. Since Michael's center had recently become an official Buddhist center, different Tibetan monks would often come to visit. There was now also another person living permanently in the center, and another would be arriving shortly.

After Rinpoche's visit, I again returned to solitude and continued with my practices. The Shakti once again became very powerful. But it was soon Christmas and I decided to come out of my retreat to spend the holidays with Michael's family, and the center's residents. After a few days, I once again returned to my solitude.

My Move To California

During my periods of solitude, I would maintain silence, meditate for long periods of time, chant a lot, and perform japa. This period lasted until about the third week of April 1987.

During the last portion of my solitude, I came to know that there soon would be a change of residence for me. However, I did not yet know where that change would take me. In May, I spoke to Michael and Margaret about my desire to go. At first I thought of going on a trip to California, as well as some other places and visit friends.

However, after speaking with Michael and Margaret, this initial plan was postponed. But by June, I had finally decided to leave Michigan for California. I had planned to stay for only a few months. But frankly I did not know where I was being led. I had a few invitations, but I decided not to make any decisions on them for the time being.

I had been invited to stay at a friend's home in the Bay Area, who was going to be on vacation, and so the house would be empty. The house belonged to Thelma, my ex-Mother-in-law. She was living alone in a large house, and was kind enough to allow me to stay there. Although she had no personal interest in meditation, or the spiritual life, she had met Baba a number of times through her daughter Lakshmi. She liked Baba very much. She is also a very kind-hearted person, and allowed me the freedom to continue my practices undisturbed.

Interestingly, my friendship with Thelma became much closer after Baba called me to his room one day in 1975, and told me to help her with some project she wanted to do. This was an unusual request, but I took it as his command, and did whatever she asked me to do as if I were doing it for Baba himself. Little did I realize at the time what a great blessing he was bestowing on me.

Besides continuing with my sadhana, I also began taking

care of Thelma's garden while she was away. I have always enjoyed gardening. I also visited some old friends and devotees of Baba living in the area.

Before leaving Michigan, an acquaintance had invited me to move to upstate New York, and start a meditation center. I had not yet accepted the invitation and was waiting for some inner inspiration before making any commitment. Since there was a doubt about it in my mind, I had decided to wait and see what developed.

Towards the last week of July, Swami Nityananda, who was once again teaching, was planning to hold a week long retreat in northern California, and had invited me to attend. I decided to go and visit him, but I stayed only one night. This was the first time we had seen each other since New York, a year and a half earlier. However, we had spoken on the phone once or twice. Since then, he had been living in India, but had recently moved to southern California.

By the end of August, I still did not know where I was going to go next, but it had become clear that I should not move to upstate New York. After a few weeks, I decided to take a short trip up the California coast. My mind was a bit agitated and I felt anxious about what I should do. I prayed to Baba for guidance but no response came. I felt there was nothing to do but wait. The life of the sannyasi is, after all, in God's hands.

After her trip, Thelma began planning another one for October, and invited me to stay until her return. After she returned, she again extended the invitation until the following spring. Meanwhile, another friend had offered me a cottage somewhere in the Pennsylvania Pocono mountains. I thought that I would travel back east sometime in the spring and visit family and friends, as well as go and see the cottage.

The Pocono mountains are located just north of where my family lived, and I thought I would drive there while visiting them. Where I would end up living was still a pressing question. Nevertheless, for the moment, some of the pressure had been removed.

On Thanksgiving night in 1987, Thelma was away celebrating the holidays with family members. I was home alone. I had been sitting for meditation for sometime, when suddenly the events of my life began to appear before my inner eye, as if I were watching a movie. The vision started with the first mystical experience I had which led me to India in search of a Guru, and then proceeded to reveal, in great detail, my experiences with Baba over the years. As I viewed this, I heard my Guru's voice say, "Write these experiences down."

At first this seemed strange, because ever since my arrival at the ashram, Baba had always encouraged me to remain silent about my spiritual experiences. And it was for this reason that I never gave any talks, nor wrote any articles about my experiences, or even what had brought me to Baba in the first place. Amma, the editor of the ashram magazine, *Gurudev-Vani*, asked me many times to write an article. But I had received similar instructions from an inner voice at the start of my journey not to speak about my spiritual experiences. However, I was now being instructed by Baba to reveal some of my experiences.

I suddenly felt inspired to start writing this autobiography. After my meditation, I immediately began writing. Within a month, the basic outline was completed.

When that was completed, the inspiration to continue writing left me. At the time, it was not my intention to publish the book. It was simply for my own benefit. No longer feeling inspired, I put the project aside, knowing that it would come up again on its own.

I spent the winter quietly. Then in March, I drove down to Los Angeles and stayed for a few days with a friend. I also visited Nityananda who at the time was living just south of Los Angeles. By April, I still had not made any plans to visit the east coast. Thelma was about to retire from her job, and she was thinking of building a cottage for herself in the back of the house, and asked if I would help her. I agreed to help. This would be a long project.

Then in the first week of May, I again felt inspired to work on this book. But this burst of creativity lasted for only about three weeks, at which time I again put the project aside.

In June, I received word from my brother that my father was ill, having been diagnosed with Alzheimer's disease. Recently I had found it more and more difficult to communicate with him on the phone. So in July, I decided to fly to Philadelphia and visit him and my family.

I found that he was easily distracted and could not communicate with others very well. It appeared that he was withdrawing more into himself, and there was also some depression. Obviously, all symptoms of the disease. This was very difficult for my mother, who initially would lose patience with him, since she did not yet understand the nature of the disease. It was sad to see him in this condition, especially since he always had an inquisitive and active mind.

During my visit, I also met with some old friends who lived in the area. And I went to the Poconos to look at the cottage which a friend had offered. The Poconos, located about a hundred miles north of Philadelphia, is a very beautiful area with its mountains and lakes. It would have been an ideal place for an ashram. It is similar to the Catskills in upstate New York. Unfortunately I discovered that the cottage would not be suitable.

After a few weeks, I returned to California. As summer ended and the fall months approached, I once again started to feel the pangs of spiritual separation. I had not spent any time in solitude for awhile, and had also cut my meditation down a bit. My mind was a bit agitated, and doubts about my spiritual work began to arise.

Then around the beginning of October, while in that mood of uncertainty about my life, I prayed to Bhagavan Nityananda for his help and guidance. A few nights later, I began feeling a deep desire to go to India and attend the *Kumbha-mela*, a religious festival which was scheduled to be held in the city of

Allahabad, in January 1989. I initially felt that this inspiration came directly from Bhagavan Nityananda.

However, the next day the inspiration was not as strong, and I began to doubt it. Besides, my funds were extremely limited. I therefore decided to wait and see if the experience would repeat itself. I recall that at the time I did not really feel one way or the other about going. My attitude was that if it was meant to happen, it would happen on its own, otherwise not.

But by the second week of November, the experience and presence of Bhagavan Nityananda became very powerful again. It was now clear that it was indeed he who was calling me, and I knew I had to go. I immediately began planning for my departure, and thought of leaving by mid-December. But December, January, and February are the busiest months for traveling to India, and all the flights for December were already booked. I did not want to leave in November, and so I decided to wait, thinking that if I could not get a seat for December, then I could leave at the beginning of January.

However, the earliest flight I could find was for the 8th of January. But I was placed on a waiting list for an earlier flight. Then, by mid December, not having heard anything from my travel agent, so I decided to call another agent. While on the phone with him, there was suddenly a cancellation for a flight leaving on the 1st of January, which I immediately booked.

It was a direct flight from San Francisco, arriving in Mumbai early on the morning of the 3rd of January, my birthday. I felt this was an auspicious start to my pilgrimage. I already had my visa and was ready to go.

Now that I had an arrival date, I could also plan my journey to Allahabad. The mela would officially start on January 14th with the entrance of the sun into the constellation of Capricorn, and would last approximately seven weeks. I did not plan to stay there the whole time, since millions of people were expected to attend. I had planned to visit other places in the area, including Varanasi.

Kumbha-Mela
(The Pot of Nectar Festival)

I left for the Kumbha-mela from San Francisco on the morning of January 1, 1989. The flight was long and uneventful. I had been invited by Anoop to stay at his home while I was in Mumbai, so I went there on my arrival in the early hours of January 3rd, my birthday. My plan was to immediately go to Ganeshpuri for Baba and Bhagavan's darshan. I had planned to stay there for four or five days.

Over the years I had heard about many of Baba's old devotees not being welcomed at the ashram. While in Mumbai, I was told that Swami Chidvilasananda was at the Ganeshpuri ashram at the time, but all of my previous attempts to remain friendly with her had been ignored.

I was uncertain of the reception I would receive at the ashram, so when I arrived in Ganeshpuri late that afternoon, I decided to take a room in town.

Because of such feelings, I decided to go for darshan of Baba's samadhi-shrine only during the hours the ashram was opened to the public. But having arrived late on that first day, after the public hours were over, I bowed to Baba from the street as I passed the ashram on my way to Ganeshpuri. That afternoon and evening I spent a number of hours at Bhagavan's samadhi shrine.

The next morning I went to the ashram for Baba's darshan. When I arrived, I noticed that some function was being held inside the front hall, and everyone was sitting there. I walked directly through the main courtyard and into Baba's samadhi shrine. It felt wonderful to be there. After bowing and walking around the tomb three times in a clockwise direction, I sat quietly for meditation. I sat for only about half an hour, and then left for Ganeshpuri, feeling inspired by Baba's presence.

As I left the ashram and was walking towards town, I heard

someone calling out to me. I turned and saw it was one of the ashram swamis, whom I knew. I waited for him to catch up, and after the usual preliminary greetings, a conversation ensued.

He began questioning me about the reason for my visit to India and Ganeshpuri. Apparently, Swami Nityananda had visited Ganeshpuri the previous day, and they were therefore certain that I was traveling with him. They also seemed sure that I was in Ganeshpuri for some diabolical purpose. The Swami made it clear that I was not welcomed at the ashram. I tried to explain to him that he was mistaken, and that I was on my way to the Kumbha-mela alone. He did not believe me, and as he turned to walk away he said, "Don't think you can make fools of us."

I thought to myself, "You don't seem to need any help. You are doing such a good job yourself."

The next day, I again stopped at the ashram for Baba's darshan on my way to the town of Vajreshwari. But when I reached the gate, I was stopped by the guard, who told me I was not allowed inside. When I asked the reason for it, he could not give me one, but told me that that it was the order he was given by the ashram management.

I then asked if I might at least fill my water bottle from the taps, located just inside the front gate. I had been suffering from a kidney stone for months, and drinking lots of water was the only thing which gave me some relief. I was denied even that. But someone standing nearby took pity on me, and took my bottle and filled it for me.

As I stood there, reflecting on the sad state of affairs, I suddenly recalled what one of Baba's trustees had once told me after Baba's mahasamadhi. When Baba told him the spot where he wanted his body to be interred, the trustee said that Baba told him why he wanted it there. He said that Baba told him, "One day you will not be allowed to enter the ashram. And from there, I can see the street, and see those who come."

Looking towards Baba's samadhi shrine from the road, I

folded my hands in reverence, and bowed my head in silence to Baba. I then continued on my way to Vajreshwari.

I stayed in Ganeshpuri for four days. In the early hours of the morning, I would meditate at the samadhi shrine, and later would participate in the arati. I also spent a great deal of time in the mahasamadhi room.

On the morning of my departure from Ganeshpuri, I felt Baba's presence very strongly. I also felt that he wanted me to write a letter to Chidvilasananda about my experience at the ashram. Among other things, I asked her why she did not allow Baba's devotees to have darshan of his samadhi shrine?

I first wrote the letter by hand, and thought I would mail it when I returned to America. However, that day in Mumbai, I unexpectedly met an old friend who was going to the ashram the very next day. He agreed to take the letter to Swami Chidvilasananda for me. Since I wanted to make sure that she received it personally, I asked him to place it directly in her hands.

Before sending the letter, I wanted to have it typed. So I searched for someone with a typewriter. I found a person near Anoop's house. He said that he would type it for me. He had a very old typewriter and did the best he could.

Even though I had asked Chidvilasananda a number of questions in the letter, I did not expect a reply, and never received one.

Meanwhile, I got my train ticket for Allahabad, and I was scheduled to leave in two days. Before going to Ganeshpuri, I had heard that Maharaj (Swami Brahmanandaji) was at his ashram in Vile Parle, so I went to pay my respects to him on my way to Ganeshpuri. This was indeed fortunate since he was leaving for Allahabad that very night. He was very kind to me, and when he heard that I had come specifically for the Kumbhamela, he graciously invited me to stay at his camp. At the time I did not realize what a great blessing this was.

I had reserved a berth on the Calcutta Mail, leaving Mumbai

at 9 p.m.. It would arrive at Allahabad just over 24 hours later. All transportation to Allahabad was heavily booked, so the train was packed with pilgrims. I arrived in the city late at night, and began searching for a hotel room, thinking it would be easier to go out to Maharaj's campsite the next morning.

It gets quite cold, damp, and foggy in Allahabad during the winter months. There was lots of fog that night and visibility was very poor. It had been many years since my last visit to that city, so I did not know my way around very well.

After inquiring at two or three hotels, things did not look very promising. But I finally found a room in the next hotel where one was being vacated just as I was talking to the hotel manager. After waiting about twenty minutes for the room to get ready, I finally laid down to sleep.

Early the next morning, I went to the *mela* grounds and found Maharaj's camp. Swami Nityananda was also there with a few of his devotees. He had planned to stay for only two days, and then travel to Delhi, where he planned to hold some programs.

I had arrived a few days before the official start of the Kumbha-mela, which would occur on the morning of the 14th. On that day the sun would enter the constellation of Capricorn, which is called *Makara Sankranti*. It is on this day that the mela at Allahabad is officially started. That day is considered the first auspicious day for taking a ritual or royal bath known as a *Shahi-snan*. There are about five such days spread over the seven week period of the mela.

The *Maha Kumbha-mela* occurs once in twelve years at one of four locations in northern India. It is timed by the transit of the planet Jupiter into one of the four fixed astrological signs: Taurus, Leo, Scorpio, and Aquarius. The mela is held at Allahabad or Prayag, the city's ancient name, when Jupiter is in Taurus, and the sun and moon are in Capricorn. When Jupiter transits Aquarius, and the sun and moon are in Aries, the mela is held at Haridwar.

Although the festival can be traced back at least two thousand years, it has grown tremendously in the 20th century, particularly after India's independence. Initially five million pilgrims were expected at this *mela*, but as it turned out, some thirty million attended.

Originally the festival was a gathering of mainly sadhus who would come from all parts of India, Nepal, Tibet, and even China. Today, however, the majority of pilgrims are lay persons. Nevertheless, seekers come from all parts of the world. In the next seven weeks, millions of people would live on the banks of the two sacred rivers, the Ganga and Yamuna. And at the spot where they merge, known as the *sangam* is where they will take their ritual bath. According to tradition, a third river, a tributary of the Sarasvati, also merges at this spot. Although it is now invisible, and flows underground. In fact, this legend may be a further indication of the mela's great antiquity, since we now know that the Sarasvati river dried up around 2000 B.C.E.

During the mela, everyone lives in temporary tents and huts which are set up by the various religious institutions on the dry river beds. I was very impressed by the overall organization and facilities of the temporary city. There was even running water and a decent sewage system. All these facilities were of course temporary, and would be dismantled after the *mela* was over. Once the monsoon season started, the whole area would be under water.

As this was my first *mela*, I started wandering around the campgrounds, seeing the sights, and meeting different sadhus and pilgrims that had gathered there. Camps had also been set up by most of the well known ashrams.

With all the loudspeakers and many lectures going on at the same time, at times the festival took on a carnival appearance. Nevertheless I felr an atmosphere of spirituality which pervaded the place. There were sadhus from all over India, as well as other parts of the world, and so I felt very much at home.

On the morning of the 14th, I awoke at around 3:30 a.m. and got myself ready. There would be a procession to the river bank by the seven main Shaiva monastic groups called *Akhadas* (or *Akaras*).

The Dashanami or 'ten name' monastic orders established by Adi Shankaracharya is also divided into seven Akhadas. These are: Maha Nirvani, Niranjani, Juna, Avahan, Agni, and Atal. Since Brahmananda belonged to the Maha Nirvani Akhada, that day his camp would be the first to take the *Shahi-snan* or royal bath.

These days a strict protocol is followed as to the bathing order of the Akhadas. Unfortunately, there had often been disagreements in the past over who should bathe first. Such disagreements have often led to violence and even death. After all of the akhadas have taken their bath, it is then the turn of the lay pilgrims.

The procession started at around 5 a.m. that first morning, and began moving slowly towards the river. Along the way we chanted various mantras and hymns. It was a cold, damp, and foggy morning. And because of the fog, we could hardly see ten feet ahead of us.

Moving in starts and stops, I began reflecting on why I was there. I looked around and wondered what it was that had brought all of us there. We were shivering in the cold morning air, but were nevertheless ready to take a dip in the river's chilly water. I also wondered whether we were all mad. Such were the thoughts that arose in my mind as we approached the confluence of the sacred rivers.

It had taken almost an hour to reach the river. I could now just barely see it ahead of us. Then something strange began to happen. My eyes suddenly opened very wide, and they became completely focused on the river in front of me. As this occurred, my legs started walking quickly towards the river, taking longer and longer strides each time. Gradually this became a slow run, leaving the others behind. Although I was fully aware, my body appeared to move as if under the control of some invisible force.

(*above*) Overview of the temporary Kumbha-Mela city 1989;
(*below*) Mela crowds.

As I ran, I also began to remove my clothing, and stuffing them mechanically into a small red plastic bag I had brought with me. All this occurred completely spontaneously. I no longer felt the cold, or noticed anyone else around me. It was as if I was being drawn towards the river by a powerful magnet. I was in an ecstatic state.

Upon reaching the river, I walked out until the water was about chest high. I then submerged myself three times, remembering my Guru, and his Guru, Bhagavan Nityananda, and all the Siddhas. I thanked them for their continued blessings.

Up to then, I had been completely withdrawn and unaware of my surroundings. But as I completed my ablutions, and turned to walk out of the water, I was suddenly overwhelmed by the thousands upon thousands of people, who were now standing on the banks, removing their clothing, or putting them on, having already had their sacred dip. It was absolutely jammed packed.

It was now dawn, and one could at least see what was in front of them. But as I walked out of the water, I suddenly realized that I had no clue where I had laid the red bag containing my clothes and camera.

Still in an ecstatic state, I walked towards Swami Nityananda and the others, who had watched me and wondered what was happening to me. I told them that I did not know where my bag was. And as I stood there joyfully, but without any clothes, they all began laughing, saying that I would never be able to find my bag. But just then, once again I felt that mysterious force taken control of my body, and suddenly I turned around, and began walking for about thirty or forty feet, and I came to a stop. I then looked down, and there was my red bag. After grabbing it, I raised it over my head in triumphant, showing my friends that I had found it. I shouted, Sadgurunath Maharaj ki Jai!

We soon started back to our camp. I felt very happy to be there and it appeared that this feeling was shared by everyone. As we left the river bank, others would arrive. This process would continue until late morning

Later that morning, I again walked around the mela grounds meeting the many sadhus. One of the most colorful groups of monks are the *Nagas* or naked sadhus, who make up the various Akhadas. These sadhus live very austere lives.

The Nagas were originally organized for the protection of sannyasis, and the Hindu religion in general, which was coming under the onslaught of Islam. The mela is a very important event for the Nagas. Interestingly, it is only during the *Kumbha-mela* that a seeker is initiated as a Naga sadhu.

Throughout the day and night, one could hear lectures and hymns coming from all parts of the mela grounds. Sadhus gathered everywhere for *satsang*. I felt that if I were to leave right then, it would have been worth the trip. But I had decided to stay for approximately two weeks.

It was estimated that over two million people were there on the first day alone, but more and more were arriving daily. The authorities were soon saying that about five to ten million pilgrims had arrived.

With so many people at the Kumbha-mela, after about ten

(*below*) Naga sadhus huddled around the warm morning fire.

(*above*) Mahamandaleshwars sitting for lunch; (*below*) The author with some friends at the Kumbh-mela.

days I decided to leave for Varanasi. I initially thought I would stay for about a week, but this was extended to two.

The two rivers: Ganga and Yamuna, which merge at Allahabad, continues on as the Ganga in an easterly direction. It eventually passes through the city of Varanasi, which is built on its western bank. You will recall that I had visited the city a number of times in the past, but that had been many years ago.

I have always enjoyed the peaceful meditations on the river's bank, and the powerful experiences I had at the burning ghat. During my stay, I again visited the Buddhist site at Sarnath.

My stay in Varanasi was a time for deep reflection. My meditations were also very powerful, and I started to become more and more aware of my Siddha lineage. It was as if for the first time I became fully aware of my real relationship with the Siddhas.

In the previous year or two, I had felt uncertain about my role in life. I lacked all interest in external activities. The feeling of my close association with the Siddhas began at the Kumbha-mela, and was now crystallizing in Varanasi. I now felt the guidance and power to continue my Guru's work.

I also felt Bhagavan Nityananda's presence, which brought a feeling of inner inspiration and renewal. I felt blessed by Baba, Bhagavan Nityananda, and all the perfected masters before them.

Feeling spiritually rejuvenated from my pilgrimage, I left Varanasi for New Delhi on the 7th of February. I had planned to stay in the capital for about two weeks. While there I stayed with Anoop's sister, Amita, her husband Sanjay, and their two young children.

While in Delhi, I met some old friends and Baba devotees as well. At one satsang, I was asked to speak about Baba and my experiences with him. I also met with Mr. T. N. Khana, owner of the Claridges Hotel, and an old devotee of Baba's. He sang a beautiful hymn to Goddess Durga for me. He sang with such great devotion that tears of joy began rolling down his cheeks.

One of the main reasons I was in Delhi was to spend some time at Amma's (Swami Prajnananda) ashram at Bhati. Amma had invited me to visit after she heard that I would be attending the Kumbha-mela. You will recall that the ashram had been built by Baba's Delhi devotees, and I had accompanied Baba to both the ground breaking ceremony, as well as its inauguration.

Amma had been with Bhagavan Nityananda, and became Baba's disciple in the late 1950's. She soon became Baba's secretary. But she not only preserved Baba's words, she was a photographer like her brother, Pappa. She was also instrumental in recording Baba chanting various hymns. Therefore, Baba's devotees owe her a great debt for preserving Baba's voice, words, and images.

After Baba's mahasamadhi, Amma went to live at her brother's house (not Pappa, but another brother) in the state of Gujarat. Things went well for a few years, but then, according to Amma, the SYDA Foundation convinced her brother to ask her to move out. So she was forced to move.

Not knowing where she would go, some Delhi devotees came to her rescue, and asked her to move into the ashram outside of Delhi, which had been inaugurated by Baba. That is how Amma moved there. As it was a beautiful ashram, I told her that she was going to be very happy there. In fact, just before Baba's death, he had actually told her that he thought she should move into that ashram after his death. But she thought she would be happier near her family in Gujarat.

Nevertheless, even after she moved to the Delhi ashram, the foundation continued to harass her by having different people write her nasty letters. Many of which I read personally. Some of the people writing the letters did not surprise me as I knew their nature. What saddened me was seeing people's names who I thought were more noble, or at least good individuals. People who would never associate themselves with such mean spirit

(*above*) The author with Swami Prajnananda (Amma), Delhi 1989.

activities. Nevertheless, in spite of all of that, Amma was very happy in that ashram.

I have always enjoyed reading spiritual books, particularly the lives of great beings. I have also always been a student of world religions. So whenever I visited India, I would always visit the many bookshops in Mumbai, Delhi, Varanasi, and in fact wherever I traveled. While in Delhi, I would visit all the local bookstores, including Motilal Banarsidass and Munshiram Manoharlal, at the time the two largest publishers of books on Indian culture and spirituality. I had in fact become friendly with N. P. Jain of Motilal's ever since I had made arrangements for him to meet Baba just before Baba's mahasamadhi. Now whenever I visited their Delhi shop, he would always invite me to have lunch with his family.

I left Delhi and arrived in Mumbai about the third week of February. My flight to San Francisco was not until the 3rd of March. I was told by someone that Maharaj was at his Vile Parle ashram at the time, and so I again went to pay my respects.

Period of Writing

When I returned to California in March of 1989, Thelma and I began the process of building her cottage. Plans had to be drawn up and submitted to the city council for approval. Then a contractor had to be found. Etc.. This was going to take months. I soon began to clear the site so that proper measurements could be taken, and prepare the area ready for construction.

I had taken many slides at the Kumbha-Mela, and soon a number of people became interested in seeing them. So I decided to make a slide-show, and showed them once or twice at the weekly satsangs I was holding at the time. I also showed them to a spiritual group who had requested it. During that period I also work on this book whenever I was inspired to do so.

After getting the plans together for the cottage, they were submitted to the city council. This took months to process. After that was done, a contractor had to be found. It was not until October or November that someone was found. Work finally got started during the last week of November.

I was kept very busy with all the preparations, and before I knew it, the year was almost over. Then, towards the end of December, I received a Christmas card from an old friend and Baba devotee, who was now living in Hawaii. She invited me to visit the island of Kauai. Her name is also Lakshmi, so in order to avoid any confusion between her and my ex-wife, I will refer to her as "Kauai Lakshmi." She had been Baba's cook for many years.

I called her at the beginning of the year thanking her for the invitation, and we made some tentative plans for my visit. Then in the third week of February, I left for the beautiful island of Kauai, on the first of many visits.

A few days after my arrival, on the night of Mahashivaratri, Lakshmi and I visited the Hindu temple and monastery, founded by Sivaya Subramuniyaswami. Swamiji was also the publisher

(*above*) The author (on left) with Sivaya Subramuniyaswami, founder of Kauai's Hindu Monastery

of the well known magazine, *Hinduism Today*. Lakshmi and I participated in the Shivaratri celebrations until late into the night, chanting and meditating.

That evening Subramuniyaswami invited me to visit the ashram again two days later, on Sunday morning, when I would be able to meet him privately. That Sunday, after enjoying a delicious lunch with him and a few of his close disciples, I had the opportunity to walk around their beautiful ashram in a more leisurely manner.

This was not my first meeting with Subramuniyaswami. I had actually met him briefly in 1972, when he and about 75 of his disciples came to visit Baba in Ganeshpuri. I also had a more recent contact with one of his disciples, Sivanatha Ceyonswami, who is the ashram's astrologer. He had contacted Matrix Software, the astrological software company founded by my friend Michael, inquiring about astrological software which would calculate charts according to the Vedic system of astrology. Since I had been closely associated with the development of such a program at Matrix when I was living in Michigan, my friend Michael turned the letter over to me. So Swamiji and I spoke briefly on the phone.

But as I was just starting a period of solitude and silence, and because the program Matrix was developing was for the PC, and not for the Mac, the contact went no further. I therefore made it a point to meet Sivanatha Ceyonswami in person while I was there. We had a wonderful conversation.

While visiting the ashram, I also had a long conversation with Sadasivanatha Palaniswami, the editor of *Hinduism Today*. I felt an immediate kinship with him. In fact, all of the swamis treated me with great kindness, and over the years I would visit Swamiji and his disciples many times. A mutual love and respect developed between us.

Initially I had planned to stay on the island for only two weeks. But it was however extended for another week when another friend, Jeff, invited me to stay in his guest cottage. Jeff had spent some time with Baba, and so I had known him for a number of years as well.

By the time I returned to California, Thelma's cottage was nearing completion. Once it was done, I would have to move out, and so the thought of where I was going to live was heavy on my mind again. I had absolutely no clue where I would be going, which made me feel somewhat anxious, but I had faith that Baba and Bhagavan Nityananda would provide what was needed.

Then an old friend named Maheshwara, invited me to move into his house with him. We had known each other for a number of years, and he had been very supportive of me ever since I had taken sannyasa. But as we had very different personalities, at first I was hesitant to accept his kind invitation. Like Baba, I placed a great deal of importance on self-discipline. I thanked Maheshwara for his kind offer, but I warned him that it was not easy to live with a sannyasi.

But frankly, I had no other choices. A sannyasi has surrendered himself to the will of the divine. From that moment on he trusts that the Lord will provide for all his or her needs. He must also be ready to bear any hardships which may come his way. But I had complete faith in God, and Baba.

A few days later I finally received some guidance. I had a dream-vision in which I saw myself sitting in Maheshwara's living room holding *satsang*. I then clearly heard Baba's voice telling me, "Go and stay at Maheshwara's for now."

The next day I called Maheshwara, thanked him again for his kind offer, and told him that I would be happy to move in with him. I moved in about the middle of April of 1990.

Not long after my move, Maheshwara began encouraging me to hold weekly satsangs at his home. But as the house was somewhat run down, I asked him if we could first clean and paint the living room, and generally get the house cleaned. He agreed, and we began painting and carpeting the two rooms. When the work was done, the room in which the programs were going to be held looked and felt like a temple. The first program was held on the auspicious day of Guru Purnima, which occurred on the 7th of July that year. I then began having weekly satsangs. Maheshwara even placed an ad in a local Indian magazine.

At the time, I was also working on a manual of Vedic Astrology, which I had started while still living at Thelma's house. The project got started in an interesting way. Although I still had an interest in astrology, and had many astrologer friends, I no longer practiced it myself. Then, in the fall of 1989, during a two month period of solitude and silence, I had a dream-vision in which I was sitting with Baba. We were having a casual conversation discussing various topics. Then at the end of our conversation, as I was about to leave, Baba looked at me and said that I should write a book on Vedic Astrology. I felt no interest or inclination in writing such a book, and I tried to politely decline. But seeing my hesitation, Baba just laughed and said, "You *will* write such a book!"

The next morning, after my meditation, I suddenly felt a surge of creative energy arising within me, and I immediately started working on the book on Vedic astrology. Within a few weeks the foundation of the book was completed, and in the following months, whenever the inspiration arose, more work would be done.

As the book took shape, I envisioned it as a manual on Vedic astrology. I had to also calculate the various charts, graphs, and tables used in the Vedic astrology system. Although I was using the software which we had developed at Matrix, it unfortunately did not have all of the necessary calculations, and so I had to do them all by hand. The work was very tedious but necessary in order to give the reader a clear understanding of what the process entailed.

Towards the end of August, I received a phone call from my elder brother who told me that my father had been hospitalized. Since he was not doing very well, he suggested that I go and visit him. So in the first week of September, I traveled to Philadelphia to visit my father and family. I stayed for about three weeks and then returned to California.

Not long after my return, I was invited to speak at the local Shanti Mandir center in October, on the anniversary of Baba's mahasamadhi. Shanti Mandir is the organization which was started by Swami Nityananda after his break with SYDA Foundation. I decided to accept the invitation and gave a short talk.

Then at the end of October, I received an unexpected telephone call from Sadasivanatha Palaniswami, the editor of *Hinduism Today* magazine. He told me that they were doing research on an article for their November 1990 issue. The subject was on the practice of trade marking public domain yoga terms by various religious and spiritual groups. One of the articles focused on the recent threats of lawsuits from SYDA Foundation against the Shiva-Shakti ashram and its founder, Swami Savitripriya, over the term "Siddha Yoga", which the foundation had trademarked. Swamiji wanted to know if I had any thoughts on the subject.

I was of course hesitant to get involved, not wishing to speak negatively of the foundation. However, I was also aware of how over the years the foundation seemed to harass not only Swami Nityananda, but other devotees as well.

I personally did not agree with the whole idea of ownership of such terms. And I was quite familiar with the history of the term "Siddha Yoga." When the ashram lawyers first applied for the trademark, it was explained to Baba that it was mainly to protect the foundation. They told him that if someone else trademarked the term before they did, that group could legally stop SYDA Foundation from using the term. It was never Baba's intention to stop someone else from using it.

In any case, I told Swamiji that I wanted to think about it. I did not have to think about it very long, because within a week, I received a telephone call from one of SYDA Foundation's lawyers, whom I knew personally. He informed me that I was using the term 'Siddha Yoga' illegally in my ad, the one placed by Maheshwara. He went on to say that if I did not stop immediately, I would be sued for trademark infringement. I told the lawyer that as a disciple of Baba's, and a follower of Siddha Yoga, that I had the right to use the term. He of course did not agree.

I had already decided to cancel the ad Maheshwara had placed for other reasons, but after receiving the call from the lawyer, I decided to extend it. I was also inspired to write a letter to Sadasivanatha Palaniswami, relating what had happened to me, as well as my thoughts on the subject. When he received the letter, he immediately called me asking my permission to print the letter in their newspaper, which I gave.

When the January 1991 issue of *Hinduism Today* came out with my letter, the paper began receiving numerous letters from SYDA staff members. The letters condemned the *Hinduism Today* article, and my letter, and tried in numerous ways to discredit me. The Kauai swamis showed me the letters, which were mostly written by people I did not even know, but who claimed to know me. A few even questioned whether I was really Baba's disciple at all. Soon after that I also started receiving nasty and threatening phone calls from foundation supporters.

But there were also calls of support. Some of the Indian newspapers in the Bay area contacted me, asking for interviews, which I politely declined. With all of this going on, I decided to observe silence for a few weeks. I did not feel the need to defend myself, and for Baba's sake, I did not want to be in a position to damage the reputation of SYDA Foundation. I did not understand their perceived need to "protect" Baba's teachings by preventing his devotees from sharing them.

During that period of solitude, there was still a pressing question which I had to try and resolve. As I had feared, my stay at Maheshwara's home was not working out, and I could see that my presence there was now disturbing him. This was therefore weighing heavily on my mind. But where could I go? I had no funds.

Then one night in a dream-vision, I saw myself flying south from Maheshwara's house near Berkeley. I was flying above one of the Bay Area's major highways, until I reached the city of Fremont, about forty miles south. Beneath me, I could see the highway traffic and all the homes along the way. I then saw myself doing some work in a house there that belonged to Thelma. This dream would turn out to be absolutely true.

When I came out of solitude, I received a phone call from "Kauai Lakshmi," inviting me to once again visit the island. I told her that since I was about to move out of Maheshwara's house, and did not yet know where I was going, I wasn't sure about visiting the island that year. But she suggested that I go and stay in Kauai for a few months. I told her that I would seriously think about it.

Around the middle of January, I decided to speak to Maheshwara and tell him that I felt it best if I moved out. I could see the relief on his face and knew that I had made the right decision. I had a lot of love for him and did not wish to cause him any distress.

I would not be able to leave for Kauai for at least a month. Then, while all this was going on, one day I happened to speak on the phone with Thelma and my ex-wife Lakshmi. I told them of my decision to move out of Maheshwara's.

"But where will you go?" they asked concerned.

I told them about the invitation to go and stay in Kauai for awhile, and I said that I would probably put my things in storage for now. But to solve my immediate problem, Thelma suggested that I go and stay at her Fremont house until I left for Kauai.

When I was living with Thelma in Mountain View, Lakshmi, and her current husband Ed, were living in the Fremont house. After the cottage was built, Ed and Lakshmi moved into the front house where Thelma had been living. While Thelma moved into her new cottage behind the main house. Meanwhile, the Fremont house had been put on the market to be sold. But I was told that it had not yet sold, and so I could stay there for the few weeks before I left for Hawaii.

Interestingly, I had stayed in that house briefly many years earlier, and so I had some history with it. I moved to the Fremont house within a few days. While waiting to leave for Kauai, I decided to do some work on the house. I began painting it so that it would look more presentable to potential buyers.

I left for Hawaii in February. "Kauai Lakshmi" had made arrangements for me to stay at Jeff's guest cottage since he was going to be away for about a month.

I again went to Kauai's Hindu temple and monastery for

Mahashivaratri, which occurred that year just four days after my arrival. Shortly afterwards, I received a call from Sadasivanatha Palaniswami, informing me about the fallout of their article. He told me that they too had now been threatened with lawsuits by SYDA Foundation lawyers. One of the ashram swamis, accompanied by two lawyers, even showed up at the Kauai office of *Hinduism Today*, and made verbal threats. This is of course unbecoming for any sannyasi.

Ironically, this was all occurring just a few miles from where I was staying. In fact, it was the same swami who had been sent to speak to me when I visited the Ganeshpuri ashram on my way to the Kumbha-Mela. It seemed that he was still going around making a fool of himself, along with the foundation. During the Kumbha-Mela, I even saw another of the ashram swamis follow and harass Swami Nityananda the whole time he was there. He then followed him to Delhi. This was not the behavior that swamis vow to uphold when they take sannyas initiation, and it saddened me to think that some of Baba's swamis were acting like common thugs.

I personally knew that Swami, and had once thought highly of him. But I then began scolding him and reminded him of the elevated path he had chosen. Although these swamis were following the wishes of the current head of the Foundation, their actions were not representative of Baba Muktananda's teaching. Baba began every program with the phrase, "*I welcome you all with love and respect.*"

I decided to remain quiet about the whole affair. I also continued to work on a book of stories which I had started the previous summer while living at Maheshwara's house. These were stories and parables, some of which are thousands of years old, that Baba used in his public talks and lectures. I had heard him tell these stories many times over the years, and had started writing them down shortly after my arrival at the ashram. I had gathered quite a collection, and had incorporated many of them into my own talks over the years. I had also used them during the years when I did astrological counseling.

Baba loved stories, both reading and telling them. I had even given him a number of books which had interesting stories in them. A number of people suggested that I publish these stories in book form. And since the book on Vedic astrology was very heady stuff, I felt like this would be a fun project. So I decided to gather all of the stories together and see what I came up with. I began going through them, trying to retell them exactly the way that I remembered Baba telling the story. Of course, Baba was a master story teller, so I am in no way comparing myself to him. Nevertheless I tried my best.

During my stay at Jeff's guest cottage that year, I also had an unusual experience. While meditating one morning, I had the vision of Bhagavan Nityananda sitting right in the middle of the room. It was not Nityananda's actual form that I saw, but his statue, a replica of the same statue that is in the Ganeshpuri ashram. It sat there peacefully looking out towards the ocean. I never told Jeff about this experience, but interestingly, about three years later, he decided to install a replica of this same statue on his property.

My visit to the island that year was a pleasant one. There was still the pressing question on my mind of where I was going to live after Kauai. Then, after almost two months on the island, Thelma called me one day and said that she still had not sold the Fremont house. and was thinking of taking it off the market for now. She wondered if I would be interested in staying there for awhile. I felt this was Baba's blessing, and thanked her for her generous offer.

Try as I may, it seemed that I could not avoid dealing with SYDA Foundation. Maheshwara called me while I was in Kauai to tell me that someone from the foundation had contacted him asking for my address, and he asked me whether he should give it to them or not. I told him he could.

A week later, Lakshmi called me to tell me that I had received a registered letter from the foundation lawyers. But the letter was not addressed to Swami Prakashananda but to my pre-sannyasi name. I received an inner message from Baba not to accept the letter, so I told Lakshmi to return the letter, writing on it that there was no one there by that name.

Whenever someone took sannyasa, Baba would tell everyone that they should no longer call that person by their previous name, as this is considered disrespectful. Sannyasa initiation is considered a new birth, and the person is now dead to their past.

When the foundation lawyers got the letter back, someone called Maheshwara again saying that the address was wrong. He gave them the same address, and pointed out to them that perhaps it was because they had not addressed the letter properly. It was a couple of months before they realized that their letter was not going to be accepted as it was addressed.

The letter was an order to stop using the term "Siddha Yoga," as well as other terms which they claimed to have the rights to. A number of my friends urged me to challenge the foundation's trademark claims, and *Hinduism Today's* lawyer even offered to defend me at a substantially reduced fee after foundation lawyers had threatened him as well.

However, I was a poor sannyasi, with no means of income, and could not even afford his reduced rate. Indeed, I was existing only through the generosity of a few friends, whom I felt Baba had inspired to help me. But the more important question was whether this was what Baba wanted me to do. After reflection, I concluded that it was not.

I returned to California about the middle of April of 1991, uncertain about my future. Thelma told me that she did not know how long it would be before the house was sold, so I lived there ready to move at any moment. But then one night, after some prayers for guidance, I had a dream-vision in which Baba told me not to worry, and that I should live there quietly, and continue my sadhana. He also indicated that I would be living in that house for a number of years.

However I never mentioned any of this to Thelma, since I did not wish to influence her in any way, and so I continued to live there ready to move at any moment. Since Baba had told me to live there quietly, I decided not to hold satsangs. I did however celebrate Baba's birthday with some friends, and observed his Mahasamadhi anniversary. I also continued with my writing projects.

Months went by, and in the second week of December, my brother called and told me that father was not doing very well. A few weeks later he passed away. I flew to Philadelphia for his funeral, and remained for a few weeks to comfort my mother.

In June 1992, I received an inner inspiration to start writing Baba's biography. Amma (Swami Prajnananda) had also been encouraging me to write such a book for some time. Then, sometime in the fall, I received a premonition that Amma may be leaving her body soon. Interestingly, shortly after this, I heard from Amma, and she told me that she had been diagnosed with bone cancer. I therefore decided to go to India to visit her, and I thought I would also do some research for Baba's biography. I left for Mumbai on November 24th.

Amma was scheduled to arrive in Mumbai from Delhi about a week after my arrival. So I decided to go and stay in Ganeshpuri for a few days. I again took a room in the town of Ganeshpuri, but this time I made no attempt to go to Chidvilasananda's ashram. As I passed the ashram gates, I would stop and bow my head towards Baba's samadhi shrine, and then continue on my way.

I also had a number of errands to do in Mumbai, but when Amma arrived, I went and visited her regularly. We spent many hours together. She told me that she was not in pain, but I could see the effects of the disease on her body.

She told me that she was planning to write a book on Bhagavan Nityananda, which she said would be written in Gujarati. However, I recommended that she write the book in English as I thought it would have a greater audience. She agreed.

I knew that she had already done a lot of research on Bhagavan, and felt it would be a very interesting book. We also discussed my project, and went over some dates and events in Baba's life.

While in Mumbai, I also met a number of old Baba devotees, and interviewed some of them for Baba's biography. I was once again staying at Anoop and Jayshree's apartment.

Anoop subscribed to a daily newspaper. On the 7th of December, when I opened the morning paper, I was shocked to read the headlines. They all pointed to the destruction of the centuries old, but abandoned mosque in Ayodhya, known as the Babri-masjid. It was torn down on the previous day by radical Hindus. They had gathered at the disputed site in order to attempt to start building a temple dedicated to Lord Rama.

The mosque is believed to have been built over a destroyed Hindu temple by the Mughal invader, Babar, in the 16th century. Coincidentally, I had just been reading an English translation of the book *Chachanamah*, which is a Muslim account of the conquest of Sind and Hind by Muslim invaders in the 7th and 8th centuries of the C.E.. The book related how Muhammad Kasim would destroy local Hindu and Buddhist temples, and then build mosques over them. This was apparently a common practice among Muslim invaders. One can certainly sympathize with the victims of such atrocities, but can one correct a wrong with another wrong?

Newspapers reported that Hindu radicals had broken through the minimum security barrier, and started creating havoc on the mosque. Within hours, roofs were collapsing and sections were being systematically destroyed. About five hours later, all three domes had collapsed and only rubble remained. Out of frustration, revenge, and years of political wrangling, these people appeared to go mad. The action, however, did not appear spontaneous but seemed to have been planned.

Leaders of the various political and social organizations

which had gathered there, i.e. the BJP, VHP and RSS, did nothing to stop the destruction. Indeed, there were reports that some of them even cheered the mob on. The fact is that for the previous five years these same political leaders had helped to feed the frenzy.

Immediately, riots broke out between Hindus and Muslims in the alleyways of the ancient town of Ayodhya. *The Times of India* reported that Muslim homes were being set on fire. The state of Uttar Pradesh (UP) was immediately placed under President's rule. Many accusations began to be hurled in all directions in the political arena. The then leader of the BJP, Mr. L. K. Advani, was arrested on charges of helping to incite the Kar Sevakas, the group responsible for the destruction. There were other arrests as well.

As news of the events at Ayodhya spread, riots broke out in a number of India's major cities like Delhi, Mumbai, Jaipur and Amedabad. Riots also broke out in Dacca and Chittagaon in neighboring Bangladesh. There were also riots in Karachi and Lahore, Pakistan, where Hindu temples were demolished and burned. By the time it was over, it was reported that over two hundred Hindu temples had been destroyed in Pakistan alone.

In Mumbai, shops immediately started closing and rioting was being reported in various parts of the city and suburbs. I could hear sirens blaring in the area where I was staying. Shops remained closed for the next few days, and even telephones were not working very well. A curfew was also enforced in certain parts of the city for many days afterwards.

In Ayodhya, government troops did not regain control of the town and the disputed sites until two days later. By then, it was reported that there were over 200 deaths throughout the country, with 46 in Mumbai alone. Most appear to have been killed by the police and troops. There was going to be a lunar eclipse in just two days, which indicated powerful emotions. As the sun and moon occupied the constellations of Scorpio and Taurus, it indicated that such emotions were deep rooted, and could not be easily changed. Two weeks later there would also be a solar-eclipse. And when there are two eclipses in one month, it does not bode well for governments.

About three weeks after my arrival in Mumbai, I left for Delhi, where I continued meeting with old friends, and Baba devotees. I also met with the owners of Motilal Banarsidass and Munshiram Manoharlal publishers, inquiring about the possibility of publishing or printing my books. Mr. N. P. Jain at Motilal appeared quite interested, particularly in Baba's biography. The owner of Munshiram also appeared interested, especially with the book on Vedic astrology. I had in fact already started looking into the possibility of publishing my books the previous year. I had been thinking of self-publishing rather than looking for a publisher.

From Delhi I had planned to go and stay at the forest ashram

(*below*) The author sitting around the morning fire with some sadhus in the forest ashram.

near Lucknow for a week or two. Afterwards, I would stop at Kanpur on my way back to Mumbai, and see if I could find my old friend Shiva Dutta Mishra. You may recall that I had stayed with his family during my first trip to India in 1969.

Over the years we had lost contact with each other, and I did not really have his correct address. I was not sure whether I would actually be able to find him. Kanpur, after all, is a very large industrial city. But feeling certain that I had not come all this way for nothing, So I went searching for them shortly after I arrived in the city.

I soon found a rickshaw, and after making inquiries about the different sections of the city, thinking that it would perhaps jog my memory, I gave him some general directions. We then started our search.

When we reached a certain area, I had a vague recognition of the place, and after a few wrong turns, I found myself on the very street they lived on. As the rickshaw was whizzing past homes, I suddenly noticed an address I recognized. I yelled for him to stop. Then, just as he was turning around, I noticed Mrs. Mishra just about to go inside her front gate. She looked towards my direction, and a smile of recognition soon appeared on her face. She then ran inside to call her husband who came out shortly. They were happily surprised at my unexpected visit. We went inside and sat down to talk. After awhile, Shiva Dutta took me to see his son, Ram Rajesh, who was now working at a local bank.

I spent about a week with the Mishras. One day Shiva Dutta, his wife Deviji, and a Mr. Khanna, a retired military man and local friend of the Mishras, and I, took a trip out to the ancient town of Bithoor. It is a beautiful spot located on the banks of the river Ganga, about 20 miles west of Kanpur. Away from the city's noise and pollution, the area is very pleasant and peaceful. Today it is mainly a pilgrimage site, as well as a place for a simple outing.

We drove out in a taxi called a Tempo, which actually looked like a stretched three wheeler. It was a poorly made vehicle, and it looked quite dangerous. To add to the danger, even though the taxi was allowed only six passengers, this limit is never adhered to. The taxis are therefore always overloaded. At one point, Mr. Mishra counted thirteen passengers in our taxi.

When we arrived at Bithoor, we first went to the site believed to have been sage Valmiki's ashram. It was there that Valmiki, considered to be India's first poet, wrote the now world famous *Ramayana*, or the story of Rama, prince of Ayodhya. It was also there that Sita was left by her brother-in-law, Lakshman, and where her two sons, Kush and Luv, were born.

From there, we started walking to the town proper, stopping at the various temples and ashrams along the way. Mrs. Mishra did not go with us but instead went to the home of their friend, a Mr. Harish Chandra Dixit, where we would meet her for lunch after our walk. Along the way, a farmer who had come to the town to sell some grains also joined our party, apparently taken by the Western sadhu. He stayed with us until we left Bithoor.

(*above*) Bithoor overview.

(*above*) A Temple dedicated to Sita, and her sons Kush and Luv.

After lunch, Mishra and Deviji stayed in the house to rest, while Mr. Khanna, myself and the farmer went to the spot called *Brahma-varta*, which is believed to be the center of the world, and the very spot where Lord Brahma created the universe. There is a small shrine on the banks of the river, with the exact spot being indicated by a silver spike.

From there, we went to visit a nearby ancient temple, where the young boy Dhruva is believed to have sat in meditation after leaving home in search of his spiritual father.

After walking around the town, particularly at this old temple and the Brahma-varta spot, I had the strong impression that this place must have once been an important astronomical center. This is perhaps the real meaning of the Brahma-varta site. And there is also an ancient astronomical-astrological system known

(*left*) The "Center of the World" Bithoor. Exact spot is covered with flowers; (*below*) The author with the Mishra family. He is sitting next to Shiva Dutta Mishra, while, Ram Rajesh sits to Swami's left. Ram's daughter, Shweta, is sitting next to her grandmother at the opposite end.

as the Dhruva system. In any case, we spent a lovely day visiting temples and ashrams.

On the day I was to leave Kanpur, Ram told me that his mother was feeling very sad. I asked why? He told me that she was unhappy about my departure, because, he said, she saw me as her own son. In fact, the Mishra's had asked me to postpone my trip as there were riots in Mumbai in the aftermath of the demolition of the Babri-masjid. It was unclear whether trains were even being allowed into Mumbai.

After assuring them that nothing would go wrong, they finally gave me their blessings to leave. But I had to promise to write them a postcard on my arrival in Mumbai.

I was going to leave that evening. As we said our good-bye's, everyone was overwhelmed with tears. They told me many times to return soon, as they loaded me down with many *ladoos*, and other sweets from that day's Ganesh puja. I told them that Ganesh would certainly remove any obstacles in the way.

Ram then took me to the train station and insisted on waiting with me until the train departed. The train was not only late in arriving from Lucknow, it was over an hour late in leaving Kanpur.

I reached Mumbai late the next night, and made my way to Anoop's apartment without any difficulties. The next day, I could see the carnage left by days of rioting. Burnt buses and cars littered the streets. It was indeed a sad site.

A few days after my arrival, I again visited Amma. She seemed to be in good spirits, and we had a long conversation.

My flight back to California was not until January 26, 1992, so I decided to go on a pilgrimage for a few days to Jnaneshwar's samadhi shrine at Alandi. I have always enjoyed my visits to that shrine, but it had been some years since I last visited the place.

Before long I was back in California. Soon, Lakshmi invited me to Kauai, in what was now becoming a yearly visit. But since

I had just returned from India, I told her that I would like to wait until the end of March, or the beginning of April to visit.

By May, I began writing to various printers asking for quotes on my different books. I also did research on how to self-publish. I was mainly trying to learn something about publishing. Someone had recently made a generous donation, and I thought that perhaps this was an opportunity to publish one of my books.

At the end of August, I received word that Amma had suffered a stroke, and had entered into a coma. After a three week stay in a Delhi hospital, she was moved to a hospital in Mumbai. She was then taken to her nephew's home a week later, where I had last seen her. Then, on the night of December 14, 1993, she left her body peacefully. Her remains were interred in the river Narmada at Bharuch, in the state of Gujarat, as per her wishes. A few weeks later, I had a beautiful dream in which she appeared, and told me that she was very happy.

In 1994, I finally decided to publish one of my books. This was to actually be an experiment. I wanted to see what it took to publish a book from start to finish. Since I had been working with a computer for many years, I began using a desktop publishing program that the printing industry supported.

I decided to start by publishing my book of Baba stories. I felt that this was the least difficult of my books to publish, since there would be no photographs, but only simple graphics. I gave the book the whimsical title, *Don't Think of a Monkey – and Other Stories My Guru Told Me*.

The title was the name of one of the stories in the book, which pointed out the fickle nature of the mind. The book was completed and printed by that fall. Unfortunately, its publication took all of the funds I had, so I was now penniless again. I was again dependent on the generosity of a few friends, who kept me going until the book started to sell.

Since I had no money, I was also not able to market the book properly. But I did take advantage of any of the complimentary advertisements offered by the few distributors who had agreed to carry the book. I also did a mailing to bookstores sending them information on the book, as well as a copy of the book's cover.

The staff at *Hinduism Today* magazine were also kind enough to write a beautiful review of the book, and there were a few others who did as well. All in all, I was happy with the results, and people seemed to enjoy it. Little did I know, however, that this would invite more problems from SYDA Foundation.

Period of Intense Sadhana

I continued living quietly at the Fremont house working on my books. And I also ended up doing all the work on the house that I had seen myself doing in the dream-vision. I also increased my meditation.

I continued visiting Kauai each year, being invited by either Lakshmi or Jeff. While there, I would hold at least one program. But over all, I felt that Baba wished for me to pursue my sadhana quietly. The programs that I held either in Kauai or in California, were held only after having received some inner inspiration to do so from Baba. In fact, I always look for some sign from Baba before performing any action. My mind became more and more focused on his presence, and I would experience a deep peace while going about my daily activities. My love for God and Baba continued to grow more and more. Indeed, I saw no difference between the two. For me God is the Guru, and the Guru is God.

Although I tried to remain ever ready to move out of the house, I must confess that the uncertainty of where I would go next did disturb me at times. I had full faith that the Lord was looking after me, but because of the tendency to doubt, the mind always gives us trouble.

In the dream-vision I had shortly after my move to the Fremont house, Baba had indicated that I would live there until at least 1998-99.

At the beginning of 1998, I observed silence for about six weeks. Then in February, I was invited to Kauai by Jeff. Jeff knew that I may have to move at any time and had on a number of occasions told me not to worry, and that he would provide a place for me to stay. I was grateful for his kind offer.

Then in October of that year, Lakshmi and Thelma told me that they were thinking of putting the Fremont house back on the market. But a few months went by, and they had still not done so. Then, in the third week of February of 1999, I was again invited to Kauai by Jeff. Originally I was scheduled to stay for only three weeks, but once I was there, my stay was extended for two more weeks.

Although my mind was generally calm, every once in a while the thought of my impending move would disrupt its peacefulness. I even called Thelma from Kauai to find out if she had made any decision yet. She told me that she had not, and that everything was ok, and that I should come home.

But a few nights later, I had a dream-vision in which Baba appeared to me. He was standing on a small rock protruding just above the ocean water, while I was standing on dry land. Baba then called me to come to him, which I did.

The place reminded me of a nearby beach near Jeff's home, which I used to visit. When he called me to him, Baba told me that something would soon happen, but that I should not worry about it, because everything would be alright in the end. He then proceeded to show me in great detail what was about to occur. Not only in the upcoming months, but also in the next few years. The scenes appeared before me like a movie projected on a screen.

But at the end of the preview, Baba told me, "You have seen everything, but now you must forget everything that I have shown you."

Having said this, he told me to go, and I immediately awoke. Finding that I could not recall a single thing that I had just seen, I spent the whole day trying to remember even the smallest detail. But I could not.

Feeling anxious about not knowing what was about to happen, I began praying desperately to Baba and Bhagavan Nityananda to help me. That night, once again Baba appeared to me, and tried to encourage me by saying, "Don't worry, everything will be alright. Don't try to remember what you saw. Whatever is meant to happen will happen."

But when I awoke the next morning, I continued trying to

recall the events I had seen. At the same time, I continued to pray to Baba for help and clarity. That night, once again Baba appeared to me, but this time only for a moment. Just long enough for him to say, with a tinge of impatience, "I told you not to worry, everything will be all right."

Well it did not take long for me to find out what was going to happen. Within just a few weeks after returning to California, Lakshmi and Thelma came to the Fremont house and told me that they were going to put the house on the market, and were in fact meeting a realtor there that very afternoon. Interestingly it was Baba's lunar birthday when they told me.

After that, everything began to occur very quickly. The house was placed on the market within a few weeks. I felt that the house would probably take about two to three months to sell, which it did.

I still did not know where I would be going. As already mentioned, Jeff in Kauai had known for a number of years that one day this would happen, as did I. He had told me a number of times that he would bring me to Kauai to live. But since it was so far from the mainland, initially I felt hesitant to go. And besides, Jeff was now on vacation, so I could not even speak with him.

I finally heard from him towards the end of July, and I told him the situation. We discussed it, and he said that he would make some arrangement for me to live on Kauai. As I had no funds, I surrendered to whatever Baba had in store for me. And in September, I was off to Kauai.

Initially I stayed on the property where Jeff lived. A cottage was being built on another property he owned, and about six months later I moved there. There were no trees or shrubbery on the property and so I began to develop the area. I began planting bananas, papaya, avocados, and a variety of trees and shrubs, including a Banyan and Bodhi tree. I also grew Rudraksha trees from seeds that I had gathered at the Kauai Hindu temple's Rudraksha forest.

The divine Shakti began to manifest more and more powerfully in my body, which began generating a great deal of heat. But I felt great physical strength, and spent hours each day working in the garden. I felt driven by Mother Kundalini.

But by the spring of 2000, I was in financial straits. The little money that I had when I arrived on the island was now depleted. It had been financially difficult ever since I had taken sannyasa, but now I began going through a period of extreme financial difficulty.

Because a sannyasi has surrendered himself to God's will, he has to learn to look with equanimity to whether something comes to him or it does not. I saw all beings as a manifestation of God, and therefore, when a person was inspired to assist me, I felt it was the Lord himself who was assisting me. But at the same time, when someone was not inspired to help, I felt that that too was the Lord's wish.

Nevertheless, it is not an easy life, especially when ling in the west, unless of course the person is associated with some institution. But what was I to do? I did not wish to ask for anything, but to accept gratefully whatever came to me naturally. So now I could only complain to Baba and God.

Interestingly, this outer misfortune soon became a catalyst. The more difficult my outer circumstances became, the more powerful were my inner experiences. Indeed, these very difficult circumstance actually became the trigger for my internal struggle for spiritual unity. Once again I was overwhelmed with painful feelings of spiritual separation.

During such periods of deep anguish, I would mentally complain bitterly to God about my outer circumstances, as a child cries to its parent. Why did He not help me, I would ask in tears. Wasn't I also His child? As the Lord of the universe, surely he could take care of my few needs.

Even having been brought to that small island served to inflame this inner anguish. I felt isolated and deserted on that small piece of rock, out in the middle of the ocean, without even the means to leave. I even felt abandoned by my friends. I thought, why had Baba brought me to this island, if not to abandon me?

I now realized why Baba had erased the memory of what he had shown me of the future in the dream-vision the previous year. But now I was recalling the scenes with each occurring event. If I would have known what was in store for me perhaps I would not have come at all. But I knew that there was a reason for all of this, so I continued on.

Now I should explain here, that although these experiences may appear to be a case of ordinary depression and anxiety, let me assure you that this is not the case at all. When not in that *bhava* or mood, I was not sad or gloomy, but felt great joy. Nor were my feelings of isolation directed towards any person or thing, but was directed at the inner Self. Indeed, because of such feelings, my inner joy and contentment only grew. Can one say this about ordinary depression? In fact, Kauai is a beautiful island, and I have always enjoyed visiting it. I was also living in a lovely cottage. But none of these mattered.

No, the divine mood that I am describing here is actually a manifestation of supreme Bhakti or divine devotion and love for God, according to the *Narada Bhakti Sutras*. Sage Narada says that the essential characteristics of Bhakti or devotion is the consecration of all one's activities to the Lord through self-surrender, and the feeling of extreme anguish arises when God is forgotten. Indeed, supreme love for the Lord is actually considered a manifestation of spiritual liberation.

I agree, however, that if one does not handle life's ups and downs properly, they will surely become depressed. But the devotee offers all of life's circumstances, good or bad, at the Lord's feet, and accepts cheerfully whatever comes. Then an intimate relationship begins to arise between the devotee and the Lord. It is this intense feeling for the divine which makes the devotee feel entitled to the Lord's full protection.

Sage Narada further states that the Lord dislikes it when a

seeker relies only on his own unaided self-effort. But likes it when the seeker feels misery which arises from the sense of total helplessness in his inability to achieve liberation. Such helplessness actually is meant to destroy the ego which is the cause of the sense of separation in the first place. These feelings also serve to draw the Lord's grace to the seeker. This mysterious process is not easy to understand, but must be experienced.

Soon such feelings were present at all times of the day and night. Even my sleep became disturbed, and I would awake a bit earlier each day. Sometimes as early as 1 or 2 a.m.. Such feelings sometimes would build up for many days at a time, until they reached a crescendo, at which time I would experience the exalted state of oneness with the God. Then, the awareness of "I Am That" would arise spontaneously within me. This would bring ecstatic joy and a deep calm and peace.

Soon the inner Shakti began to manifest even more powerfully. Besides having kriyas that I had previously experienced, there were also a number of new *kriyas* taking place, including various types of *pranayama* and *mudras*, which I had not experienced before.

One such pranayama occurs when the lips are puckered, as if one were going to whistle. This forms a small hole through which the prana is drawn in and out. First slowly, then quickly. This process would produce a continuous whistling sound which sounded similar to an ambulance siren. In another pranayama, the breath is quickly inhaled down to the stomach, and is then released in small increments. Bhagavan Nityananda compared this type of pranayama to the dropping of a bucket into a deep well, and then slowly pulling it up in a jerking motion.

I also experienced various subtle tastes and odors, something I had experienced before. Sometimes the mantras "Om", "Guru Om", "Om Namah Shivaya", or simply "Shiva" would be repeated spontaneously. Sometimes my eyes would remain wide open, unable to close them. One day this lasted for over an hour. At times I felt like shouting, or I would roar like a lion. At other times I would feel like dancing, or I would cry for hours, feeling that I could not bear the pain of separation any longer. Sometimes I would start laughing uncontrollably. At such times I felt I was going insane. But all of these were the manifestations of Mother Kundalini.

As difficult as things were already in my outer circumstances, they were to get worse before getting better. In October of 2001, I was informed that the property I was living on was to be sold, and I would have to move. Since there was no place for me to move to, and I had no money to leave the island, I thought for certain my end had come. As weeks went by, the situation became more difficult. But then one morning, after a powerful meditation session, I received an inner message from Baba telling me that things would soon get better. This occurred just after I had bitterly complained to him about my situation.

I have a pair of Baba's shoes which he had given me. For years I kept two one hundred dollar bills in them. They were the first donation I had received after taken sannyasa, and so I had offered them to Baba, and kept them in the shoes. But recently I had to use the money, and so I complained about this to Baba. The day after this occurred, I received a phone call from an old friend living on the mainland. He used to call me regularly, but I had not heard from him in over a year. This person has a good heart, but he is not always reliable. Nevertheless, he has a lot of love for me. When he asked me how things were going, I told him about my financial situation, and how I was going to have to move soon.

"Where are you going?" he asked concerned.

Of course I did not know. But then, as if in direct response to my prayer to Baba on the previous day, he began telling me that he had been saving up some money for me, and now had several thousand dollars. And, out of the blue, he said that he had been keeping the money in a pair of Baba's shoes that he had. When I heard this, I began crying uncontrollably. If this was not an answer to my prayers, nothing was.

However, Baba would test me for a few more weeks yet. At first my friend did not send the money when he said he was going to. Then even after he said he sent a check, it never arrived. However, I had already received Baba's assurance, and although it was becoming somewhat comical, I saw it all as Baba's play.

Finally, everything came together, and I left Kauai in the third week of January 2002. I returned to California and went and stayed temporarily with Maheshwara, who had invited me to move in with him again after he had heard I was returning to the Bay Area.

A few months later, I was invited to attend Baba's birthday party celebration at the home of Lakshmi and Ed Collins. At one point, Lakshmi took me aside and told me that she, her husband Ed, and Thelma wanted to invite me to come and live in a room on their property. I was quite touched by their generosity, and all that they had done for me over the years.

Interestingly, it was now exactly three years since Lakshmi and Thelma had told me that the Fremont house was going to be sold. Which, as you may recall, also occurred on Baba's birthday.

At the time that Lakshmi made the offer, I did not make any commitment, but a few months later, circumstances forced me to move from Maheshwara's.

My spiritual practices were still very intense. And near the end of my stay on Kauai, a thought kept arising in my mind that perhaps Baba had brought me to the island to leave my body. The feeling that I was going to die became very powerful.

In fact, I felt that if God had no work for me to do here on earth, then death would be better. Indeed, my prayer ever since Baba's mahasamadhi had been that he make me an instrument of his divine grace. Otherwise, he should allow me to leave this body, for I felt no worldly ambitions. Although I preoccupied myself with meditation, study, writing and teaching, I felt all of these to be insignificant. I did not care to be a burden on anyone, therefore I would pray to God to make me a giver and not a taker.

Then one day, while meditating, I saw a vision in which I was walking in a cemetery. I soon noticed a tombstone a short distance in front of me, and I began walking towards it. When I reached the spot I could read the inscription on the tomb. It read: "Here lies Swami Prakashananda."

The feeling of death I was experiencing indicated not the death of the body, but the death of the ego. It was a symbolic death which had started with my sannyasa initiation, and culminated in Hawaii with the vision of a tombstone. After this experience, a deep feeling of contentment and calm arose within me, which has remained ever since.

Dear reader, God dwells within your own heart. Search for Him there. Realize Him there. Experience His joy within yourself. Buddha was a man who found this divinity within his own heart. He called it *Nirvana*. Jesus experienced it within his own heart and spoke about it to others as the "Kingdom of God." All mystics have experienced this divinity within themselves. The Vedas have proclaimed it in the great statement, *Aham Brahmasmi*, meaning, "I am Brahman, the Absolute." And my Guru taught, "God dwells within you as you."

Again and again redirect your mind within. At the beginning, because of the many past impressions, the mind continues to wander. There will be periods when one loses faith, and may even lack interest in the spiritual life altogether. However one must not stop. Always continue to move forward. Eventually the mind will become steady, and a deep calm and joy will be experienced. At those moments there will be no doubts, all will be perfectly clear to you.

When the inner Lord is revealed, the awareness of Ham'Sa, "I am That," will be experienced naturally. There is no need to go here or there. Everything is within you. Therefore my prayer is that you experience that divinity within your own heart. May God and the Siddhas bless you. Sadgurunath Maharaj ki Jai!

Glossary

A

A'ba: Aramaic word meaning "father," identical to the Hindi word Baba.

Acharya: A spiritual teacher; one who instructs in religious practices; a title affixed to names of learned men.

Advaita: (a + dvaita) The word *dvaita* literally means "two" and signifies two principals. The word therefore indicates duality, dualism, and a dualistic perspective. In Sanskrit, when an 'a' is placed before a word, the letter takes on the meaning of "not", meaning that it is not what the word it precedes means, e.g. A-dvaita literally means "not two." In the Hindu philosophy, Advaita Vedanta is therefore a non-dualistic philosophy. It negates any possibility of a second principal independent of the Absolute Brahman. It therefore teaches that in reality there is no difference or separation between an individual soul and Brahman.

Aghori: Non-terrifying; the merciful Shiva; also, a Shaivite sect.

Aham: Literally, 'I Am'; the pure inner Self; the pure 'I' consciousness; the experiencing subject.

Ahimsa: Non-injury; the practice of non-violence or injury, either physical or mentally towards all living beings.

Ajna Chakra: The spiritual center situated between the eyebrows, which is often called the third eye; the seat of the Guru; also called the command center.

Ananda: Spiritual joy, bliss; usually added to a swami's name, e.g. Nitya + ananda, and Mukta + ananda.

Apana: Incoming breath; inhalation; the vital air which goes downward towards the anus; one of the five vital-airs (*vayu*) which governs excretion of waste from the body.

Arati (or Aarthi): 'The waving of lights'; the ritual waving of oil lamps before an altar, image of a deity, or a saint. It represents God as divine light, brilliance, and luminosity. It is considered an auspicious act indicating divine protection and the triumphant of light over darkness. Afterward, the flame is offered to devotees, who pass their hands over it, and then touch their eyes with the hands. This is repeated three times.

Asana: A seat or posture; in Hatha Yoga certain postures are performed in order to strengthen the body and purify the nervous system (*nadis*); one of the eight limbs or practices in Patanjali's Yoga Sutras.

Ashram: Place of striving, from *sram*, 'to exert energy'; a place of refuge from worldly concerns; the abode of a saint or holy man; a community where spiritual disciplines are practiced; also, a name for the traditional Hindu concept of the four stages of life: student, married life, retirement from worldly concerns, and *sannyasa*.

Ashramite: One who lives in, and follows the rules of the ashram.

Atman *(or Atma)*: The eternal and unchanging Self, the inner Spirit; one's true nature or Self. According to the *Brihadaranyaka Upanishad*, the Self should be realized by reflection and meditation after hearing about it from one's Guru. Not to be confused with the ego sense, which is referred to as *Ahamkara*.

AUM: see OM

Avadhuta: Literally, 'one who has shaken off, discarded, or expelled' all attachments to the world; one who has transcended body-consciousness and is beyond the mind. One who always lives in the highest spiritual state. Such a being wanders freely, completely free from all social conventions; an Avadhuta is one who has achieved the highest state of renunciation, which is neither attachment nor detachment, but is beyond both. He seeks nothing, nor avoids anything; also, a name of Guru Dattatreya, believed to be an incarnation of the trinity: Brahma, Vishnu, and Shiva.

Avatara: Literally, 'coming down or descending'; Incarnation; the descent of the Lord into a human form in order to perform some particular action for the benefit of *dharma*, and the upliftment of humanity.

B

Baba *(or Babaji)*: Respected father. A term of affection for a saint, especially one's Guru.

Bandhas: Literally, 'binding, fastening, or a lock'; a *hatha yoga* exercise used in conjunction with certain types of breath control (*pranayama*). At such times certain organs of the body are contracted or locked in order to control and direct the life force (*prana*) into the *sushumna nadi*.

Bhadrakali: *Bhadra* 'auspicious' + *kali* 'the dark Goddess'; Shakti; a name of the Divine Mother. Baba Nityananda erected a temple dedicated to her at the entrance to the town of Ganeshpuri.

Bhagavad Gita: Literally, 'the song of God'; One of India's greatest scripture. It is a dialogue between Lord Krishna and his disciple Arjuna just before the start of the Mahabharata war. He speaks on *dharma*, *yoga*, knowledge. the spiritual path, and the performance of one's duty.

Bhagavan: (or Bhagawan) Literally, 'one who possesses the six attributes,' viz., infinite spiritual power, righteousness, glory, splendor, knowledge, and renunciation; the Lord; God; also, a term used when addressing a revered person such as Bhagavan Nityananda.

Bhajan: Devotional song or hymn.

Bhakta: A devotee and lover of God; a follower of *Bhakti Yoga*, the path of love and devotion.

Bhakti: As in *Bhakti Yoga*; The yoga of devotion leading to union with God; a state of intense devotional love for God, or one's Guru, and the desire to be united with Him; also, the constant feeling of being united with God or Guru.

Bhartrihari: (5th or 6th century C.E.?) A great philosopher and poet king who renounced his kingdom and became a great yogi.

Bhastrika: Literally, 'like a bellows'; a type of *pranayama* where the breathing is done with the diaphragm, and is inhaled and exhaled forcefully, resembling a bellows.

Bhava: Literally, 'becoming, being'; a spiritual mood or attitude of identification or absorption. In this state the devotee identifies totally with the object of their devotion, whether a deity, or one's Guru.

Bhimeshwar: Literally, 'Bhima's Lord'; the name of the lingam in the Shiva temple in the town of Ganeshpuri.

Bilva: (also called *Bel*). The wood-apple tree (Aegle Marmelos); a species of tree sacred to Lord Shiva. Its unripe fruit is used for medicinal purposes, and its leaves are used in the worship of Lord Shiva.

Bindu: Literally, 'dot, spot, or point.' The *neela bindu* or blue dot; Baba Muktananda called this the blue pearl. It is a brilliant blue dot which appears to the meditator. It is actually the subtle abode of the inner Self; also, in *yogic* terminology, the word is often used to also indicate semen.

Bramacharya: Continence; A religious student who practices celibacy. In its wider sense the word stands for abstinence not only from sexual indulgence, but freedom from all sensual cravings. Also, according to traditional Hindu society, it is the first of four stages of life, that of a student.

Brahman: In the Upanishads, God as Transcendental and Absolute is called Brahman. From the root *brih*, to 'grow, expand, increase.'

Brahmin: Literally, 'one who knows Brahman'; the first of four main castes according to the ancient Vedic social system. It indicates the spiritual man of society.

C

Chakra: Wheel, circle, disk; the seven main spiritual centers within the subtle body.

Chinmudra: A gesture in which the thumb and index fingers are joined. This *mudra* helps in controlling and maintaining the *prana* within the body. (see *mudra*)

Chitshakti: The Supreme Power of Consciousness.

Chitshakti Vilas: "Play of Consciousness". The title of Baba Muktananda's spiritual autobiography.

Chitta: "Mind stuff"; it is associated with the mind, intellect, heart, and sub-conscious mind; As used in yoga philosophy, it indicates consciousness and 'mind-substance'; It is comprised of the three subtle inner instruments of consciousness, viz. the Intellect (*buddhi*), Ego (*ahamkara*), which gives the sense of 'I am so and so,' and the mind (*manas*), which is associated with the senses, and is made up by an assortment of thoughts and emotions. Actually *chitta* comprises all the levels of mind, and indicates the quality of awareness and consciousness.

D

Dal: A kind of split pea soup and staple in the Indian diet which is eaten with rice, or bread, called *roti* or *chapati*.

Dandapranam: Literally, 'prostration like a stick'; a full body prostration where one lays flat on the ground with the arms and hands joined and outstretched overhead, thereby resembling a stick (*danda*).

Darshana: Literally, 'seeing or looking at,' from the root *Drsh*, which means 'to see'; vision, perception, observing, meeting, an audience; to be with, or have the sight or vision of a deity, saint, or sacred place; a philosophical perspective, thereby referring to the six traditional philosophical systems of India: Yoga, Vedanta, Sankhya, Mimamsa, Nyaya and Vaisheshika.

Dashanami: Literally, 'ten names'; the ten orders or branches of *sannyasis* started by Adi Shankaracharya. These are: Giri, Parvata, Sagar, Puri, Bharati, Sarasvati, Vana, Aranya, Tirtha and Ashram. Muktananda, and all of his *swamis*, belong to the *Sarasvati* (also spelled Saraswati) branch or order of monks.

Deva: Literally, 'shining one'; a celestial being and cosmic protector; they are similar to angels in the Judaic, Christian and Islamic religions.

Devi: Literally, 'shining one'; the feminine form of Deva; The Goddess; a name used to indicate the Divine Mother; also, a name for *Kundalini*.

Dharma: From the Sanskrit root *dri*, 'to sustain'; divine or cosmic law; the law of righteousness; religion; duty and obligation to one's family and society; one of the four life goals of traditional Hindu society. *Dharma* has traditionally been divided into four types:
1. *Rita* - This is Universal *dharma*, it is cosmic law and order.
2. *Varna dharma* - This is social *dharma*. It is the duty and responsibilities one has towards society,
3. *Ashrama dharma* - This consists of the traditional four stages of life according to Vedic culture. These four are: student, householder, retirement, and religious pursuits.
4. *Svadharma* - This is one's own personal *dharma*, and is determined by one's *karmas*, or the good and bad actions from past lives, as well as the influence of the above three *dharmas*.

Dharmashala: A building which houses pilgrims.

Diksha: Any religious initiation; in Siddha Yoga it means *Shaktipat* initiation received from the Guru, in which he transmits his spiritual power into the disciple by either look, touch, word (*mantra*) or thought.

Diwali *(or Dipavali)*: 'a row of lights'; festival of lights; depending on the part of India, a two or three day festival starting on the 13th day of the dark fortnight, in the month of Karttika (October-November). Diwali proper is the 15th day, or the day of the new moon, and according to some north Indian calendars, it is the first day of the Hindu New Year. There are various origins attributed to this festival. Some say that they are celebrating the marriage between Lakshmi and Lord Vishnu. The festival also commemorates the day Sri Ram returned to Ayodhya after his triumphant victory over the demon Ravana; it is the celebration of light over darkness or good over evil.

Durga: Shakti; the Universal Mother; a form of the goddess shown riding on a lion, or tiger. An image which indicates an awakened Kundalini.

Dvaita: Literally, the word means 'two', thereby indicating two principles. Duality; dualism. In Hindu philosophy it indicates the Dvaita Vedanta or the dualistic philosophy which asserts the separation or differences between the individual soul and Brahman.

F
Faqir *(or fakir):* Literally, 'poor'; an Arabic word to designate a mendicant, *sufi*, ascetic, or yogi.

G
Ganga (or *Ganges*): The most sacred river in India today, flowing from the Himalayas, and across the plains of Northern India; as a celestial river, the Ganga represents the Milky Way.

Gita: A song or poem, like the Bhagavad Gita, Guru Gita, Anu Gita, etc.

Guna: In the Samkhya philosophy, it indicates the three qualities or attributes which makes up the primordial cosmic substance known as *Prakriti*. These are the qualities of intelligence (*sattva*), activity (*rajas*) and inertia or ignorance (*tamas*).

Guru: Literally, 'one who removes darkness'; weighty, heavy, large: the spiritual teacher or preceptor; also, in Hindu astrology, *Guru* is the name for the planet Jupiter, along with the name *Brihaspati*.

Guru-bhava: The mood or mystical attitude of identification with one's Guru as the inner Self; also, 'he who feels or thinks about the Guru.'

Gurudev: Literally, 'the divine Guru'; God as Guru; an affectionate, yet respectful term used to address one's Guru.

Guru Gita: Literally, 'the song or poem of the Guru'; a hymn extolling the greatness of the Guru, and the Guru-disciple relationship.

Guru Purnima: Literally, 'the Guru's full moon.' The word *purnima* means, "full, complete, whole," and is used to indicate the full moon. This festival falls in June-July, and is the day when one's Guru, or any true Guru, is honored. It is also called "Vyasa's full moon" in honor of that ancient sage, since it is said it was on the full moon day of July when he achieved enlightenment, and also started writing the Brahma Sutras, a treatise on Vedanta. Traditionally, during the four months of the rainy season following this date, wandering monks stay in one place to meditate and study.

H

Ham'Sa (or So'Ham): Literally, 'I am That'; the natural mantra which is continuously going on within each individual, with each incoming and outgoing breath; an individual soul; a swan, or more accurately, the wild Indian goose which symbolizes an adept class of renunciates or yogis called *Paramahamsas*.

Hatha-Yoga: Literally, 'the forceful yoga'; various physical and mental exercises practiced specifically for purifying the countless network of *nadis*, and to bring about the even flow of the incoming (*prana*) and outgoing (*apana*) breath; also, the syllables *'ha'* symbolizes the 'sun,' and *'tha'* the 'moon.' Therefore, the word *hatha* also means 'the Sun-Moon Yoga,' which symbolizes the yogis ability to experience himself to be beyond the rhythm of ordinary time, indicated by the sun and moon.

Hatha-Yoga-Pradipika: Literally, 'light on the forceful yoga.' A famous treatise on hatha yoga by Svatmarama, who lived sometime in the mid-fourteenth century C.E. The work seeks to integrate the physical discipline with the higher spiritual practices of Raja Yoga.

I

Ida: Subtle channel (*nadi*) in which *prana* flows. It is located on the left side of the body and is said to be feminine in nature, indicating emotions and feelings. It is associated with the lunar principle.

Ishta Devata: One's chosen ideal form of God.

Ishvara: (also *Ishwara*) The Lord; God as Creator, Preserver, and Destroyer.

J

Japa: Recitation, repetition. The devotional repetition of the *mantra*, often while counting on a rosary. It may be done aloud or silently. For meditation, *japa* is usually performed silently.

Ji: A suffix used after a person's name or title, not only to show respect, but it also indicates a personal intimacy. It is pronounced jee, as in Babaji, Swamiji, Nityanandaji, etc.

Jiva: Literally, 'alive, living, existing.' From *jiv* 'to live.' The individual soul or embodied spirit, conditioned by the body and the mind, and bound by the three *malas* or impurities of *anava*, *karma* and *maya*.

Jnana: Enlightened wisdom; the highest yogic knowledge

Jnaneshwari: A famous commentary on the Bhagavad Gita written originally in Marathi by the 13th century poet/saint Jnaneshwar.

Jnani: 'One who possesses knowledge (*jnana*)'; a man (or woman) of enlightened wisdom and knowledge.

K

Ka'ba: The house of *Allah* (God). Islam's most sacred spiritual center. This Arabic word actually means "cube" and indicates the square building housing the sacred stone in the Arabian city of Mecca. All Muslims face Mecca when praying. The *Ka'ba* was an ancient place of pilgrimage even before Islam. Tradition tells us that the sacred stone was originally brought to Mecca from Sri Lanka by the Biblical Adam, while others say it was given to Abraham by the archangel Gabriel. It seems, however, that there is sufficient evidence to indicate that this shrine was originally a Shiva temple, with the black stone as the emblem (linga) of Lord Shiva.

Kailash: A mountain peak in the Himalayas, located in Western Tibet, known as the abode of Lord Shiva. It is sacred to both Hindus and Buddhists alike; the name of Baba Nityananda's ashram in Ganeshpuri; Also, in yogic terminology, the word indicates the highest spiritual center, located in the crown of the head, the thousand petal lotus (*sahasrara*).

Kali: Literally, the 'dark one'; time; a name of the Divine Mother; *Shakti*; a form of the goddess symbolizing the destructive quality of time; also, the destroyer of ignorance.

Karma: Action or deed, both mental and physical; the law of cause and effect; the reservoir of past impressions; the belief that an individual will reap the fruits of their own past actions, whether in the present life, or in some future one; results of one's past actions; destiny; *Karma* is generally divided into three categories: *Prarabdha-karma*, *Kriyamana-karma* and *Sanchitta-karma*.
   1. *Prarabdha-karma* (*pra* = 'before' + *rabh* = 'begin') is the fruits of one's past actions which are now operative in the form of the present life conditions. It is this category of karma which is often referred to as one's destiny.
   2. The second category is called *kriyamana-karma* ('being done'). This *karma* indicates the new actions which are being performed by the person in the present life, often in response to life's circumstances.
   3. Some of the *kriyamana-karmas* will bear fruit in the person's present life, but most will be stored in the *Chitta* for future births. These stored actions are called *sanchitta-karma* (*san* = 'together' + *chitta* = 'mind substance').

Karmapa: The spiritual head of the Kagyu sect of Tibetan Buddhism founded in the 12th century. Gyalwa Rangjung Rigpe Dorje Karmapa was the 16th Karmapa in this lineage (1923-1981). He visited Muktananda's ashram in Ganeshpuri in 1973.

Kashmir Shaivism: Shaivism as practiced in Kashmir. Vasugupta (circa 800) is considered the founder of this tradition. In this philosophy, the Lord (Shiva) is considered both immanent and transcendent. In this tradition God-realization depends on the grace of the Sadguru. Traditionally, the method of spiritual transmission is through *Shaktipat*.

Kripa: Divine grace, compassion, mercy.

Krishna: Literally, 'blue-black'; the central figure in the Indian epic, the Mahabharata, of which the Bhagavad Gita forms one chapter. Krishna is considered an incarnation (*Avatara*) of God; also, Krishna was Swami Muktananda's childhood name; another meaning of the word is, 'one who attracts, or draws one near by his captivating qualities.'

Kriya: Literally, 'action, movement'; in Siddha yoga it means a spontaneous physical or mental action or movement which occurs after receiving *Shaktipat* initiation and the awakening of *Kundalini*.

Kula: Undifferentiated Energy; a name for the *Kundalini Shakti*; also, a spiritual tradition or school of Kashmir Shaivism.

Kumbhaka: Literally, 'like a pot'; retention of breath; a process of *pranayama* or breath control practiced in hatha yoga, whereby the breath is retained in an expanded stomach. This form is called inner *kumbhaka*. When the breath is completely exhaled, and then held, it is called external retention. Although these are the two best known forms, the author of *Hatha Yoga Pradipika* gives eight types. An advanced form of *kumbhaka* actually is not practiced at all, but occurs spontaneously when *Kundalini-Shakti* is awakened. It occurs without inhalation or exhalation, but happens naturally without any strain. This type is called *kevala-kumbhaka*.

Kumbha-Mela: Literally, 'the pot festival'; an ancient spiritual gathering which occurs in a cyclical manner on the banks of sacred rivers at Haridwar, Allahabad (Prayaga), Nashik, and Ujjain according to the transits of the planet Jupiter.

Kundalini: Literally, 'the coiled one'; the serpent power; the feminine form of *Kundala*, meaning 'coiled' or 'circular'; the Primordial Energy (*Shakti*) or cosmic power that lies coiled like a serpent at the base of the spine of every individual. Through the Guru's grace, or the intense practice of yoga, it is awakened and is made to rise through the central *nadi* (*sushumna*) to the spiritual center in the crown of the head (*sahasrara*).

L

Lakshmi: The Universal Mother as the goddess of wealth and prosperity; *Shakti*.

Lama: Literally, 'superior one'; a Tibetan word with the same meaning as *Guru*; a title for any Tibetan Buddhist monk, but specifically for advanced and experienced adepts.

Langoti (also called *Kaupin*): Two pieces of cloth, one wrapped around the waist, and the other covering the private parts; a loincloth.

Linga: 'Mark, sign or emblem.' (see *Shiva-linga*)

M
Maha: A prefix meaning 'great, supreme, paramount.'

Mahamandaleshwar: Literally, 'the great lord of a community, province, or regiment (*mandal*)'; a religious title which is usually bestowed on a spiritual leader by the community of Mahamandaleshwars. When Adi Shankaracharya (788-820 C.E.?) organized the monastic order into ten branches, he is also believed to have organized the *Naga sannyasis* into seven groups called Akhadas (or *Akharas*), namely: Mahanirvani, Niranjani, Juna, Atal, Avahan, Agni and Ananda. These naked *Naga* monks were allowed to bear arms for the protection of not only the ten monastic branches of *sannyasis*, but also the Hindu religion, which was coming under attack by the invading Muslims. Centuries later, a controversy broke out between the Shankaracharyas of the time and the Akhadas. Instead of guiding them, the often class conscious successors of Adi Shankaracharya, appeared to ignore the lower caste *Nagas*. It was at that time that the Akhadas, in a unanimous vote, decided to accept *Paramahamsa sannyasis* as their spiritual guides (*Acharyas*). *Paramahamsa sannyasis* consider themselves free of all dogmas and orthodoxy, and will accept worthy disciples from any caste. At first, seven were chosen, one for each Akhada. They were called Mandaleshwars. As time passed, more were appointed, and when any of their disciples also became Mandaleshwars, the Guru would then become known as Mahamandaleshwars.

Maharaja: Literally, 'great king'; an Indian title for a great king or monarch; one who is ranked above a normal king *(raja)*; also, a term of address for great gurus or holy men.

Maharashtra: The Indian state where the town of Ganeshpuri, and Baba Muktananda's ashram is located.

Mahasamadhi: Literally, 'the great *samadhi*'; the final transcendental experience of a great being; the conscious exit from the physical body by a realized soul; death.

Mahashivaratri: see Shivaratri.

Mahavira: Literally, 'the great hero, or adept'; the title and name of the 24th Guru in the Jain religion (6th century C.E.).

Mahayajna: The 'great fire sacrifice.'

Mahayoga: Literally, 'the Great Yoga' (Maha = 'Great'); It is called the 'Great Yoga' because when it is activated by a Siddha through *Shaktipat* initiation, it spontaneously sets in motion the other yogas such as: hatha-yoga, mantra-yoga, bhakti-yoga, jnana-yoga, laya-yoga, and raja-yoga. It is also known as Kundalini Maha Yoga, Siddha Yoga, and Guru Kripa (kripa = grace). In this yoga, the Guru initiates the disciple through the method known as *Shaktipat*, in which he or she transmits their own spiritual energy into the disciple by either touch, word (*mantra*), look, or thought in order to awaken the dormant *Kundalini*.

Mala: A string of beads, similar to a rosary, used to keep count the number of times a mantra is repeated. The material which the beads are made from vary according to sectarian traditions, but they may be seeds, wood, or mineral. The number of beads are usually 108; also, a garland made of flowers; a term used to indicate the impure layers or coverings of the spirit.

Mandap: From *mand*, 'to adorn, decorate'; an open hall or temple compound; an opened building or structure where the fire ritual (*yajna*) is performed.

Mandir: A Hindu temple, or place of worship.

Mantra: 'Instrument of thought'; A mystical or sacred word, verse, or formula given by the Guru at the time of initiation. When given by a Sadguru, it is said to be a 'conscious' *mantra*, and becomes a vehicle for the transmission of the Guru's spiritual power. *Mantras* may be repeated aloud or silently.

Marathi: The language spoken in the modern state of Maharashtra.

Marga: Literally, 'path or way'; the spiritual path.

Moksha: Spiritual liberation.

Mosque: A Muslim hall of prayer; a gathering place for religious worship and instructions; French derivative of the Arabic *Masjid*.

Mouna: The observance of silence; a yogic discipline practiced during one's spiritual practices.

Mudra: Literally, 'seal'; various advanced hatha yoga techniques; symbolic hand gestures used to control and direct the vital airs (*prana*) in the physical body. After receiving *Shaktipat* these gestures may occur spontaneously, expressing ecstatic feelings. Among the best known are: 1. *Chin-mudra* (also known as *jnana-mudra* and *yoga-mudra*) where the thumb and index finger touch, forming a circle, while the other fingers are extended; 2. *abhaya-mudra*, in which the fingers are extended and the palm faces forward. This is the gesture of fearlessness (*abhaya*); 3. *shambhavi-mudra*, 'the ecstatic mood.' In this *mudra* the eyes may become wide open, or, the eyes become focused within, even though they remain half opened; 4. *Anjali-mudra*, the two hands are joined together in reverence at the level of the heart, eyes, or above the crown of the head.

Muktananda: *Mukta* = 'set free, released' + *ananda* = 'bliss, joy'; the joy of spiritual freedom and liberation; the name of the author's Guru.

Muladhara: *mula* = 'root' + *adhara* = 'support'; the root center; the spiritual center at the base of the spine where the *Kundalini* resides, symbolically represented as a coiled serpent, it indicates the spiritual potential when awakened.

N

Nada: Literally, 'sound'; divine music or sound; the various spontaneous inner sounds heard during advanced stages of meditation, i.e. drum, flute, thunder, running water, the sound of bees, etc..

Nadi: Physical and subtle channels through which *prana* flows. According to *Bhuti Suddhi Tantra* there are 72,000 nadis; the *Prapancha Sara Tantra* gives 300,000, while the *Shiva Samhita* says there are 350,000 *nadis*. In any case, this merely indicates that there are countless *nadis* in the human body, but the *sushumna*, *ida* and *pingala* are considered the three most important *nadis*.

Nagas: An order of naked monks who have traditionally wandered throughout India, particularly in the Himalayas. However, today many live in ashrams.

Namaskara (or Namaste): Literally, 'homage to the divine within you'; the Indian greeting which honors the divine in others, and is performed by joining the hands at the level of the heart (*anjali-mudra*). It is also used to show reverent devotion to an image of a deity, or one's Guru.

Neem: A bitter tree with medicinal value, and whose twigs have traditionally been used for brushing one's teeth.

Nityananda: Literally, 'Eternal bliss'; *Nitya* = 'eternal, constant' + *ananda* 'supreme bliss'; The great Siddha and Guru of Baba Muktananda, and the author's grand-guru.

Nivritti *(or Nivrittinatha)*: 'non-activity, renunciation'; without mental modifications; the elder brother and Guru of Saint Jnaneshwar (1273-1297 C.E.).

O

Om: (pronounced as: *AUM*); The sacred syllable; the Word; the Transcendent; in Hinduism the mystical and sacred syllable representing the Absolute (Brahman). It is also the symbol representing the fourth state of consciousness, the transcendental state; In the Chandogya Upanishad it is associated with *prana*, and is therefore also called *pranava*; it may also be used in daily language to mean yes, as it also indicates agreement, or concurrence.

Om Namah Shivaya: Salutations (or homage, adoration) to Shiva (God); I bow to Shiva; The great mantra of Shaivism known as the *Panchakshari*, or 'five syllable' *mantra*, which is found in the Krishna Yajur Veda.

Om Tat-Sat: Literally, 'That is the Truth'; *Tat* = 'That' + *Sat* = 'truth, being, reality'; the Vedic *mantra* 'Om Tat Sat.'

P

Pali: An ancient language derived from Sanskrit, used mainly in the Indian state of Bihar. Most early Buddhist scriptures were written in Pali.

Parsi: Literally, 'Persians' in the Gujarati language. A follower of the ancient Zoroastrian religion. Descendants of a Zoroastrian community who migrated to India around the 8th or 9th century, after the Islamic conquest of Iran. No longer allowed to practice their religion freely, they settled in the western state of Gujarat, where they were welcomed, and have prospered. Today they are mainly living in Mumbai, as well as in Gujarat, and make up three fourths of the world's approximately one hundred thousand Zoroastrians.

Patanjali: An ancient sage (circa 2nd century B.C.E.?) who compiled a treatise on yoga called, the Yoga Sutras.

Pingala: Subtle channel (*nadi*) in which *prana* flows, located on the right side of the body. It is said to be masculine in nature, indicating intellectual and mental energy. It is symbolized with the solar principal.

Pradakshina: Circumambulating an image, shrine, saint, or one's Guru in a clockwise direction.

Prajapati: Literally, 'Lord of Creatures'; God as Creator; a name of Shiva.

Prakasha: Literally, 'light, illumination'; from *pra* - 'forth' and the root-verb *kash* - 'to shine'; shining forth; luminous; in Kashmir Shaivism, it is the principal of Self-revelation; consciousness; the principal by which everything else is known; Lord Shiva.

Prana: Literally, 'breathing forth'; vital air; life force or vital energy, from the root *pran*, 'to breathe.' This indicates the life sustaining force of the individual's body, as well as the whole universe. Also, the first of five vital airs (*vayus*). *Prana* in the human body manifests as five vital airs or winds (*vayus*), each performing a specific function, viz., *prana* (outgoing breath) *apana* (incoming breath), *samana* (equalizing breath), *udana* (ascending breath) and *vyana* (separating breath).

Pranapratishtha: The ritual of enlivenment or installing an image with the life force (*prana*).

Pranayama: Literally, 'restraining the breath'; the control of *prana* or life-force. Certain types of *hatha-yoga* techniques to bring about the even flow of *prana* in order to still the mind. When the *Kundalini* is awakened, these may occur spontaneously without any conscious effort on the part of the individual.

Prarabdha karma: 'Actions set in motion'; it is this type of *karma* which has created one's current birth; that *karma* which has become active, and has brought about the present life, and its conditions; It is what is called destiny. (see *karma*)

Prasad: Purity, grace, blessings; a word which means, 'containing blessings or sacred power'; consecrated food and other offerings which has been first offered to the deity, saint, or one's Guru; also, anything given by a saint or one's Guru is called *prasad*, such as a gift, or *mantra*.

Pratyabhijnahridayam: Literally, 'the heart of the doctrine of Self-recognition'; an 11th century treatise by Kshemaraja, which summarizes the Pratyabhijna philosophy of Kashmir Shaivism.

Puja: Worship; actions performed with the feelings of devotion towards God, or one's Guru; also, an altar with images of the Guru or deity, and other objects used in worship.

Punyatithi: An auspicious lunar day (*tithi*), a day for gaining merit; An anniversary of a sacred event.

Puranas: Literally, 'ancient, old'; sacred books of the Hindus containing ancient stories, legends and hymns about the creation of the universe, the incarnations of God, the history of kings, and the instructions of various deities and sages. There are 18 major *Puranas*.

R
Rama: The 'joyful or delightful'; hero of the Sanskrit epic poem, the Ramayana, composed by sage Valmiki. According to the Vaishnavites, Sri Rama is believed to be the 7th incarnation (*Avatara*) of Vishnu. He represents the ideal son, king and husband.

Rinpoche: Literally, 'precious one.' A title added to the names of highly advanced Tibetan spiritual teachers, usually of those who are recognized as incarnate *lamas*. Both the Karmapa and his disciple, Shamar Rinpoche, were recognized as incarnate *lamas (tulku)*.

Rishi: 'Seer, sage'; the Vedic seers; a term for an enlightened being, emphasizing a visionary wisdom. The Rig Veda mentions seven *rishis* who guide mankind throughout its countless life-cycles.

Rishikesh: Literally, 'the place of *rishis*'; a famous town at the foothills of the Himalayas not far from Haridwar.

Rudra: Literally, 'the howler, or one who roars'; One who bestows strength or power; a Vedic name of Shiva.

Rudraksha: Literally, 'the eye of Rudra'; multi-faced reddish-brown seeds from the species *Eleocarpus ganitrus*. They are sacred to Shiva (*Rudra*) and are used to make rosaries for *mantra* repetition.

S

Sadhana: Spiritual practices; a technique used to achieve a desired goal, such as meditation, yoga, japa and austerities. The practice or discipline which produces success or perfection (*siddhi*), from *Sadh*, meaning 'to go straight to the goal.'

Sadhu: The holy or virtuous; an ascetic or holy man. From *sadh*, meaning 'one who goes straight to the goal.' According to Adi Shankaracharya, a *sadhu* is one who is endowed with *sattva-guna*, the quality of purity, has good conduct, and who is well versed in every branch of learning. A *sadhu* may or may not be a yogi or *sannyasin*.

Sahasrara: The highest spiritual center located at the crown of the head. The seat of the Supreme Lord, symbolized as a thousand petal lotus.

Samadhi: Literally, 'even, sameness'; It is samadhi when *'dhi'* (*Buddhi* or intellect) attains *'sama'* (equanimity); Intense or sustained concentration; the state of profound meditative union with the Absolute; according to yoga philosophy, the last stage in the eight limbs of Patanjali's yoga. There are two main types of *samadhi*, *savikalpa* (with seed or form) and *nirvikalpa* (without seed, formless); also, the tomb or burial shrine of a saint.

Samadhi Shrine: A saint's tomb or burial shrine.

Sanatana dharma: The eternal, or perennial religion. It is the oldest name for the Hindu religion.

Sannyasa: Literally, to 'throw down or abandon'; the Hindu monastic path of renunciation; also, the fourth and last stage of life according to ancient Hindu culture.

***Sannyasi* (or *sannyasin*)**: Literally, one who 'throws down or abandons'; one who has renounced or abandoned the worldly life in favor of the monastic life. *Sannyasa* is a personal dedication to the path of God-Realization and service to humanity.

Saptah: Literally, 'seven'; also, the event of continuous chanting of God's name for seven days.

Sarasvati: From *saras* 'flowing' + *vati* 'having'; the flow of consciousness; flowing with speech and knowledge; the Universal Mother as the Goddess of learning and the arts; *Shakti*; name of an ancient sacred river mentioned in the Vedas which flowed from the Himalayas to the Arabian Sea, but which is now dried up; one of the ten orders (*dashanami*) of *sannyasins* started by Shankaracharya. The monastic order to which Swami Muktananda belonged to, as well as all his renunciate disciples.

Sadguru (or *Satguru*): The true Guru; one who has realized the ultimate truth and is able to lead others along the spiritual path; a spiritual preceptor of the highest attainment, considered to be an embodiment of God.

Sadgurunath-Maharaj-ki-Jai: Sad = true + Guru + Natha = lord + Maharaj = great king + ki Jai = victory to. 'Victory to the true Guru, the Lord and great king'; an expression or exclamation of joy, gratitude, and love towards one's Guru.

Satsang: Literally, 'the company of Truth'; the company or association of saints and devotees; a group of people coming together to hear scriptures, chant, meditate, or just to sit in the presence of the Guru.

Seva: Literally, 'service'; selfless service; work performed with an attitude of detachment towards the fruits of one's actions.

Shaivite: A follower of Shiva; one who worships Shiva as the Supreme Being.

Shakta: Worshippers of *Shakti*; one who worships God as Goddess or Universal Mother.

Shakti: Power; energy; strength; skill or ability; active power or energy; the Supreme Primordial Energy (*Parashakti*) which creates, maintains, and dissolves the universe; a term for the *Kundalini Shakti* within each individual.

Shaktipat: Literally, 'descent of *Shakti*': the power of grace; the descent of grace; a specific method of initiation in the lineage of Siddhas. The transmission of spiritual power (*Shakti*) from the Guru to the disciple in order to awaken the dormant *Kundalini*.

Shankaracharya *(also Sri Shankara)*: (788-820 C.E.?) Although many modern scholars place Shankara in the 8th century, this date is disputed by many of his successors. But unfortunately they do not all agree with each other, given dates that range from around the 5th century B.C.E., to the 2nd century C.E.. Adi Shankar, philosopher and saint, taught the non-dual (*Advaitic*) system of Vedanta. He also founded the ten orders (*dashanami*) of *sannyasins*, and established *ashrams* (*mutts*) in the four corners of India through his four main disciples: Padmapada, Hastamalaka, Totaka (Anandagiri) and Sureshwara. In his short life of 32 years, he wrote commentaries on the principle Upanishads, Brahma Sutras and Bhagavad Gita, as well as several poems and numerous other works, including the Atma-Bodha and Viveka Chudamani. In the following verse Shankara expresses the core of all his teachings:

Brahma Satyam Jagan'Mithya,
Jivo Brahmai'va Naparah

Brahman is true, the universe illusory;
The individual soul is verily not different from Brahman.

Shanti: Peace, calm; mental peace or tranquility.

Shiva: Literally, 'the auspicious, kind, gracious or compassionate One.' The name given to the Absolute when viewed as the dissolver of the universe. According to Shaivism, the Supreme Lord who is transcendent, as well as immanent. In His immanent form He is the Creator, Preserver and Destroyer of the universe.

Shiva-Linga: An emblem, mark or sign of Shiva; a symbol representing the Absolute Being in his unmanifested state. A rounded, elliptical, aniconic image made of stone, metal, crystal, wood, or any natural substance, either carved or naturally formed.

Shivaratri: Literally, 'the night of Shiva'; the 14th night of each dark lunar month (from full moon to new moon); this night, when falling in February-March, is called Maha-Shivaratri. It is celebrated by fasting, meditation and chanting throughout the night.

Shivasutras: The main scripture of Kashmir Shaivism, said to have been found by Sage Vasugupta (circa 800) written on a huge rock, after its whereabouts were revealed to him in a dream by Lord Shiva Himself.

Siddha: A perfected being; one who has attained the highest spiritual goal, from the verb-root *sidh,* 'to attain, to accomplish'; one who has attained or achieved *siddhis* or mystical powers; a perfected spiritual master of great purity and power. A Siddha is one who lives in a state of total freedom. His mind is completely steady, and he always maintains the awareness, 'I am pure consciousness.'

Siddhapitha: The place, abode, or seat of a Siddha.

Siddhi: 'Perfection, accomplishment, attainment'; the achievement or completion of the spiritual goal; also, supernatural powers attained through *mantra* repetition, meditation, austerities, and other yogic techniques.

Sita: Wife of Lord Rama. Sita was kidnapped by the demon Ravana, and Rama had to rescue her. The story is retold in the epic *Ramayana*.

So'Ham: Literally, 'That I Am'; the natural mantra which is going on within each individual. (same as *Ham'Sa*.)

Stupa: Originally a mound housing the remains or relics of the Buddha, and his followers.

Sufis: The mystics within the religion of Islam. From *suf*, 'wool', believed to indicate the simple woolen robe worn by the *Sufis*.

Sushumna: The central, and most important subtle nerve (*nadi*) located within the spinal column, which extends from the base of the spine to the top of the head. The awakened *Kundalini* travels upwards within the *sushumna* towards the highest spiritual center located in the crown of the head.

Swami or Swamiji: Lord; 'One who is lord of his senses'; he who knows himself; a prefix to a sannyasin's name; a religious title of a Hindu holy man, usually a *sannyasin*; also, a term of respect for any sadhu.

T

Tandra: An inner state of consciousness between waking and dreaming, in which one may have visions of gods and goddesses, future events, lights, or sees other objects during meditation.

Tantra: Loom or methodology: a scripture in general; a revealed work; a book of knowledge dealing specifically with spiritual practices (*sadhana*).

Tapas *(or tapasya)*: Literally, 'to create heat'; severe austerities or penance;

bearing or enduring the pairs of opposites; performing difficult tasks; in order to purify the ego, the person practices *tapas* willingly, and accepts any pain or suffering which comes naturally in the course of life.

Turiya: The transcendental state; the state of witness consciousness; the fourth state beyond waking, dream and deep sleep, in which the true nature of reality is directly perceived; the state of *samadhi*.

Turyatita: *turiya* + *atita*; Literally, 'gone beyond the fourth state (*turiya*) of consciousness.'

U
Upanishad: Literally, 'sitting near'; also meaning 'esoteric knowledge'; the scriptures embodying the teachings of the ancient sages of India, and which are a part of the Vedas. Traditionally, the number of Upanishads is given as 108, but only ten to sixteen are considered to be the 'major' or 'principle' Upanishads.

V
Vaikuntha: 'The Savior'; the 405th name of Lord Vishnu given in 'the Thousand Names of God' (*Vishnu Sahasranama*); it also indicates the celestial realm or abode of Vishnu (Heaven); the name of Bhagavan Nityananda's first ashram in Ganeshpuri.

Vaishnavite: Followers of Lord Vishnu (God); one who worships Vishnu as the supreme being.

Vajreshwari: *Shakti*; A name of the goddess indicating one who holds the thunder-bolt (*vajra*); a town near Ganeshpuri where a temple to the goddess is located.

Veda: 'Knowledge, wisdom'; the revealed scriptures of the Hindus; the world's oldest scriptures; there are four Vedas: Rig, Yajur, Sama and Atharva.

Vedanta: Literally, 'ultimate knowledge, the final conclusion of the Vedas'; Vedic philosophy or knowledge indicating ultimate wisdom; one of the six orthodox schools of Indian philosophy, arising from discussions in the Upanishads about the nature of the Absolute. The three main scriptures of this philosophy are: the Upanishads, Brahma Sutras, and the Bhagavad Gita.

Vishnu: 'All-pervasive'; a name given to the Absolute when viewed as the sustainer of the universe; He is conceived of as having his special abode in the realm or region known as Vaikuntha (Heaven).

Vishnu Sahasranama: The "Thousand Names of Vishnu (God)"; a hymn chanted in Muktananda's ashram.

Vyasa: Literally, 'the compiler'; a great sage who is credited with compiling the four Vedas, and is the author of the great epic the Mahabharata, as well as all the Puranas. He was the son of sage Parashara, and himself had a son named Shukadev muni. His given name was Krishna Dwaipayana. There is said to be a Vyasa at the end of every third age (*Dvapara yuga*).

Y

Yajna: From the root *yaj*, 'to worship, to sacrifice'; a sacred ritual; sacrificial fire ritual in which different materials, such as fragrant wood, *ghee*, spices, and different grains are offered to the flames while sacred *mantras* are chanted; also, any work done in the spirit of surrender to the Lord.

Yoga: Literally, 'union'; from *yuj*, to 'yoke or join'; one of the six systems of Hindu philosophy. Yoga teaches the means by which the individual spirit can be joined or united with the universal Spirit.

Yoga Sutras: 'Aphorisms on Yoga'; A systematic treatise on yoga by the sage Patanjali (circa 2nd century B.C.E.?).

Yogi: One who practices yoga, usually a male; also, one who has achieved yoga or union. The name for a female practitioner of yoga is *Yogini*.

Z

Zarathustra: The ancient sage of Persia and founder of the Zoroastrian religion. Some say he was the last of a long line of prophets of that religion. Although most modern scholars place him around the sixth century B.C.E., the early Greeks placed him millenniums earlier than themselves. One can find many similarities in the rituals and practices of the Zoroastrians, and those of the Vedic people. The early Zoroastrians also performed the yajna or fire ritual.